PERSPECTIVES ON
LEARNING AND MEMORY

COMPARATIVE COGNITION
AND NEUROSCIENCE

*Thomas G. Bever, David S. Olton, and
Herbert L. Roitblat, Series Editors*

Roitblat/Bever/Terrace: Animal Cognition

Nilsson/Archer: Perspectives on Learning and
Memory

Kendrick/Rilling/Denny: Theories of
Animal Memory *(in press)*

Schusterman/Thomas/Wood: Dolphin
Behavior and Cognition *(in press)*

PERSPECTIVES ON LEARNING AND MEMORY

Edited by
LARS-GÖRAN NILSSON
TREVOR ARCHER
University of Umeå, Sweden

 LAWRENCE ERLBAUM ASSOCIATES, PUBLISHERS
1985   Hillsdale, New Jersey   London

Copyright © 1985 by Lawrence Erlbaum Associates, Inc.

Lawrence Erlbaum Associates, Inc., Publishers
365 Broadway
Hillsdale, New Jersey 07642

Library of Congress Cataloging in Publication Data
Main entry under title:

Perspectives on learning and memory.

(Series in comparative cognition and neuroscience)
Papers from the conference ''Perspectives on animal
learning and human memory—the Umea conference,'' held
at the University of Umea, Sweden, June 17–21, 1984.
Includes bibliographies and indexes.
1. Learning—Physiological aspects—Congresses.
2. Memory—Congresses. I. Nilsson, Lars-Göran,
1944– . II. Archer, Trevor. III. Series.
QP406.P465   1985   153.1   85-10360
ISBN 0-89859-628-9
ISBN 0-89859-698-X (pbk.)

Printed in the United States of America
10 9 8 7 6 5 4 3 2 1

Contents

Foreword

Studies of cognitive processes in humans and in other animals have often proceeded independently of each other. Consequently, advances made in each of these fields have not had as much impact as they should on studies in the other, and a true comparative cognition has been slow in developing. This series reflects a renewed interest in rectifying this problem. It includes volumes examining cognition in many different species, in the hope that this comparative analysis will foster the interchange that has traditionally been lacking and, thereby, promote the advancement of an integrated approach to mind, brain, and their evolution.

This volume presents the results of a conference designed to achieve these goals. The chapters discuss cognitive processes in both animals and humans. The introductory chapter by the organizers of the conference, and the summary chapter at the end of the book, both provide an overall integration of this material. Many common themes run through these chapters and help to interrelate the results obtained from the different species.

This series seeks to reduce the high cost of publication and to increase the speed of publication. Consequently, we plan to use a series of computerized word processing procedures wherever possible. These allow rapid publication of two editions, one of which is considerably less expensive than the usual hardbound version. We hope that these measures will help return academic publishing to the control of academics.

T. G. Bever
D. S. Olton
H. L. Roitblat

Preface

The conference "Perspectives on Animal Learning and Human Memory: The Umeå conference" was held at the University of Umeå, Sweden, June 17–21, 1984. The prime objective of the conference was to assemble prominent scientists to discuss and develop a common ground for conceptualizations in animal learning and human memory.

It is well known by anyone in any field of science that communication with researchers in other fields at times could be very difficult. This is of course not surprising if the two fields, seeking closer communication have had divergent development, and the knowledge bases of the researchers of one field are only roughly understood in the other field. However, what *is* surprising is that communication problems may be overwhelming, although the two disciplines are basically very close together. This is the case when attempts are made to establish a penetrating communication between research practitioners in animal learning and human memory.

Few would probably deny that learning and memory are closely related and few would probably argue against the notion that both animals and humans are biologically related to each other. Throughout the years of development of psychology as a science there has been much interaction between the two fields. Supposedly, the researchers within one of the two fields have also been able to talk with the researchers in the other field since we historically, in fact, have seen direct influence in both directions between the two fields. Still, as witnessed by many, there are considerable problems when trying to understand what the main issues, what the methods, concepts, models, and theories are in the other field. The aim of the present conference was to try to find common grounds for communication between researchers in these two fields, which should have and actually also do have so much in common.

The conference was made possible by economical support from the University of Umeå, the City of Umeå, Stiftelsen Seth M. Kempes Minne, The Swedish Council for Research in the Humanities and the Social Sciences, The Swedish Medical Research Council and several companies including AB Ferrosan, AB Leo, AB Volvo, ASTRA Läkemedel AB, Boliden Mineral AB, CIBA-GEIGY, Ferring AB, IBM Svenska AB, Linjeflyg, SCA, and Searle Research and Development. The support from these institutions and companies is gratefully acknowledged.

We are indebted to the following persons for invaluable help in organizing the conference: Lars Bäckman, David Chalom, Sven-Åke Christianson, Lars Fällman, Agneta Herlitz, Margaretha Json-Lindberg, Tomas Karlsson, Annacari Lundquist, Björn Lyxell, Timo Mäntylä, Tommy Nordqvist, Kjell Ohlsson, Ulrich Olofsson, Jerker Rönnberg, Karl Sandberg, Jan Skoog, Michael Swedberg, and Jan-Åke Åkerlund. We are also grateful to Per-Olov Svärd for encouragement and support.

Lars-Göran Nilsson
Trevor Archer

LIST OF CONTRIBUTORS

Trevor Archer, ASTRA Läkemedel AB, R & D lab., S-151 85 Södertälje, Sweden.

Robert C. Bolles, Department of Psychology, University of Washington, Seattle, WA 98195

Ronald L. Cohen, Department of Psychology, Glendon College, York University, 2275 Bayview Avenue, Toronto, Ontario, Canada M4N 3M6.

Fergus I. M. Craik, Department of Psychology, University of Rotonto, Erindale College, Mississauga Ontario, Canada L5L 106.

Robert G. Crowder, Department of Psychology, Yale University, New Haven, CN 06520

Anthony Dickinson, The Psychological Laboratory, University of Cambridge, Downing Street, Cambridge CB2 3EB England.

William K. Estes, Department of Psychology and Social Relations, Harvard University, William James Hall, 33 Kirkland Street, Cambridge, MA 02138.

David Gaffan, Department of Experimental Psychology, University of Oxford, South Parks Road, Oxford 0X1 3UD England.

Graham J. Hitch, Department of Psychology, University of Manchester, Manchester M13 9PL England.

N. J. Mackintosh, The Psychological Laboratory, University of Cambridge, Downing Street, Cambridge CB2 3EB England.

Lars-Göran Nilsson, Department of Psychology, University of Umeå, S-901 87 Umeå, Sweden.

Kjell Ohlsson, Department of Technical Psychology, Luleå University of Technology, Sweden.

David S. Olton, Department of Psychology, Johns Hopkins University, 34th & Charles Streets, Baltimore, MD 21218

Robert A. Rescorla, Department of Psychology, University of Pennsylvania, 3815 Walnut Street, Philadelphia, PA 19104.

Jerker Rönnberg, Department of Education and Psychology, University of Linköping, Sweden.

David Shanks, The Psychological Laboratory, University of Cambridge, Downing Street, Cambridge CB2 3EB England.

Endel Tulving, Department of Psychology, University of Toronto, 100 st George St. Toronto, Ontario, Canada M5S 1A1.

INTRODUCTION

1 Perspectives on Animal Learning and Human Memory

Lars-Göran Nilsson
Trevor Archer
University of Umeå and ASTRA Läkemedel AB

BACKGROUND

Learning and memory are related areas that benefit from some degree of common treatment. Irrespective of theoretical orientation, few psychologists would deny the obvious links between learning and memory. Some manner of learning or acquisition must be assumed if material is to be remembered. Similarily, without a memory of some sort there can be no expression of anything more than very simple forms of learning. Logically there has to be some retention from one training session to the next, if there is to be any learning or gradual build up of accuracy or speed of response. From an evolutionary point of view the organism has to learn to adjust to various aspects of the environment and, understandably, it is assumed that the organism will use this memorized information on a later occasion in order to survive or cope successfully with the various changes exerted by the environment.

Current research on learning and memory stem from somewhat different traditions. At times the two fields have been very much apart; at other eras of the development of psychology as a science learning and memory research have merged closer together. This difference in tradition is reflected, among other things, in the predominant use of animals as subjects in current learning research and the predominant use of humans in current memory research. The present state of affairs brings us to the core issue of this chapter and the book, viz. the extent to which we can find commonalities between animal learning and human memory. There are certainly many differences between animal and human behavior, but in this context our main focus is on possible similarities, although we will when necessary, emphasize the constraints brought about by differential characteristics.

A philosophical issue of long standing is whether or not animals and humans should be regarded as basically similar or different in a qualitative sense. Ever since Aristotle and antiquity there has been a general tendency within the philosophical domain to argue for a sharp line of demarcation. The primary rationale for this viewpoint has been that humans, on the basis of spoken language, had the ability to think, whereas animals, lacking such a language, did not have this ability. At the start of a more modern era Descartes continued to maintain the same type of division and, on a philosophical basis, this issue has survived up to the present in about the same way as the mind-body dichotomy.

From time to time this basic issue has also been considered as being of crucial importance for broad psychological theories. Whenever arguments have been made for a psychological distinction between animal and man, it appears as if the basic rationale has been essentially the same. Because animals, in contrast to man, do not use a spoken language and therefore cannot think, reasonably they cannot be obeying the same basic laws or principles as man. Moreover, when teaching introductory courses in psychology we often feed our students with this philosophical background and, at times, both textbooks and teachers seem to find reasons for warning the students to generalize from animal to man. By virtue of the philosophical roots it would somehow be more self-evident in general and more honest to tell students about the danger of such generalizations than to tell about the apparent potentials in bridging the gap between psychological studies on animals and humans.

In actual psychological research, however, by which we mean the experimental analysis of behavior approach, the distinction between animal and man has been much less pronounced. Classical psychological theories, often with a biological orientation developed during this century, explicitly claimed to be valid for both animal and human behavior. This was certainly the intention and legacy of the behaviorist era and, to a considerable extent, it is reflected in current theorizing as well. Not surprisingly, the trend towards such a generality has been especially prevalent in learning theory.

In spite of the striving towards conceptual frameworks, applicable to both animal and human behavior, a basic difference between the earlier behaviorist approach and modern approaches ought to be attended to. The general assumption from S-R theories was that behavior, no matter how elaborate and complex, could always be reduced to some configuration of reflexes, stimuli and responses in which cognitive processes were relegated to the wings. The order of the day was that little could be gained from reference to a hypothetical mental life within the organism. The main objective of the behaviorist was to isolate environmental variables, which, through experimental manipulation, could be demonstrated to control behavior. Perhaps the most obvious example of this particular underlying rationale for generality across species was the research inspired by Skinner. The same basic, noncognitive, principles were assumed to hold for simple conditioning, complex language acquisition, and problem solving. Commonly, the actual direction of influence during these years was from simple to more complex forms of learning. Concepts, theories, and principles were first developed within the animal learning domain and were then applied to human learning situations.

The classical learning theorists explicitly avoided the concept of memory in their models. This was true also for those who, in retrospect, may be called the predesessors of present day memory theorists and it is understandable, since their energy was expanded upon the physical parameters of the stimuli and their associated responses. The valuable conceptual and methodological tools developed in animal learning were readily grasped by the initial theorists within the verbal learning domain. Having reached this stage of development during the forties and fifties there appeared ample opportunity for animal and human learning research to merge with a common ground for communication about theory and data.

It appears that this development did not quite come to pass. Time was not yet ripe for a joint enterprise in trying to uncover the basic principles in learning. Division of labor was apparently necessary. Those scientists with a primary interest in biological or neurophysiological approaches to learning found their inspiration in classical learning theory and they continued to use animals as subjects in their experiments.

Other workers, more interested in the level of sophistication offered by analysis of verbal behavior used human subjects in their experiments. Consequently, some departure from the behaviorist tradition was inevitable. With the advent of the information processing approach, a new niche had been carved out for those seeking an investigation of higher cognitive functions. Despite some efforts to the contrary, the divergence of animal learning and human memory proceeded, and perhaps there is justification for neglect of joint enterprises if we consider the amount of energy expenditure required.

SOME CRITICAL EXPERIMENTS

Given the close relationship between learning and memory, and the fact that both animals and humans are biological systems with, supposedly, many basic similarities in their ways of adjusting to the environment, it was inevitable that experimental designs led to results that stimulated the convergence of animal learning and human memory at a conceptual level. Thus, the scene was set during the late sixties and early seventies, for a handful of critical experiments to open new horizons. We have chosen several examples, which have influenced our own approach to this enterprise.

One of these examples concerns the interpretation of the Kamin blocking effect: Conditioning to a stimulus A followed by conditioning to the stimulus compound AB resulted in lesser conditioning to the stimulus B during subsequent testing. Thus, stimulus A was said to have blocked conditioning to stimulus B, the Kamin blocking effect (1969). It is quite true to assume that the

Kamin effect has had enormous and lasting influence upon the current theorising within cognitive associationism (see especially Rescorla, this volume, but also Estes, Dickinson, and Mackintosh). Paradoxically, it appears that the blocking phenomenon is sometimes difficult to obtain and in fact an "anti-blocking" or "unblocking effect" (e.g., Rescorla & Colwill, 1983) has been demonstrated. Among others, there are two special points we draw attention to in this regard: (1) the great diversification of conditioning procedures that are available and have to be overcome for generality to be demonstrated, (2) the need to seek parallels between animal learning and human memory once a phenomenon, e.g., blocking, has been proven to be significant and robust.

The second example illustrating how animal learning and human memory are welded together profitably, is taken from the theoretical presentations inherent to the Rescorla-Wagner model (1972), its development by Mackintosh (1975), and the model of memory and conditioning proposed by Estes (1973). Estes' model was taken as a starting point of our own research. In this model CS, US and contextual events are represented by associations via higher-order control elements. One control element, C_1, is assumed to combine CS with context while a second control element, C_2, combines US with its particular context. Another control element, C_{12}, at a still higher-order level is then assumed to combine the lower level control elements, C_1 and C_2 with the general context of the experimental situation, i.e., CS and US become associated to each other in the common experimental context through this higher-order control element.

There have been long and intense debates in the psychological literature concerning whether or not animals do, in fact, have memory. None can state it better than Mackintosh (1974) when he jested ". . . laboratory animals, like elephants, never forget." In retrospect these debates seem pointless. Mackintosh (1974) goes on, "As with many myths, this one rests on a small core of truth surrounded by a larger mass of casually reported and uncritically accepted data" (p. 472). Given the logical relationship between learning and memory with the benefit of hindsight it seems remarkable that the pioneering learning theorists were so neglectful of parameters to measure memory and cognitive functions. On the basis of the successful applications of cognitive concepts in, for example, the Rescorla-Wagner—Estes and Mackintosh models, we are now seeing several examples of the application of cognitive concepts in learning theory. Bolles (1975) commented that learning theory was undergoing a revolutionary change and that, for this reason, the learning theorists are particularily receptive to new concepts and ideas. If one might isolate a point in time to give substance to this claim, it seems reasonable to suggest Kamin's blocking experiment as a critical operation.

The historical origins of the conference and this particular book on animal learning and human memory are to be found in an effect produced in our own laboratory. The theoretical starting point was inspired by Estes' model just mentioned. The paradigm chosen for the application of the model was taste aversion learning, the Garcia effect, as described by Garcia and Koelling (1966).

Rats were presented with a compound CS composed of taste, auditory, and visual elements, which was paired with either an electric shock or an illness-producing US. During subsequent testing, rats which had the compound paired with illness avoided only the taste element, whereas rats which had the compound paired with shock avoided only the auditory-visual element. In our experiments we varied some aspects of contextual stimuli in a systematic fashion during the phase of acquisition and extinction of taste aversion. We were able to demonstrate that rats learn about other aspects of the situation as well as the explicit taste CS, when given a number of unreinforcing postconditioning presentations of the taste + some conditioning context stimulus.

Theoretically, the implications from the Garcia effect were traumatic for established learning principles and "preparedness" reared its ugly head. Thus, we were told that rats by virtue of the evolutionary status were prepared to associate taste and illness, but contraprepared to associate external cues with illness. Cognitive functioning in this respect was stringently denied. To us, this offered the unique opportunity of falsifying Estes' model. Thus, we used saccharin as the taste stimulus and an exteroceptive context as the external cues within which taste and poison were combined. Since we knew, or thought we knew, that rats could not associate those contextual elements with malaise there could be no possibility of Estes' context, modulating the degree of taste aversion obtained. We received a great shock from our very first experiment (Archer, Sjödén, Nilsson, & Carter, 1979), since the contextual elements were shown to control taste-aversion conditioning and extinction to a considerable extent.

In a later experiment (Sjödén, & Archer, 1981), the CS saccharin was presented either in a novel context or in a familiar context at conditioning. Two groups received the novel context and two groups received the familiar context. During extinction trials, one of the novel context groups and one of the familiar context groups received saccharin in a different context from that of conditioning, the other novel context group and the other familiar context group received saccharin in the same context as for conditioning. The results of this experiment are seen in Fig. 1.1.

N-D in Fig. 1.1 refers to the rats that received novel context at conditioning and were then switched to a different context during extinction; the N-S group remained in the same context during extinction. F-D refers to rats that received a familiar context at conditioning and were switched to a different context during extinction; F-S groups remained in the same context during extinction. For the first two preference tests the original conditioning context was reinstated for all four groups.

The results from the extinction phase describe a conditioning dependent context effect that was greater when a new context had been presented at conditioning. However, the extinction dependent context effect, to be seen at T_1 and T_2 was equally great for both the novel and familiar conditions. Note finally that the reversal of context at T_3 once again controlled the strength of the saccharin aversions. Thus, happily with this experiment and several others we failed to

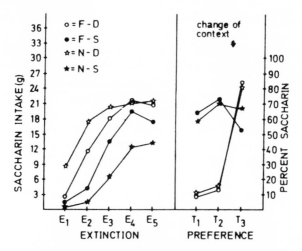

Fig. 1.1.   Saccarin intake during extinction phase (left) and percentage saccarin preference on preference tests (right). (Copyright 1985 Academic Press, Inc. Reprinted by permission of the publisher from P.-O. Sjödén and T. Archer, Associative and non-associative effects of exteroceptive context in taste-aversion conditioning with rats, *Behavioral and Neural Biology*, 1981, *33*, 74–92).

falsify Estes, Rescorla-Wagner and Mackintosh, a matter of some significance for the parsimony of a general theory of learning.

What we wish to emphasize is that the procedure used to study the Garcia effect would probably be one of those paradigms, where the expectation of finding an influence of cognitive factors would be very low. Thus, the rationale is, that if one could demonstrate an influence of cognitive factors in such a ''primitive'' learning situation as taste aversion learning, one would probably be able to demonstrate the influence of cognitive factors in almost any learning situation even with animal subjects.

Thus, there are good reasons to agree with those workers who have already adopted this cognitive orientation in learning theories (Kesner, 1973; Kesner & Conner, 1972; Westbrook, Bond, & Feyer, 1981) and we believe that this new wave of convergence between animal learning and human memory might be a profitable point of departure for a future understanding of the basic principles underlying both learning and memory. This is not to say that we are unaware of or ignore the inherent pitfalls. One simply cannot produce parallels between human memory and animal learning *ad infinitum* and then point to the result and suggest that these are really the same thing. The cautionary requirement is carefully outlined in Gaffan's chapter (this volume) and we agree. The question remains: Which parallels should we seek? A simple answer is: The six topics under which we have organised this volume.

It is true that human memory research has flourished during the last couple of decades or so, and some human memory theorists might argue that there is nothing to be gained from seeking company with animal learning research. However, the historical evidence concerning these two fields may suggest that this is not a very wise attitude to adopt. Medicinal and theoretical reasons force us to face the problem of solving the neuropharmacological, neurophysiological, and biochemical bases of learning and memory, which hardly could be carried out solely on humans. This work confronts the psychologists, whose research must be carried out in the laboratory with various species. To avoid any unfortunate misunderstandings we hasten to add that this does not entail the abandonment of successful psychological methods of studying memory. On the contrary, this approach is expected to continue to the same extent as before, and hopefully as a complement to the neurobiological-conditioning analysis.

The influence of animal work on human learning research during the heyday of behaviorism, appears to be progressing in the opposite direction in present day research. Is this an indication that the animal learning researchers in general might currently be more knowledgeable about human memory than the average human memory researcher is about animal learning? At any rate, a closer integration between animal learning and human memory should be profitable for future advancements of knowledge in these two fields.

Although the realization of a need for an integration might be a first important step, it is not enough simply to hope for such an integration. There are many obstacles that may hinder people from taking further integrative steps. Interdisciplinary communication constitutes one such primary difficulty and the main objective of this book has been to assemble prominent scientists to discuss and develop common grounds for conceptualizations in animal learning and human memory with the ultimate goal of promoting advancement of knowledge in our science.

If it appears from this introduction that we have neglected the labors of the human memory theorists our intentions were meant to be worthy, since the successful and substantial contributions of the human memory theorists have caused their animal learning colleagues to consider established behaviorist concepts in a cognitive light.

In order to promote further integrative steps between animal and human research on learning and memory processes we might be wise to take a more biological approach than we have done before. The time may now be ripe for striving towards a more interdisciplinary orientation towards various problems of learning and memory. Biochemistry, neuroanatomy, neuropharmacology, neurophysiology, and psychology are some of the disciplines that should complement each other in forming the basis for a broader scientific approach to learning and memory than never would be possible when taking each of these disciplines separately. In proposing this we are of course aware of the great resistence such an approach may invoke among single scientists within each of these disciplines.

Often, it has been argued among researchers in one area that they could gain very little, if anything, from other fields. For example, neurobiologists may claim that psychological measures are far too crude for ever being able to match the exact biological measures used. Or, psychologists have said that there is, as of yet, not one single case in the literature that has demonstrated that, for example, neurophysiological findings have been able to fertilize psychological theorizing. It is argued here that both these statements are examples of a way of thinking that could be avoided if we were striving towards goals of a common neurobiological discipline rather than worrying whether one of these subdisciplines could fertilize another. Rather than taking a protectionistic attitude a more humble and open-minded view should be preferred when seeking common grounds and common goals in trying to solve common problems. Moreover, as stated elsewhere (Nilsson, 1984), new technological inventions in the neurosciences may open up new fields of common interest which may be difficult to forsee at the present stage. Some psychologists may still resist but the exploding technological development appears to be here to stay and it would seem unwise to utilize for a further expansion of the psychological field as well. The CAT brain scan is one such invention, which already has had both important theoretical and more pragmatic value for (literally speaking) the mapping of the brain. Studies of cerebral blood flow by means of the intra-arterial 133 Xenon clearance technique (Ingvar, 1979), neuroendocrinological research, and a brain surgery breakthrough are other examples, which probably will bloom even more in the future.

This strive towards finding common grounds and common goals for basic problems in learning and memory should not, however, be taken as an indication that we see such an integration as an absolute goal in itself. We should also pose the question that in some cases and for some problems it is quite unreasonable to seek parallels and commonalities. As is seen in the remaining chapters of the book both similarities and differences are pointed out. Whenever any type of relation is proposed we should be alert to its potentials and consequences.

The chapters of this book are organized around six topics and are presented with the purpose of providing a basis for future integration between animal learning and human memory. For each topic there is one chapter written by a researcher within the human memory area and one chapter written by a researcher within the animal learning field. The idea behind such an arrangement was that one representative from each of these two research traditions should give the perspective on the topic in question from a human memory or an animal learning point of view. In an enterprise of this sort the selection of topics is of essential importance. It can probably always be argued that some other topics should have been included than those that actually were. Therefore, the selected topics should be regarded as *perspectives* with the implicit indication that they are not mutually exclusive and that those topics chosen are not meant to exclude other areas which could have been included if there were even a slightly different theoretical orientation at the outset of our endeavors or if there had been another group of authors contributing to the book. The six topics selected for our purposes are: Basic theoretical concepts, classification of concepts, short-term memory and attention, connecting models, experimental paradigms and ecology, and general empirical laws.

BASIC THEORETICAL CONCEPTS

As mentioned earlier learning and memory are related areas and the theoretical concepts used within each field should supposedly share some resemblance. Even when we further specify the two fields to be animal learning and human memory we should expect some degree of overlap in the theoretical concepts. However, as we all know from what history has shown this is hardly the case. The basic concepts used are different and this difference makes communication between the two fields very difficult. As witnessed by many of the contributors to this book and by others, it is very difficult for, say, an active researcher within human memory to come to grips with the fine grains of the concepts used in animal learning even though this representative for human memory took graduate courses in animal learning, even though he or she has taught such advanced courses to other graduate students, and possibly, even though this representative him or herself during some period of time has been running animal learning experiments. It is one thing to know as a representative of human memory what is meant by unconditioned and conditioned stimuli, by blocking effects, latent inhibition paradigms, and the like, but it is quite another matter to know how these and other similar concepts fit into a program by an animal learning researcher in claiming that a certain series of experiments were designed to study how the animal is acquiring knowledge about the world. Sometimes it is as if there are two completely different cultures which try to meet. The same thing of course holds true when an animal learning researcher tries to understand how comparisons of data from experiments on free recall, word completion, and lexical decision tasks would have to say anything about the distinction between episodic and semantic memory.

Thus, the purpose of including this topic in the book was to try to find a common conceptual platform for communication and understanding between researchers in the two fields. There might be functional similarities between the concepts used in the two fields that have been unnoticed or overlooked in spite of the fact that there are profound differences between the concepts in the two fields at a nominal level.

CLASSIFICATION OF CONCEPTS

In preparing the conference that preceded this book the title of this topic was phrased quite differentially. The title was systems of representation. The idea was that we should be dealing with the various ways in which we conceive of how knowledge and experience is represented in the storage system of the organism, whether it be a human being or an animal. As a result of considerable thought and extensive discussions we agreed with the contributors to this topic, Tulving and Olton, about the need in a context like this to give some thought and effort to a somewhat broader topic, viz. the problem of classification. We thought such a change of the original plans was appropriate especially since systems of representations were consequently dealt with by several of the other contributors in their chapters.

And indeed, the problem of classification is an important one that has not been dealt with in our science to the extent it actually deserves. This topic obviously relates to the previous one (i.e., basic theoretical concepts) in the sense that it seeks to organize the conceptual tools used within the learning and memory domains.

SHORT-TERM MEMORY AND ATTENTION

Some may wonder why there is a topic specified to the extent that the present one is. It could possibly be argued, following the traditional memory terminology that because there is coverage of short-term memory there should be a specific topic on long-term memory too, perhaps on sensory storage as well, and on episodic memory, on semantic memory, and so on. However, our purpose with including short-term memory and attention was not to initiate a full comparative coverage of various hypothetical memory structures. Rather, the ambition was to give full recognition to the concept of short-term memory as one which has played probably the dominating role, when, as pointed out initially, cognitive concepts emanating from the human memory domain has successively been incorporated in frameworks used by animal learning theorists.

By tradition attention is a concept very much related to short-term memory, and this concept too, in its own right, has been used extensively in theories of human cognition and during the last few years also in animal learning theories. Thus, both short-term memory and attention are concepts, which actually have been employed by both human memory and animal learning theorists and these concepts may therefore be regarded as priming concepts for the integrative development we would like to reflect with this book.

CONNECTING MODELS

It may be argued that commonalities between human memory and animal learning for single concepts may provide very little of a more profound basis for an integration between the two fields. Integration on the basis of single concepts may provide an important first step but one may argue that an integration that would be of any lasting importance would seem to require more substance. Specific models which relates a certain empirical phenomenon to a particular mechanism may have more of an impact in promoting an integration between human memory and animal learning research.

The purpose of this topic is therefore to evaluate whether there are common empirical phenomena in both fields which can be explained by common mechanisms proposed within the two fields. It may also be the case that similar empirical phenomena within the two fields are explained by quite different mechanisms in human memory and animal learning models, and that different phenomena within the two fields are explained by quite similar mechanisms in animal learning and human memory models. If such cases exist they may very well serve the purpose of shedding light on both similarities and differences within the two fields, which in turn may serve as a basis for a future integration.

EXPERIMENTAL PARADIGMS AND ECOLOGY

It is a well known fact that experimental paradigms and methods within animal learning and human memory research are quite different. Actually, the different methodological tools within the two fields constitute much of the impediment for an efficient research communication between the practioners within the two fields. Thus, it seems as if much effort in trying to integrate the two fields should be devoted to considering the research methods proper.

Animal learning and human memory research resemble each other in a sense that they have been attacked because the laboratory methods, used within both fields, have been claimed to have very little to say about learning and memory in animal and man in more ecologically valid situations. This critique in itself in both fields may serve the purpose of making it easy to find a common methodological platform for a future integration.

GENERAL EMPIRICAL LAWS

This final topic has been included in the organization of the book with the contention that general empirical laws within the two fields should exist if learning and memory really are related. If there is a close relationship between learning and memory it should be evident in general empirical regularities. It would seem crucial to look for such regularities since they, supposedly, are more fundamental than any similarities which can be found for concepts, models, and other theoretical constructs. Presumably, such empirical regularities ought to reflect some biological commonalities between various species within the whole animal kingdom. Theoretical constructs on the other hand need not reflect the same underlying laws, but may be a result of Zeitgeist and various other preconceptions of the theorists themselves.

In the final chapter of the book an attempt is made by Rönnberg and Ohlsson to integrate the rich harvest of ideas produced during the working conference. Thus, they discuss a number of points brought up during the final days, when the speakers reviewed each others' formal presentations. Rönnberg and Ohlsson have used the Task Analysis orientation as a frame of reference from which to treat the issues raised during the working conference.

REFERENCES

Archer, T., Sjödén, P.-O., Nilsson, L.-G., & Carter, N. (1979). Role of exteroceptive background context in taste-aversion conditioning and extinction. *Animal Learning and Behavior, 7*, 17–22.

Bolles, R. C. (1975). *Learning theory*. New York: Holt, Rinehart & Winston.

Estes, W. K. (1973). Memory and conditioning. In F. J. McGuigan & D. B. Lumsden (Eds.), *Contemporary approaches to conditioning and learning*. Washington, D.C.

Garcia, J., & Koelling, R. A. (1966). Relation of cue to consequence in avoidance learning. *Psychonomic Science, 4*, 123–124.

Ingvar, D. H. (1979). Patterns of activity in the cerebral cortex related to memory functions. In L.-G. Nilsson (Ed.), *Perspectives on memory research*. Hillsdale, NJ: Lawrence Erlbaum Associates.

Kamin, L. J. (1969). Predictability, surprise, attention and conditioning. In B. A. Campbell & R. M. Church (Eds.), *Punishment and aversive behavior*. New York: Appleton-Century-Crofts.

Kesner, R. P. (1973). A neural system analysis of memory storage and retrieval. *Psychological Bulletin, 80*, 177–203.

Kesner, R. P., & Conner, H. S. (1972). Independence of short- and long-term memory: A neutral system analysis. *Science, 176*, 432–434.

Mackintosh, N. J. (1974). *The psychology of animal learning*. New York: Academic Press.

Mackintosh, N. J. (1975). A theory of attention: Variations in the associability of stimuli with reinforcement. *Psychological Review, 82*, 276–298.

Nilsson, L.-G. (1984). New functionalism in memory research. In K. M. J. Lagerspetz & P. Niemi (Eds.), *Psychology in the 1990s*. Amsterdam: North Holland Publishing Company.

Rescorla, R. A., & Colwill, R. M. (1983). Within-compound associates in unblocking. *Journal of Experimental Psychology: Animal Behavior Process, 9*, 390–400.

Rescorla, R. A., & Wagner, A. R. (1972). A theory of Pavlovian conditioning: Variations in the effectiveness of reinforcement and nonreinforcement. In A. H. Black & W. F. Prokasy (Eds.), *Classical conditioning II: Current research and theory* (pp. 64–99). New York: Appleton-Century-Crofts.

Sjödén, P.-O., & Archer, T. (1981). Associative and nonassociative effects of exteroceptive context in taste-aversion conditioning with rats. *Behavioral and Neural Biology, 33*, 74–92.

Westbrook, R. F., Bond, N. W., & Feyer, A. M. (1981). Short- and long-term decrements in toxicosis-induced odor-aversion learning: The role of duration of exposure to an odor. *Journal of Experimental Psychology: Animal Behavior Processes, 7*, 362–381.

BASIC THEORETICAL CONCEPTS

Lars-Göran Nilsson
Trevor Archer

As stated in the introductory chapter an attempt to integrate animal learning and human memory research should start preferably with a discussion of conceptual matters. To what extent are the basic theoretical concepts within the two fields similar, parallel, or tangent to each other, or to what extent do they differ? To what extent are these concepts based on the same premises? Do we need a large set of basic concepts in the two fields, or is it enough with only a few? As will be seen in the chapters by Crowder and Rescorla, who are the representatives of human memory and animal learning, respectively, for this topic, the two fields appear quite different with respect to basic theoretical concepts. The difference is no surprise since each field of research owes its conceptual basis to the development of particular methodologies and with differential emphasis placed upon usage of operationalism. Where Crowder presents several concepts as being the most basic ones in human memory research, Rescorla's position seems to suggest that the animal learning researcher can do very well with only one, viz. the concept of the association.

This conceptual difference mirrors quite clearly the actual state of the art within a substantial portion of the two fields. In human memory research there has been an obvious tendency to generate concepts for building models. At one time there was almost a one to one ratio between models and the phenomena these different models were set to explain. For obvious reasons the building of all these models has created a large number of concepts and Crowder has grouped them into three large sets, viz. as concepts related to representation of information, concepts of various types of processing, and concepts connected to the notion of capacity limitations.

The animal learning area on the other hand can be characterized as demonstrating a much higher degree of conservatism in the sense that the concept of the association has, at least in the last 15–20 years, assumed the status of a cardinal concept to which other minor concepts in one way or another have been related. It is certainly true that there have been discussions of nonassociative learning, but yet as Rescorla claims in his chapter there has been little evidence in the field that the association should be replaced by another concept incorporating all forms of learning but even associative/nonassociative discussions (Garcia, 1978; Mitchell, 1978; Revusky, 1977) served to underline the very central and fundamental role of the association (Logue, 1979). With several notable exceptions (see Bolles' chapter, this volume), there is scant evidence within the field that the animal learning researchers would be better off if they were to diverge the concepts to sets of concepts as in the human memory field. This does not mean that such attempts have not been made and this should not blind us to the fact that an unrealistic explanatory burden is placed upon the association (see Gaffan's chapter, this volume). Recent formulations of conditioning effects in animal learning have used the theoretical flexibility of memory models to characterise the phenomena (Wagner, 1976, 1978). On the other hand, we should also point out the movements aimed at dissecting the association concept into an ecological-dependent set of "specialized associations" (Rozin & Kalat, 1971; Seligman, 1970; Shettleworth, 1972), movements that have certainly increased our awareness of a fragility within the concept of association.

Although there are differences between the two fields with respect to the number of basic concepts used, there are similarities as well. One such similarity is very striking and it seems worthwhile to dwell on this before proceeding to chapters by Crowder and Rescorla. It is obvious that the dominating view of storage in human memory research for quite a long time has been based on a spatial metaphor. For many years memory has been conceived of as an entity—a receptacle—in which information is encoded and stored and from which the information is later retrieved when needed. According to this view each to-be-remembered item is stored in a localized fashion. That is, given items can be searched and located if the address to this item in memory is known. Although this view is still by far the most dominating one, recent years have witnessed an alternative conception of storage, namely that of nonlocalized or distributed storage (e.g. Anderson, Silverstein, Ritz, & Jones, 1977; Hinton & Anderson, 1981; Kohonen, 1977; Metcalfe-Eich, 1982; Murdock, 1979, 1982, 1983; Pribram, Nuwer, & Baron, 1974). One way of conceptualizing how information is stored in a distributed-storage system is to regard the information as being composed of attributes of features and that these aspects of the information are stored in points of the storage system which are distributed (cf. Nilsson, 1980, 1984). In order to make sense of this contention of storage with respect to how a subject can put all these aspects together, thereby understanding the information presented, one has to assume some kind of associative relationship among the features of the information and among the points in which features are stored (cf. Anderson et al., 1977). Much work still has to be carried out in order to get any empirical data of which these features are and how they would combine to form single items, that the subject encode at study and retrieve and respond with later at test. The animal learning approach to the locus of storage in memory has of tradition and circumstance been a neurobiological/neuropharmacological one, with all the concomitant hazards of such an enterprise (Bammer, 1982). Empirical evidence seem to suggest the hippocampus as the site of encoding or retrieval, or both, whereas the cerebral cortex is associated with storage (Squire, 1982). From these assumptions, the search has been towards locating the biochemical basis of memory storage (cf. Lynch & Baudry, 1984). Thus, although the information processing concepts are applied, once again the emphasis is upon operationalism rather that conceptualization.

It seems there is a conceptual similarity between this new way of thinking about storage within the human memory domain and the essentials of what Rescorla argues for in this associationistic framework. Rescorla suggests that the overall objective for research in animal learning is to study how the organism acquires knowledge about the world. His own contention concerning this respondent-analysis appears to involve the acquisition of knowledge by means of the formation of associations between various aspects of a complex environment. In the same way as for human memory, and to the best of our knowledge, no taxonomy of the environment has yet been worked out, but it is striking to see such a close conceptual resemblance between human memory and animal learning in spite of the fact that both areas are still lacking in data supporting the notion that items, events or situations should be seen as a complex compound of aspects forming these events.

REFERENCES

Anderson, J. A., Silverstein, J. W., Ritz, S. A., & Jones, R. S. (1977). Distinctive features, categorical perception, and probability learning: Some applications of a neural model. *Psychological Review, 84,* 413–451.

Bammer, G. (1982). Pharmacological investigations of neurotransmitter involvement in passive avoidance responding: A review and some new results. *Neuroscience and Biobehavioral Reviews, 6,* 247–296.

Garcia, J. (1978). Mitchell, Scott and Mitchell are not supported by their own data. *Animal Learning and Behavior, 6,* 116.

Hinton, G. E., & Anderson, J. A. (Eds.). (1981). *Parallel models of associative memory.* Hillsdale, NJ: Lawrence Erlbaum Associates.

Kohonen, T. (1977). *Associative memory: A system-theoretical approach.* Berlin: Springer-Verlag.

Logue, A. W. (1979). Taste aversion and the generality of the laws of learning. *Psychological Bulletin, 86,* 276–296.

Lynch, G., & Baudry, M. (1984). The biochemistry of memory: A new and specific hypothesis. *Science, 224,* 1057–1063.

Metcalfe-Eich, J. (1982). A composite holographic associative recall model. *Psychological Review, 89,* 627–661.

Mitchell, D. (1978). The psychological vs. the ethological rat: Two views of the poison avoidance behavior of the rat compared. *Animal Learning and Behavior, 6,* 121–124.

Murdock, B. B., Jr. (1979). Convolution and correlation in perception and memory. In L.-G. Nilsson (Ed.), *Perspectives on memory research.* Hillsdale, NJ: Lawrence Erlbaum Associates.

Murdock, B. B., Jr. (1982). A theory for the storage and retrieval of item and associative information. *Psychological Review, 89,* 609–627.

Murdock, B. B. Jr. (1983). A distributed memory model for serial-order information. *Psychological Review, 90,* 316–338.

Nilsson, L.-G. (1980). Methodological and theoretical considerations as a basis for an integration of research on memory functions in epileptic patients. *Acta Neurologica Scandinavica, 62,* (Suppl. 80), 62–74.

Nilsson, L.-G. (1984). New functionalism in memory research. In K. M. J. Lagerspetz & P. Niemi (Eds.), *Psychology in the 1990s.* Amsterdam: North-Holland Publishing Company.

Pribram, K., Nuwer, M., & Baron, R. (1974). The holographic hypothesis of memory structure in brain function and perception. In D. Krantz, R. C. Atkinson, R. C. Luce, & P. Suppes (Eds.), *Contemporary developments in mathematical psychology. Vol II.* San Francisco: Freeman.

Revusky, S. (1977). Correction of a paper by Mitchell, Scott and Mitchell. *Animal Learning and Behavior, 5,* 320.

Rozin, P., & Kalat, J. W. (1971). Specific hungers and poisoning as adaptive specializations of learning. *Psychological Review, 78,* 459–486.

Seligman, M. E. P. (1970). On the generality of the laws of learning. *Psychological Review, 77,* 406–418.

Shettleworth, S. J. (1972). Constraints on learning. In Lehrman, D. S., Hinde, R. A. & Shaw, E. (Eds.), *Advances in the study of behavior,* (Vol. IV, pp. 1–68). New York: Academic Press.

Squire, L. R. (1982). The neuropsychology of human memory. *Annual Review of Neuroscience, 5,* 241–273.

Wagner, A. R. (1976). Priming in STM: An information processing mechanism for self-generated or retrieval-generated depression of performance. In T. J. Tighe & R. N. Leaton (Eds.), *Habituation: Perspectives from child development, animal behavior and neurophysiology.* Hillsdale, NJ: Lawrence Erlbaum Associates.

Wagner, A. R. (1978). Expectancies and the priming of STM. In S. H. Hulse, H. Fowler, & W. K. Honig (Eds.), *Cognitive aspects of animal behavior.* Hillsdale, NJ: Lawrence Erlbaum Associates.

2 Basic Theoretical Concepts in Human Learning and Cognition

Robert G. Crowder
Yale University

The research traditions of animal learning and human learning are tightly connected. The connection was announced by Watson and Rayner (1920) and then given rich intellectual substance by Dollard and Miller (1950). It thrives today in such explicit clinical applications of basic learning research as that of Seligman (1975) on learned helplessness. Other basic research in animal learning, such as that of Rescorla (1980) on second-order conditioning, promises new applications and theoretical connections. The topic of this conference was quite different from these clinical-personality applications and quite audacious—to interconnect animal-learning work with modern approaches to *human memory*. This is audacious because the flow of history seems to be going just the wrong direction. The study of human memory and learning were comfortable with their animal-learning roots (though sometimes in second-class citizenship) when I was beginning graduate school, in what we now know to have been the last days of stimulus-response dominance in psychology. Subsequently, under successive waves of influence from linguistics, information theory, digital computers, and artificial intelligence, we memory people distanced ourselves from these roots.

The estrangement of animal learning and human memory has little or nothing to do with reductionism, however; the phylogenetic reductionism practiced in the former is no less strenuous than the *task reductionism* practiced in the latter. Recall the vice-like grip of the paired-associate task Bower (1962) clamped on his subjects in confirming his one-element learning model. Recall then the seemingly trivial task variation (second-guessing with three rather than two alternatives) that falsified the model. So a predilection for reductionism is not at stake. (I am assuming here that we should provisionally leave apart from this discussion those members of the animal-learning community whose target interest is the "real life" behavior of lower animals. Even there, however, pressures towards ecological sensitivity of method are quite comparable in the animal [Shettleworth, 1978] and human [Neisser, 1976] domains.)

My goal is to identify a set of basic theoretical concepts from the area of human memory, broadly defined, concepts that could possibly be held against a comparable list from animal learning. The challenge of this goal is to avoid concepts so narrow (Speech Recoding in Short Term Memory) that they undermine in advance the effort to bring animal and human work together, or so broad (Inhibition) that they apply almost surely to all forms of animal life and make the effort trivial. (Is Association in this category?) My compromise between these extremes has led me to organize my review around headings of (1) Representation, (2) Processing, and (3) Capacity Limitations. Compromises never lead to unqualified joy and I shall explain why I am uncomfortable with this particular organizational scheme before I proceed cheerfully to use it:

For one thing, by classifying concepts as either Representational or Processing, this organization seems to make official a solution to the ancient opposition of structure and function. I readily concede that these are groupings of convenience and I have not solved the structure/function problem. Furthermore, capacity limitations should properly be subsumed under Representation or Processing principles, pointing respectively representation resources that are too small or to processing rates that are too slow. Finally, I worry that my list of principles, organized this way, are not "basic" enough; others might propose that they can be derived from more abstract First Principles.

Why, then, have I worked within this organization? Because it suits the particular level of explanatory concept I am trying to deal with in this paper. I have avoided First Principles partly because I don't think I know the right ones and, if I did, they would probably be either too inclusive (inhibition), too molecular (synaptic change), or beside the point (adaptation to the environment). I think it might be easy for us all to reach agreement about First Principles but it might not make much difference.

That leaves the level of concept I am interested in here, concepts that an active scientist uses on a day-to-day basis for resolving contradictions, generating specific predictions, reading critically the literature in his area, and finding order in his own data. These are theoretical in the sense that they are explanatory principles, but I am convinced they are inherently metaphorical and provisional. These last qualities make them none the less more basic than would be the elusive First Principles if we knew them. The concepts I describe are basic in the sense that they form the basis of *scientific problem-solving*.

PRINCIPLES OF REPRESENTATION

The first concepts I discuss all concern what the memory trace "contains" as it were. How does it reflect prior organized knowledge? How does the memory trace of an experience differ from regular knowledge?

Codes and Schemata

You don't need visual illusions to be convinced that sensory evidence generally allows a variety of parsings. The same holds for the verbal-linguistic domain. There are no more elementary concepts in human memory than that of coding, the idea that the memory trace retains whichever alternative organization was somehow selected at the time of learning. Certainly there is a neurochemical level at which information coding is all the same in memory; had we been too worried about this truism, we would all have gone into a different line of work, however.

Functional coding distinctions answer whether an isolated word like SEA-GULL brings to mind another word like REGAL or one like HERON. Fisher and Craik (1977) have shown that retrieval cues stressing exactly these two dimensions of a memorized word are differently effective depending on what aspect of the word was processed originally at learning.

The historical influences that shaped our ideas of coding begin perhaps with the controversy over Gestalt versus linguistic coding of visual form (Riley, 1962). The much more recent "imagery argument" merely continues that debate (Kosslyn, 1980; Shepard, 1978). Conrad's (1964) evidence on speech-based coding for visual memory of letters provided a vivid instance of internal *recoding*, in which information registered in one modality (visual letters) gets transformed to the stimulus dimensionality of a radically different modality (speech coding) for storage and recall later. Speech recoding has been the single most important concept in the field known as short-term memory ever since. Proponents of *schemata* don't usually talk to people interested in coding, but codes and schemata are really instances of the same concept—alternate bodies of world knowledge that guide the way new information is received and stored.

Traditional ideas of stimulus selection and sampling may be found in animal learning sources, but they do not really capture the idea here, for in them the selectivity is not tantamount to a fundamental reorganization of the information. Perhaps Lawrence's (1950) proposals for acquired distinctiveness of stimulus dimensions were a step in this direction, but this work seems to have been greeted over the years with more respect than investors.

The Spatial Metaphor

Roediger (1980) has documented with care how spatial ideas of storage have dominated our thinking and our very terminology about memory. I don't propose to repeat those particulars here. To an amazing degree, we think of memory as storage areas, into which entities are placed and from which they are later extracted. Everyday experience provides all too handy a metaphor for memory storage, as when we put objects into places and then fetch them later.

Entrenched as the spatial-storage metaphor may be in folk psychology, recent developments have advanced it even more among memory psychologists: The distinction among learning, retention, and retrieval, suggested in different words by Kohler (1947) and Melton (1963), was a breakthrough in analytical thinking about memory. It opened the way for the experimental investigation of retrieval, which must surely rank as one of our chief accomplishments. But the learning-retention-retrieval analysis probably increased the allure of library or spatial storage metaphors.

Broadbent's Y-tube model for selective attention (Broadbent, 1958) showed how information-processing models could be realized in spatial notations that were another advance in analytical clarity. And just as short-term memory experiments were first being reported, the notion of buffer storage was becoming familiar to psychologists knowledgeable about digital computers. It is no wonder that under these influences, the age of the *memory store,* was inaugurated. Memory stores are dedicated parts of the mental apparatus whose only purpose is holding information passively over time. Whether leading these trends or in response to them, neuropsychology has in the meantime supplied ample evidence of localization of function, specificity of loss, and the like.

Hierarchical and network models of memory organization are no less committed to the spatial metaphor than ''flow-diagram'' models. Although they presume no stores, they do propose a metric of proximity upon spatially-organized knowledge (Collins & Quillian, 1969) or episodic memories (Estes, 1972).

Even with consciousness raised about the dominant spatial perspective among memory scientists, more than vague uneasiness is required to question this basic concept. Beginning at least with Lashley (1950), there have been calls for alternative ideas about memory representation. Neisser (1967) voiced an articulate possibility when he suggested a bank of tuning forks prepared to resonate to different frequencies as a model for memory storage. Newer and more meticulously worked-out thoughts on distributed memory (Hinton & J. A. Anderson, 1981; J. M. Eich, 1982; Murdock, 1982) have been aimed at showing how the nonspatial models can handle traditional facts of human memory, largely through simulation. The complexity of these models makes them less handy as sources of viable concepts for day-to-day problem-solving. But this confession may tell more about my own cognitive development, in the Piagetian sense, than about the models: A problem for all of us is to separate the formal properties of a model from our limited abilities to think in really abstract terms. Here is one ironic example: Ratcliff's explicitly distributed, nonspatial theory of retrieval is based on the resonance metaphor (Ratcliff, 1978) and yet he uses, among other assumptions, the almost irresistably spatial mechanism of a random walk.

I think the spatial mode of thought is less entrenched in the field of animal learning. This may be because acquisition, storage, and retrieval are not so frequently distinguished in that field. In particular memory storage per se is perhaps less emphasized. An apologist for the field of human memory might suggest the difference is because theory is less advanced in complexity in animal learning. I know people in the latter area, however, who would maintain that the "cognitive revolution" has led to sloppy, mentalistic theories and we deserve the mess we've produced.

Episodic Memory

The extraordinary restrictions Tulving (1983) has recently placed around his original (Tulving, 1972) distinction between episodic memory and what I like to call generic knowledge (semantic memory, for Tulving) have not prevented virtually universal acceptance of the "pragmatic" distinction between the two. When we are testing retrieval of information planted in memory by deliberate design of an experiment, we may be dealing with a different set of problems than when we are testing retrieval of information people gained in "real life" prior to experimental intervention. If this pragmatic distinction between episodic memory and knowledge seems like a cheap concession, one should recall how equally plausible was the alternative assumption that "memory is memory."

Three historical phases should probably be separated. Ebbinghaus (1885/1964) must have been convinced that, by using unfamiliar materials, he was effecting the *tabula rasa* of his philosophical roots, bypassing the knowledge system altogether. (The really brilliant contributions of Ebbinghaus are usually overlooked, ironically enough, in textbook citations. These sources carry on instead about his invention and use of the nonsense syllable, which we now see as a misguided blunder.) Scattered voices in the wilderness notwithstanding, the field fell in behind Ebbinghaus, on this matter, for a long time. The second phase came with appreciation, led largely by Underwood (1957), that experimental learning is laid against, and interacts with, a rich background of exterior language and learning. Here we find the "memory is memory" assumption and its implicit companion, strength theory. Assuming the combination of pre-experimental and experimental habits, interference theorists did experiments trying to show episodic memories overcoming prior generic knowledge and then falling away against spontaneous recovery of the latter afterwards. These experiments had failed notoriously to show episodic memory as continuous with prior knowledge in the predicted ways (Postman & Underwood, 1973) by the time Tulving's own experiments (for example Thomson & Tulving, 1970) brought the issue into sharp relief. Tulving's encoding specificity principle had its basis in experiments showing that pre-experimental strength of an association counted for nothing as compared to whether or not it had been somehow involved in the learning episode. Alternatives exist for coping with this fact, but it does represent a third stage of rationalizing how memories lie among knowledge in the mind. We now can no longer speak of simple additivity between pre-experimental and episodic "strengths."

Acceptance of the pragmatic distinction between episodic memory and knowledge sets the stage for a lively debate about whether episodic memory should be considered a temporary marking of the knowledge structure (Anderson, 1976) or a separate system altogether (Tulving, 1983). Should this distinction and the ensuing debate be an urgent priority for animal-learning theory? I think not, for an interesting reason: The research enterprise in human memory sticks almost exclusively with learning materials that are thoroughly familiar elements of their subjects' outside lives. I stand ready for correction but I think this is not the case in animal learning, with its buzzers, illuminated keys, elevated runways, and double-avoidance boxes. It may be more true than false to claim that human (verbal) learning is essentially transfer and more false than true to claim the same for animal learning.

PRINCIPLES OF PROCESSING

Spreading Activation

The assumption that knowledge is laid out spatially in accord with semantic (or episodic) distances has generated heuristic assumptions about information processing. Convenient techniques for measuring response speed have animated these assumptions. Again, Collins and Quillan (1969) seem to have been among the first to exploit notions of spreading semantic activation with their predictions of verification speed based on assumed subset and property networks of concepts. Question-answering time was faster when concepts could be presumed to be close in the concept network than when remote. Meyer, Schvaneveldt, and Ruddy (1975) extended similar ideas to lexical decisions. Following their work, spreading activation has been a seminal concept in the psychology of reading.

Several authors suggested, during the 1970s, that automatic spreading activation was really only the passive half of a two-process, passive/active principle of knowledge activation. The form of the hypothesis varied from source to source, but the assumption was usually that there is an initial, passive wave of excitation followed later by a consciously-controlled selective search (Atkinson & Juola, 1973; LaBerge & Samuels, 1975; Posner & Snyder, 1975; Shiffrin & Schneider, 1977). In a later section (Strategies), the active half of this type of theory will receive attention.

People using the idea of spreading activation have generally been interested in generic or semantic knowledge structures. One exception was the spreading activation assumed by Estes (1972) for recall from serially ordered lists in episodic memory. In the hands of J. R. Anderson (1976), spreading activation has made contact with both episodic memory and natural language understanding. Anderson's experiments vary the number of artificially-learned propositions emanating from lexical nodes, showing that responses are slow to constituents that are "loaded" with multiple associations. Challenges to the underlying idea of spreading activation have been rare enough to make me think it must be a basic concept in our field. Spread of activation is a testable proposition, however, and dissent exists: Ratcliff and McKoon (1981) found that facilitation between remote concepts differs from facilitation between close concepts more in the ultimate *level of facilitation* than in the speed this facilitation reaches asymptote. Although Anderson (1983) has accommodated this result in the newest version of ACT, it should cause restless nights for those who depend on a more casual spatial-spread metaphor.

Top-Down and Bottom-Up Influences

That we often perceive and remember things as coherent wholes depends on a balance of elementary sensations and memories coupled with world knowledge that is already organized as coherent wholes. Recognition of this central issue cuts across specialties as diverse as reading, speech perception, category-abstraction, and reconstructive memory. For memory theory the principle is simply that you can't smugly assume an organized pattern of retrieval represents organized learning and storage of the episodic memories you are interested in. The organization might be imposed by a retrieval process that adds organization based on world knowledge to essentially fragmentary memory traces.

How seriously to take the top-down influences is a dimension that separates memory workers today. One view is that remembering is inherently a problem-solving activity (Neisser, 1976; Schank, 1982) and that experimental safeguards against reconstructive processes in recall are tantamount to throwing out the baby with the bathwater (or in Robert Abelson's more elegant simile, like throwing out the baby and clinging tenaciously to the bathwater). I still believe it is useful to separate the memory and problem-solving aspects of retrieval, but anyone who denies the latter altogether is being unrealistic.

I return again to the possibility that human learning is more based on transfer than animal learning. If the knowledge base which animals bring into the laboratory is thinner than that for humans, it should be no wonder that our animal-learning colleagues can ignore the matter relatively. I wonder whether a case could be made that the proper comparison is with biological-evolutionary forces as the top-down constraint or influence. For example, that some species typically freeze in response to danger and others locomote (Bolles, 1970) would seem to me to be a top-down influence of great importance to the understanding of avoidance conditioning.

Strategies

Indispensible as it is to the everyday conceptual life of the cognitive psychologist, *the strategy* is seldom examined experimentally itself. So that we may be sure to know what we are talking about, I present here a prototype example of explanation based on strategy. A famous experiment by Rubenstein, Lewis, and Rubenstein (1971) established that people performing a lexical decision task are unexpectedly slow (as against appropriate controls) to affirm that letter strings like YOKE are indeed English words. The interpretation was that this is because of the fact that YOKE is a homophone to another word, YOLK. Because the task was visual-motor, this homophone effect suggested an involvement of speech in a silent-reading task (task reductionism again). Some years later, Davelaar, Coltheart, Besner, and Jonasson (1978) showed that the homophone effect depended crucially on the overall experimental design. In the Rubenstein et al. experiment the nonwords had all been pronounceable items like SLINT, and these nonwords were never confusable with real words on the basis of sound. Thus, some form of saying the candidate test items internally would serve to establish their lexicality. Davelaar et al. had the insight that the internal-speech "strategy" might be a poor one if the experiment included substantial numbers of items of the form BRANE, pseudo-homophones to real words. With items of the BRANE type coming up frequently, subjects *if they had the option* might choose to ignore the reference to internal speech and decide on the basis of the visual appearence of the item. Davelaar et al. (1978) were able to show, as had Rubenstein et al. (1971), that with nonwords exclusively of the SLINT variety and none of the BRANE type nonword, YOKE was indeed an especially slow item. However, when the experimental materials were changed so as to include BRANE-type items intermixed in the experimental session, YOKE was no slower than nonhomophonic control items. Thus, the reference to inner speech during lexical decision-making was shown to be a strategy available to subjects in flexible response to the experimental design, not an inevitable mediating stage, as some investigators had claimed all through the history of research on reading.

Sorting out which of our phenomena are "hard wired" and which depend on strategies is a major preoccupation of the psychology of memory and related fields. Perhaps the use of visual imagery in mental rotation (Shepard & Metzler, 1971) is not strategically optional in this sense. The discovery that our particular favorite experimental outcome is "only a strategy" causes us to swallow hard; most cognitive experimenters would prefer to have the controlling hand in how their subjects process information.

This attitude is irrational. Strategies do not celebrate free will, they force us to reformulate simpler experimental effects as higher-order interactions. The process by which people are sensitive to overall experimental situations, the nature of the nonwords in our example, is seldom studied. It reminds me of the early experiments on place learning and response learning in which rats proved sensitive to laboratory cues that were at first ignored by experimenters. Paying attention to sources of incidental light in the laboratory must surely qualify as a strategy under any definition of the term that does not disqualify animals *a priori*.

In human memory work, particularly developmental work, strategies are grouped with *metacognitive* skills. A refreshing attitude towards developmental memory has been that young children are perhaps not deficient at all in memory capacity but rather are unskilled in strategic, metacognitive operations. This suggests a promising avenue for following continuity of process between animal and human work. The comparisons should be the performance accomplishments of lower animals held against those of young children. For certain species, primates, for example, there is overlap. The question to ask is what monkeys can do as compared with normal young or mentally retarded human subjects. This approach has been used recently by Buchanan, Gill and Braggio (1981) in a study of a chimpanzee's serial position and clustering effects.

Procedural Knowledge

I have been resisting the temptation, in this survey, to promote currently fashionable concepts that have not stood the test of time. On the other hand, I see no reason to conceal what may be a breakthrough just because it is recent; especially when the idea may help in our goal of in comparing basic concepts in animal and human research:

J. R. Anderson (1976, Chapter 4) may have been first to emphasize the distinction between declarative and procedural knowledge for psychological audiences. He was, of course, following leads from philosophy and artificial intelligence. Although the distinction was explicit and even fundamental to Anderson's ACT theory, proceduralism has been advanced more by several other recent developments.

One influence was a change in direction for memory theory during the 1970s, turning away from multistore models towards a conception of memory as the byproduct of perceptual activity. I read this proceduralist message easily into the famous Craik and Lockhart (1972) paper, but it was especially explicit in Kolers' work in the 1970s, (for example, Kolers & Ostry, 1974; see Kolers & Roediger, 1984). Kolers' proceduralism emphasized that all perception involves more-or-less skilled operations on the stimulus and that, consciously or not, there is persistence of those operations *as applied to those stimuli*. His experimental demonstrations showed surprisingly good memory for superficial encoding operations (reading transformed typography) carried out on verbal materials.

The brain centers used for perceptual analysis should surely remain active in response to specific perceptual processing for some moments after offset of the stimulus, which parts remaining active depending on which forms of analysis were applied to the stimulus (that is, what form of coding occurred). For this lingering, patterned activation of the overall system to be our sole agency for memory, even after days, months, and years, is farfetched. Proceduralism needs some distinction, like Hebb's (1949), between the *activity trace and structural trace*. The stipulation to make such a proposal truly procedural would be that the locus of memory, whether the active, persistent, residue of perception or the ensuing structural changes, is in the information-processing apparatus used for perception or encoding in the first place. Terms like short- and long-term memory may be useful once more, to cover this distinction. They would be purely classificatory terms in that each possible form of coding would carry its own activity and structural traces, though. Memory would thus be the by-product of the skills engaged in perception.

The topic of skill (motor skill) had of course been a part of mainstream learning theory in Hullean days, but was then for years an increasingly insulated subspecialty, estranged from both the human-memory and animal-learning fields. The attitude that motor skills were incidental to "real" human learning and (verbal) memory made it possible to regard as isolated curiosities reports that these skills were spared in otherwise severe amnesia (Corkin, 1968). In parallel with Kolers' and others' proceduralist view of verbal learning and memory, this distinction, between verbal and motor skills, has broken down too: Warrington and Weiskrantz (1974) demonstrated a while ago that amnesics perform normally on verbal materials when the manner of testing is procedural rather than declarative (word completion rather than, say, recall or recognition). But some time passed before work of Squire and others (Cohen & Squire, 1980; Graf, Squire, & Mandler, 1984) made the point dramatically. Amnesics who are a total loss in conventional memory tests show up *absolutely unimpaired* when the same episodic information is measured by word-completion or perceptual thresholds. The amnesia work is another indication we need a concept such as procedural memory.

Meanwhile, work by Jacoby and others (Jacoby, 1983; Jacoby & Dallas, 1981) on verbal memory in normal subjects showed in various ways that perceptual fluency (procedural knowledge) was not necessarily correlated across experimental operations with normal (recognition-recall) memory measures. The interpretation of these "dissociations" is subject to debate (Graf, Squire, & Mandler, 1984; Jacoby, 1983; Tulving, Schacter, & Stark, 1982), but these data affirm that there is now an aspect of unconscious memory for verbal experiences that was previously unsuspected.

Unconscious perception has returned to respectable psychology. The meaning of a word can be perceived and shown to affect perception of a related word under conditions where the perceiver does not know the first word was even presented (Marcel, 1983). I was trained to resist as nonsense suggestions of perceptual defense or subception when I was in graduate school. But the evidence now available from several laboratories makes resistance difficult. Furthermore, the procedural/declarative distinction makes unconscious perception sensible. If our conscious, declarative knowledge is part of a separate system from a concealed mental life that rattles off skilled perceptual procedures automatically, as Marcel (1983) has assumed, then it becomes an open question whether these procedures could become conscious and subject to retrieval. In any case, the old issue of "learning without awareness" can be considered settled (not that it was ever an especially popular issue in animal learning!).

This talk of proceduralism in human learning and memory could be important for the goals of this conference. If humans have these dual memory systems, procedural and declarative, systems that behave differently in response to factors like amnesia, experimental conditions, perceptual clarity and the like, then the suggestion is that we should look for common principles between animals and humans in some places but not in others: Declarative knowledge, as contrasted with procedural, may be inherently metacognitive, if not downright epiphenomenal, and as such, *perhaps uniquely human*. This speculation relies on consciousness as the criterion for declarative knowledge perhaps more than is warranted. I am thinking of the amnesic who cannot achieve deliberate access to memories that are otherwise quite intact by procedural measures. More complete analysis of the procedural/declarative distinction would not disqualify lower animals from declarative knowledge (see Adams & Dickinson, 1981).

Almost exclusive study of the human declarative system, up to now, may have been unfortunate: The declarative, conscious system may be systematically misleading in some sense, as regards what we know and what makes us behave as we do. So argue Marcel (1983) and Nisbett and Wilson (1977), from entirely different empirical contexts. In both of these statements, the human is pictured as a naive cognitive psychologist, trying to make and test plausible process assumptions *a posteriori* about why his behavior turned out the way it did. These process assumptions, whether from naive or sophisticated cognitive psychologists, should probably not be the ones held as candidates for generalization across species differences.

PRINCIPLES OF CAPACITY LIMITATION

From the precipitous forgetting curve of Ebbinghaus (1885/1964), to the reconstructive memory errors of Bartlett (1932), the unlearning and competition hypotheses of interference theory (Postman, 1961), and down to Tulving's recognition failure of recallable words (Tulving & Thomson, 1973), students of human memory and learning have focused hard on performance breakdowns. Our colleagues specializing in animal learning have not ignored breakdowns, by any means; consider the Hullean ideas of reactive inhibition (Hull, 1943), Harlow's "error factor" explanations of learning set (Harlow, 1949), and the more recent blocking and overshadowing paradigms (Kamin, 1969). The emphasis on acquisition in animal work and on forgetting in human work make it natural, however, that decremental principles are much more highly elaborated in the latter than in the former. Efforts at *rapprochement* between animal and human work should include sober attention to this difference in emphasis. Even if our theoretical languages were much more compatible with each other than they seem to be, the emphasis in one field on gradual acquisition and in the other field on decrements could make the best-intentioned conversations among us awkward. Current concepts of performance limitation in human cognition, learning, and memory fall under headings of input, storage, and output. As before, these are divisions of expediency. I appreciate that, at some level, these three are hard to distinguish.

Input Limitations

Estes (1959) and Broadbent (1958) both advanced explicit models for perceptual selection in the 1950s, the former drawing on a background of research in animal learning and the latter on emerging work in communication theory (dichotic listening, to be specific). (By the way, I try to be careful in reserving the term "model" for sets of assumptions that are explicit and internally consistent—that "work" demonstrably, either in the mathematical sense or by analogic physical criteria [in Broadbent's case, the Y-tube].) Both models stressed that some early selection process limited what information could become accessible to later processing resources. These claims set the stage for decades of experimental debate about "early" versus "late" selection (Deutsch & Deutsch, 1963; Treisman & Geffen, 1968). The serial versus parallel processing argument, which has been another focus of attention in information-processing, really boils down to the same issue, for processing at the level of sensory transduction is manifestly parallel and at the response stage it is just as manifestly serial (only one response at a time). Serial processing of information received in parallel is an assumption that meshes smoothly with others of our basic concepts, particularly that of the buffer memory: It is *because* subsequent processing stages must handle information serially that we need to have earlier buffer memories. Buffer memory can act as a waiting room where surplus information—information exceeding serial input limitations—can wait its turn. This idea motivates Broadbent's S and P systems (our first flow diagram, Broadbent, 1958), Sperling's model for preliminary iconic storage (Sperling, 1963), and, really, the entire concept of primary memory or short-term storage (Atkinson & Shiffrin, 1968; Waugh & Norman, 1965), all of which have been absolutely fundamental to modern thinking about human learning and memory.

The classical buffer stores are fading fast in popularity these days (Crowder, 1982, 1983; Haber, 1983). Correspondingly, the serial/parallel issue is losing its innocent appeal: J. R. Anderson (1976) and Townsend (1971) claimed, with mathematical demonstrations, that the serial/parallel issue was not capable *in principle* of being decided by data. Turvey (1973) with his "concurrent-contingent" model of information processing and, later, McClelland (1979) with his proposal of cascaded stages of information processing, further complicated what had seemed elegant simplicity in guiding theory with data (for example, Sternberg, 1966).

But the issue still lives. The most extreme version of late selection ever proposed has recently come from Marcel (1983), when he asserted that everything (given some minimal sensory registration) progresses completely, automatically, and in parallel, through the information processing system all the way to meaning. Marcel (1983) contrasts this unconscious, unlimited parallel processing with a second, subsequent, conscious process which is the basis for our awareness of events and deliberate responses. Earlier notions of awareness (LaBerge & Samuels, 1974) had assumed what I call the "flashlight metaphor"—that we can scan our mental operations but only with a narrow-focus device that illuminates isolated regions of the whole machinery. Marcel's radical proposal is that we never really can know our information-processing routines. We can only construct and test hypotheses about how the information-processing might have worked in order to yield the results that ensued. Because this proposal is radical, it brings into relief a set of assumptions that were inarticulate for being taken for granted. However, there is not space to dwell on this theme here.

Storage Limitations

If having buffer stores helps to overcome serial processing bottlenecks, a forgetting mechanism is provided by their limited capacity to hold information. Miller's (1956) paper on chunks and the limitation of memory span to 7 plus-or-minus 2 items was a pivotal contribution. It made a transition between the classical, psychometric concept of the memory span and modern information-processing approaches to memory. The limitation on memory span has usually been handled through the assumption that when stores get overloaded new information can be admitted only through displacement of old information. Displacement thus emerged as an authentic principle of forgetting, a reason to expect retention to decrease across time delays, independently of acquisition and retrieval conditions.

Estes (1980) complained that notions of buffers and slots result from an erroneous assumption that the mind resembles hardware arrangements in the digital computer. Erroneous as it might have been, the concept of buffer-limitations was the cornerstone of massive research efforts in applied memory theory: Analytic techniques for measuring numerical capacities of Primary Memory, for example, were used to determine whether memory deficits owing to childhood, advanced age, or amnesia might not be attributed to buffer capacity. Case and his colleagues (Case, Kurland, & Goldberg, 1982) have used such an approach to good advantage recently in the study of children's reasoning.

Forgetting in so-called long-term memory ought to be among the most intensively studied phenomena in the field, one might think. By forgetting, I mean specifically why retrieval failures grow with the passage of time since learning, when conditions of acquisition and conditions of retrieval are kept constant. In the early decades of the century, this was indeed a thriving research area, first as workers hurried to replicate Ebbinghaus' forgetting curve and then as experiments on retroactive inhibition (McGeoch, 1942) became popular. This approach flourished in the intricacies of S-R interference theory (Postman, 1961) and then ground to a halt as these same intricacies became unwieldy (Postman & Underwood, 1973).

Buffer models for short-term memory bypassed the problem neatly by assuming that there simply *is* no loss from long-term memory (Waugh & Norman, 1965). This principle certainly makes life easier for the theorist and it seems to be accepted widely, if tacitly. Perhaps the depth of processing and retrieval-based accounts of performance failure seemed so powerful, we have questioned whether an authentic *forgetting* principle for long-term memory were necessary. There are isolated exceptions: Bahrick (1984) has recently proposed experiments as tests of the permanent-memory hypothesis, generally endorsing it. Loftus and Loftus (1980), on the other hand, deplored psychologists' and laymen's acceptance of permanent storage on the basis of the flimsy evidence. With these exceptions, the field is content to embrace, as sort of an antiprinciple, that loss from long-term memory is nothing to worry about. Few of our basic concepts are so bad a mismatch with what the intelligent public might expect of a modern scientific psychology of memory.

Output Limitations

Minimizing the importance of outright forgetting in all but the sensory and buffer memories poses a major explanatory problem, because retrieval failures are so obvious a part of our lives as scientists and as laymen. This gap has been filled for nearly 50 years by the proposition that the performance breakdowns come from retrieval, from difficulty in gaining access to available memories. From the beginnings of interference theory, McGeoch (1942) was clear that interference at recall was a blocking of one response by another response attached to the same stimulus. Only the unlearning mechanism (which produced a temporary unavailability of competing prior associations through an analogue of experimental extinction) located response failures at the retention, rather than retrieval phase. And although unlearning was a retention mechanism rather than a retrieval mechanism, its role was restricted to retroactive inhibition. (In retroactive inhibition, a subsequent learning experience interferes with a prior one.) Unlearning played no role at all in proactive inhibition, which Underwood (1957) demonstrated to the satisfaction of many was the more important factor in forgetting. Proactive inhibition had to be exclusively a consequence of inaccessibility of available responses. So again the limiting stage was retrieval. The response-set-suppression hypothesis of Postman, Stark, and Fraser (1968) was a theoretical departure from orthodox interference theory, but it left intact the nearly axiomatic faith that observed performance failures occur because of retrieval dynamics and not because memory traces had been lost.

Tulving's early experiments on retrieval cues (for example, Tulving & Pearlstone, 1966) gave a fresh perspective on the accessibility/availability distinction. These experiments emphasized retrieval processes to a new generation of psychologists, largely unfamiliar with interference theory. Tulving's ensuing work on encoding specificity (Tulving & Thomson, 1973; see review in Tulving, 1983) stressed that retrieval failures should be addressed as jointly caused by the exact nature of what was learned at encoding and what cues were present at the time of attempted retrieval. Encoding specificity in Tulving's work makes explicit and testable the very basic but very slippery concept of *context* as a factor in human learning and memory. Contextual learning is a concept we cannot do without, especially as it provides a nonmystical way of talking about what changes in an orderly way with the passage of time. Successful experimental programs have stressed what might be called "sledge-hammer" manipulations of context—room shifting (Smith, Glenberg, & Bjork, 1978), dramatic external environments (Godden & Baddeley, 1975) or state-dependent learning in distinctive internal conditions (J. E. Eich, 1980). As far as the flow of time without such radical interventions, contextual drift is more an article of faith than it is an operational concept.

J. R. Anderson's "fan effect" (Anderson, 1976) is the contemporary grandchild of McGeoch's interference concept. It combines assumptions of (1) a propositional network for storing knowledge and episodic memories, (2) spreading activation at retrieval, and (3) limited-power to invest in the branching activation process. These assumptions entail that retrieval will be worse the more associations there are connected with a particular memory node. However, this cost is realized in the time required for retrieval as well as perhaps in retrieval accuracy. Beginning in the middle 1960s with Sternberg's (1966) experiments on memory search, the analysis of retrieval has been shifting to the latency domain, perhaps acnowledging that apparently inaccessible memories usually do come out sooner or later.

CONCLUDING REMARKS: IMPEDIMENTS TO CONSTRUCTIVE DISCUSSION

My survey here has been terse and so I cannot see myself summarizing it further. Instead, I shall collect here at the end several circumstances that I think are impediments to a fruitful dialogue between the human and animal investigators. These are all cases of our apparently working and thinking at cross purposes, mismatches between our two conceptual languages. They all became evident as I was reviewing this material and I think we will be better off to have them on the table. Indeed, these may be good issues on which to start: They transcend our individual experimental activities and yet they do not seem completely intractable.

First, the military, linguistic, and cybernetic influences under which cognitive psychology has been molded for the last 25 years have moved it towards a central concern with communication and away from the central concern of learning with adaptation to the environment. Would it be interesting for animal workers to tackle problems of learning in animal-communication situations?

Second, human learning and memory research uses materials that are almost always highly familiar to subjects, whereas the discriminanda and manipulanda of animal laboratories typically are not familiar to the subjects using them. What memory principles would we be entertaining if our materials were unfamiliar odors, visual designs, or snowflake patterns?

Third, top-down influences on animal behavior in typical learning research are largely biological-evolutionary, whereas in human research, top-down influences are largely linguistic and experientially based.

Fourth, our concepts of human learning and memory, to the present, are largely guided by data on declarative knowledge, whereas it is reasonable that the procedural system just now coming under study is the one to compare with animal concepts. If skill learning and perceptual fluency were the reference tasks in human memory research, would ideas like strength—which do so badly for declarative memory—have been rejected so readily? Would such ideas form a better fit to animal-learning concepts?

Fifth, theory in the animal domain has been responsive mainly to the growth of performance in acquisition, whereas theory in the human domain is more responsive to performance breakdowns. Can we find common ground by considering forgetting in animals and acquisition in humans?

ACKNOWLEDGMENT

Preparation of this paper was supported partially by NSF Grant BNS 8219661. I greatly appreciate the comments of Robert L. Greene on an earlier draft.

REFERENCES

Adams, C., & Dickinson, A. (1981). Actions and habits: Variations in associative representation during instrumental learning. In N. E. Spear & R. R. Miller (Eds.), *Information processing in animals: Memory mechanisms (pp. 143–165)*. Hillsdale, NJ: Lawrence Erlbaum Associates.

Anderson, J. R. (1976). *Language, memory and thought*. Hillsdale, NJ: Lawrence Erlbaum Associates.

Anderson, J. R. (1983). A spreading activation theory of memory. *Journal of Verbal Learning and Verbal Behavior, 22,* 261–295.

Atkinson, R. C., & Juola, J. F. (1973). Factors influencing speed and accuracy of word recognition. In S. Kornblum (Ed.), *Attention and performance IV.* London: Academic Press.

Atkinson, R. C., & Shiffrin, R. M. (1968). Human memory: A proposed system and its control processes. In K. W. Spence & J. T. Spence (Eds.), *The psychology of learning and memory, Volume 2.* New York: Academic Press.

Bahrick, H. P. (1984). Semantic memory content in permastore: Fifty years of memory for Spanish learned in school. *Journal of Experimental Psychology: General, 113,* 1–29.

Bartlett, F. C. (1932). *Remembering: A study in experimental and social psychology.* Cambridge, Eng.: Cambridge University Press.

Bolles, R. C. (1970). Species-specific defense reactions and avoidance behavior. *Psychological Review, 77,* 32–48.

Bower, G. H. (1962). An association model for response and training variables in paired-associate learning. *Psychological Review, 69,* 34–53.

Broadbent, D. E. (1958). *Perception and communication.* New York: Pergamon.

Buchanan, J. P., Gill, T. V., & Braggio, J. T. (1981). Serial position and clustering effects in a chimpanzee's "free recall." *Memory & Cognition, 9,* 651–660.

Case, R., Kurland, M. D., & Goldberg, J. (1982). Operational efficiency and the growth of short-term memory span. *Journal of Experimental Child Psychology, 33,* 386–404.

Cohen, N. J., & Squire, L. R. (1980). Preserved learning and retention of pattern-analysing skill in amnesia: Dissociation of knowing how and knowing that. *Science, 210,* 207–210.

Collins, A. M., & Quillian, M. R. (1969). Retrieval time from semantic memory. *Journal of Verbal Learning and Verbal Behavior, 8,* 240–247.

Conrad, R. (1964). Acoustic confusions in immediate memory. *British Journal of Psychology, 55,* 75–84.

Corkin, S. (1968). Acquisition of motor skill after bilateral medial temporal-lobe excision.*Neuropsychologia, 6,* 255.

Craik, F. I. M., & Lockhart, R. S. (1972). Levels of processing: A framework for memory research. *Journal of Verbal Learning and Verbal Behavior, 11,* 671–684.

Crowder, R. G. (1982). The demise of short-term memory. *Acta Psychologica, 50,* 291–323.

Crowder, R. G. (1983). The purity of auditory memory. *Philosophical Transactions of the Royal Society of London, B, 302,* 251–265.

Davelaar, E., Coltheart, M., Besner, D., & Jonasson, J. T. (1978). Phonological recoding and lexical access. *Memory & Cognition, 6,* 391–402.

Deutsch, J. A., & Deutsch, D. (1963). Attention: Some theoretical considerations.*Psychological Review, 70,* 80–90.

Dollard, J., & Miller, N. E. (1950). *Personality and psychotherapy.* New York: McGraw Hill.

Ebbinghaus, H. E. (1885). *Memory.* (Translated by H. A. Ruger and C. E. Bussenius.) New York: Dover (Reprint), 1964.

Eich, J. E. (1980). The cue-dependent nature of state-dependent retrieval. *Memory & Cognition, 8,* 157–173.

Eich, J. M. (1982). A composite holographic associative recall model. *Psychological Review, 89,* 627–661.

Estes, W. K. (1959). The statistical approach to learning theory. In S. Koch (Ed.), *Psychology, the study of a science, Volume 2.* New York: McGraw Hill.

Estes, W. K. (1972). As associative basis for coding and organization in memory. In A. W. Melton & E. Martin (Eds.), *Coding processes in human memory.* Washington, D.C.: Winston.

Estes, W. K. (1980). Is human memory obsolete? *American Scientists, 68,* 62–69.

Fisher, R. P., & Craik, F. I. M. (1977). Interaction between encoding and retrieval operations in cued recall. *Journal of Experimental Psychology: Human Learning and Memory, 3,* 701–711.

Godden, D. R., & Baddeley, A. D. (1975). Context-dependent memory in two natural environments: On land and underwater. *British Journal of Psychology, 66,* 325–332.

Graf, P., Squire, L., & Mandler, G. (1984). The information that amnesics do not forget. *Journal of Experimental Psychology: Learning, Memory, & Cognition, 10,* 164–178.

Haber, R. N. (1983). The impending demise of the icon. *The Behavioral and Brain Sciences, 6,* 1–54.

Harlow, H. F. (1949). The formation of learning sets. *Psychological Review, 56,* 51–65.

Hebb, D. O. (1949). *Organization of behavior.* New York: Wiley.

Hinton, G., & Anderson, J. (1981). *Parallel models of associative memory.* Hillsdale, NJ: Lawrence Erlbaum Associates.

Hull, C. L. (1943). *Principles of behavior.* New York: Appleton-Century-Crofts.

Jacoby, L. (1983). Remembering the data: Analyzing interactive processes in reading. *Journal of Verbal Learning and Verbal Behavior, 22,* 485–508.

Jacoby, L., & Dallas, M. (1981). On the relationship between autobiographical memory and perceptual learning. *Journal of Experimental Psychology: General, 3,* 306–340.

Kamin, L. J. (1969). Predictability, surprise, attention, and conditioning. In B. A. Campbell & R. M. Church (Eds.), *Punishment and aversive behavior.* New York: Appleton-Century-Crofts.

Köhler, W. (1947). *Gestalt psychology.* New York: Liveright (Meuter).

Kolers, P. A., & Ostry, D. J. (1974). Time course of loss of information regarding pattern analyzing operations. *Journal of Verbal Learning and Verbal Behavior, 13,* 599–612.

Kolers, P. A., & Roediger, H. L. (1984). Procedures of mind. *Journal of Verbal Learning and Verbal Behavior, 23,* 425–449.

Kosslyn, S. M. (1980). *Image and mind.* Cambridge, MA: Harvard University Press.

LaBerge, D., & Samuels, J. (1974). Toward a theory of automatic activation in reading. *Cognitive Psychology, 6,* 293–323.

Lashley, K. S. (1950). In search of the engram. *Symposia of the society for Experimental Biology, 4,* 454–582.

Lawrence, D. H. (1950). Acquired distinctiveness of cues: II. Selective association in a constant stimulus situation. *Journal of Experimental Psychology, 40,* 175–188.

Loftus, E. F., & Loftus, G. R. (1980). On the permanence of stored information in the human brain. *American Psychologist, 35,* 409–420.

Marcel, A. J. (1983). Conscious and unconscious perception: An approach to the relations between phenomenal experience and perceptual processes. *Cognitive Psychology, 15,* 238–300.

McClelland, J. L. (1979). On the time relations of mental processes: An examination of systems of processes in cascade. *Psychological Review, 86,* 287–330.

McGeoch, J. A. (1942). *The psychology of human learning.* New York: Longmans Green.

Melton, A. W. (1963). Implications of short-term memory for a general theory of memory. *Journal of Verbal Learning and Verbal Behavior, 2,* 1–21.

Meyer, D. E., Schvaneveldt, R. W., & Ruddy, M. (1975). Loci of context effects on visual word recognition. In P. M. A. Rabbitt & S. Dornic (Eds.), *Attention and Performance V.* London: Academic Press.

Miller, G. A. (1956). The magical number seven plus or minus two: Some limitations on our capacity to process information. *Psychological Review, 63,* 81–97.

Murdock, B. B., Jr. (1982). A theory for the storage and retrieval of item and associative information. *Psychological Review, 89,* 609–626.

Neisser, U. (1967). *Cognitive psychology.* New York: Appleton-Century-Crofts.

Neisser, U. (1976). *Cognition and reality.* San Francisco: Freeman.

Nisbett, R. E., & Wilson, T. DeC. (1977). Telling more than we know: Verbal reports on mental processes. *Psychological Review, 84,* 231–259.

Posner, M. I., & Snyder, C. R. B. (1975). Facilitation and inhibition in the processing of signals. In P. M. A. Rabbitt & S. Dornic (Eds.), *Attention and Performance V.* London: Academic Press.

Postman, L. (1961). The present status of interference theory. In C. N. Cofer (Ed.), *Verbal learning and verbal behavior.* New York: McGraw Hill.

Postman, L., & Underwood, B. J. (1973). Critical issues in interference theory. *Memory & Cognition, 1,* 19–40.

Postman, L., Stark, K., & Fraser, J. (1968). Temporal changes in interference. *Journal of Verbal Learning and Verbal Behavior, 7,* 672–694.

Ratcliff, R. (1978). A theory of memory retrieval. *Psychological Review, 85,* 59–108.

Ratcliff, R., & McKoon, G. (1981). Does activation really spread? *Psychological Review, 88,* 454–462.

Rescorla, R. A. (1980). *Pavlovian second-order conditioning: Studies in associative learning.* Hillsdale, NJ: Lawrence Erlbaum Associates.

Riley, D. A. (1962). Memory for form. In L. Postman (Ed.), *Psychology in the making.* New York: Knopf.

Roediger, H. L. (1980). Memory metaphors in cognitive psychology. *Memory & Cognition, 8,* 231–246.

Rubenstein, H., Lewis, S. S., & Rubenstein, M. A. (1971). Evidence for phonemic recoding in visual word recognition. *Journal of Verbal Learning and Verbal Behavior, 10,* 645–657.

Schank, R. C. (1982). *Dynamic memory.* Cambridge, Eng.: Cambridge University Press.

Seligman, M. E. P. (1975). *Helplessness.* San Francisco: Freeman.

Shepard, R. N. (1978). The mental image. *American Psychologist, 33,* 125–127.

Shepard, R. N., & Metzler, J. (1971). Mental rotation of three-dimensional objects. *Science, 171,* 701–703.

Shettleworth, S. J. (1978). Reinforcement and the organization of behavior in golden hamsters: Punishment of three action patterns. *Learning and Motivation, 9,* 99–123.

Shiffrin, R. M., & Schneider, W. (1977). Controlled and automatic human information processing: II. Perceptual learning, automatic attending, and a general theory. *Psychological Review, 84,* 127–189.

Smith, S. M., Glenberg, A. M., & Bjork, R. A. (1978). Environmental context and human memory. *Memory & Cognition, 6,* 342–353.

Sperling, G. (1963). A model for visual memory tasks. *Human Factors, 5,* 19–31.

Sternberg, S. (1966). High-speed scanning in human memory. *Science, 153,* 652–654.

Thomson, D. M., & Tulving, E. (1970). Associative encoding and retrieval: Weak and strong cues. *Journal of Experimental Psychology, 86,* 255–262.

Townsend, J. T. (1971). A note on the identifiability of parallel and serial processes. *Perception and Psychophysics, 10,* 161–173.

Treisman, A. M., & Geffen, G. (1968). Selective attention and cerebral dominance in perceiving and responding to speech messages. *Quarterly Journal of Experimental Psychology, 20,* 139–151.

Tulving, E. (1972). Episodic and semantic memory. In E. Tulving & W. Donaldson (Eds.), *Organization of memory.* New York: Academic Press.

Tulving, E. (1983). *Elements of episodic memory.* London: Oxford University Press.

Tulving, E., & Pearlstone, Z. (1966). Availability versus accessibility of information in memory for words. *Journal of Verbal Learning and Verbal Behavior, 5,* 381–391.

Tulving, E., Schacter, D. L., & Stark, H. A. (1982). Priming effects in word-fragment completion are independent of recognition memory. *Journal of Experimental Psychology: Learning, Memory, & Cognition, 8,* 336–342.

Tulving, E., & Thomson, D. M. (1973). Encoding specificity and retrieval processes in episodic memory. *Psychological Review, 80,* 352–373.

Turvey, M. T. (1973). On peripheral and central processes in vision: Inferences from an information-processing analysis of masking with patterned stimuli. *Psychological Review, 80,* 1–52.

Underwood, B. J. (1957). Interference and forgetting. *Psychological Reveiw, 64,* 49–60.

Warrington, E. K., & Weiskrantz, L. (1974). The effect of prior learning on subsequent retention in amnesic patients. *Neuropsychologia, 12,* 419–428.

Watson, J. B., & Rayner, R. (1920). Conditioned emotional reactions. *Journal of Experimental Psychology, 3,* 1–14.

Waugh, N. C., & Norman, D. A. (1965). Primary memory. *Psychological Review, 74,* 89–104.

3 Associationism in Animal Learning

Robert A. Rescorla
University of Pennsylvania

INTRODUCTION

Modern theories of learning in infrahuman organisms are primarily concerned with how animals come to represent their world accurately. Because it is especially important that organisms be able to forecast the coming of pleasureable and painful events on the basis of other events, theories have concentrated on the manner in which they learn relations among events. It is common to identify two examples: the learning of relations among two events both located in the world (Pavlovian conditioning) and the learning of relations between the animal's own behavior and events in the world (instrumental training).

The single theoretical term which is central to explanations of both types of learning is the association. Theories of animal learning attempt to represent virtually all of the learning of relations in terms of the formation of an association between two elements. Moreover, the notion of association which they employ differs little from that described in the 19th century by British philosophers. When two elements become associated, then the activation of the representation of one element leads to the activation of the representation of the other. Associations are primarily seen as differing from each other quantitatively (in strength), rather than qualitatively (in type). A major attempt of theories of nonhuman learning has been to describe all the relational learning across a wide range of species and settings in terms of degrees of association among entities.

Experimental evidence clearly shows that organisms can develop a very rich knowledge of the world. But modern theories have not seen that richness as deriving from a corresponding multiplicity of learning mechanisms. Instead that richness is captured by the way that this single learning mechanism is viewed as operating. In my view, there are three features which modern theories bestow upon the association which allow it to have the needed explanatory power. First, the circumstances that govern the development of associations turn out to be quite complex. Although the organism is not viewed as learning *about* complicated relations it is viewed as learning *because of* those relations. Second, theories acknowledge a wide range of elements which might enter into associations. Moreover, they often attribute to the animal considerable power to process those elements, with the consequence that the elements of an association are often quite complex. Consequently, much of the richness of the animal's knowledge is represented not in terms of its learning different relations among elements but in terms of its learning a single relation among multiple and complexly processed elements. Third, current thinking allows associations to influence the animal's behavior in multiple ways. Those multiple influences allow the animal to maximially exploit that knowledge which associations give him.

I have elsewhere (e.g., Rescorla, 1980) emphasized that any theory of learning must deal with three questions: What are the circumstances which produce learning? What are the contents of that learning? How does that learning affect performance? It seems to me that these are just the sorts of questions that modern theories address with respect to an elementary notion of association. It is in the richness of their answers to those questions that the simplicity of an associative notion is preserved. Consequently, in what follows those three questions are used to organize some of the ideas which are current in theories of learning.

One final introductory point needs to be made. The discussion that follows repeatedly uses phrases such as "the organism" and "the animal," often without reference to the species actually under consideration. This usage betrays an important characteristic of theories in this field. Those theories are constructed to describe learning in an idealized, abstracted organism. Interest often centers on specifying what any organism must know about its world and detailing the ways in which that learning might be achieved. The notion persists that learning mechanisms will share a great many features across species and settings. Modern theories have been more interested in capturing those shared features than in detailing the variation in learning which obviously occurs across species. Consequently, there is a sense in which those theories may not be applicable to any particular species. Rather they might be viewed as a framework whose output describes many of the features which any learning process must have. They serve as a kind of abstract model system which may form the basis upon which variations for specialized systems may be built.

CONDITIONS PRODUCING ASSOCIATIONS

The study of infrahuman learning has been dominated by the issue of what circumstances result in the formation of associations. It is just in the attempt to answer that question that our thinking has most dramatically changed in recent years. Historically, of course, the principal condition under which two events were thought to become associated was their contiguous occurrence. But considerable modern experimentation has forced the conclusion that a simple notion of contiguity fails to capture the exquisiteness of the animal's sensitivity to its environment. In order to associate two events animals often demand more than contiguity; they demand what one might casually call an informational relation between them. I am fond of an analogy which is flawed, but nevertheless useful, between the circumstances producing association and those under which scientists identify causal relations. One does not overestimate many animals by claiming that they will associate two events under just those curcumstances which would lead a scientist to conclude that one event causes the other.

Clearly such an analogy suggests that the animal requires further conditions between two events than their simple cooccurrence in order to associate them. In this first section I note two sets of such further conditions which have been extensively studied and which have influenced our theories of associative learning. One set of conditions might be labeled "formal" conditions because, like the simple notion of contiguity, they describe event relations which can be characterized abstractly, without reference to the events themselves. The other set might be labeled "qualitative" because they make reference to the events associated. Rescorla & Holland (1976) use the terms "extrinsic" and "intrinsic" for this same distinction.

Formal Relations

The finding that has given the greatest impetus to the informational orientation which is current in animal learning is Kamin's (1968, 1969) blocking effect. If one offers an animal the opportunity to associate a compound conditioned stimulus (CS) with an unconditioned stimulus (US), it will typically form associations between that US and several of the components of the signaling CS. However, Kamin found that if one component of the signal had previously been separately paired with the US, then when compounds containing that component are paired with the US, other components develop relatively little association. That is, an AX+ trial may lead to little conditioning of X if the animal has a history of A+ treatment. However, that same AX+ trial is capable of yielding substantial conditioning of X in animals lacking the A+ treatment. This observation is important because both sets of animals share the same contiguity between X and the reinforcer but they differ substantially in the amount of conditioning it produces. Most interpretations of that result have identified the difference in new information which X gives about the reinforcer as the operative factor. In animals for which A was pretrained, A alone forecasts the reinforcer, making X redundant; in the control animals lacking prior conditioning of A, both A and X are informative.

There are several other results which have seemed to fit with this orientation. One is the observation made in my laboratory (e.g., Rescorla, 1968) about the same time as Kamin reported blocking, that the degree of CS/US correlation importantly influences conditioning. The critical finding is that a Pavlovian CS/US contiguity which is adequate to produce associative learning could be rendered ineffective by the simple expedient of presenting the US frequently at times when the CS is absent. Indeed, if the rate of the US occurrence is arranged to be the same whether or not the CS is present, little conditioning of the CS is observed. That outcome occurs despite the fact that such a procedure can result in a large number of joint occurrences of the CS and US. This sort of finding occurs in a wide range of learning situations, including contingency judgments by humans (Dickinson, this volume). These findings too indicate that contiguity is insufficient to produce conditioning: but the information value of the CS seems important to the formation of an association.

The third observation is that of conditioned inhibition. Once one thinks of the CS as providing information about the US, it is natural to ask about cases in which that information is negative, rather than positive. What happens when the CS tells the organism that a US will not be presented? This can be arranged in several ways, but the most frequent is to reinforce a stimulus when it is presented alone, but not when it is accompanied by another stimulus. Such an $A+/AX-$ procedure typically produces an association between A and the US which enables A to evoke a response; but it also produces an association between X and the US which enables X to inhibit performance. Moreover, detailed investigations have suggested that in order for X to have this power it is not enough that it be presented without the US; instead it must inform the organism that an otherwise anticipated US will not occur. That, of course, is just what the $A+/AX-$ paradigm arranges (cf. Konorski, 1948, 1967).

These three observations, blocking, the importance of correlations, and conditioned inhibition, are now touchstones of Pavlovian conditioning. Although fewer Pavlovian preparations have been examined than one might like, these results have a striking generality and hence seem to identify something fundamental about the formation of Pavlovian associations. They seem to represent general principles of Pavlovian associative learning (cf. Cohen, this volume).

Modern theories of associative learning have accommodated informational findings of this sort by what amounts to a reformulation of the notion of contiguity. Consider, for instance, blocking, in which a contiguity between X and US fails to produce associative learning. Some theories (e.g., Mackintosh, 1975; Pearce & Hall, 1980) attribute that failure to inadequacy of processing of the CS. For instance, one might view the animal as having a limited processing capacity for which A and X compete. Then pretraining of A might reduce attention to X, with the result that X is not well-represented at the time of the US and hence benefits little from the contiguity. Various rules have been suggested for how the organism might learn to attend to A, but most appeal to A's ability to predict the US. Alternative theories (e.g., Rescorla & Wagner, 1972) attribute blocking to the inadequacy of processing of the US. According to such views, a US which is well-predicted is less effective at producing further learning. The A stimulus then blocks conditioning of X because A renders the US less effective. In some formulations, the degree of processing is represented in terms of the length of time an event remains in a short term memory (e.g., Wagner, 1981).

What it means in all of these theories for a US to be well-predicted is for it to be preceded by a CS with a strong association allowing activation of a representation of the US. Then informativeness is measured in terms of the absence of a discrepancy between the US anticipated and the US delivered. Note that whether the theory views this information value as modulating the conditionability of a CS or the conditioning power of a US, the informativeness itself is a condition of learning, not part of its content. In each case, the issue is how strong is the resulting association.

It may be helpful to give an example of how such approaches allow a relatively complex relation to be encoded. Consider the correlational result mentioned above, in which a US occurs at a higher rate during a CS than in its absence. This is a relatively complex relation between two events, and one might suppose that the organism encodes this relation itself, learning different correlations depending on the relative frequencies of the US in the presence and absence of the CS. But most modern theories have instead viewed the animal as acquiring a single associative entity which varies in its strength. Moreover, they see that as accomplished by what is basically a modified contiguity mechanism. Most theories suggest that when a US occurs contiguously with a CS there develops some increment in the strength of the association between them. However, when the US occurs in the absence of that CS it does not directly modify the CS-US association. Instead those USs act to condition the stimuli with which they *are* contiguous, namely the general background stimuli. Those background stimuli remain present when the explicit CS occurs and, because they are partially conditioned, they partially predict the USs which occur during that CS. As a result they effectively block conditioning of the CS. That blocking may result because the CS is reduced in salience or because the US is reduced in effectiveness; but whichever the mechanism, conditioning as a result of the CS/US contiguity is reduced. The point is that when the organism is exposed to varying probabilities of the US in the presence and absence of the CS, it does not learn different overall relations between the CS and US. Rather it forms a simple association with varying degrees of success, based on contiguity mechanisms.

This sort of theorizing has been immensely successful in generating a wide variety of predictions and accounting for considerable data in surprising quantative detail (see Mackintosh, 1983; Rescorla, 1972). I mention here just one experiment recently conducted by Durlach (1983) to illustrate its power. According to such accounts, the adverse effect of these extra (between CS) USs comes not so much because they occur but rather because their occurrence conditions the background stimuli. Thus if we could present those USs in such a way as to prevent them from conditioning the background, they should not disrupt conditioning of the CS. Modern theories provide such a way: precede all of the offending USs with another signal; that other signal could then become associated with the US and block the ability of the US to condition the background stimuli. Under those circumstances, one should be able to deliver the extra USs, thereby destroying the overall relation between the original CS and the US, and yet preserve conditioning of that CS.

Durlach (1983) conducted an autoshaping experiment to investigate this deduction. Autoshaping is a standard Pavlovian conditioning preparation in which pigeons are given keylight CSs and food USs. As they learn the association between CS and US, they exhibit pecking at the CS. Durlach asked two questions of this conditioning. First, would the delivery of extra foods in the absence of the CS undermine conditioning of the CS? Second, would that undermining be reduced if those extra USs were preceded by another signal, a tone? Figure 3.1 shows her results, which imply an affirmative answer to both questions. That figure shows acquisition data from three groups of pigeons. All three groups underwent a treatment in which a 10-sec keylight terminated in food on 25% of its occasions; they differed in what occurred between those trials. For Group 25, there were no intertrial events and conditioning was rapid. For Group Unsignaled, food was delivered between CSs at a rate sufficient to make that CS uninformative. It is clear that this had a profoundly detrimental effect on conditioning. The difference between Group 25 and Group Unsignaled is the main effect of contingency; the groups are matched on simple CS-US contiguity but differ in contingency. However, the data of primary interest are those from Group Signaled, which received the same intertrial food presentations as Group Unsignaled but each food was itself signaled by a tone. Despite the fact that they too had the overall relation between the keylight CS and food attenuated, they showed substantial conditioning of that keylight. That result follows from molecular accounts of contingency in which the background plays an important role in mediating basically contiguity mechanisms. It supports the view that a rather complex overall performance, in which the animal might seem to be encoding a rich relation, can be understood in terms of simple associations having rather complex conditions under which they occur.

Theorizing has followed a similar path for the case of conditioned inhibition, where again a more complex relation between CS and US seems to occur. Again a revised form of contiguity is normally invoked. Most theorists have argued that in the $A+/AX-$ paradigm, A becomes capable of activating a representation of the US through its own excitatory association. Then X is presented contiguously with that activated US representation, but the US itself is absent. That combination of representation but no event is then seen as an occurrence contiguous with X which makes X become a conditioned inhibitor. There remains some disagreement over just what it means for X to become a conditioned inhibitor. Some theorists have shown a willingness to expand on the notion of association by assuming that X develops an inhibitory association with the US (e.g., Rescorla &

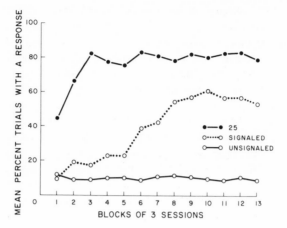

FIG. 3.1. The effect of CS-US contingency in autoshaping. Responding is shown to a keylight CS during the course of acquisition. All animals received food with a probability of .25 after a keylight CS. Group 25 had no other food; Group Unsignaled received unsignaled food between keylight presentations: Group Signaled received signaled food between keylight presentations. From Durlach (1983).

Wagner, 1972). That association has been described as raising the threshold for the activation of the US representation (e.g., Konorski, 1948), thereby making excitors less effective. Others (e.g., Konorski, 1967) have favored the view that the organism creates a new event representation (the no-US event) which enters into an excitatory association with X.

Whichever view one adopts, the notions of excitation and inhibition have become central to modern theories of association. But the point of interest here is that theories have reduced the circumstances for their establishment to an elaborated form of contiguity. Although differing in detail, those theories share a core theoretical idea: that the organism forms associations to the degree that it is surprised. The animal is viewed as sensitive to the discrepancy between expected and obtained outcomes, with conditioning occurring only when a discrepancy occurs. It is contiguity with that discrepancy, rather than contiguity with an event, which generates both excitatory and inhibitory conditioning. Those theories in turn have been responsible for generating a host of other phenomena which appear to support the original informational approach (See Rescorla & Holland, 1982).

Qualitative Relations

Another condition which has been identified as affecting the formation of associations concerns not the formal relations among events but rather their qualitative relations. The discussion to this point has followed the tradition of describing the events abstractly, without attention to their actual identity. The reasoning may be thought of as applying to *any* two potentially associable events. However, considerable modern evidence suggests that not all pairs of events which bear the same formal relations to each other develop associations equally. Some pairs seem to become associated more readily than others. I will just cite two examples.

The first is by far the more famous and is the result which is largely responsible for attention to nonformal relations among events. That is the result, originally reported by Garcia (e.g., Garcia & Koelling, 1966), that when internal and external aversive stimuli are the USs, conditioning depends heavily on whether they are paired with signals in the taste or auditory-visual modalities. A taste is apparently relatively more easily associated with an illness-inducing agent than with a shock; however, an auditory-visual event has the reverse preference. Analytic experimentation is sufficiently difficult in this case that we still do not know how in detail to characterize these stimulus classes; nor can we be certain about the relative contributions of associative and nonassociative processes to the performance differences observed. But most experimenters have concluded that indeed the qualitative relation between the events associated affects the success of associative learning (e.g., Domjan & Galef, 1983; LoLordo, 1979).

The preceding example arose from attention to a discipline on one side of animal learning, biology. The second example arose from attention to a discipline on the other side, human learning and perception. Gestalt psychologists, notably Kohler (1941), have suggested that such qualitative relations as perceptual similarity can promote the formation of associations. He argued that similars are more associable than are arbitrarily selected stimuli. Recent evidence from the Pavlovian literature has provided strong evidence supporting that proposition, under circumstances which control for various alternative interpretations. That evidence comes from a variety of kinds of similarity. One is especially worth noting, similarity in terms of identity of spatial location. We have argued elsewhere (e.g., Rescorla, 1980) that it is by viewing spatial contiguity as an example of similarity that one can bring it back into associative theories of learning. But in any case similarity among the elements is an important condition for the formation of an association. Some authors (e.g., Rescorla, 1980) have argued that this is only one example of how perceptual conditions affect associations.

There has been some confusion about the implications to be drawn from these findings on qualitative relations. Some authors have suggested that when different qualitative relations are involved the nature of the learning process is different. The proposition is that either different learning entities or different processes are involved when different qualitative relations obtain. But systematic investigation has suggested a more modest conclusion: qualitative relations modulate the success of conditioning, but may not change its nature. For instance, the various informational phenomena described earlier seem applicable to stimulus pairs of varying degrees of relatedness (see Rescorla & Holland, 1982).

It is worth reemphasizing an important feature of the way in which thinking about associative learning processes has reacted to fresh data on the circumstances producing learning. Certainly current theories envision the animal as reacting to a wide range of relations among events in its environment. But those different relations do not result in different associative entities; rather they result in different amounts of a single entity. There is a complexity in the worldly relations which occasion associative learning, but that richness is not represented in the learning itself. The analogy to the scientist may again be useful. It is as though the animal sifts through the evidence to decide whether or not one event causes another; but no matter how demanding he is of the evidence and no matter what features he examines, he only acknowledges one type of causality. This reaction is nowhere more obvious than in the way theorizing and experimentation reacted to the finding that qualitative relations affected learning. Modern theories continue to recognize only the kinds of association across those different relations.

ELEMENTS OF THE ASSOCIATION

A second way in which theorists have widened the power of a single associative mechanism has been to acknowledge the range and complexity of elements that may participate in associative learning. By multiplying the number and types of entities which can become associated with each other, theories have gained considerable applicability for an associative mechanism. This tactic has been employed by theorists since the British associationists, who envisioned a heirarchical structure in which the product of one association could itself enter as a unit into other associations. Like modern theorists they also appealed to the multiplicity of associative connections as responsible for the richness of encoding of information. Also like modern theorists, they generally assumed that this could all be accomplished with a single associative mechanism operating at multiple levels and on multiple entities. This tradition was carried on by such dominant figures as Hull (1943) and Guthrie (1952) who also imagined that concatination of associative structures could generate complex representations. This section provides some examples of how this tradition continues in modern Pavlovian experiments.

When we think of Pavlovian conditioning we naturally think of the organism forming an association between a US and a signaling CS. And we normally think of evidence for that association coming from the ability of the CS to evoke a response anticipatory to the occurrence of the US. Such responding is indeed a serviceable index of standard Pavlovian associations. But there are many instances of associations which are not well displayed in this way. Recently exploited techniques suggest that the organism forms a rich array of associations which cannot be detected simply by examining anticipatory responding.

We have found one technique particularly valuable for exposing the range of associations. In this procedure, animals are given the opportunity to form an association between the elements of interest. Then one of those elements is endowed with a new property, perhaps the ability to evoke some response. Then the animal's behavior to the other element is tested; to the degree that it too has that new property, we infer the formation of an association between the elements. This sensory-preconditioning-like procedure has proven to have substantial value in detecting associations which previously had not been documented. The following discussion describes examples of its use to detect three types of associations: within-event, between an event and its context, and between a response and an outcome.

Three Examples

The first example comes from a potentially quite important instance, in which a multifaceted event serves as the signal in a Pavlovian experiment. Traditionally, we have been most concerned with the degree to which each of those facets becomes associated with the eventual US. That has been quite important to modern theories of conditioning and is apparently easily evaluated: present the elements individually after conditioning and examine the magnitude of the CR they evoke. But it should be obvious that when two features of an event co-occur there is also the opportunity for them to become associated with each other.

Consequently, several years ago we began a series of studies seeking evidence for such within-event associations (Rescorla & Cunningham, 1978). Our initial studies picked stimulus events which we knew to be highly salient for our rat subjects: flavors. Thirsty animals were exposed to fluids having two mixed flavors, and asked to associate those flavors. For instance, some rats received the opportunity to drink a sweet-sour solution of sucrose and hydrochloric acid (SH) on some occasions and a salty-bitter solution of NaCl and quinine (NQ) on other occasions. Other rats received instead SQ and NH compounds. Then, to detect the presence of any within-event associations, we endowed one of the flavors (H or Q) with a new property—aversion induced by its pairing with a toxin. Finally, we gave the rats the choice between S and N, expecting that an SH association would be revealed by rejection of S when H was poisoned but not when Q was poisoned; similarly an NQ association would be revealed by the opposite result. Our expectations were amply confirmed, as is indicated in Fig. 3.2. That figure shows the intake of S and N, separated according to the particular compounds the animals had experienced (SH and NQ or SQ and NH) and whether H or Q was subsequently poisoned. A within-event association is indicated by the reduced intake of substances indexed by the cross-hatched bars.

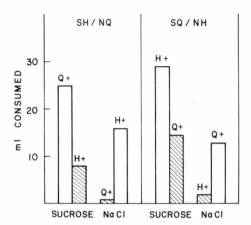

FIG. 3.2. Within-event learning. Intakes of sucrose and salt solutions after exposure to either sucrose-hydrochloric acid (SH) and salt-quinine (NQ) or SQ and NH compounds. Either H or Q had been paired with a toxin prior to the test. Intakes of flavors whose partners had been poisoned are cross-hatched. From Rescorla and Cunningham (1978).

This sort of result has now been confirmed with a range of stimuli (e.g., auditory and visual events in rodents, visual compounds in pigeons). Moreover, it occurs in many different Pavlovian conditioning preparations and in many standard procedures (see Rescorla & Durlach, (1981). For instance in the cases of blocking and conditioned inhibition described above, not only does the organism form associations between the US and the individual A and X elements; it also associates those elements. In fact, the available evidence suggests that whenever the organism experiences two stimulus features jointly it forms an association between them.

Such findings are important for several reasons. First, these associations can have profound effects on performance to the individual stimuli. In fact, we have collected a number of instances in which performance to one stimulus of a compound is so profoundly influenced by its association with another that experimenters have been misled about the degree to which that stimulus is associated with the US. Second, this kind of experiment can be conducted with stimuli which are initially relatively neutral. Indeed, some unpublished results suggest that these associations are just as well formed among neutral as among potent stimuli. Since most of the stimuli which an animal encounters are neutral, this greatly expands the kinds of events among which associations are formed. Third, notice that in the Rescorla and Cunningham experiment (and in most experiments on this problem) the events which are associated occur simultaneously. In fact, Rescorla (1981) has argued that when the issue is properly assessed, the strength of an association may be greater with simultaneous presentation than with sequential presentation. It may be that the priority which standard Pavlovian experiment give to sequential presentation is more a matter of their detection of associations than of their presence. Finally, this kind of experiment can be used as a model for the formation of event representations. Recall that the British Associationists built their between-event associations on just such within-event associations as those described here. The fact that the animal apparently can readily form multiple associations of this sort lends plausibility to this idea. I will return to that heirarchical possiblity below.

The second example of associations other than that between the CS and US involves the context. The fact that associations are always formed in a context has long been acknowledged in an informal way; the literature on animal learning has regularly made appeal to changes in the context to explain effects on learning and performance. However, in recent years the role of context has received increasingly explicit empirical and theoretical attention (see Mackintosh, this volume). The most frequent assertion is that during conditioning associations are formed between the context and the US. Such associations are relatively easy to document empirically since the context often evokes a different response after a US has occurred in its presence (e.g., Rescorla, Durlach, & Grau, 1985). As noted earlier, context-US associations have been accorded theoretical roles in governing both learning about explicit CS-US relations and performance to previously conditioned stimuli. There seems little doubt about the existence and importance òf this sort of context-US association.

But there is also evidence that the organism associates the context with neutral events, such as CSs. Like the cases already discussed, the simple formation of an association between context and CS is not necessarily exhibited by a change in performance. But the technique used above can also be applied here. Recent studies in our laboratory (e.g., Rescorla, 1984) have found that pigeons which receive two different CSs presented in discriminably different contexts will exhibit quite different levels of activity to those contexts if the CSs are separately given different excitatory values by pairing with food. Moreover, those different levels of contextual excitation appear to modulate learning and performance in just the way that associations with USs do.

The third kind of association I want to mention is important in the understanding of instrumental performance. Classical accounts of instrumental training emphasized a particular kind of association, that between an antecedent stimulus and the instrumental response itself. Such S-R theories can be contrasted with a different account which has been less popular until recently. That second account sees instrumental learning as the formation of an association between the response and its consequence. Adams and Dickinson (1981) have argued that the S-R account is analogous to procedural learning and the second account to declarative learning, as the terms are sometimes used in human learning (cf. Crowder, this volume). The S-R (procedural) account has been favored because of the demonstrable fact that a stimulus seems to evoke a new response after instrumental training. However recent evidence suggests the presence of the second (declarative) association as well. The techniques which have been used to expose that response-outcome association are the same as those described earlier for exposing otherwise hidden associations. For instance, Colwill and Rescorla (1985) recently conducted an experiment which is the analogue to the Rescorla-Cunningham experiment. They trained rats to make two different responses, lever pressing and chain pulling, each leading to a distinctive outcome, Noyes pellets or sucrose. Then they presented one of those outcomes separately and followed by it by a poison, until the rat was no longer willing to consume that outcome. Finally they gave the rats the choice between the two manipulanda in the absence of either outcome. Figure 3.3 shows the results of that manipulation. The rats showed a strong preference for responding on the manipulandum whose outcome had not been poisoned. That provides clear evidence for the existence of response-outcome associations. Only if the animal knows which outcome follows each response can it show such differential performance. The circumstances under which response-outcome and stimulus-response association each occur and their relative contributions to instrumental performance remain to be explored.

The point of interest here is that if one uses somewhat different procedures, he can find evidence that a wide variety of events enter into associations. I have tried to show that features of an individual event, contexts in which those events occur, and behaviors generated by the animal all participate in associative connections. One of the ways in which a learning theory which appeals to only one associative mechanism can survive is precisely to note that this multiplicity makes for substantial richness of encoding of the environment. But of course, the precise description of how the organism integrates this array of associations into a coherent representation remains to be worked out.

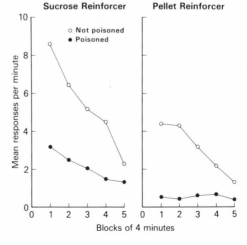

FIG. 3.3. Response-outcome learning. Performance during an extinction test on two responses, one previously reinforced with sucrose and one with pellets. Either the sucrose or the pellets were paired with a toxin between training and test. From Colwill and Rescorla (in press).

Hierarchical Organization

One of the important implications of this multiplicity of associations is the possibility for the construction of more hierarchical structures. We noted earlier that one way to think about the Rescorla-Cunningham data is as the organism forming a representation of a complex flavor event. But we gave an associative interpretation of the structure of that event representation. The implication is that the organism can use more complex structures, themselves created by associations, as the basis for further associative connections (cf. Gaffan, this volume). Such building greatly expands the power of the associative model and will, at least in some instances, provide an account of phenomena which apparently demand that the animal learn other than simple relations.

To illustrate that point, this section shows some evidence that more complex structures can in fact enter into associate connections, both as signals and as consequents. The demonstration that they participate as signals is relatively simple and has been available for many years (e.g., Konorski, 1948; Saavedra, 1975; Woodbury, 1943). In Pavlovian settings animals are typically capable of learning such complex discriminations as negative patterning (A+, B+, AB−), and conditional discriminations (AC+, BD+, BC−, AD−). In the former, the elements of the AB stimulus are reinforced when presented separately but non-reinforced when presented jointly. In the latter, each elemental stimulus is reinforced half the time in such a way that only certain combinations lead to the US. Neither of these discriminations can be learned simply on the basis of associations between the individual elements and the US which summate to yield behavior to the compounds. Rather, the animal must respond to the combinations themselves. One might view successful performance in terms of the animal learning more complex relations between an element and the US. For instance, one may describe the conditional discrimination as follows: A signals that C rather than D will be reinforced whereas B signals that D rather than C will be reinforced. But it is also possible to view the joint presentation of two stimuli as generating a new entity which in turn becomes associated with the US. That new entity may take several forms, but a particularly successful approach has been the suggestion that joint presentation of A and B results in an additional element, unique to the compound. Some experiments suggest that such an element allows Pavlovian theories not only to deal with the basic phenomena but to make some novel predictions (e.g., Rescorla, 1973). It is natural to think of such an element as emerging from an association between A and B. This account is one form in which stimulus recoding (cf. Crowder, this volume) has been seen as occurring in the nonhuman learning literature.

With a little more effort one can also find evidence that events on the other end of a Pavlovian association are complexly encoded. This can be illustrated with a procedure related to that used above, second-order conditioning. In a second-order experiment, one first pairs one stimulus, A, with a US and then uses A as the reinforcer for another stimulus, X. Associations between X and A are easily developed in this way and can have profound effects on behavior. One advantage of this technique is that it allows one to construct second members of an association to his taste and so study the nature of learning about consequents. In one experiment we used such a procedure to search for complex structures for consequents (Rescorla, 1980). We did this by composing our own consequent which had multiple features we could identify and modify; this allowed us to ask whether the organism formed a complex representation of a consequent which entered into association with prior events. In this experiment, pigeons were first given Pavlovian autoshaping in which two keylights (red and yellow) were paired with food. The birds pecked these keylights as evidence of their learning the association. Then we presented the red (R) and yellow (Y) stimuli together for the first time as side by side components of a compound. That RY compound was signaled by a horizontal stripe pattern (H); consequently, the birds rapidly came to peck H. The question of interest concerns the nature of the association which H has acquired. Is H associated with the individual R and Y elements or has the organism formed a more complex representation of RY which constitutes the second member of the association? This can be answered using the procedures described above: change the current value of various aspects of the RY compound and ask what impact those changes have on performance to H. In this particular experiment we taught some animals a discrimination of the form RY+, R−, Y− and we taught others a discrimination of the form RY−, R+, Y+. If RY has been represented as a unit, then responding to H should be higher in the former case; if R and Y have separately been associated with H, responding should be higher in the latter case.

Figure 3.4 shows the primary results of this experiment. To the left is shown responding to the second-order H after initial H-RY pairings, separated according to which discrimination treatment the animals would subsequently receive.

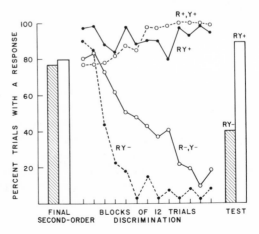

FIG. 3.4. Heirarchical organization of between and within event learning. The left-hand panel shows performance in two groups of birds both given second-order conditioning of a grid pattern (H) by a compound color (RY) reinforcer. In the middle panel, one group received an RY+, R−, Y− discrimination; the other received the concerse. The right-hand panel shows responding to H as a function of this discrimination. From Rescorla (1980).

Clearly, considerable second-order conditioning of H occurred. The middle panel shows the development of the discrimination between RY and its elements, R and Y; in both cases the discrimination was well within the animal's competence. Of most interest, are the results of responding to H after those different discriminations, shown in the right-hand panel. Responding was greater after reinforcement of the compound than after reinforcement of the elements. This suggests that to some degree the animal had organized the consequent RY in the way it organizes antecedents of an association. Since we know that animals associate the elements of the consequent under these conditions, that association is a natural candidate for the basis of this organization.

This discussion is intended to illustrate the degree to which modern theories of conditioning allow the CS and the US to be complexly represented. As I noted previously, it is partly through such introduction of complexity into the events associated that theories have avoided introducing complexity into the association itself. But it is important to note that in the cases I have described associations themselves may form the basis for generating more complex elements.

EFFECTS ON BEHAVIOR

The third way modern theories expand the domain of associations lies in the effects they have on behavior. Historically, the role of the association in producing performance was quite limited. Its primary function was to enable a stimulus to elicit a conditioned response (CR). One of the ways modern theorizing has expanded the domain of association is to acknowledge that it has a range of consequences other than elicitation. This section mentions some of those other roles.

Response Elicitation

It is important to note first that even the notion of elicitation has been elaborated considerably. Classical descriptions of Pavlovian conditioning emphasized the ability of a CS to evoke behaviors like those originally evoked by the US. But modern discussions have been considerably more liberal in accepting responses in a wide variety of forms as indices of association. Many would adopt a quite operational view in which any change in the behavior which a CS elicits as a result of its being presented in a conditioning relation with the US would be acceptable evidence of the formation of an association. Several observations have encouraged this change. One important result is that in many conditioning preparations the response which the CS evokes is quite different from that evoked by the US. In some dramatic instances the two responses are actually antagonistic (see Mackintosh, 1983; Rescorla & Holland, 1982).

Another important result is that the nature of the CR is affected not only by the choice of US but also by the choice of CS. There are now a number of well-documented instances in which the same consequent when paired with different signals establishes quite different behavior patterns to those signals. This is particularly well-documented for cases of appetitive USs. For instance, Holland (1977) has reported that when rats receive a visual CS for food, the CR takes on one form (e.g., rearing) whereas when an auditory CS signals that some food the CR takes on another form (e.g., excited head-jerking). Similarly, a localized keylight which signals food for a pigeon evokes directed pecking; a tone signaling that same food evokes only general activity. Recently, Boakes, Poli, Lockwood and Goodall (1978) and Timberlake (1983) have reported quite complex behaviors to small portable objects which signal food, behaviors quite different from those evoked by diffuse CSs. Finally, there is one striking instance in which the nature of the CS paired with an aversive US determining the form of the response. When shock is signaled by a diffuse CS in rat subjects, the dominant behavior is inactivity during that CS (freezing); however, several authors (e.g., Pinel, Treit, & Wilkie, 1980) have reported that when a shock is signaled by a localized object, such as a prod, the dominant behavior is approach and covering of the object. Such results have sometimes been interpreted in terms of Pavlovian conditioning giving a CS access to a preorganized response pattern appropriate to the US that is anticipated and the CS signaling that US (e.g., Timberlake, 1983). We are only beginning to arrive at accounts of this variability in performance. But what evidence we have suggests that the learning which produces these diverse behaviors follows similar acquisition laws and responds similarly when assessed by procedures not involving the ability of a CS to evoke a response (see Holland, in press). Consequently, it appears that the same associative structure can show itself in various response topographies.

But the liberalization in our thinking about how associations affect behavior extends beyond acknowledging the different response topographies which they can elicit. There are two other classes of effects which associations seem to have. They influence behavior by influencing both the *acquisition* and *exhibition* of other learning which the organism can undergo.

Effects on Acquisition by Other Stimuli

This section indicates some of the ways in which the association which a stimulus has allows it to influence learning about other stimuli. First, an associated stimulus can serve as a *signal* which affects the learning of other stimuli. Perhaps the most celebrated example is the interference effect known as blocking, described earlier. It is now clear that the formation of an association between one CS and a consequent can have profound detrimental effects on other learning about that consequent. This effect is powerful and widespread; it applies not only to discrete CSs, but also to more diffuse stimuli such as contexts. Of more relevance here, some authors have suggested that the ability of one CS to block conditioning of another can be a more sensitive index of the associative structure of that CS than is its ability to evoke a response (e.g., Rescorla & Holland, 1982).

Second, an associated stimulus can act as a *reinforcer,* as in the case of second-order conditioning. One index of the presence of an A-US association is the ability of A to condition another stimulus, B. In some cases even when A does not evoke a conveniently measurable response, its association with the US can be readily detected by using it to condition B. Moreover, current results suggest that a wide variety of properties of A can be transferred to B in this way. Not only A's excitatory association with the US, but also its inhibitory association can be transferred. An extreme possibility, not incompatabile with current data, is that when B is associated with A it adopts in some measure all of A's properties.

An unpublished experiment we recently did with autoshaping encourages this possibility that an association allows one stimulus to substitute for another. We trained birds on a configural discrimination, like that described above, AB−, A+, B+. Then we used A and B in a second-order paradigm, as associates of X and Y, respectively, We then asked whether X and Y could substitute for A and B in controlling performance; consequently we tested XY, AY and XB. Although we observed substantial behavior to X and Y individually, none of the compounds evoked responding. In contrast, control animals, which had received A and B reinforced but another compound nonreinforced, showed substantial performance to the XY, AY, and BX compounds. This suggests that X and Y acquired a sufficiently detailed set of the properties of A and B to permit them to serve as replacements in governing performance.

Third an associated stimulus can act as an *activator,* rearousing the representation of another stimulus, so as to permit that representation to undergo additional learning. That is, one function of an association might be to rearouse memory representations sufficiently well that they can have new associations attached to them. One result which encourages that view is a recent report by Holland (1981). Holland conducted Pavlovian conditioning in which he paired an auditory and visual CS each with a distinctive flavor. Then he paired one of the auditory or visual CSs with a toxin and tested the responding to the flavors. This is, of course, quite like the procedures described above, but it has an important wrinkle: as we noted, other results suggest that the auditory-visual CSs are substantially less successful signals for the toxin than are the flavors with which they were paired. And indeed, Holland found that poisoning the auditory and visual CSs had little impact on responding to them. However, their poisoning had a strong differential impact on subsequent consumption of the flavors. A natural interpretation is that the CS-flavor association had allowed the CS to activate representations of the flavor at the time of poisoning, so as to permit direct flavor-toxin associations.

Consequently, we have evidence that an association endows a stimulus with a variety of impacts on subsequent learning: it can produce interference, it can act as a reinforcer, and it can reactivate representations of other stimuli.

Effects on Performance to Other Stimuli

An associated stimulus can also have an impact on the performance which other stimuli produce. This section briefly mentions a few ways this can happen. One possibility, of course is direct combination of associations from multiple sources can augment performance by summation. Another is on processing of the CS. It takes no imagination to anticipate that to the degree the organism attends to one stimulus, because of its associations, it will attend less to other stimuli.

Finally, an association may affect performance by affecting processing of the US. For instance, one way of thinking about inhibitory associations is that they make it more difficult for excitatory associations to activate a representation of the US, perhaps by raising the threshold for such activation. That is, conditioned inhibition may be described not by postulating a new type of association, but a rather new function which that association might play: raising the threshold for US activation. As Rescorla (1979) noted, this view, originally suggested by Konorski (1948), has much to recommend it in dealing with otherwise re-calcitrant data. Moreover, recent evidence suggests that some associative train-ing paradigms can result in stimuli with the opposite properties, lowering that threshold. In some recent experiments (Rescorla, 1985), we have found pro-cedures in which a CS-US association results not in that CS eliciting behavior itself but rather in its acting to permit other stimuli to elicit behavior. For instance, a pigeon may be given autoshaping with a keylight CS and a food US, such that they are paired only in the presence of a tone. Under those conditions, the tone does not evoke a direct pecking response of its own, but it does promote pecking to the keylight. Moreover, that facilitation transfers in interesting ways which suggest that the tone makes the US more readily accessible to activation by a variety of keylights. That is, some associations with a US may not result in evocation but rather in modulating the ability of other stimuli to evoke.

As this discussion indicates, modern theorizing has increasingly seen the association as having multiple effects on learning and performance. Associations can interfere with or promote learning and performance to other stimuli. That is, associations can adopt a variety of functions. One of the ways in which theories have preserved the unitariness of an association in the face of complexity of performance is to give that association multiple roles to play.

CONCLUSION

The previous discussion has focused on the ways in which current theories have preserved the integrity of the association, at the expense of elaborating it. But it is worth raising two questions about this effort: First, can one really expect to have a theory with only one connective mechanism? Second, should one think of all learning as the connecting of initially disparate things?

I doubt that one would find much unanimity in the answer to the first question. Certainly there are some subdomains in the study of learning which reject the singularity of an associative notion. Others, as we have seen, doggedly cling to the notion of a single mechanism. Part of the problem is that it is not entirely clear what counts as evidence for multiplicity of learning mechanisms (cf. Tulving, this volume). Certainly the simple fact that similar methodologies are employed does not imply a common process (cf. Bolles, this volume). However, we could try to characterize a particular mechanism in terms of a cluster of attributes (e.g., dependence on contiguity, sensitivity to frequency of exposure, evidence of competitive processes, etc.). What little evidence is available indeed suggests that the various instances to which we have here applied the term association do share similar rules. But one could anticipate that a diversity of learning mechanisms would nevertheless share many of these attributes. After all, any learning mechanism must be sensitive to many of the same properties of the world which it is intended to represent. Moreover, theoretical notions of associative are not static; they evolve when new data emerge. And it is often unclear whether new data demand new theoretical mechanisms or simply modification in our conceptions of old ones. For instance, the cue-to-consequence results described by Garcia were originally taken by many to demand a new learning process, but current thinking views them as simply demanding the acknowledgement of a new parameter in an old process. Similarly, the initial reaction to our contingency data was to suggest a rejection of a contiguity notion; but instead they led to a reformulation of that notion to give it broader application. Consequently, what appear to be contrary data at any given point in the development of our understanding may well prove instead to inform our understanding of accepted mechanisms. In my view, the decision about number of learning mechanisms should be made on the grounds of what one finds to be an effective heuristic which leads to profitable analysis. For many students of animal learning the notion of a single mechanism has proven to be heuristic. This partly accounts for a bias which that field has against the introduction of new theoretical notions.

The second issue is whether it is sensible to view all learning as involving some connecting mechanism. Of course, associative learning has dominated American studies of nonhuman learning. This is partly the result of an historical effort to separate modification due to learning from that due to other kinds of interaction with the environment. But the term ''nonassociative'' has often carried the connotation of "nonlearned." However, there are signs in recent years of a break in this monopoly. Perhaps the strongest sign is the interest in habituation and sensitization processes, which seem to represent learning simply as a result of exposure to a single event. In part their acceptance reflects the hope that they will yield to neurobiological analysis. But some theoretical analyses of habituation, while admitting to a nonassociative temporary modification, envision long-term habituation as fundamentally an associative process (e.g., Wagner, 1981). Another indication that nonassociative processes are being taken seriously is the attention recently given to mechanisms of short-term memory in animals (Bolles, this volume; Hitch, this volume). Theoretical treatments of such memory phenomena typically do not make appeal to associations. The tasks used apparently demand only that the animal remember which of several items has recently occurred, not which of several relations has obtained among those elements. As a result, theories typically view these phenomena in nonassociative terms. Finally, another sign of a break with pure associationism is the frequency with which students of animal learning use the term "representation." For many it has seemed that we need to provide an account of how the animal represents the events among which he forms associations. In some instances, those representations seem themselves to be the product of experience. Again, there are attempts to describe event representations as associations among components (see above), but there are also suggestions that the process may not be fundamentally associative. Indeed, over the years various authors have argued that the fundamental process in event representation is not the connecting of originally disparate parts but rather the discrimination of elements out of an initially unitary representation (e.g., Rescorla, 1981). Whether this kind of learning will prove heurisitic for further work in the study of animal learning remains unclear. Historically it has had less success than the associative model.

It should finally be emphasized that animal learning is a field which is fundamentally conservative. It adds learning processes only when the data overwhelmingly force that addition; even then it may only modify already accepted processes. It is willing to tolerate unexplained phenomena without losing hope that existing mechanisms will eventually provide an account. It is as much in this matter of style as in matters of substance that it differs from adjacent fields studying learning.

REFERENCES

Adams, C., & Dickinson, A. (1981). Actions and habits: Variations in associative representations during instrumental learning. In N. E. Spear & R. Miller (Eds.), *Information processing in animals: Memory mechanisms.* Hillsdale, NJ: Lawrence Erlbaum Associates.

Boakes, R. A., Poli, M., Lockwood, M. J., & Goodall, G. (1978). A study of misbehavior: Token reinforcement in the rat. *Journal of the Experimental Analysis of Behavior, 29,* 115–134.

Colwill, R. M., & Rescorla, R. A. (1985). Post-conditioning devaluation of a reinforcer affects instrumental responding. *Journal of Experimental Psychology: Animal Behavior Processes, 11*, 120–132.

Domjan, M., & Galef, B. G. Jr. (1983). Biological constraints on instrumental and classical conditioning: Retrospect and prospect. *Animal Learning and Behavior, 11*, 151–161.

Durlach, P. J. (1983). Effect of signaling intertrial unconditioned stimuli in autoshaping. *Journal of Experimental Psychology: Animal Behavior Processes, 9*, 374–389.

Garcia, J., & Koelling, R. A. (1966). Relation of cue to consequence in avoidance learning. *Psychonomic Science, 4*, 123–124.

Guthrie, E. R. (1952). *The psychology of learning*, New York: Harper.

Holland, P. C. (1977). Conditioned stimulus as a determinant of the form of the Pavlovian conditioned response, *Journal of Experimental Psychology: Animal Behavior Processes, 3*, 77–104.

Holland, P. C. (1981). Acquisition of representation-mediated conditioned food aversions. *Learning and Motivation, 12*, 1–18.

Holland, P. C. (in press). Origins of behavior in Pavlovian conditioning. In G. Bower (Ed.), *The psychology of learning and motivation*, New York: Academic Press.

Hull, C. L. (1943). *Principles of behavior*. New York: Appleton-Century-Crofts.

Kamin, L. J. (1968). Attention-like processes in classical conditioning. In M. R. Jones (Ed.), *Miami Symposium on the prediction of behavior: Aversive Stimuli* (pp. 9–32). Coral Gables, Fl: University of Miami Press.

Kamin, L. J. (1969). Predictability, surprise, attention, and conditioning. In B. Campbell & R. Church (Eds.), *Punishment and aversive behavior* (pp. 279–298). New York: Appleton-Century-Crofts.

Kohler, W. (1941). On the nature of associations. *Proceedings of the American Philosophical Society, 84*, 489–502.

Konorski, J. (1948). *Conditioned reflexes and neuron organization*. Cambridge, Eng.: Cambridge University Press.

Konorski, J. (1967). *Integrative activity of the brain*. IL: University of Chicago Press.

LoLordo, V. M. (1979). Selective associations. In A. Dickinson & R. A. Boakes (Eds.), *Mechanisms of learning and motivation*. Hillsdale, NJ: Lawrence Erlbaum Associates.

Mackintosh, N. J. (1975). A theory of attention: Variations in the associability of stimuli with reinforcement. *Psychological Review, 82*, 276–298.

Mackintosh, N. J. (1983). *Conditioning and associative learning*. Eng.: Oxford University Press.

Pearce, J. M., & Hall, G. (1980) A model for Pavlovian learning: Variations in the effectiveness of conditioned but not of unconditioned stimuli. *Psychological Review, 87*, 532–552.

Pinel, J. P. J., Treit, D., & Wilkie, D. M. (1980). Stimulus control of defensive burying in the rat. *Learning and Motivation, 11*, 150–163.

Rescorla, R. A. (1968). Probability of shock in the presence and absence of CS in fear conditioning. *Journal of Comparative and Physiological Psychology, 66*, 1–5.

Rescorla, R. A. (1972). Informational variables in conditioning. In G. Bower (Ed.), *The psychology of learning and motivation*. New York: Academic Press.

Rescorla, R. A. (1973). Evidence for a unique-cue account of configural conditioning. *Journal of Comparative and Physiological Psychology, 85*, 331–338.

Rescorla, R. A. (1979). Conditioned inhibition and extinction, A. Dickinson & R. A. Boakes (Eds.), *Mechanisms of learning and motivation*, Hillsdale, NJ: Lawrence Erlbaum Associates.

Rescorla, R. A. (1980). *Pavlovian Second-Order Conditioning: Studies in Associative Learning*, Hillsdale, NJ: Lawrence Erlbaum Associates.

Rescorla, R. A. (1981). Simultaneous Associations, In P. Harzem & M. Zeiler (Eds.), *Advances in analysis of behavior (Vol. 2)*, New York: Wiley.

Rescorla, R. A. (1984). Associations between Pavlovian CSs and context, *Journal of Experimental Psychology: Animal Behavior Processes, 10*, 195–205.

Rescorla, R. A. (1985). Conditioned inhibition and facilitation, in R. R. Miller & N. S. Spear (Eds.), *Information processing in animals: Conditioned inhibition,* Hillsdale, NJ: Lawrence Erlbaum Associates.

Rescorla, R. A. & Cunningham, C. L. (1978). Within-compound flavor associations, *Journal of Experimental Psychology: Animal Behavior Processes, 4,* 267–275.

Rescorla, R. A., & Durlach, P. J. (1981). Within-event learning in Pavlovian conditioning. In N. E. Spear & R. Miller (Eds.), *Information processing in animals: Memory mechanisms,* Hillsdale, NJ: Lawrence Erlbaum Associates.

Rescorla, R. A., Durlach, P. J., & Grau, J. W. (1985). Contextual learning in Pavlovian conditioning. In P. D. Balsam & A. Tomie (Eds.), *Context and learning,* Hillsdale, NJ: Lawrence Erlbaum Associates.

Rescorla, R. A., & Holland, P. C. (1976). Some behavioral approaches to the study of learning. In M. R. Rosenzweig & E. L. Bennett (Eds.), *Neural mechanisms of learning and memory* (pp. 165–192). Cambridge, MA: MIT Press.

Rescorla, R. A., & Holland, P. C. (1982). Behavioral studies of associative learning in animals. In M. R. Rosenzweig & L. W. Porter (Eds.), *Annual Review of Psychology, 33,* 265–308.

Rescorla, R. A., & Wagner, A. R. (1972). A theory of Pavlovian conditioning: Variations in the effectiveness of reinforcement and nonreinforcement. In A. H. Black & W. F. Prokasy (Eds.), *Classical conditioning III* (pp. 64–99). New York: Appleton-Century-Crofts.

Saavedra, M. A. (1975). Pavlovian compound conditioning in the rabbit. *Learning and Motivation, 6,* 314–326.

Timberlake, W. (1983). The functional organization of appetitive behavior: Behavior systems and learning. In M. D. Zeiler & P. Harzem (Eds.), *Advances in the analysis of behavior (Vol. 3),* Chichester: Wiley.

Wagner, A. R. (1981). SOP: A model of automatic memory processing in animal behavior. In N. E. Spear & R. Miller (Eds.), *Information processing in animals: Memory mechanisms.* Hillsdale, NJ: Lawrence Erlbaum Associates.

Woodbury, C. B. (1943). The learning of stimulus patterns by dogs. *Journal of Comparative and Physiological Psychology, 35,* 29–40.

CLASSIFICATION OF CONCEPTS

Lars-Göran Nilsson
Trevor Archer

As mentioned in the introductory chapter, the rubric of this topic was originally planned to be "systems of representation." The intention was that the contributors to this topic should deal with the various ways, which have been proposed to account for representation of experience and knowledge in memory. Among other conceptualizations we had in mind that dichotomies like episodic and semantic memory (cf. Tulving, 1972, 1983) should be dealt with as well as the dichotomy between working and reference memory proposed by Olton (1978; Olton, Becker, & Handelmann, 1979). Tulving and Olton, who were invited to be the two contributors to this topic, soon discovered that a somewhat broader topic was more urgent to discuss in a context like the present one, viz. the problem of classification of concepts. We agreed that this broadening of the topic was actually to an advantage and especially so when we found out that, for example, the semantic-episodic memory distinction would be dealt with anyhow and that some chapters under other topics would touch upon various aspects of representation of experience and knowledge as well.

Tulving's message in his chapter is that research workers in both animal learning and human memory should devote more of their time and efforts to try to construct a natural classificatory system of varieties of learning and memory. Tulving states that such an enterprise may or may not foster closer integration between the two main fields under discussion here, i.e., animal learning and human memory.

In spite of considerations of this nature, the object of this enterprise is to assume that the achievement of a closer integration is within our grasp and that classification must proceed apace. However, it is not at all certain whether the best possible solution in constructing such a classifcatory system is to seek similarities in behavior between species. Tulving's own contention seems to be that a more straightforward path to success in this vein is to begin such a classification by focusing on humans and animals separately. This may well be, but again a prime task for us as scientists is to discover regularities and lawfulness and it is also a major task to determine the boundaries within which the regularities are assumed to hold.

A good deal of attention in Tulving's chapter is given to the concept of task. Tulving uses task to exemplify all problems and difficulties which may be involved in constructing a classificatory system. We certainly find that Tulving's warnings are worthwhile taking into account. However, as witnessed by several of the contributors to this volume, analyses of tasks have apparently caught much recent attention of the contributors' efforts. We concur with the importance of this emphasis and we believe that an important progress has been made in both animal learning and human memory, if the development of both these fields will in one way or another be contingent upon a more pronounced emphasis on task analysis than previously has been the case in psychology. However, our own bias is that task analysis will have to be coupled with some biological principles in order to be meaningful and fruitful in future research.

As we have argued previously in the introductory chapter and in the introductory remarks to the topic on Basic Theoretical Concepts we conceive of learning, memory, and remembering as interactions between available cognitive capabilities of the organism and specific demands of the current task. We have proposed this in opposition to the traditionally dominating view of memory as an entity or a ''thing'' in the head (cf. Craik, this volume). Thus, we would like put more emphasis on the task and the task demands than previously has been the case; we see a danger in focusing on a hypothetical memory entity only. However, we certainly do not advocate a view in which too much focus is placed on the task per se at the cost of the biological system under scrutiny; after all the task has little or no interest for a psychologist, if it is not related to an organism and its cognitive capabilities. It is the joint contribution of the task and the cognitive capabilities that we should focus on. In this vein we concur with Tulving (chapter 4) when he claims that a neuropsychological approach should be the most profitable one in a classificatory endeavor. The general principle of such a neuropsychological criterion, according to Tulving, is to show that behavioral expressions of various forms of learning and memory correlate systematically with variations in brain activity which reflects ''species differences, developmental stages, lesions, electrical stimulation, or changes in biochemistry.''

The probability of finding an extensive classificatory system in learning and memory, for example, like the one proposed some 250 years ago by the Swedish biologist Carl von Linné for plants, animals, and minerals (*Systema Naturae*), may be quite low. However, the ambition is that it should be a "natural" classificatory system and psychologists will have to realize that much of the inspiration will have to picked up in the biological sciences. The consequences of descriptive precision are invaluable for learning and memory experimental endeavors. A descriptive sophistication of neurobiological processes may prove to be a crucial complement to purely psychological analyses.

REFERENCES

Olton, D. S. (1978). Characteristics of spatial memory. In S. H. Hulse, H. F. Fowler, & W. K. Honig (Eds.), *Cognitive aspects of animal behavior* (pp. 342–373). Hillsdale, NJ: Lawrence Erlbaum Associates.

Olton, D. S., Becker, J. T., & Handelmann, G. E. (1979). Hippocampus, space, and memory. *The behavioral and Brain Sciences, 2*, 313–322.

Tulving, E. (1972). Episodic and semantic memory. In E. Tulving & W. Wickelgren (Eds.), *Organization of memory*. New York: Academic Press.

Tulving, E. (1983). *Elements of episodic memory*. Oxford: Oxford University Press.

4 On the Classification Problem in Learning and Memory

Endel Tulving
University of Toronto

The purpose of the conference whose proceedings the present volume represents was to discuss and develop a common ground for conceptualizations in animal learning and human memory. This mandate is important and timely. On both historical and rational grounds, the fields of (animal) learning and (human) memory should have a good deal in common, their facts and theories should be mutually relevant, and practitioners in each of the two fields should find it easy to benefit from what those in the other have accomplished and what they are doing. Nevertheless, the two seem to represent separate cultures: they begin with different pretheoretical assumptions, they are concerned with apparently different problems, they employ different methods, and they speak different languages. In the animal learning literature, there are very few references to work in human memory; in the human memory literature there are even fewer mentions of work in animal learning.

A COLLABORATIVE ENTERPRISE

How should we go about meeting the challenge that the objective of the conference presents? How do we change the insularity of the two disciplines? How do we get a typical, busy student of animal learning to take an interest in, say, theoretical speculations surrounding the concept of levels of processing, or in the empirical findings concerning the retention of names and faces of one's fellow high-school students from 40 years ago? How do we make an equally chronically preoccupied student of human memory appreciate the relation between autoshaping and superstitious behavior in pigeons, or the latest "hot data" on the second-order fear conditioning?

67

Appeals to the good will of the practitioners on the other side of the fence, suggestions to read the other's literature, discussing one's work with the members of the other culture, at specially organized conferences or even in one's own department—these and other obvious devices are unlikely to be successful. At best they can be expected to produce a temporary arousal of curiosity. Even making available for deep study and thought the proceedings of the deliberations of a number of well-meaning practitioners from both cultures at the Umea conference holds only a little more promise of success. A highly motivated and open-minded reader may improve his or her understanding and appreciation of the strange customs and difficult language of the other culture, but it would be a miracle if, as a result of the exercise, a conversion to the unified field of animal learning and human memory took place. Such a field does not yet exist, and even several conferences such as ours will not bring about a rapid change. Any bridging of the current chasm will take time. All we can do now is to try to plant some seeds for the future development of a unified science of learning and memory.

In this chapter, I would like to propose that one possibly fruitful approach to the problem of bridging the two fields may lie in a collaborative enterprise aimed at solving a problem that is:

(a) *new* in the sense that it has not yet been (seriously) approached in either field,

(b) *relevant* in the sense that existing knowledge and previous accomplishments in both fields can be brought to bear on the effort,

(c) *important* in that the problem is perceived as having to do with basic and fundamental objectives of both fields,

(d) *pertinent* in that the pursuit of the problem can be imagined to lead to genuine progress in the understanding of learning and memory, and

(e) *difficult and challenging,* in that it is not at all obvious, at least at the outset, how the problem is to be solved.

A problem that satisfies these criteria is what I refer to as *the classification problem* of learning and memory. It parallels the classification problem in biology, with the difference that biological classification is concerned with living organisms—animals and plants—whereas in our case it would be concerned with varieties of learning and memory. A successful solution of the classification problem of learning and memory would take the form of a classificatory scheme, or system, embodying and expressing the relations among all varieties of learning and memory. Such a classificatory system would constitute an overall framework within which empirical phenomena and theoretical ideas regarding learning and memory can be integrated in a manner neither possible nor conceivable today. Ideally, we would have but a single classificatory system, one that in some real sense corresponds to nature, one that "carves nature at its joints."

Systematic research directed at the classification problem of learning and memory would entail the development of *systematics* as a new branch of the science of learning and memory, analogously with systematics in biology. In the course of such development, many subproblems of taxonomy would emerge and would have to be solved.

Thus, the proposal is for the undertaking of a collaborative venture: a broadly based attack on the classification problem within a new branch of study, the systematics of learning and memory. Such an undertaking would constitute, and bring about, a new perspective on learning and memory, one that would complement and enhance the value of the perspectives that have characterized the field for the better part of the last 100 years.

The chapter expands on the theme of the classification problem, describes the objectives of classification research in the field of learning and memory, discusses some of the problems that are likely to arise in the pursuit of the problem, and makes some tentative suggestions for general rules of procedure. We begin with a brief survey of some of the relevant features of the current scene.

EXPLANATION AND CLASSIFICATION: PRESENT STATE

Explanation in Learning and Memory

There are three major classes of explanation in life sciences, including psychology. They correspond to three kinds of questions that can be asked about biological phenomena: How does it work, what is it like, and where does it come from (cf. Bruce, in press; Solbrig, 1966). One is explanation in terms of underlying *causes*: postulation of mechanisms, processes, intervening variables, hypothetical constructs, and various kinds of hypothetical structures and functions that account for what is observed about the relation between behavior and situation. When we ask a question such as, "What causes forgetting?", or "Why is reinforcement effective?", we usually expect to be given such a causal explanation. The causal explanation has been the norm in the field of learning and memory. Acquisition and extinction of habits, strengthening and weakening of associations, generalization and discrimination, transfer and interference, retention and forgetting have usually been accounted for in terms of hypothetical happenings—functioning structures, mechanisms, processes, intervening variables, hypothetical constructs, and the like.

The second kind of explanation is one where a phenomenon of learning or memory is accounted for in terms of the *properties* of the organism exhibiting the learning or memory. We could refer to these as property explanations. Questions such as "Why can some tasks be learned more readily than others?", or "Why do older children learn Tasks X, Y, and Z faster than younger ones?" usually evoke responses specifying certain (other) characteristics of tasks or individuals under scrutiny.

The third explanation constitutes an extension of a part of the second: The characteristics of learners and rememberers are related to their *history*: previous experiences, individual development through growth and maturation, or the evolution of the species to which the organism belongs. Thus, differential ease of learning of different tasks is accounted for by transfer, differential learning abilities are interpreted in terms of age-related characteristics of the nervous system (neural, conceptual, or otherwise), and species-specific learning abilities are attributed to evolutionary selection pressures. We can refer to this form of explanation as historical. Property explanations and historical explanations have figured less prominently in learning and memory.

Explanations of events, effects, phenomena, or relations between variables, whatever their kind, are usually expressed in terms of more or less formal theories, models, and hypotheses. In principle, each of them is expected to do two things: (a) provide an explanation, and (b) specify the *domain* of the explanation, that is, state *what it is* that the theory, model, or hypothesis accounts for. The many theories, models, and hypotheses that we have in learning and memory have met the first expectation better than the second. Indeed, the domains of our theories, models, and hypotheses usually are either left implicit or specified in terms of arbitrary categories accidentally derived from historical practices of our research field.

A prerequisite for informed specification of domains of explanations is a classificatory system of different varieties of learning and memory. The creation of such a system is the objective of systematics of learning and memory.

Consider a single example of the current state of affairs in the matter of classification, although many others could be given. A recognized problem of fundamental importance in human memory concerns the relation between recall and recognition, attested to by the existence of a flourishing experimental and theoretical literature. (For a representative sample, see the references in Gillund & Shiffrin, 1984, and in Tulving, 1982.) The question of interest in the context of the present discussion is this: What is the domain of theories and models of recall and recognition (e.g., Gillund & Shiffrin, 1984; Tulving, 1982)?

The answer to the question seems to be straightforward: The domain is a collection of phenomena defined in terms of comparisons between recall and recognition in a variety of situations (Gillund & Shiffrin, 1984, pp. 6–7; Tulving, 1982, pp. 140–142). Problems emerge, however, when we ask additional questions: Is the domain of a given model limited to recall and recognition of verbal material, or even just discrete verbal items, or does it extend to other kinds of materials? Is it limited to college-student subjects, or adult humans, or all humans? Do the models have anything to say about recall and recognition in animals? Indeed, can one distinguish between recall and recognition in animals, either in the same way as in humans, or in some comparable fashion? If not, why not? If yes, why do we not have models of recall and recognition in the animal learning or animal memory literature? What kind of learning and memory is involved in comparisons between recall and recognition, and why do we seem to have it in humans but not in animals? If recall and recognition are two forms of retrieval, and if retrieval processes exist in animal learning (e.g., Spear, 1971, 1984), what kinds of models of retrieval processes in animal learning correspond to models of recall and recognition in humans?

We could go on in this way for a long time, asking question after question about the domains of existing theories and models in both (human) memory and in (animal) learning, without much hope for satisfying answers. But this sample makes the point: Existence of explanations does not imply that we always know the boundaries of their domains. If so, establishment of such boundaries would constitute an important research objective. Systematic classification of varieties of learning and memory would contribute to the attainment of that objective: The paramount purpose of classification is to describe the structure of relatedness of objects of interest, a structure within which general statements can be made (Sokal, 1974).

Thus, it could be argued that orthogonal to the three basic kinds of explanation mentioned earlier there exists, or there exists a need for, a fourth kind, that we could refer to as categorical explanation. An event, effect, phenomenon, or relation between situation and behavior is accounted for by identifying it as a member of a particular class or *category* of events, effects, phenomena or relations whose known properties include those requiring explanation in a given instance. For instance, questions such as, "Why is the slope of the forgetting curve flatter for primed fragment completion than for recognition?" and "Why can amnesics do as well as control patients in completing fragmented pictures or words although their recognition performance is very much poorer?" could be answered by identifying the two specific performances (fragment completion and recognition) as manifestations of different memory systems, one whose information is lost relatively rapidly and that is affected by the kind of brain damage that causes amnesia, and another that retains information for a much longer time and that is relatively unimpaired in amnesia (Tulving, Schacter, & Stark, 1982; Warrington & Weiskrantz, 1982). Categorical explanation presupposes the existence of (a) an empirically valid and theoretically sound classificatory system, and (b) theories and models that are known to hold for whole classes, specifiable parts of the system, rather than only for individual phenomena. Thus, classification would provide a basis for categorical explanation, not as a substitute for causal explanations and historical explanations of phenomena of learning and memory, but as a necessary precursor for their generality.

Why Classify?

Classification in all fields of human activity can serve either or both of two purposes. One is practical. Facilitation of communication, reduction of the memory load in handling knowledge, and optimization of storage and retrieval of information provide ready examples of such a pragmatic function of classification.

The second purpose of classification is theoretical. As discussed earlier, it is of much greater interest in our field. A classificatory system of learning and memory would guide functional research on learning and memory, it would help formulate theoretical objectives, aid in the evaluation of conceptual achievements, and provide a basis on which generalizations about learning and memory can be made.

Let us briefly mention a number of specific ways in which both the activity and the results of classification can be of value to the field. In summarizing these payoffs, I will assume a reasonably successful outcome of the classification research, that is, the existence of an acceptable and useful classificatory system, although it goes without saying that anything even resembling such a finished product is unlikely to be available in the foreseeable future.

1. The major contribution of a classificatory system would lie in the enhancement of *comprehensive understanding* of learning and memory. It would constitute one way in which theorists and students could perceive and describe the totality of learning and memory functions in a particular species in relation to the detailed structure and finer components of such a totality. It would facilitate the construction, evaluation, and description of functional models and theories of learning and memory. The classificatory system would represent one kind of manifestation of the overall regularity and order that students of learning have always been seeking.

2. A classificatory system would greatly facilitate selective delimitation of *conclusions* drawn from experiments and other kinds of empirical observation of particular varieties of learning and memory. More often than not, generalizations of empirical facts, and phenomena of learning and memory, to conditions other than those under which the observations were made—if such are explicitly made at all—are based on intuition and private theories.

3. In a closely related vein, the boundary conditions within which *theoretical* claims are assumed to hold, could be specified objectively and more precisely with the aid of a classificatory system. At the present time, neither the writers nor the readers necessarily know the range of situations in which a theoretical statement is expected to hold. In a developed science of learning and memory, we would expect to find statements of the following sort: "The model (or theory) described here applies to all varieties of learning (or memory) in (name of a specific category of learning or memory), and it may also hold, albeit less faithfully, for (names of some other classes). No claims are made that it applies to any other class." Today such statements do not exist in the literature, presumably partly because of the absence of any accepted classificatory system of learning and memory.

4. A classificatory system would provide economical ways of describing *deviations* from specified "norms." For instance, different kinds of amnesic

syndromes (Rozin, 1976; Moscovitch, 1984; Cohen, 1984) could be described in terms of the extent to which functioning of learning and memory of particular classes is impaired. Similarly, age-related changes in learning and memory capabilities in children and in older people may be describable succinctly and economically in terms of levels and branches in a hierarchical taxonomic tree.

5. Reasonably complete *descriptions of learning and memory abilities* of individual organisms or groups of organisms, free from unnecessary redundancies, might become possible by constructing tests and tasks that systematically sample—with any desired degree of thoroughness—the varieties of learning and memory organized by the classificatory system.

6. Existence of an accepted classificatory system would make it easier to construct a more rational *nomenclature* of varieties of learning and memory. In the absence of such a system, we see in the literature anomalies like "cued free recall" and "negative priming effects," expressions comparable to "a six-legged quadruped" and "negative expenditure of energy." While other life sciences devote a good deal of institutionalized and international effort to problems of terminology (e.g., Mayr, Linsley, & Usinger, 1953, *Appendix*; World Health Organization, 1974), students of learning and memory have retained the *laissez faire* attitude that served our science well in its formative years but which is unlikely to remain workable in the longer run. The creation of a useful, stable, and generally accepted terminology would be more likely if we had in existence an acceptable classificatory system.

These, then, are some of the reasons for undertaking the classification enterprise in learning and memory, stated in rather general and somewhat abstract terms. To illustrate the need for a useful classificatory system in more concrete terms, let us contemplate a simple exercise.

Intuitive Decisions About Relatedness

Suppose you are a specialist in learning and memory, and someone asks you the question, "How closely related are X and Y?" where X and Y refer to varieties of learning and memory. Can you answer the question? Always? Sometimes? If yes, on what basis do you do it, and on what sort of a scale do you provide the answer? If you cannot answer the question, why not?

Consider some possible concrete examples of X and Y in the question about the relatedness of X and Y. When in doubt, assume that in the situations described we are talking about performances following appropriate "training."

1. University students recalling words from a studied list versus recognizing words from the same list.
2. Rats turning left in a T-maze versus turning to the brighter side in the same maze.

3. A person recalling the plot of a movie and a bird picking up seeds from various hiding places in which it had cached them earlier.

4. A university student recalling a letter trigram in the Brown-Peterson task and a monkey making the correct choice in a delayed matching-to-sample task.

5. A person imagining the face of her beloved and a pigeon pecking the key with a plus sign on it.

6. A dog jumping over the barrier in a shuttle shock-avoidance task and a mouse staying on the elevated platform in a "step-down" compartment.

7. A professor of psychology recalling the formula of the multiple correlation coefficient and a student of psychology remembering how he failed the first term test in statistics.

8. An amnesic patient recalling the response word to the stimulus word in a paired-associate task with associatively related pairs and a young woman showing perfect adaptation to the "distorted" visual world while wearing Ivo Kohler's prism-lenses.

The list contains descriptions of relatively simple and straightforward situations that are either well known to everybody from real life or represent standard experimental paradigms from learning and memory laboratories. The exercise could be expanded in scope by considering all possible 120 pairings of the 16 memory and learning performances, or a very much larger number of pairings of a much larger number of examples of what humans and animals can learn and remember. And it would not be difficult to add excitement to the game by including descriptions of situations with greater detail. One of the situations might be described as follows: "A girl of 12 years of age, with an M.A. of 15, trying to recall, to extralist semantically related cues, three-word semianomalous sentences presented auditorily at the rate of 5 sec per sentence, on two successive study trials 24 hours earlier, with 24 sentences in the list, under the conditions where her orienting task was to judge the meaningfulness of the sentences on the first trial and the plausibility of the described action on the second." The list of such concoctions, enough of which can be found in the literature, could be made arbitrarily long, and it could include many comparably complicated scenarios from real life outside the laboratory.

It is possible to imagine the existence of a world in which (a) each of the varieties of learning and memory described in our exercise can be reliably *identified* as a member of a particular class or category, (b) each such class ("species") has a name accepted as such by everyone who cares about these things, and (c) the classes of learning and memory are organized into a comprehensive classificatory system. In such a world, the problem posed in the exercise could be solved by a simple look-up procedure, comparable to that used by systematic biologists faced with questions about relatedness of plants or animals.

In the world in which we live now, just about the only thing we can do when confronted with problems of relatedness of different varieties of learning and memory is to rely on our intuition. Intuitively, guided by the wisdom distilled from watching ourselves and other people, and by whatever relevant knowledge is found in the memory and learning literature, we do make judgments concerning relatedness of tasks. Many examples could be given, but let us limit ourselves to a few.

Nicholas Mackintosh, in his chapter in this volume, suggested that classical conditioning in animals is like episodic cued recall in humans, and David Olton (1984) has argued that rats have episodic memory of the kind that allows people to remember past events, since rats can respond correctly on delayed conditional matching tasks, which, like episodic remembering, require retrieval of particular past happenings. Fergus Craik (1983) has interpreted the differential impairment in memory capabilities of the aged in terms of the extent to which the performance of tasks require "self-initiated constructive operations" or "activation of conscious operations," properties of tasks that are reflected in their listing in an ordered array. Tasks that are closer to one another on Craik's scale could be regarded as being more closely related to one another than those farther apart. For instance, free recall is more closely related to cued recall than it is to recognition. In a similar vein, the task analysis described by Rönnberg and Ohlsson in this volume can be seen as affording one basis for making judgments about relatedness of varieties of learning and memory. Then there are students of learning and memory (e.g., Baddeley, 1984; Cohen, 1984; Kinsbourne & Wood, 1975; Mishkin, Malamut, & Bachevalier, 1984; Squire, 1982; Tulving, 1983, 1985a, 1985b; Warrington & Weiskrantz, 1982; Weiskrantz, 1982), who believe in the existence of different memory systems, and who are willing to make judgments concerning relatedness of varieties of learning and memory in terms of the extent to which different systems mediate performance of different tasks.

Finally, and perhaps most relevant in the context of the Umeå conference, the many generations of students of animal learning who have pursued their research in the hope that their findings and ideas will throw light on the basic principles of human learning (Jenkins, 1979), must have had in mind assumptions regarding correspondences between particular varieties of animal and human learning and memory. In the same vein, the search for "connecting models," the topic of Estes's paper in the present volume, must be predicated not just on the assumption that common mechanisms exist in (animal) learning and (human) memory, but also on the knowledge, hypothetical or real, concerning correspondences between particular kinds of learning in different species. In the absence of such knowledge, or at least ideas, about these correspondences, the enterprise of looking for parallels between learning and memory in animals and humans could not possibly succeed.

Thus we can say that, despite the strong traditional pretheoretical belief in the unity of learning and memory (Tulving, 1984), students of learning and memory have always been willing, and sometimes obliged, to assume differences in ways in which organisms benefit from their experiences, and to make judgments about relatedness of varieties of learning and memory, both within and between species. In this (limited) sense, they have acted as taxonomists. Their judgments, however, have been based on intuition only. There has been little or no discussion of objective rules for determining relatedness, and no systematic attempts to gather evidence that would either support the intuitive conjectures or correct them.

The pursuit of an explicitly articulated classification problem would supplement pure intuition with objective empirical evidence, explicitly gathered for the purpose, and evaluated and interpreted with the aid of accepted rules of procedure. It would make explicit, general, and systematic the practices that until now have been largely implicit, local, and haphazardly followed. Let us, in the next section of the paper, ponder on the nature of relevant evidence and on the rules of procedure.

OBJECTIVES OF CLASSIFICATION RESEARCH: EVIDENCE AND METHODS

Systematics of Learning and Memory

The distant goal of the classification enterprise in learning and memory would be development of what we might refer to, borrowing the term from biology, as the *systematics* of learning and memory. Paraphrasing Simpson (1961, p. 7), we could define the systematics of learning and memory as the scientific study of the kinds, diversities, and varieties of learning and memory, and natural relations among them. We could further think of systematics as comprising three separate but interrelated specialities: classification, taxonomy, and nomenclature (cf. Savory, 1970).

The subject matter of *classification* would be kinds, diversities, and varieties of learning and memory and its objective would be the ordering of varieties of learning and memory into "natural" groups. The *taxonomy,* or taxometrics (Meehl & Golden, 1982), of learning and memory would comprise the study of the rules, principles, and bases of classifying. *Nomenclature* would be concerned with the development and application of distinctive names and labels for the resulting groups or classes of varieties of learning and memory that would be generally accepted, thereby contributing to the quality of communication between different disciplines concerned with learning and memory.

The history of problems of classification and taxonomy in other fields of science teaches us that the classification problem in learning and memory is going to be complex, difficult, and frustrating. It is also going to be controversial. The whole idea will be rejected out of hand by some, and those who accept the general objective as worthwhile will not always agree on methods, facts, or interpretations. These kinds of problems, however, are usual in any new venture, in science as well as in other spheres of human activity, and they will be overcome in time.

Lessons from Biology

There exists a rich technical literature on classification and its application in many spheres of human activity. Research on principles and procedures of classification crosses traditional subject-matter boundaries; it has benefitted from the fruits of labors of thinkers in a number of disciplines (e.g., Dahlberg, 1982; Engelien, 1971; Felsenstein, 1983; Korner, 1976; Meehl & Golden, 1982; Simpson, 1961; Sneath & Sokal, 1973; Sokal, 1974). Although the application of principles of classification creates unique problems in different disciplines, the nature of the problems, as well as that of solutions, is characterized by a good deal of generality. Thus, as we start contemplating the possibilities and problems of classification in our own field, we can benefit from the experiences accumulated by practitioners in others.

Most relevant for our own purposes are probably the lessons that biologists have learned in their attempts to come to grips with the tremendous variety of living organisms that inhabit the earth (e.g., Huxley, 1940; Mayr, 1982; Simpson, 1961; Solbrig, 1966). Systematic biology, of course, differs from systematic learning and memory in many ways. One of the more conspicuous differences is the fact that there is little difficulty in determining the to-be-classified things in biology: They are concrete things that occupy space, that have boundaries, and that have perceptually identifiable and objectively measurable characteristics. In learning and memory, it is not necessarily clear what the objects of classification are or what they should be. We return to this problem shortly. Another difference pertains to the guidance that phylogenetic knowledge has provided to taxonomists in biology: Since taxonomists in learning and memory will not have such knowledge available, they would have to adopt some other criteria that will help them to construct a natural classificatory scheme. We discuss one such criterion presently.

Although all classificatory systems are based on the idea that like objects are grouped into like classes, and that like classes are further grouped together as superordinate classes, we should probably be sceptical about the possibility of reaching our goal through what have been referred to as numerical phenetics (Mayr, 1982) or numerical taxonomy (Sneath & Sokal, 1973). These terms cover a number of procedures in which the perceptual similarity of objects to be classified is judged by human observers, either experts or others, and the results of such judgments subjected to any one of a large number of statistical techniques that convert the data in similarity or proximity matrices into structured wholes (e.g., Sneath & Sokal, 1973; Felsenstein, 1983).

We would probably not want to follow this route. The number of different classificatory systems that could be produced would be large, and there would be no reasons to believe that any of them would agree with nature. The outcomes of such exercises in some other fields have been disappointing. Thus, for instance, Meehl (1979) has said that in psychopathology, phenetic classification procedures (procedures based on phenotypical descriptions of target entities) coupled with classical techniques of cluster analysis, have *never* led to the discovery of a single taxon (taxonomic unit), and Mayr admits to knowing of not "a single substantial contribution made by numerical phenetics to the classification of any mature groups, or to classification at the level of orders, classes, or phyla" (Mayr, 1982, p. 225). Given such evaluations we would be wise not to rush to embrace these methods, despite their great popularity. Classifying varieties of learning and memory on the basis of their identifiable properties is unlikely to be more successful in our field.

We have always had, and have now, various arbitrarily defined and intuitively constituted categories of learning and memory, categories such as instrumental and classical conditioning, associative and nonassociative memory, and short-term and long-term memory, among others. (See also Gagne, 1977; Melton, 1964; Tolman, 1949). These may be useful for practical purposes, but there is no evidence that they conform to nature. Classification simply on the basis of observed characteristics of varieties of learning and memory is unlikely to be successful.

Neuropsychological Criterion

If we do not classify on the basis of observable properties of varieties of learning and memory, what do we do? One thing we can do is to take a greater interest in what is known and what will be learned in the future about the neural basis of learning and memory, and pursue the classification problem in terms of known relations between brain activity on the one hand and psychological (behavioral and cognitive) manifestations of learning and memory on the other hand (e.g., Kinsbourne, 1976; Oakley, 1981; Rozin, 1976; Squire, 1982; Weiskrantz, 1968). Thus, instead of requiring that a classificatory scheme be consistent with known facts about the phylogeny of the classified organisms, as is done in systematic biology, we could require that our classification be consistent with what is known about brain activity in learning and memory. Moreover, we could adopt the extent to which two varieties of learning and memory are subserved by the same neural mechanisms or brain processes as one of our criteria for making judgments about their relatedness. We can refer to this rule for making judgments concerning relatedness as the neuropsychological criterion.

Although relatively little is known yet about brain activity in learning and memory, additional knowledge is being gained at an increasingly rapid rate. Even now a great deal can be done with the neuropsychological criterion, if we are willing to adopt it. Changes in brain activity can be effected through lesions or stimulation, as discussed by David Olton in his chapter in this volume, and techniques for observing brain activity *in vivo* are being invented and improved all the time.

The neuropsychological criterion can be also used in situations where changes or differences in brain function accompany, or result from, evolutionary changes of the species (e.g., Bitterman, 1975) or developmental changes of individuals. For instance, it is well known that older organisms can learn things that younger ones cannot (e.g., Amsel & Stanton, 1980; Bachevalier & Mishkin, 1983) and that older ones cannot do what younger ones can (e.g., Craik, 1977; Craik & Rabinowitz, 1983). Varieties of learning and memory thus could be classified on the basis of their presence in different species and the time of their appearance in development (e.g., Schacter & Moscovitch, 1984).

Especially useful for classificatory purposes, at least during the initial stages of the enterprise, are observed dissociations of learning and memory performances. A dissociation is said to have been demonstrated if a treatment that changes brain activity affects learning or memory performance of Type X, but not of Type Y. Dissociation means that a particular structure, or a neural mechanism, constitutes one of the *necessary* neurophysiological conditions for the carrying out of a psychological function. Thus, the observation of the dissociation between performances X and Y, as a result of treatment A, permits the conclusion that the brain mechanism affected by A is necessary for learning or memory manifested in X, and that it is not necessary for Y, and that to this extent X and Y represent different *classes* of learning or memory. Treatments most commonly used in the establishment of dissociations are brain lesions, experimentally produced in animals, and resulting from disease or accidental injury, or from therapeutic surgical procedures, in humans.

Even more compelling are demonstrations of double dissociation: Treatment A affects X but not Y, whereas another treatment B affects Y but not X (Jones, 1983; Shallice, 1979; Weiskrantz, 1968). In this case, the possibility is excluded that the single dissociation reflects simply differential vulnerability of performances X and Y, and the conclusion that X and Y are mediated by different neural systems is much stronger. We will see later in this paper, however, that sometimes it is the *absence* of a double dissociation, in a situation in which a single dissociation has been established, that can provide strong evidence useful for classification.

The general principle in all these criterion procedures is the same: Behavioral expressions of different varieties of learning and memory show systematic correlations with variations in brain activity reflecting species differences, developmental stages, lesions, electrical stimulation, or changes in biochemistry. These correlations constitute one basis on which a "natural" classificatory system of learning and memory can be constructed.

Tasks as Objects of Classification?

In many ways the most difficult part of the classification problem in learning and memory lies in getting started. Before we can begin worrying about the degree of relatedness of varieties X and Y of learning or memory, we must make some preliminary decisions as to what constitutes X and what constitutes Y. Exactly what are the things that we want to compare in order to assign them to categories that then define their "identity"? What are the *objects* of our classification enterprise?

So far in the paper I have used the somewhat fuzzy expressions of "varieties" or "kinds" of learning and memory, or even "performances" and "situations," when referring to the things that we wish to classify, but what exactly do we mean by these terms? How do we delineate a particular variety, kind, performance, or situation of learning or memory? What kind of intellectual operations are necessary to create a situation where we can describe a "variety" of learning and memory, assert that it is the "object" of the classification enterprise, and pose questions about its relatedness to other "objects"?

We could take "phenomena" of learning and memory, or "effects," or "relations between behaviors and situations," or anything else, as objects of classification, and we would always have to face similar kinds of problems: How to delineate them, how to decompose behavior into the chosen units, how to define and describe them. There are no obvious solutions to these problems; they constitute a part of the larger classification problem.

To illustrate the difficulties, uncertainties, and possible frustrations inherent in the selection of *units* of learning and memory, let us consider an obvious candidate for such a unit, namely a learning or memory *task*. We can provisionally define a "task" as a situation in which a particular organism interacts with its environment in a particular way, and, as a consequence, acquires the capacity to behave differently in similar situations in the future. The concept of *task* is widely used in psychological research on learning and memory: The literature is full of descriptions of, and statements about what happens in, all kinds of tasks. Tasks are the most frequently occurring products of decomposition procedures that psychologists have used in extracting units from the stream of behavior and thought. But if we adopted tasks as objects of classification, we would immediately run into problems.

What Are Tasks?

One of the first serious difficulties with tasks as objects of classification lies in the absence of a workable definition of *task*, a definition that would enable its users to decide whether two situations represent the same task or different tasks. Although the concept of *task* has been used widely by all learning and memory theorists and experimenters, few attempts have been made to define it explicitly in relatively abstract terms, in a manner that would not create disagreements with the extant use of the term in different situations. Nor have there been many attempts to specify the rules by which decisions regarding identity and nonidentity of tasks, in different situations, could be made.

One approach to the problem of defining "task" would be through specifying its constituents or properties. Most practitioners would probably agree that such specifications should include statements about (a) the kind of organism that does the learning, (b) the conditions under which learning occurs, (c) the behavior in which the organism engages at the time of learning, and (d) the behavior through which what has been learned is expressed. Each of these aspects of a task can be, and usually is, quite complex. The last three aspects correspond closely to Rescorla's three issues with which theories of learning must be concerned (Rescorla, 1980; also his chapter in this volume). The learning organism may have to be included as a part of the definition of "task" since we cannot always assume that what appear to be similar kinds of learning in different species, or even within a species, are based on the same underlying mechanisms, a point made by Estes in his chapter in this volume (see also Estes, 1978).

But thinking of tasks in this way creates a number of questions: (a) Is the learning organism's motivational, emotional, or pharmacological "state" in any way relevant to the specification of a task? (b) Does the task change as a function of the learner's expertise or relevant prior knowledge? (c) Do different strategies that an organism may bring to bear upon its learning activities change the task? (d) Is the behavior through which the effects of learning are expressed an *obligatory* part of the definition of a task? (e) Is a task a *single* task even if we know that people's performance of it is based on different processes that can be separately identified? (f) How does the fact that identical responses to identical stimuli may reflect quite different underlying processes affect our definition of tasks?

Consider possible answers to some of these questions with the help of two concrete examples of tasks, one that can be used only with humans, and one that can be used with both humans and animals. The first is single–trial free recall: A subject is exposed to a collection of discrete items and he is instructed to recall the names of as many of the presented items as he can (e.g., Waugh, 1961). The second task is the single-object version of delayed matching to sample: A subject is exposed to an object, and after an interval of time has to choose the same object from a test set that consists of the target object and one not encountered on that trial. This task figures prominently in the research that David Gaffan discusses in his chapter in the present volume. (See also Roberts & Grant, 1976.)

What aspects of the free-recall task can we alter before we have to concede that we have changed the *task*? Does it change when we alter the length of the list, or the retention interval, or the activity of the rememberer interpolated between the study and the recall of the list? Does it change when the rememberer changes—say, from a university student to a very young child, or to an Alzheimer patient? Does it change when the to-be-remembered items change, say, from familiar words to 8-letter nonsense strings, or to 16-word sentences, or to photographs of complex scenes? Does the task become another kind of task when the experimenter instructs the subjects to record recalled words in the order in which the items were presented (e.g., Cohen, 1970), or to recall the last few items from the list first (e.g., Craik & Watkins, 1973, Exp. 2), or to recall the items by their initial letters (e.g., Murdock, 1960), or in alphabetical order (e.g., Tulving, 1962)? Is the *task* changed when subjects use the serial or alphabetical recall strategy on their own, without instructions from the experimenter? Is recalling a once-presented list of 16 familiar words 10 seconds after study the same task as recalling the names of one's schoolmates 40 years later (e.g., Bahrick, Bahrick, & Wittlinger, 1975)? What about faces of the same school-mates? What about recalling names when faces are given as cues? Does the task become a different task when subjects, at the time of recall, are given seman-tically related words as cues or prompts for the recall of words from a studied list (e.g., Bahrick, 1969)?

Let us turn our attention next to the behavior through which learning is expressed. Does the single-trial free recall task change when we ask the person to (a) reproduce the list items orally, (b) write the names down, (c) recall the words in another language with which the learner is familiar, or (d) tap the names out in the Morse code? Does the negative answer, which most people would give, imply that the overt behavior through which learning is expressed is not a defining feature of *any* task? For instance, if we think of the eyelid conditioning situation as a "task," would we be willing to concede that the exact form of overt behavior in which the learning manifests itself is immaterial? If not, does it mean that sometimes the expressive behavior is, and sometimes it is not, to be regarded as part of the definition of tasks? And if so, what determines when it is and when it is not?

If the reader is gradually becoming, or already has become, sceptical of the possibility of ever finding satisfactory answers to these questions, and hence is starting to have doubts about the usefulness of thinking of tasks as objects of classification, he or she is on the right track: The point of the exercise is to demonstrate that we have difficulty with questions that an outsider might think we answered a long time ago.

It is not only the difficulty of answering these and similar questions that should concern us. We should also be concerned with the rules or criteria that we use when we try to or do come up with answers to the questions. On what basis do we arrive at the answers? Is it possible to articulate such rules and criteria? Can we expect them to be generally acceptable?

Behind these and many other specific questions posed in this paper lurks perhaps the most telling one: How is it possible to ask all these questions that seem quite reasonable and appropriate, and yet have no place in our 100-year-old literature to turn to for the answers, or even for an enlightened discussion of the issues? What kind of perspective of the subject matter has been missing in the study of learning and memory ever since Ebbinghaus, Pavlov, Thorndike, Bryan and Harter, and other early pioneers started it all (Cofer, 1979; Hearst, 1979; Jenkins, 1979)?

Let me ask just two questions about our other task, delayed matching to sample, before we take leave of the problem of what is a task. First, does the task remain the "same" for organisms that have no language and for those that do? If yes, does it mean that possession of language does not affect the identity of *any* task? If not, when does it matter? Second, is the task the same task regardless of the nature of test objects that are used? Consider the difference between two versions of the task. One employs "trial-unique" objects, in the other the objects recur trial after trial. In the "trial-unique" procedure (e.g., Mishkin, 1978), every target object presented for inspection, and every distractor object at test, is always "new": The subject has never encountered them before. In the extreme form of the "repeated-objects" procedure there are only two objects used on successive trials of the experiment, A and B. One is selected randomly on each trial to serve as the inspection stimulus, and both are presented at test. Now, should we think of these two versions of the basic procedure as one and the same task, or do they constitute different tasks? The "same" judgment would obviate the need for any further questions concerning the relatedness of the two versions; the "different" decision would render such questions both important and meaningful.

Tasks As Categories

Although I want to emphasize problems and questions in this paper, rather than declarative ideas and suggestions, it may be useful at this juncture to try to reduce the perplexity that the long string of questions may have created. One way to do so would be to introduce the distinction between individual tasks and classes of tasks. Many a question I have posed here could have been clarified, and answers rendered less uncertain, by the specification that the question referred to a *class* of tasks and not to an individual member of that class.

Biology again provides a useful analogy here, in the form of the concept of "species." Species are taxonomic units at the lowest level of the classificatory hierarchy, being formed into larger categories at higher levels (genera, families, orders, and so on). An important property of species is that it represents a natural *population* of plants or animals. Individual members of any population may vary greatly in many of their characteristics. Only some characters are critical for the determination of whether or not an individual belongs to a species, characters such as ability to interbreed, or chromosomal structure.

When we discuss tasks, we also must distinguish between a single task as such and the population to which it belongs. Like individual members of a species, so individual tasks within a particular population need not at all be identical but may vary in a number of characters. Classes of tasks would be defined in terms of certain critical characters that its members share. The classification problem thus reduces, during the early stages of the game, to the problem of discriminating defining characters from nondefining characters of task categories.

Overt Behavior and Covert Processes

Let us return to the implications of subjects' use of different strategies for the definition of tasks, because it, and some related observations, will lead us to one of the fundamental problems in the classification enterprise. Suppose, for instance, that in a task such as free recall one subject uses a rote learning strategy, implicitly rehearsing individual items by muttering their names over and over during the presentation, whereas another person constructs interacting mental images of the named objects. Would the tasks performed by the two individuals belong to the same "species"?

The general question here has to do with the contrast between observable behavior and underlying processes as characters potentially relevant to classification. Should we go strictly by what the specified requirements are for the learner—by the observable, overt behavior—or should we take into account the covert mental activity in which the learner engages in performing the task?

Consider a slightly different version of the same question. It concerns situations where we know, or have good reasons to believe, that the performance on the task represents a combined effect of separate and experimentally differentiable mechanisms. For instance, we know now that in the single trial free recall task (e.g., Craik & Levy, 1976; Glanzer, 1972; Tulving & Colotla, 1970; Watkins, 1974) primary and secondary memory processes, or systems, contribute to the overall performance on the task that is measured in terms of the number of items recalled (cf. Crowder, 1982). The two components are differentiable in the sense that many independent variables that affect one component have no effect on the other, and vice versa. Given this knowledge, should we still treat the overall procedure as a single "task"?

A third related observation is derived from the common knowledge that one and the same response that a learner makes to one and the same stimulus may represent the effects of rather different underlying processes. For example, if in a paired associate learning task, a subject learns a pair such as *army*-SOLDIER, and later is tested with the stimulus item *army*, the learner can make the correct response SOLDIER either in terms of his remembering seeing the two words in the study list (relying on his episodic memory, as some of us might say) or simply in terms of his general knowledge of the associative structure of words, using a "free-association strategy" (or relying on his semantic memory). How does the fact that there is no unique one-to-one correspondence between underlying mechanisms and processes on the one hand and overt responses on the other affect our definitions and descriptions of tasks? Should it matter in one way or another, or should we ignore it altogether?

All three examples illustrate the almost universally accepted assumption—supported by some factual evidence—that every learning and memory task is composed of a number of components (informational units, relations among them, processes, operations, mechanisms, or whatever), and that different tasks may have both common and non-common components. This assumption creates a fundamental problem: Should we take whatever information we have about composition of tasks into account *before* we begin classifying them, or should we expect that these components will be revealed by the classificatory scheme with which we end up after we have successfully completed the mission? What would a search for *components* of learning and memory mean and entail?

Components of Learning and Memory

Concepts such as "learning" and "memory" do not represent entities that have some sort of existence in the brains or minds of organisms. They are simply broad labels assigned to describe concatenations of neural, behavioral, and mental components whose various combinations serve the function of shaping an organism's knowledge and behavior through its interactions with the world, thereby helping it to adjust and survive.

If varieties of learning and memory represent various concatenations of more elementary components, why should we not try to classify the varieties in terms of these constituent elements? The reason is simple: We do not know what the components are. We do not as yet have even a short list of "basic" processes of learning and memory that can be reliably identified and isolated across different situations. Part of the difficulty is undoubtedly attributable to the intrinsic complexity of the subject matter of our science. Another part of it may lie in the ineffective methods we use, or infertile pretheoretical and theoretical ideas that we have inherited and uncritically accepted from the past, the "curse of an angry god" that Bolles talks about in his chapter in the present volume. Many theorists (e.g., Craik, 1983, also this volume; Nilsson, 1984), indeed, might want to argue that any search for *components* of learning and memory, regardless of how they are conceptualized, is doomed to failure at the outset for the simple reason that there are *no* components of varieties of learning and memory: Learning and memory are manifestations of *interactions* between task demands and the environment, shaped by the capabilities of organisms.

I think that we should not reject ideas before we test them, or at least think hard about them. Although we may not have many compelling facts about components of learning and memory, it is possible to entertain thoughts about how they might be detected should they exist. Consider a simple example.

It is possible to identify several *logical* components of the delayed matching-to-sample task: (a) inspection of the presentation object, (b) construction of a neural (mental) representation of that object, (c) storage of the representation, (d) retention of the representation over time, (e) observation of the test objects, (f) selection of the test object that matches the representation of the target object, and (g) the making of the appropriate response to the selected test object. This description sketches the sequence of events that have to occur if the animal is to respond consistently and successfully in the task. Failure of any one of the seven processing stages will result in chance performance.

We do not know how these seven "logical" stages correspond to neural and behavioral processes that constitute the performance on the task, although we have good reasons to believe that the situation is in fact very much more complicated than the simple listing of the stages suggests. Any one of the labeled processing stages is probably mediated by a complex pattern of neural events: The apparent unity and simplicity of the operation lies in our description rather than in the underlying processes. The situation is further complicated by the fact that the processes of successive stages must run their course under the general guidance of operating procedures that define the "rules of the game" for the subject of the experiment. These are the rules that Harlow (1959) studied under the rubric of "learning sets"; they may be involved in the establishment of what others have referred to as "reference memory" (Honig, 1978; Olton, Becker, & Handelmann, 1979).

The organism's required knowledge of the "rules of the game" vary with the version of the task. With "trial-unique" objects there is no need for the organism to keep track of the temporal date of the occurrence of the inspection object, whereas in the "repeated-objects" version such temporal dating is indispensable. In the former, general "familiarity" of one of the test objects is sufficient for successful performance, whereas in the latter the "rules of the game" must include a concept like the "trial": test objects must be matched with the inspection object seen on a given trial, not on any trial. Ability to keep a specifically dated record of the appearance of objects on particular trials is mandatory for success with repeated stimuli. In the absence of such a record, performance cannot exceed chance level. According to this analysis, then, both versions of the task have a number of components in common, and they differ in that the repeated-objects version has at least one *additional* component, one that makes it possible for the organism to keep track of the temporal date of occurrence of objects.

We can schematically express the situation as follows. Both versions of the task consist of or require a number of common components, *a, b,* and *c,* and the repeated-objects version consists of or requires an additional component *d.* Given such a situation, it should be possible to find single dissociations of the kind where, say, a particular brain lesion results in the organism's inability to perform the repeated-objects version of the delayed matching-to-sample task without affecting the performance on the version of the task involving trial-unique objects. More important is another expectation derived from our logical analysis: Under the conditions as specified, double dissociation of performance on the two versions of the task would be *precluded.* Given that the components of Task Y entail those of Task X, there is no way of interfering with the operation of X without interfering with Y. The presence of one, and the absence of the other, type of dissociation would thus provide strong evidence for the existence of a particular component of learning or memory, as well as for the necessary involvement of the component in particular tasks.

The same logic applies to the distinction made by Olton and his associates (e.g., Olton, 1983; Olton et al., 1979) between reference and working memory as dissociable systems: Reference memory is required for all the tasks that the Olton group has used in their experiments whereas working memory is required only for some. Such a relation renders possible single dissociations, as demonstrated by the Olton group, and it rules out the possibility of double dissociations. The logic also has definite implications for schemes such as I have described elsewhere (Tulving, 1985a, 1985b) in which three memory systems—procedural, semantic, and episodic—constitute a class-inclusion "monohierarchy."

To what extent *logical* analyses of this kind agree with nature is unknown. Brains and minds of animals and people are complicated, and we should not be surprised to find mismatches between our simple ideas and the more complex world of facts. But such analyses do pinpoint possibilities for finding especially useful kinds of evidence. Mere demonstrations of single or double dissociations of two tasks that vary with respect to several (unknown) components, as a rule, do not tell us very much about anything and do not help us much with the classification problem. However, systematic correlations between brain function and behaviors in carefully analyzed tasks could play a decisive role in the mission of identifying components of learning and memory.

CLASSIFICATION AND EXISTING SYSTEMS

Although the classification problem in learning and memory, and the new perspective on research that it represents, is not yet a part of the scientific agenda of workers in learning and memory, we do already have various speculative proposals regarding different kinds, or systems, of learning and memory. How is the classification problem that I have discussed in this chapter related to current research and notions with respect to these systems? I briefly discuss this issue in relation to a triadic scheme that I have described more fully elsewhere, as well as to other similar schemes.

Triadic Memory

In discussing the relation between episodic and semantic memory not too long ago (Tulving, 1983), I assumed that episodic and semantic memory represent parallel subsystems of propositional (declarative) memory. Because of certain difficulties inherent in such a conceptualization, pointed out by a number of critics (e.g., Kihlstrom, 1984; Lachman & Naus, 1984; Lieury, 1979; Seamon, 1984; McCauley, 1984; Tiberghien, 1984) I have now revised these ideas and have suggested that it may be more appropriate to think of episodic memory as "growing out of but remaining embedded in" the semantic system (Tulving, 1984). The same general idea can also be extended to the relation between procedural memory and propositional memory: rather than thinking of these two as parallel subsystems of the overall memory system, it seems to make more sense to conceptualize semantic memory as subsumed by the procedural memory system (Tulving, 1985a, 1985b).

A learning and memory system refers to a particular set of neural structures, or mechanisms, or both, that subserve different behavioral and cognitive functions, that operate according to different laws and principles, and that have evolved at different times in the phylogeny of the species and evolve at different times in the ontogeny of individuals (Tulving, 1984). The overall arrangement of procedural, semantic, and episodic memory systems could be characterized as "monohierarchical": a hierarchical arrangement of varieties of learning and memory in which pocedural memory contains semantic memory, and semantic memory contains episodic memory, as a specialized subsystem. The arrangement conforms to the principle, found useful in the study of phylogeny of animals (e.g., Carter, 1961; deBeer, 1938), according to which a structure or structural feature that has developed later always must be such that it can be derived by modification of the corresponding earlier structure or structural feature. Thus we assume that in the evolutionary emergence of learning and memory systems, too, systems that have developed later represent extensions and modifications of earlier systems rather than independent, parallel developments of completely different systems.

Other tripartite divisions of memory in animals have been proposed by Ruggiero and Flagg (1976) and Oakley (1981). The category that represents the "simplest" memory in their schemes is essentially identical, or at least homologous, with the procedural system in the triadic classification I have just described, and the other two classes in Oakley's (1981) scheme, "representational" and "abstract" memories, can be regarded as analogous to semantic and episodic memory, respectively.

A number of other theorists have proposed various dichotomous divisions of learning and memory. These schemes, by Cohen and Squire (1980), Mishkin, Malamut, and Bachevalier (1984), O'Keefe and Nadel (1978), and Olton (1983), among others, fit into the triadic or tripartite schemes without undue difficulties.

"Upward" and "Downward" Approaches

There are two major differences between the classification problem as I have discussed it in this chapter and the extant speculations concerning learning and memory systems. First, attempts to subdivide the total subject matter of learning and memory into different systems, exemplified in the schemes just discussed, are reminiscent of the Aristotelian and Linnaean methods of classification of organisms on the basis of the "downward" procedure (Mayr, 1982). One begins with the total population of things to be classified, subdivides them into two classes on the basis of a criterion that defines the "essence" of classes, and then proceeds to repeat the operation at lower levels. Thus, for instance, the distinction between procedural and nonprocedural memory could be based on the presence or absence of symbolic "content" of learning. Similarly, the further division of the nonprocedural memory into episodic and semantic could be based on the presence or absence of personal reference of the symbolic content that is learned and remembered. The fact that sometimes correlations exist among these criterial features (e.g., Tulving, 1983, Table 3.1) does not change the nature of the basic approach.

The classificatory system that I am envisaging as emerging from a systematic application of the principles of taxonomy to varieties of learning and memory, on the other hand, would represent the "upward" procedure (Mayr, 1982), characteristic of the post-Darwinian approach to classification in biology. Here, one begins with the smallest units of the classification, and builds them into larger groupings on the basis of a large number of criterial characters, working from the bottom up.

The second major difference between existing schemes and the one envisaged here is one that we have already discussed: the currently existing large dichotomous and trichotomous categories are mostly products of individual scientists' intuition, albeit tempered with some empirical evidence. The approach is largely intuitive because of the absence of agreed-upon, or even reasonably widely discussed, principles and rules on which the divisions are based. There are only general rules of thumb, such as those that are used in connection with functional dissociations or double dissociations. Many relevant questions—such as those concerning components of tasks, and their weights in different tasks—can be answered only in terms of implicit rules and hunches.

The classification problem envisaged here would be accompanied and guided by the development of useful explicit rules and procedures that are worked out according to generally accepted methods of science, and it would entail the application of these rules and principles to making decisions about the relatedness of tasks, or whatever units are to be classified.

The fact that the existing classificatory schemes are "downward" and based on intuition does not necessarily mean that they are wrong, or that they will necessarily be replaced by different divisions at top levels of the hierarchical scheme that might emerge from the "upward" classification activities. It is quite possible that the present large categories, or systems, may map quite well onto the classificatory structure that will be constructed from the bottom up.

Nevertheless, an approach more systematic than the one that has been used to date is clearly called for. Even those of us who are willing to pontificate as to the nature and correspondence of components of different tasks and different memory systems, and who are willing to interpret evidence from experiments and other empirical observations in terms of our own hypothetical classificatory schemes, have very little to say about subsystems within the larger postulated systems. The classificatory structure that will be produced by the systematists in learning and memory will undoubtedly turn out to be very much richer in detail than are the existing schemes.

CONCLUSIONS

I have proposed in this chapter that students of learning and memory should devote a part of their experimental and theoretical efforts to the construction of a natural classificatory system of varieties of learning and memory. In elaborating this proposal, I pointed to gaps in our knowledge, gaps revealed by many difficult questions. Many questions I posed are of the kind that would have to be dealt with and answered in the course of the classification enterprise. The central suggestion was to adopt the neuropsychological criterion as an important basis for a natural system of classification, and as a potential deterrent to the proliferation of many arbitrary classificatory schemes.

At the beginning of the chapter I said that work on the classification problem constitutes a kind of a collaborative venture of students of (animal) learning and (human) memory that might help to build bridges between them. But the worthwhile nature of the enterprise should be clear even if we did not have to worry about the present separation of the two fields. If the systematics of learning developed independently of the systematics of memory, and if instead of collaboration we were to find ourselves engaged in a friendly but vigorous competition as to who "gets there first," nothing much would be lost.

Indeed, we must not overlook the possibility that, despite our nobler motives and aspirations, progress in classification might turn out to be easier to achieve if we initially restricted the domains of our activities by species of learners, and by broad categories of learning and memory. Many subproblems of the classification problem may become more tractable if we thought of them in connection with a particular population of learners, and a particular class of learning.

On the day when I completed the final version of this chapter, a new book entitled *Taxonomies of Human Performance* by Fleishman and Quaintance (1984) came to my attention. Although Fleishman and Quaintance are primarily concerned with taxonomic problems in those parts of psychology that are of particular interest to specalists in engineering psychology and research on human factors, their book should be required reading for all aspiring taxonomists in learning and memory. Chapter 2, for instance, provides an excellent summary of basic concepts of classification and their application in biological and psychological sciences, and elsewhere one finds a thorough discussion of the concept of *task,* the source of so much difficulty in this paper. I was pleased to see a good deal of overlap between Fleishman and Quaintance's ideas and those discussed here. It looks as if classification is coming into its own, creating new perspectives in psychological research, and that its pursuit in learning and memory is but another manifestation of the everpresent *Zeitgeist.*

ACKNOWLEDGMENT

The preparation of this paper has been supported by the Natural Sciences and Engineering Research Council of Canada Grant No. A8632, and by a Special Research Program Grant from the Connaught Fund, University of Toronto. I am grateful to Marcel Kinsbourne for the idea of the classification problem (Kinsbourne, in press), to Fergus Craik and David Olton for advice, and to Janine Law for collaboration in library research and the production of the manuscript.

REFERENCES

Amsel, A., & Stanton, M. (1980). Ontogeny and phylogeny of paradoxical reward effects. In J. S. Rosenblatt, R. A. Hinde, C. Beer, & M. Busnel (Eds.), *Advances in the study of behavior.* New York: Academic Press.

Bachevalier, J., & Mishkin, M. (1983). The development of memories vs. habits in infant monkeys. *International Journal of Psychophysiology, 1,* 116.

Baddeley, A. (1984). Neuropsychological evidence and the semantic/episodic distinction. *Behavioral and Brain Sciences, 7,* 238–239.

Bahrick, H. P. (1969) Measurement of memory by prompted recall. *Journal of Experimental Psychology, 79,* 213–239.

Bahrick, H. P., Bahrick, P. O., & Wittlinger, R. P. (1975). Fifty years of memory for names and faces: A cross-sectional approach. *Journal of Experimental Psychology: General, 104,* 54–75.

Bitterman, M. E. (1975). The comparative analysis of learning. *Science, 188,* 699–709.

Bruce, D. (1985). The how and why of ecological memory. *Journal of Experimental Psychology: General, 114,* 78–90.

Carter, G. S. (1961). *A general zoology of the invertebrates, Ch. 23.* London: Sidgwick & Jackson.

Cofer, C. N. (1979). Human learning and memory. In E. Hearst (Ed.), *The first century of experimental psychology.* Hillsdale, NJ: Lawrence Erlbaum Associates.

Cohen, N. J. (1984). Preserved learning capacity in amnesia: Evidence for multiple memory systems. In L. R. Squire & N. Butters (Eds.), *Neuropsychology of memory.* New York: Guilford Press.

Cohen, R. L. (1970). Recency effects in long-term recall and recognition. *Journal of Verbal Learning and Verbal Behavior, 9,* 672–678.

Cohen, N. J., & Squire, L. R. (1980). Preserved learning and retention of pattern analyzing skill in amnesia: Dissociation of knowing how and knowing that. *Science, 210,* 207–209.

Craik, F. I. M. (1977). Age differences in human memory. In J. E. Birren & K. W. Schaie (Eds.), *Handbook of the psychology of aging.* New York: van Nostrand Reinhold.

Craik, F. I. M. (1983). On the transfer of information from temporary to permanent memory. In D. E. Broadbent (Ed.), *Philosophical Transactions of the Royal Society of London, B.* London: The Royal Society, *302,* 341–359.

Craik, F. I. M., & Levy, B. A. (1976). The concept of primary memory. In W. K. Estes (Ed.), *Handbook of learning and cognitive processes. Vol. 4: Attention and memory.* Hillsdale, NJ: Lawrence Erlbaum Associates.

Craik, F. I. M., & Rabinowitz, J. C. (1983). Age differences in the acquisition and use of verbal information. In H. Bouma & D. G. Bouwhuis (Eds.), *Attention and performance X.* Hillsdale, NJ: Lawrence Erlbaum Associates.

Craik, F. I. M., & Watkins, M. J. (1973). The role of rehearsal in short-term memory. *Journal of Verbal Learning and Verbal Behavior, 12,* 599–607.

Crowder, R. G. (1982). The demise of short-term memory. *Acta Psychologica, 50,* 291–323.

Dahlberg, I. (1976). Classification theory, yesterday and today. *International Classification, 3,* 85–90.

Dahlberg, I. (1982). Editorial: Classification science—a true scientific discipline? *International Classification, 9,* 63.

deBeer, G. R. (1938). *Evolution: Essays on aspects of evolutionary biology.* Oxford: Clarendon Press.

Engelien, G. (1971). *Der Begriff der Klassifikation.* Hamburg: Helmut Buske Verlag.

Estes, W. K. (1978). On the organization ands core concepts of learning theory and cognitive psychology. In W. K. Estes (Ed.), *Handbook of learning and cognitive processes. Vol. 6: Linguistic functions in cognitive theory.* Hillsdale, NJ: Lawrence Erlbaum Associates.

Felsenstein, J. (Ed.). (1983). *Numerical taxonomy.* Berlin: Springer Verlag.

Fleishman, E. A., & Quaintance, M. K. (1984). *Taxonomies of human performance.* Orlando, FL: Academic Press.

Gagne, R. M. (1977). *The conditions of learning.* New York: Holt, Rinehart, & Winston.

Gillund, G., & Shiffrin, R. M. (1984). A retrieval model for both recognition and recall. *Psychological Review, 91,* 1–67.

Glanzer, M. (1972). Storage mechanisms in recall. In G. H. Bower (Ed.), *The psychology of learning and motivation: Advances in research and theory.* New York: Academic Press.

Harlow, H. F. (1959). Learning set and error factor theory. In S. Koch (Ed.), *Psychology: A study of science* (Vol. 2). New York: McGraw-Hill.

Hearst, E. (1979). One hundred years: Themes and perspectives. In E. Hearst (Ed.), *The first century of experimental psychology.* Hillsdale, NJ: Lawrence Erlbaum Associates.

Honig, W. K. (1978). Studies of working memory in the pigeon. In S. H. Hulse, H. Fowler, & W. K. Honig (Eds.), *Cognitive processes in animal behavior.* Hillsdale, NJ: Lawrence Erlbaum Associates.

Huxley, J. S. (1940). *The new systematics.* Oxford: Claredon Press.

Jenkins, H. M. (1979). Animal learning and behavior theory. In E. Hearst (Ed.), *The first century of experimental psychology.* Hillsdale, NJ: Lawrence Erlbaum Associates.

Jones, G. V. (1983). Note on double dissociation of function. *Neuropsychologia, 21,* 397–400.

Kihlstrom, J. F. (1984). A fact is a fact is a fact. *Behavioral and Brain Sciences. 7,* 243–244.

Kinsbourne, M. (1976). The neuropsychological analysis of cognitive deficit. In R. G. Grenell & S. Gabay (Eds.), *Biological foundations of psychiatry.* New York: Raven Press.

Kinsbourne, M. (in press). Systematizing cognitive psychology. *Behavioral and Brain Sciences.*

Kinsbourne, M., & Wood, F. (1975). Short-term memory processes and the amnesic syndrome. In D. Deutsch & J. A. Deutsch (Eds.), *Short-term memory.* New York: Academic Press.

Korner, S. (1976). Classification theory. *International Classification, 3,* 3–6.

Lachman, R., & Naus, M. J. (1984). The episodic/semantic continuum in an evolved machine. *Behavioral and Brain Sciences, 7,* 244–246.

Lieury, A. (1979). La memoire episodique est-elle emboitee dans la memoire semantique? *L'Annee Psychologique, 79,* 123–142.

Mayr, E. (1982). *The growth of biological thought.* Cambridge, MA: Belknap Press.

Mayr, E., Linsley, E. G., & Usinger, R. L. (1953). *Methods and principles of systematic zoology.* New York: McGraw-Hill.

McCauley, R. N. (1984). Inference and temporal coding in episodic memory. *Behavioral and Brain Sciences, 7,* 246–247.

Meehl, P. (1979). A funny thing happened to us on the way to the latent entities. *Journal of Personality Assessment, 43,* 563–581.

Meehl, P., & Golden, R. R. (1982). Taxometric methods. In P. C. Kendall & J. N. Butcher (Eds.), *Handbook of research methods in clinical psychology* (pp. 127–181). New York: Wiley.

Melton, A. W. (Ed.). (1964). *Categories of human learning.* New York: Academic Press.

Mishkin, M. (1978). Memory in monkeys severely impaired by combined but not by separate removal of amygdala and hippocampus. *Nature, 273,* 297–298.

Mishkin, M., Malamut, B., & Bachevalier, J. (1984). Memories and habits: Two neural systems. In G. Lynch, J. L. McGaugh, & G. Weinberger (Eds.), *The neurobiology of learning and memory.* New York: Guilford Press.

Moscovitch, M. (1984). The sufficient conditions for demonstrating preserved memory in amnesia. In L. R. Squire & N. Butters (Eds.), *Neuropsychology of memory.* New York: Guilford Press.

Murdock, B. B. Jr. (1960). The immediate retention of unrelated words. *Journal of Experimental Psychology, 60,* 222–234.

Nilsson, L.-G. (1984). New functionalism in memory research. In K. M. J. Lagerspetz & P. Niemi (Eds.), *Psychology in the 1990's.* Elsevier Science Publishers B.V. (North Holland).

Oakley, D. A. (1981). Brain mechanisms of mammalian memory. *British Medical Bulletin, 37,* 175–180.

O'Keefe, J., & Nadel, L. (1978). *The hippocampus as a cognitive map.* Oxford: Clarendon Press.

Olton, D. S. (1983). Memory functions and the hippocampus. In W. Seifert (Ed.), *Neurobiology of the hippocampus.* New York: Academic Press.

Olton, D. S. (1984). Comparative analysis of episodic memory. *Behavioral and Brain Sciences, 7,* 250–251.

Olton, D. S., Becker, J. T., & Handelmann, G. E. (1979). Hippocampus, space and memory. *The Behavioral and Brain Sciences, 2,* 313–365.

Rescorla, R. A. (1980). *Second-order conditioning.* Hillsdale, NJ: Lawrence Erlbaum Associates.

Roberts, W. A., & Grant, D. S. (1976). Studies of short-term memory in the pigeon using the delayed matching to sample procedure. In D. L. Medin, W. A. Roberts, & R. T. Davis (Eds.), *Processes of animal memory.* Hillsdale, NJ: Lawrence Erlbaum Associates.

Rozin, P. (1976). The psychobiological approach to human memory. In M. R. Rosenzweig & E. L. Bennett (Eds.), *Neural mechanisms of learning and memory.* Cambridge, MA: MIT Press.

Ruggiero, F. T., & Flagg, S. F. (1976). Do animals have memory? In D. L. Medin, W. A. Roberts, & R. T. Davis (Eds.), *Processes of animal memory.* Hillsdale, NJ: Lawrence Erlbaum Associates.

Savory, T. (1970). *Animal taxonomy.* London: Heinemann.

Schacter, D. L., & Moscovitch, M. (1984). Infants, amnesics, and dissociable memory systems. In M. Moscovitch (Ed.), *Infant memory.* New York: Plenum Press.

Seamon, J. G. (1984). The ontogeny of episodic and semantic memory. *Behavioral and Brain Sciences, 7,* 254.

Shallice, T. (1979). Neuropsychological research and the fractionation of memory systems. In L. G. Nilsson (Ed.), *Perspectives on memory research.* Hillsdale, NJ: Lawrence Erlbaum Associates.

Simpson, J. (1961). *Principles of animal taxonomy.* New York: Columbia University Press.

Sneath, P. H. A., & Sokal, R. R. (1973). *Numerical taxonomy.* San Francisco: Freeman.

Sokal, R. R. (1974). Classification: Purposes, principles, progress, prospects. *Science, 185,* 115–123.

Solbrig, O. T. (1966). *Evolution and systematics.* New York: Macmillan.

Spear, N. E. (1971). Forgetting as retrieval failure. In W. K. Honig & P. H. R. James (Eds.), *Animal memory.* New York: Academic Press.

Spear, N. E. (1984). Behaviours that indicate memory: Levels of expression. *Canadian Journal of Psychology, 38,* 348–367.

Squire, L. R. (1982). The neuropsychology of human memory. *Annual Review of Neuroscience, 5,* 241–273.

Tiberghien, G. (1984). Just how does ecphory work? *Behavioral and Brain Sciences, 7,* 255–256.

Tolman, E. C. (1949). There is more than one kind of learning. *Psychological Review, 56,* 144–155.

Tulving, E. (1962). The effect of alphabetical subjective organization on memorizing unrelated words. *Canadian Journal of Psychology, 16,* 185–191.

Tulving, E. (1982). Synergistic ecphory in recall and recognition. *Canadian Journal of Psychology, 36,* 130–147.

Tulving, E. (1983). *Elements of episodic memory.* Oxford: Clarendon Press.

Tulving, E. (1984). Multiple learning and memory systems. In K. M. J. Lagerspetz & P. Niemi (Eds.), *Psychology in the 1990's* (pp. 163–184). North Holland: Elsevier Science Publishers B.V.

Tulving, E. (1985a). How many memory systems are there? *American Psychologist,* in press.

Tulving, E. (1985b). Memory and consciousness. *Canadian Journal of Psychology, 26,* 1–12.

Tulving, E., & Colotla, V. (1970). Free recall of trilingual lists. *Cognitive Psychology, 1,* 86–98.

Tulving, E., Schacter, D. L., & Stark, H. A. (1982). Priming effects in word-fragment completion are independent of recognition memory. *Journal of Experimental Psychology: Learning, Memory, and Cognition. 8,* 336–342.

Warrington, E. K., & Weiskrantz, L. (1982). Amnesia: A disconnection syndrome? *Neuropsychologia, 20,* 233–248.

Watkins, M. J. (1974). Concept and measurement of primary memory. *Psychological Bulletin, 81,* 695–711.

Waugh, N. C. (1961). Free versus serial recall. *Journal of Experimental Psychology, 62,* 496–502.

Weiskrantz, L. (1968). Some traps and pontifications. In L. Weiskrantz (Ed.), *Analysis of behavioral change.* New York: Harper & Row.

Weiskrantz, L. (1982). Comparative aspects of studies of amnesia. In D. E. Broadbent & L. Weiskrantz (Eds.), *Philosophical Transactions of the Royal Society of London, B.* London: The Royal Society, 298, 97–109.

World Health Organization (1974). *Glossary of mental disorders and guide to their classification.* Geneva: WHO.

5
Memory: Neuropsychological and Ethopsychological Approaches to its Classification

David S. Olton
The Johns Hopkins University

INTRODUCTION

The correct classification of the processes involved in memory can help greatly in the analysis and understanding of them (see chapter by Tulving, this volume). However, great care must be taken when deciding how to make this classification because the validity of the resulting description is limited by the validity of the standards used to generate it. Classification is a noble goal, but if the criteria for it are inappropriate, the result will be misleading rather than informative.

This chapter reviews two biological approaches that can help lead us to correct psychological descriptions of memory. One of them involves neurology, and emphasizes the influence of brain mechanisms on memory. The other involves ethology and emphasizes the influence of the environment on memory. Both approaches have face validity as appropriate standards to help judge the organization of memory for two reasons. First, the logic of scientific investigation has often been applied more fruitfully in biology than in psychology; biological analyses have often proceeded more productively than psychological ones and are held up as "role models" for the type of enterprise that psychologists should pursue (Platt, 1964). Second, although biological analyses of learning and memory were begun only recently, they have already provided significant insights, suggesting that further consideration of the ways in which they can contribute to psychological analyses is appropriate.

Both sets of biological approaches make two contributions to the psychological analysis of memory: (1) They illustrate a general approach and suggest analytical strategies that may be adopted by psychological approaches. (2) They provide a set of converging operations (Garner, Hake, & Eriksen, 1956) that can be used to evaluate current psychological theories and suggest new ones. Both these points are addressed in turn. Special emphasis is placed on the application of these approaches to a type of memory in which the temporal context of the information to be remembered is an important component of that memory.

NEUROPSYCHOLOGICAL APPROACHES TO MEMORY

The activity of the brain influences and is influenced by behavior. Consequently, neural analyses of memory should provide some information relevant to psychological analyses of memory even if psychological descriptions cannot be reduced completely to neural ones.

Neuropsychological analyses combine neurological and psychological descriptions. If the independent variable is neurological, then the dependent variable is psychological; if the independent variable is psychological, then the dependent variable is neurological. "Neuropsychological" is an appropriate term to distinguish this type of analysis from the purely neurological (in which both the independent and dependent variables are neurological) and the purely psychological (in which both the independent and dependent variables are psychological).

This combination of levels can make important contributions to the examination of learning and memory. The first is general; it assumes that the same strategies used to examine the functional organization of neural systems can also be used to examine the functional organization of psychological systems. The second is more specific. It uses the results of neuropsychological experiments to test theories about the functional organization of psychological processes. Each of these is discussed in turn.

Characteristics of Neuropsychological Analyses

Neuropsychological analyses have differed from most psychological ones in three ways. They have (1) identified the neural structure being examined, (2) emphasized a systems analysis in which this structure is interrelated to others both in terms of its afferent (input) and efferent (output) connections, and (3) described the experimental strategies used for the functional analysis. All three of these characteristics are briefly summarized here; specific examples are offered later.

1. The brain structure being manipulated or measured in the experiment is identified. The size of the structure may be large, such as an entire cortical lobe or an entire neurochemical system, but some localization is always possible. In many cases it may be as discrete as a single nerve cell.

2. The brain structure being examined is considered as one component of a more extensive system. This emphasis on the system considers the afferents

(inputs) to and the efferents (outputs) from the structure to other structures in the system. This integrated perspective emphasizes the role of the component in the functioning of the entire system.

3. The activity of a brain structure can be manipulated directly in two ways (enhanced or suppressed) or measured. These three strategies are the only ones available to study structure—function relations, and the logic of their use has been well developed (Olton, in press-a). A neuropsychological experiment always identifies which one of these three approaches is being used to study the structure.

In contrast, psychological experiments rarely identify explicitly the component being studied, its organization into a wider system, or the experimental strategy used to examine its function. Some of these ommissions are due to the limited ways of accessing specific components in a psychological system. For example, consider a hypothetical system composed of the components A—B—C—D, each of which projects sequentially to the next in line. If these components are neural, direct access can be obtained to each of them for manipulation and measurement with the appropriate biomedical technology (electrodes, cannulae, dissections, etc.). If these components are psychological, however, such is not the case. Only A can be manipulated directly and only D can be measured directly. The situation can be helped if other inputs and outputs are present (Webster, 1973),but the general principle still holds. In a sequential system of neural components, all of them can be directly manipulated and measured, while in a sequential system of psychological components, only the first can be directly manipulated and only the last can be directly measured.

These differences between psychological and neuropsychological approaches to memory can be seen more clearly after the neuropsychological approach is described more thoroughly. The following section emphasizes the three experimental strategies because these are the crux of the neuropsychological approach. Examples are also given of explicit identification of the structure being investigated and its relationship to other structures in the system.

Strategies for Investigating the Functional Organization of the Components in a System

Three strategies have been used to examine the functional organization of a system. Two directly manipulate a component of the system. One (inhibition) decreases the function of the component being investigated, the other (enhancement) increases the function of that component. The third (recording) measures the activity of a component of the system while it functions. To my knowledge, these three strategies are the only ones that can be used to conduct a functional analysis of any system. The following sections discuss briefly the logic and rationale for each of them.

Inhibition (Lesions).   Inhibition decreases the activity of a component. Lesions of brain structures are often used to produce inhibition to decrease function. At the extreme, a lesion can completely eliminate the function. At intermediate points, a lesion may partially suppress that function so that a quantitative relationship (which is often not linear) can be established between the extent of the lesion and the inhibition of function. If a brain structure is involved in a function, inhibition of its activity ought to interfere with that function.

Dissociations are particularly important in the interpretation of the results of lesion experiments. Different types of dissociations provide information about the types of independence. Consider an experiment in which lesions are placed separately in each of two different structures (S1 and S2), and the effects of these lesions are examined on two different functions (F1 and F2). In a single dissociation, a lesion may impair one function without affecting the second. However, the opposite effect (an impairment of the second function without an impairment of the first function) is never found. Whenever a lesion impairs the second function, the first is also impaired. Thus, a lesion of S1 might impair F1 but not F2, while a lesion of S2 might impair both F1 and F2. This pattern of results indicates that F2 must have an input and an output that are independent of those of F1 (because F2 can proceed normally without F1), while F1 must have either an input or an output in common with F2 (because F1 cannot proceed normally without F2).

In a double dissociation, the lesion in each structure produces a different pattern of effects; the lesion in S1 produces an impairment of F1 but not F2, while the lesion in S2 produces the opposite pattern of results, an impairment in F2 but not F1. These results indicate that each function must have at least one input and one output that is independent of those of the other so that each can proceed effectively without the other.

Enhancement (Stimulation).   Enhancement of a component increases the effectiveness of its function if the component is not already functioning optimally and the enhancement is treated as normal activation of the component rather than disruptive intervention. Stimulation of brain structures is often used to produce enhancement and increase function. Like lesions, stimulation can vary in the extent to which it alters the activity of a structure. If a structure is involved in a function, enhancement of its activity ought to enhance that function.

Recording.   The activity of a component in the system is monitored during a function. If the component is involved in a function, then its activity ought to change in a predictable manner with the activity of the function. Dissociations similar to those found after lesions provide information about the organization of the structures into a functional system.

A Neuropsychological Application of These Strategies: Hippocampus and Memory. These three experimental strategies are the components of every functional analysis, whatever the system being studied. In neuropsychological investigations, the components in which the activity is inhibited, enhanced, or recorded are in the brain. For example, consider the application of these three strategies to the hypothesis that the hippocampus is selectively involved in some types of memory. Interference with the activity of the hippocampus through lesions or pharmacological manipulations impaired choice accuracy in tasks that required these types of memory. The pattern of behavioral impairments indicated that this behavioral syndrome was due to a true amnesia rather than to an impairment of other cognitive functions (Kesner, 1982; Mishkin, Spiegler, Saunders, & Malamut, 1982; Olton, Becker, & Handelmann, 1979). Enhancement of the activity of the hippocampus improved memory (Berger, 1984). Recording during tasks that required memory indicated that the activity of the hippocampus was affected by the types of memory required in the tasks (Deadwyler, West, & Christian, 1982; Wenk, Heplen, & Olton, 1984). Thus, all three strategies provide converging evidence that the hippocampus is involved in memory.

The hippocampus is connected neuroanatomically to a set of both cortical and subcortical structures. The three analytical strategies discussed here have been applied throughout this system to describe the functional organization of it (Mishkin, 1982; O'Keefe & Nadel, 1978; Olton, 1983). Consequently, the analysis of the role of the hippocampus in memory does not stand in isolation, but is integrated into a coordinated analysis of the structures that send afferents to it and receive efferents from it.

Psychological Applications of these Strategies. The three strategies used for functional analyses in neuropsychological experiments should also be applicable to psychological experiments. Some comparisons are readily apparent. Inhibition experiments may be used to interfere with the activity of a psychological process. For example, consider an experiment in which a person is given a list of items to be remembered and then asked to recall the items in that list. The probability of reporting an item at the end of the list is greater than the probability of reporting an item in the middle of the list, a phenomenon known as the "recency effect." The better memory for items at the end of the list has been attributed to the greater opportunity to rehearse these. To test this hypothesis, the experimental procedure was arranged so that rehearsal was prevented. At the end of the list, the person was given another task, one that prevented rehearsal of the last few items in the list. As predicted, the recency effect disappeared. Thus, inhibition of the psychological component thought to be responsible for the effect impaired the magnitude of the effect (Klatsky, 1980, pp. 14–20; Murdock, 1962; Postman & Phillips, 1965).

Procedures analogous to stimulation also have been used. The priming experiment is one in which exposure to a stimulus increases a certain type of memory processing that would otherwise be less activated (Tulving, 1983). Instructions emphasizing visual or semantic associations may also selectively influence memory processing (Kosslyn, 1983).

In the examples above, the logic is similar to that of the equivalent neuropsychological strategy, even though the experiments do not say so explicitly. If the memory process being manipulated (either inhibited or enhanced) is independent of other memory processes, then the manipulation ought to affect it but not the others (Platt, 1964).

Psychological equivalents of the recording strategy used in neuropsychological experiments are difficult to suggest. Indeed, I am not even certain of how to conceptualize the appropriate experimental design. In neuropsychological experiments, the distinction between the neural structure and the psychological function is clear; the neural structure can be easily identified, its activity can be measured directly by biological procedures and described in biological terms. Thus, experiments using the enhancement strategy (which manipulates the activity of the structure directly and records elsewhere) can be distinguished clearly from experiments using the recording strategy (which records directly the activity of the structure and stimulates elsewhere). Such is not the case in psychological experiments. Arguments for the analysis of "remembering" rather than "memory" may reflect this difficulty (see Craik, this volume).

In some psychological experiments, the other two characteristics of neuropsychological analyses are also apparent. A working computational model attempts to specify the psychological components and their interrelationships (Anderson & Bower, 1980; Gibbon, Church, & Meck, 1984; Kosslyn, 1983; Olton, 1978) in the same way that neuroanatomical analyses specify neural structures and their afferent and efferent connections.

Implications of Neuropsychological Analyses of Memory for Psychological Analyses of Memory

Neuropsychological analyses of memory can make two contributions to the psychological analyses of memory: (1) They illustrate a general approach that can be adopted by psychological analyses of memory. (2) They provide specific information about the ways in which some memory processes are organized. Each of these are discussed in turn.

General Principles for the Systematic Analysis of Memory

With only a few exceptions (Anderson & Bower, 1980; Gibbon, Church, & Meck, 1984; Kosslyn, 1983), the vast majority of psychological analyses of memory do not specify explicitly the three types of information (see p. 96–97) that are inherent in almost all neuropsychological analyses. Psychological experiments do describe the parametric aspects of the experiment, of course, but these are rarely related to a more comprehensive systematic analysis similar to that used for neuropsychological experiments.

The steady progress of biology, as compared to the more circular and tortuous course of psychology, may reflect in part biology's successful application of systematic functional analyses (Platt, 1964). Psychology has made progress defining the procedural variables that influence behavior. The extensive applications of psychological principles in behavioral medicine, sports, and business are more than ample proof of these contributions. But, describing the mechanisms and the representations of the processes that are involved is still very difficult. One can ignore these problems and take a strictly empirical, behavioral approach, but this endeavor leaves unspecified everything in the "black box" between the stimulus and the response. Certainly, one level of understanding of a system is a descriptive one, indicating the output that results from a given input. But, a given input can be transformed into a given output in many different ways, a fact well known to every computer programmer who has tried to debug someone else's program. Consequently, a more complete level of understanding describes the mechanisms responsible for producing the output from the input.

Neuropsychological analyses explicitly seek to specify all the mechanisms intervening between the neural equivalent of a stimulus (the receptor) and a response (the effector). If this mechanistic analysis is indeed more complete than the simpler black box one, then psychological analyses should profit by attempting to incorporate into their design the general characteristics of neuropsychological experiments. Each experiment would identify explicitly the psychological component being manipulated or measured, the interconnections of this component with each of the others in the system, and the strategy used for this manipulation (inhibition or enhancement) or measurement (recording). In essence, one wants a complete, working, computational model that identifies each of the relevant components and their organization. This goal may not be obtainable immediately, but it should not be ignored. If researchers keep these characteristics in mind and attempt to incorporate them into experimental designs whenever possible, psychological analyses may proceed more effectively than they have in the past.

A failure to attain an adequately precise description may have significant consequences. If neuropsychological analyses of memory can provide a more detailed statement of the processes involved in memory than purely psychological ones, the neuropsychological approach may displace the psychological one. Considerable debate has taken place about the reduction of the psychological level of analysis to the neural level of analysis (see reviews in Churchland, 1985; Olton, in press-b). Such a reduction requires equally detailed theories at both levels. When one theory provides not only a different explanation, but a more complete or more accurate one, it often displaces the other theory, which is subsequently ignored. Unless psychological analyses of memory can become sufficiently sophisticated, neuropsychological analyses may displace them and render them relatively unimportant.

A Neuropsychological Analysis of the Memory for Temporal Context

Some of the information in memory can be useful without reference to the context in which it was learned (learning context) or the context in which it is to be applied (application context). Much of our information about the general characteristics of the world in which we live can be used without reference to either of these contexts.

In contrast, some types of information in memory must be associated with one or both of these contexts in order to guide behavior appropriately. "Episodic memory" (Tulving, 1983), "working memory" (Honig, 1978; Olton, 1978), and "dispositional memory" (Thomas & Spafford, 1984) have all been used to refer to the memory system that requires information about the temporal context of the item to be remembered. I use a more empirical term, "trial dependent memory," to describe this memory in the rest of the Chapter.

For example, remembering the fact that cars are left in parking lots rather than vegetable gardens is information that is useful without specific reference to when it was learned or when it is used. In contrast, remembering where you parked your car in the morning (learning context) when you wish to go home at night (application context) is useful only if this memory includes the appropriate contexts (assuming the car is parked in a different place each day). Remembering where the car was parked this morning will not help you find it tomorrow (a different application context), and remembering where the car was parked yesterday morning will not help you find it today (a different learning context).

Theoretical analyses suggest that trial-dependent memory and trial-independent memory may be separate systems (Honig, 1978; Olton, 1978; Thomas & Spafford, 1984; Tulving, 1983). Neuropsychological analyses have provided a great deal of support for this conclusion, and have begun to describe the mechanisms that might be involved in this memory. The neuroanatomical systems that have received the most intensive analysis are those involving the temporal lobe and frontal lobe.

Lesion analyses show consistent single dissociations following damage to the structures in the hippocampal system. Choice accuracy in tasks involving trial dependent memory is impaired, especially as the importance of the memory in these tasks increases (Jarrard, 1975). In contrast, choice accuracy in tasks involving trial independent memory often proceeds normally. The results demonstrate that trial-dependent memory is built onto the trial-independent memory; its input or output must go through those of trial-independent memory. In contrast, the trial-independent memory must have functional inputs and outputs to the rest of the system independently of those of the trial-dependent memory system; trial-independent memory proceeds normally even while trial-dependent memory is markedly impaired (Olton, 1983).

Unit recording analyses also support these conclusions. For example, the activity of single units in the inferotemporal cortex, an area that has projections to the hippocampus, was correlated with performance in a delayed conditional discrimination (DCD). Monkeys were given a visual stimulus to remember at the beginning of a trial. This sample stimulus had both a color and a symbol on it. If the sample had the symbol "=" on it, the correct response at the end of the trial depended on the color of the sample. If the sample had the symbol "O" or "X", the correct response at the end of the trial depended on the symbol of the sample. Some of the units responded to the color of the sample stimulus only if it was relevant for correct performance at the end of the trial. Other units responded primarily during the delay interval between removal of the sample stimulus at the beginning of the trial and presentation of the comparison stimuli at the end of the trial. Thus, unit activity reflected different requirements of the task, and a sequential analysis of the different types of response patterns provided information about how the brain handles the different components of this task (Fuster & Jervey, 1981).

Similar results were obtained from units in the hippocampus of rats as they solved a DCD with black or white sample stimuli. Many of the units had activity preferentially associated with these stimuli. Others responded to particular combinations of the color of the stimuli, their position in the testing apparatus, and their significance in the task (a sample stimulus to be remembered at the beginning of the trial or a comparison stimulus for a response at the end of the trial). These data show that unit activity in the hippocampus can indicate the ways in which this structure responds to the different aspects of a DCD. The systematic application of this approach to adjacent neural structures should indicate the ways in which the cellular components of this neural system respond to the different demands of this memory task (Findling, Shapiro, & Olton, 1983).

ETHOPSYCHOLOGICAL APPROACHES TO MEMORY

The environment also has face validity as an important factor related to memory. Consistent environmental contingencies provide evolutionary pressure for certain types of learning and memory. Consequently, analyses of an animal's behavior in its natural habitat can help suggest ways in which learning and memory can be classified. Indeed, these types of analyses are necessary to be certain that the arbitrary experimental tasks that we give to animals in the laboratory have some validity as procedures to assess meaningful aspects of memory. "Ethopsychological" is an appropriate term to distinguish this type of analysis from purely ethological ones (which consider only environmental factors) and purely psychological ones (which consider only psychological factors).

Characteristics of Ethopsychological Approaches to Memory

Ethopsychological analyses combine an ethological and psychological approach to the study of memory. The characteristics of the animal's natural environment are analyzed to determine the ways in which they might influence the characteristics of the animal's memory. For example, many animals face a situation in which they should go to a place, retrieve some food, and then use this experience to guide their subsequent choice behavior. In some cases, the optimal strategy is to remain in the same area or return to it because having found food during the initial visit increases the likelihood that food will be obtained on a subsequent visit. In other cases, the optimal strategy is to leave the area and go elsewhere for the immediately subsequent visits because the likelihood that food will be obtained on an immediate visit after having found food during the initial visit is small (Goss-Custard, 1981; Kamil, 1978; Kamil & Balda, in press; Kamil & Yoerg, in press; Kamil, Peters, & Lindstrom, 1982; Kamil & Sargent, 1981; Olton, 1985; Whitham, 1977).

This type of environment puts selective pressure on the development of a specialized memory system to perform appropriately. The logic of this argument is as follows. Food is not distributed randomly in time and space, but in patches; it is more likely to be in some locations at some times than in other locations and at other times. Efficient foraging in this environment reduces costs (expenditure of energy, loss of time for other activities, exposure to predators, etc.) and increases benefits (calories, time available for other activities, etc.). Consequently, animals that forage efficiently should have an adaptive advantage over those who forage inefficiently. Some "patchy" environments have been stable for many generations. To the extent that efficient foraging has a genetic basis, the more numerous offspring of the efficient forager should result in a predilection for the species to develop appropriate strategies to search for food (See reviews in Kamil et al., 1982; Kamil & Sargent, 1981; Krebs & Davies, 1978).

Selective pressure for a certain characteristic does not ensure that it will actually appear. The number of extinct species is silent testimony to the ability of the environment to produce demands that are significantly beyond the capability of the species. However, the behaviors of animals in both natural habitats and in laboratory discriminations suggests that they have responded to these pressures with the development of appropriate behaviors and cognitive systems. Consequently, a second means of developing strategies for the classification and analysis of memory is to examine the types of discrimination problems faced by animals in their natural habitats.

Examples of Ethopsychological Analyses

An example of this type of approach may be found in a comparative analysis of the tendency to *stay* or *shift* after finding food (Cole, Hainsworth, Kamil, Mercier, & Wolf, 1982). Two variations of a delayed conditional discrimination (DCD) were presented to hummingbirds (*Archilochus alexandri*). In both of them, a stimulus was presented at the start of the trial and then removed. At the end of the delay interval, the bird was given a choice between responding to this stimulus or responding to a different one. In the *stay* discrimination, a response to the stimulus originally presented as the sample was reinforced. In the *shift* discrimination, a response to the other stimulus was reinforced. Thus, these two discriminations were identical in all respects except the response-reinforcement contingencies.

Hummingbirds normally obtain nectar from flowers. The bird usually depletes the nectar during a visit. Consequently, the optimal strategy following a visit is to shift and go elsewhere to search for nectar until sufficient time has passed for the flower to replenish its nectar supply. This consistent environmental pressure for shifting after a visit should produce a species-specific search strategy, a predilection to shift after obtaining food at a given location.

This hypothesis was supported by laboratory experiments comparing the rates of acquisition in the two discriminations described above. The birds reached criterion performance more rapidly in the shift discrimination than in the stay discrimination because they (a) had a preference to shift even at the start of the experiment and (b) had an increased rate of learning in the shift discrimination (Cole et al., 1982).

Differences in the reactions of two species of birds when obtaining hoarded seeds may also illustrate the effects of environmental pressures on memory. Both species were given a group of seeds to hoard and retrieve in a naturalistic environment. The Clark's nutcrackers (*Nucifraga columbiana*) had cups filled with sand placed on the floor of their aviary (Kamil & Balda, in press). The marsh tits (*Parus palustris*) had holes drilled into branches of artificial ''trees'' placed throughout their aviary (Shettleworth & Krebs, 1982).

At the beginning of each trial, a container of seeds was placed in the aviary. A bird was released into the aviary to take seeds from the container and hide them in the available hoarding sites (cups of sand or holes in the trees). The bird was then removed from the aviary for a delay interval. The container of food was removed. At the end of the delay, the bird was allowed back into the aviary to search for food among the hoarding sites.

Both species of birds accurately restricted their visits to sites in which they had hoarded seeds and avoided other sites in which they had not placed seeds. However, the marsh tits rarely went back to a site after they had removed the food from it. In contrast, the Clark's nutcrackers often returned to previously visited sites (in which no food remained). Thus, both species made few errors by going to sites in which they had not hoarded seeds. However, the Clark's nutcrackers made many errors by returning to sites from which they had removed the seeds, while the marsh tits made very few of these types of errors.

This striking dissociation of choice accuracy in the two species may be related to the way in which they hoard seeds in their natural habitat. A marsh tit usually places only one seed in each site, while a Clark's nutcracker may often place many seeds in a single site (Balda & Turek, 1984). Thus, a return visit to a cache from which a seed has been removed will rarely be reinforced for a marsh tit, but may often be reinforced for a Clark's nutcracker. A definitive test of this hypothesis awaits a more controlled test procedure, but the presently available results suggest that the behavior of these birds may provide another example of the way in which response-reinforcement contingencies in the environment may produce strong cognitive predispositions that influence how animals approach many different types of problems.

TRIAL-SPECIFIC MEMORY AND EPISODIC MEMORY

Both neuropsychological and ethopsychological approaches suggest that trial-dependent memory processes in animals may be independent of other types of memory. This type of memory in animals may be similar to episodic memory in humans (Tulving, 1983). However, conceptual and practical differences complicate this analysis. One of the questions is the extent to which animals use episodic memory (Tulving, 1984). An answer to that question requires an analysis of the ways in which experimental procedures testing animal memory with context-specific information differ from the ones used to test episodic memory in humans. Such a comparative analysis with animals requires that the experimental designs and verbal material used with people be translated into a more general procedure that can be used with animals and nonverbal material. As Tulving (1983, p. 146) has commented, "Words to the memory researcher are what fruit flies are to the geneticist: a convenient medium through which the phenomena and processes of interest can be explored and elucidated." If such a statement is true, then the characteristics of the words themselves are unimportant, the general principles used to conduct the experiment are of most concern, and translating the verbal material used with humans into nonverbal material that has the necessary characteristics for use with animals should not be difficult.

One of the ways of developing a rapprochement between studies of animal memory and studies of human memory is to work with situations that have face validity for both species. This similarity provides the opportunity to apply equivalent conceptual developments to the study of different species. Of particular importance is knowing that the application of the procedure to the different species is appropriate. One of the dangers of a comparative approach that applies the same general procedure to many different animals is that the information obtained may reflect more about the procedure than it does about the animal. This danger is especially relevant when different animals perform in the same way. Consequently, the procedure must be justified for each species, and checked carefully to be certain that the information obtained from the test procedure is indeed reflecting characteristics of the animal being tested and its cognitive processes.

To a large extent, the procedures used for testing animals and humans have been different (see the section that follows). Consequently, the development of relatively independent conceptual frameworks should not be surprising. The question of interest has to do with the reason for these different frameworks. On the one hand, it might reflect different cognitive processes in animals and humans. Alternatively, it might reflect the characteristics of the procedures being used. If so, adaptation of the procedures that are used for animals to humans (and vice versa) might lead to similar conceptual frameworks.

A specific example of convergence between animal and human research is the delayed conditional discrimination (DCD), particularly as applied to the learning of lists of items. The initial studies of memory by Ebbinghaus relied heavily on the analysis of the types of errors that occurred when remembering lists of words and other items. When animals are given more than one item to remember in a DCD, that situation provides the same type of task for analysis as the list learning did for Ebbinghaus (D'Amato, 1973; Mishkin, 1982; Olton, 1978; Roberts & Smythe, 1979; Roitblat, 1982).

Most experiments studying memory in people use words or other verbal information as the stimuli to be remembered (but see Sidman, Stoddard, & Mohr, 1968, for an exception). To the extent that the phenomena being studied in people require a verbal analysis, their application to results from experiments with animals must be limited. An analysis of the tasks in such a way that the general characteristics of them can be emphasized, rather than their specific procedures, can help design tests for animals that are equivalent to those for people. A major contribution to those who study animals would be the conduct of experiments with humans using nonverbal stimuli and procedures similar to those used for animals (see chapter by Dickinson).

Animal experiments must explicitly define the response alternatives at the time of testing. The experiments examine the ability of the animal to choose from among the items presented by the experimenter rather than the ability to generate these items (with the possible exception of sign language). This procedure does have one advantage over free recall; the experimenter is able to provide better control over the experimental situation and determine accurately the chance level of performance. However, it does severely limit the ability to investigate how animals generate the information to be remembered (as distinguished from choosing among the available information to find the correct response).

One of the general problems here has to do with the comparative analysis. The comparison of performance of different kinds of animals is a classic one in psychology. It cannot be solved simply by giving different species the same kind of task. The object is to assess the same processes in both animals and humans. The emphasis on representation (Roitblat, 1982) facilitates this integration of the animal work with that from humans because the results of experiments can be described in a similar frame of reference. Even so, similar ends can be attained by markedly different means; similar performance on a memory task does not necessarily guarantee the use of a similar representational process.

Recognition and Recall

"Recognition" and "recall" have been used to describe two different experimental procedures assessing memory. These procedures have been distinguished in terms of the type of information present at retrieval and the type of response required. In recognition, the information during retrieval includes a real copy of the item that was to be remembered and the person simply indicates whether this item is familiar or not. In recall, these explicit cues from the original stimulus are not present (although other cues for recall obviously are), and the person is asked to reproduce the item to be remembered.

As indicated by Tulving (1983, p. 303), given two types of retrieval cues and two types of responses, four tasks are possible. These are outlined in Table 5.1.

As can be seen in the Table, recognition and recall occupy the diagonal positions, indicating the intersection of two different variables. In experiments with animals, the most common procedure is that in the top right hand corner. The cues present at the time of retrieval are identical to those when the item to be remembered was first presented, and the animal reproduces the response originally made to them.

An interesting alternative to this procedure would be to try to create for an animal a task which has the equivalent of a yes–no response to indicate familiarity. Thus, the animal would make one response if the stimulus had occurred before, and would make another if it had not. The same two responses would be used for all stimuli. This procedural change would probably make the task more difficult. The question is whether or not this change would elicit a fundamentally different cognitive process. Certainly, another conversion is required. The animal must not only retrieve the correct stimulus from memory, but also determine the response that should be made to it.

Symbolic matching (see Roitblat, 1984) is a variation not represented in Table 5.1. The cues at retrieval are not identical to those at the beginning of the trial. Nonetheless, they are functionally the same in that they have been associated with the stimuli at the beginning of the trial. A paired associate task is added to the other requirements.

Even though the experimental procedures for testing recall and recognition may differ, the retrieval processes in each may be basically the same. Potential

TABLE 5.1
Procedures for Recognition and Recall

		Response	
		Familiarity	Identification
Cues Present at Retrieval	Copy	Recognition	
	Noncopy		Recall

stimuli must be reviewed, and a decision about each stimulus must determine whether or not it is correct.

The experimental procedures typically labeled as recognition and recall do not represent mutually exclusive alternatives. Rather, they are both made up of many different processes. The combination of these varies in the procedures of recognition and recall. However, many other types of combinations of the relevant variables are possible. Consequently, the procedural distinction between recognition and recall is an arbitrary one based on the combination of the variables involved. The two procedures may not be fundamentally distinct in terms of their processes. Procedural differences do not necessarily imply fundamentally distinct psychological processes. Furthermore, many different factors influence the way in which information is retrieved. Thus, the procedural dichotomy of recognition and recall may have blinded us to more important factors by emphasizing two arbitrary combinations of variables that are used in testing procedures, rather than focusing on the different psychological processes that must be involved.

In retrieval, the experimenter may ask for an item from a list that the individual is supposed to remember, or just ask for whatever item pops into the individual's head (Graf, Squire, & Mandler, 1984). Asking for an item from a list emphasizes the previous episode and directs the individual to a possible set of cues. Experiments with animals typically use this type of procedure. Asking for familiarity simply requests free association without reference to any particular preceding event. This latter type of retrieval may be very hard to arrange for animals.

In summary, the procedures used to measure trial-specific memory in animals and episodic memory in humans differ. One step towards the rapprochement of analyses of memory in animals and humans is the development of tasks that use procedures eliciting the same balance of memory processes in the retrieval of the information to be remembered. An analysis of the experiments from a theoretical rather than procedural viewpoint suggests that equivalent representational processes in both animals and humans can be elicited by the appropriate experimental procedures (Dickinson, this volume; Olton, 1985; Roitblat, 1982).

WHY EXAMINE MEMORY IN NONHUMAN ANIMALS?

In our own anthropocentric way, we have little difficulty justifying the investigation of behavior and psychological processes in humans. But questions about human behavior and cognition can often be addressed most effectively by experiments with animals. Thus, the information obtained from comparative analyses can help explain behavior and cognitive processes not only in the animal being studied, but also in people. This section reviews three examples of this type of comparative approach.

Neuropsychology

Although this book focuses mainly on the psychological analysis of learning and memory in humans and animals, neuropsychological approaches can assist in the analysis of normal learning and memory, as outlined earlier in this chapter. Neuropsychological analyses with people are severely limited by primary concern for the immediate therapeutic treatment of the individual being studied rather than the acquisition of basic knowledge to help understand the organization of cognitive processes. As in any scientific endeavor, the accuracy of the conclusions is limited by the accuracy of both the independent and dependent variables. Experiments with animals are critical for the controlled neurological manipulations and measurements necessary for precise analysis of cognitive function.

Using the results of neuropsychological analyses to draw conclusions about the characteristics of normal learning and memory requires careful logic in the best of cases. To generalize from animals to humans is even more difficult, and requires close attention to the psychological demands of the task given to the animals. With these qualifications, however, experiments with animals provide us the opportunity to gain better control of neurological variables, which in turn can provide us better information about the organization of the cognitive processes involved in learning and memory.

Environmental Influences on Cognitive Processes

Animals often exhibit very sophisticated adaptations to the environment in which they live. Specialized coloring, morphology, and physiology are common, as are specific sensory and motor abilities. All these examples reflect an ability of the animal to adapt to the demands of its environment.

Selective pressure for certain types of learning and memory may also be exerted by the environment (see p. 104). Ethological analyses of foraging behavior in the natural environment show that certain types of search strategies are more effective than others. Resources are not distributed equally throughout the environment, temporally or spatially. Thus, a predator can obtain a selective advantage by being in the right place at the right time. If the environmental pressures are consistent for many generations, then a species has the opportunity to develop a predisposition to follow a search strategy that is appropriate for the environment.

Determining whether or not environmental pressures actually do produce species with specialized cognitive processes is very difficult with people. All aspects of the comparative process are complicated by the rapidly changing environments in which people live and the many different ways in which groups of people differ from each other.

In contrast, the spatial and temporal distributions of resources in some environments have remained consistent for many generations. Furthermore, the many different varieties of animals offers an opportunity to control for the effects of variables other than the one currently being studied (Kamil & Yoerg, in press; Kamil, Peters, & Lindstrom, 1982).

The analyses describing the behavior of the different species of birds when foraging for food indicates how this type of analysis can be carried out (see p. 105). The results of these experiments show that environmental characteristics have a strong influence on the characteristics of memory exhibited by the animals who live there. This type of analysis can provide us information about the ways in which environments influence memory, and also supports the use of ethopsychological analyses as a means of classifying memory.

CONCLUSION

Working computational models that specify the psychological components of the system being studied and their interrelationships are necessary if we are to understand memory and classify it appropriately. Although psychological analyses of memory have provided us much information about the variables that affect behavior, they have not consistently attempted to go beyond this relatively simple statement of parametric manipulations and effects to specify such a model. Neuropsychological analyses have not *solved* the problem of memory either, but their approach naturally incorporates many of the steps necessary to produce a functional model. Consequently, neuropsychological approaches provide an example of the ways in which psychological approaches might proceed, and produce specific suggestions about the organization of the psychological components involved in memory.

Ethopsychological analyses of memory are also helpful. They can determine the extent to which our laboratory procedures reflect problems naturally encountered by animals, and can suggest new types of tasks to assess ethologically relevant memory processes. Although they do not necessarily emphasize the components of the system as neuropsychological analyses do, they can provide an effective standard for assessing the validity of psychological analyses.

REFERENCES

Anderson, J. R., & Bower, G. H. (1980). *Human associative memory: A brief edition.* Hillsdale, NJ: Lawrence Erlbaum Associates.

Balda, R. P., & Turek, R. J. (1984). The cache-recovery system as an example of memory capabilities in Clark's nutcracker. In H. L. Roitblat, T. G. Bever, & H. S. Terrace, *Animal cognition* (pp. 513–532). Hillsdale, NJ: Lawrence Erlbaum Associates.

Berger, T. (1984). Long-term potentiation of hippocampal synaptic transmission affects rate of behavioral learning. *Science, 224,* 627–629.

Churchland, P. S. (1985). ,*Neurophilosophy: Towards a unified understanding of the mind-brain.* Cambridge, MA: MIT Press.

Cole, S., Hainsworth, F. R., Kamil, A. C., Mercier, T., & Wolf, L. L. (1982). Spatial learning as an adaptation in hummingbirds. *Science, 217,* 655–657.

D'Amato, M. R. (1973). Delayed matching and short-term memory in monkeys. In G. H. Bower (Ed.), *The psychology in learning and motivation: Advances in research and theory* (Vol. VII). New York: Academic Press.

Deadwyler, S. A., West, M. O., & Christian, E. P. (1982). Neural activity in the dentate gyrus of the rat during the acquisition and performance of simple and complex sensory discrimination learning. In C. D. Woody (Ed.), *Conditioning: Representation of involved neural functions* (pp. 63–73). New York: Plenum Press.

Findling, R. L., Shapiro, M., & Olton, D. S. (1983). Single unit activity in the hippocampus of rats: Behavioral correlates in a nonspatial delay match-to-sample task. *Society for Neuroscience Abstracts, 9*(1), 646.

Fuster, J. M., & Jervey, J. P. (1981). Inferotemporal neurons distinghish and retain behaviorally relevant features of visual stimuli. *Science, 212,* 952–954.

Garner, W. R., Hake, H. W., & Eriksen, C. W. (1956). Operationism and the concept of perception. *The Psychological Review, 63*(3), 149–159.

Gibbon, J., Church, R. M., & Meck, W. H. (1984). Scalar timing in memory. In J. Gibbon & L. G. Allan (Eds.), *Annals of The New York Academy of Sciences.* New York: New York Academy of Sciences.

Goss-Custard, J. D. (1981). Feeding behavior of Redshank, *Tringa totanus,* and optimal foraging theory. In A. C. Kamil & T. D. Sargent (Eds.), *Foraging behavior: Ecological, ethological, and psychological approaches.* New York: Garland Press.

Graf, P., Squire, L. R., & Mandler, G. (1984). The information that amnesic patients do not forget. *Journal of Experimental Psychology: Learning, Memory, and Cognition, 10*(1), 164–178.

Honig, W. K. (1978). Studies of working memory in the pigeon. In S. H. Hulse, H. Fowler, & W. K. Honig (Eds.), *Congitive processes in animal behavior.* Hillsdale, NJ: Lawrence Erlbaum Associates.

Jerrard, L. E. (1975). Role of interferendce in retention by rats with hippocampal lesions. *Journal of Comparative and Physiological Psychology, 89,* 400–408.

Kamil, A. C. (1978). Systematic foraging by a nectar-feeding bird, the Amakihi (*Loxops virens*). *Journal of Comparative and Physiological Psychology, 92,* 388–396.

Kamil, A. C., & Balda, R. P. (in press). Cache recovery and spatial memory in Clark's nutcrackers (*Nucifraga columbiana*). *Journal of Experimental Psychology: Applied Behavioral Psychology.*

Kamil, A. C., & Yoerg, S. I. (in press). Learning and foraging behavior. In P. P. G. Bateson & P. Klopfer (Eds.), *Perspectives on ethology* (Vol. 5). New York: Plenum Press.

Kamil, A. C., Peters, J., & Lindstrom, F. J. (1982). An ecological perspective on the study of allocation of behavior. In M. L. Commons, R. J. Herrnstein & H. Rachlin (Eds.), *Quantiative analyses of behavior* (pp. 189–203). Cambridge, MA: Ballinger Publishing Company.

Kamil, A. C., & Sargent, T. D. (Eds.). (1981). *Foraging behavior: Ecological, ethological, and psychological approaches.* New York: Garland Press.

Kesner, R. P. (1982). Mnemonic function of the hippocampus: Correspondence between animals and humans. In C. D. Woody (Ed.), *Conditioning: Representation of involved neural functions* (pp. 75–88). New York: Plenum Press.

Klatzky, R. L. (1980). *Human memory: Structures and processes.* San Francisco, CA: W. H. Freeman and Company.

Kosslyn, S. M. (1983). *Ghosts in the mind's machine.* New York: W. W. Norton & Company.

Krebs, J. R., & Davies, N. B. (1978). *Behavioural ecology.* Oxford: Blackwell Scientific Publications.

Mishkin, M. (1982). A memory system in the monkey. *Philosophical Transcripts of the Royal Society of London, 298B,* 85–95.

Mishkin, M., Spiegler, B. J., Saunders, R. C., & Malamut, B. L. (1982). An animal model of global amnesia. In S. Corkin et al. (Eds.), *Aging: Alzheimer's disease: A report of progress* (Vol. 19, pp. 253–247). New York: Raven Press.

Murdock, B. B., Jr. (1962). The serial position effect of free recall. *Journal of Experimental Psychology, 64*, 482–488.

O'Keefe, J., & Nadel, L. (1978). *The hippocampus as a cognitive map.* Oxford: Oxford University Press.

Olton, D. S. (1978). Characteristcs of spatial memory. In S. H. Hulse, H. F. Fowler, & W. K. Honig (Eds.), *Cognitive aspects of animal behavior* (pp. 342–373). Hillsdale, NJ: Lawrence Erlbaum Associates.

Olton, D. S. (1983). Memory functions and the hippocampus. In W. Seifert (Ed.), *Neurobiology of the hippocampus* (pp. 335–373). New York: Academic Press.

Olton, D. S. (in press-a). Interventional approaches to memory: Lesions. In J. L. Martinez & R. P. Kesner (Eds.), *Learning and memory: A biological view.* New York: Academic Press.

Olton, D. S. (in press-b). Expansionism: Its contribution to the mind-brain solution. In M. Gazzaniga & H. Killackey (Eds.), *Neuropsychological approaches to the study of memory.* Cambridge, MA: MIT Press.

Olton, D. S. (1985). The temporal context of spatial memory. *Annals of the Royal Society of London. B 308*, 79–86.

Olton, D. S., Becker, J. T., & Handelmann, G. E. (1979). Hippocampus, space, and memory. *The Behavioral and Brain Sciences, 2*, 313–322.

Platt, J. R. (1964). Strong inference. *Science, 146*, 347–353.

Postman, L., & Phillips, L.(1965). Short-term temporal changes in free recall. *Quarterly Journal of Experimental Psychology, 17*, 132–138.

Roberts, W. A., & Smythe, W. E. (1979). Memory for lists of spatial events in the rat. *Learning and Motivation, 10*, 313–336.

Roitblat, H. L. (1982). The meaning of representation in animal memory. *The Behavioral and Brain Sciences, 5*, 353–372.

Roitblat, H. L. (1984). Representations in pigeon working memory. In H. L. Roitblat, T. G. Bever, & H. S. Terrace (Eds.), *Animal cognition* (pp. 79–97). Hillsdale, NJ: Lawrence Erlbaum Associates.

Shettleworth, S. J., & Krebs, J. R. (1982). How marsh tits find their hoards: The roles of site preference and spatial memory. *Journal of Experimental Psychology: Animal Behavior Processes, 8*(4), 354–375.

Sidman, M., Stoddard, L. T., & Mohr, J. P. (1968). Some additional observations of immediate memory in a patient with bilateral hippocampal lesions. *Neuropsychologia, 6*, 245–254.

Thomas, G. J., & Spafford, P. S. (1984). Deficits for representational memory induced by septal and cortical lesions (singly and combined) in rats. *Behavioral Neuroscience, 98*(3), 394–403.

Tulving, E. (1983). *Elements of episodic memory.* New York: Oxford University Press.

Tulving, E. (1984). Precis of *Elements of episodic memory. The Behavioral and Brain Sciences, 7*, 223–268.

Webster, W. G. (1973). Assumptions, conceptualizations, and the search for the functions of the brain. *Physiological Psychology, 1*, 346–350.

Wenk, G. L., Heplen, D., & Olton, D. S. (1984). Behavior alters the uptake of (3H)-choline into acetylcholinergic neurons of the nucleus basalis magnocellularis. *Behavioral Brain Research, 13*, 129–138.

Whitham, T. G. (1977). Coevolution of foraging in Bombus and nectar dispensing in Chilopsis: A last dreg theory. *Science, 197*, 593–596.

IV SHORT-TERM MEMORY AND ATTENTION

Lars-Göran Nilsson
Trevor Archer

A core concept in theories and models inspired by the information processing approach is the concept of short-term memory. In this particular realm the concept has been around at least since Broadbent's book *Perception and Communication* was published in 1958 and since John Brown and Lloyd and Margaret Peterson at the same time and independently of each other invented a technique to study short-term memory experimentally (Brown, 1958; Peterson & Peterson, 1959). As is well known this method, subsequently referred to as the Brown-Peterson paradigm, has later been used extensively to study various aspects of short-term memory.

Throughout the 1960s and 1970s short-term memory was a major target of investigation in human memory research. While studies of memory functions using the same short-term memory paradigms have continued also during the last 10 years or so, the theoretical tools have successively reached a higher level of sophistication and maturity. As stated by Hitch in his chapter the concept of a unitary short-term memory appears untenable and should be replaced by a more complex notion proposing a working memory which consists of separate but interacting subsystems. Such an approach, according to Hitch, fosters the possibility of making interesting and potentially fruitful comparisons between human and animal memory. The comparisons made by

115

Hitch are focused on rehearsal and recency effects, and indeed the comparisons made promise a great deal for the future with respect to an integration between the fields of animal learning and human memory.

With respect to short-term memory the research on humans during the last 25 years has witnessed an impressive degree of inventiveness. Many experimental paradigms have been worked out and tested and at least at one time there was a strong tendency to emphasize method and data rather than theory. Little was said about what the empirical phenomena really could mean in a sense of understanding learning and memory in broader terms. As noted several times elsewhere, at one time there was almost a one-to-one relationship between phenomena and models.

At the end of the 1960s and early 1970s when the information-processing approach (developed within the human memory domain) was adopted to the animal learning field as well, there was a clear tendency to repeat the explicit focus on method and data and to pay less attention on broad theoretical outlooks. To judge from Bolles' chapter this distribution of attention still holds and Bolles expresses his sincere unhappiness with the fact that animal learning researchers to a far too strong degree are methodologists rather than theorists.

Attention is a concept closely related to the concept of short-term memory. This is the way it has been in human memory research and apparently this is also the general line of development which has occurred in animal learning. It is interesting to note that the concept of attention per se has been developed and adjusted to fit the general requirements of animal learning research. As Mackintosh (1974) has stated "The implication is that the strength of attention to a particular stimulus may change with the subject's experience of the validity or redundancy of that stimulus—although there is no necessary implication that changes in attention to one component of a compound are accompanied by equal and opposite changes in attention to all other components" (p. 589). Thus, the concept of attention has been used freely to explain various conditioning effects in neuropharmacological and neurophysiological research (Aston-Jones & Bloom, 1981; Mason & Iverson, 1978; Mair & McEntee, 1983; Robbins, 1984; Robbins, Everitt, Fray, Gaskin, Carli & de la Riva, 1982).

REFERENCES

Aston-Jones, G., & Bloom, F. (1981). Norepinephrine-containing locus coeruleus neurons in behaving rats exhibit pronounced responses to non-noxious environmental stimuli. *Journal of Neuroscience, 1,* 887–900.

Broadbent, D. E. (1958). *Perception and communication.* London: Pergamon Press.

Brown, J. A. (1958). Some tests of the decay theory of immediate memory. *Quarterly Journal of Experimental Psychology, 10,* 12–21.

Mason, S. T., & Iverson, S. D. (1979). Theories of the dorsal bundle extinction effect. *Brain Research Reviews, 1,* 107–137.

Mair, R. G., & McEntee, W. J. (1983). Korsakoff's psychosis: Noradrenergic systems and cognitive impairment. *Behavioral Brain Research, 9,* 1–32.

Mackintosh, N. J. (1974) . *The psychology of animal learning.* London: Academic Press.

Peterson, L. R., & Peterson, M. J. (1959). Short-term retention of individual verbal items. *Journal of Experimental Psychology, 58,* 193–198.

Robbins, T. W. (1984). Cortical noradrenaline, attention and arousal. *Psychological Medicine, 13.*

Robbins, T. W., Everitt, B. J., Fray, P. J., Gaskin, M., Carli, M., & de la Riva, C. (1982). The roles of the central catecholamines in attention and learning. In M. Spiegelstein & A. Levy (Eds.), *Behavioral models and the analysis of drug action.* Amsterdam: Elsevier.

Short-term Memory and Information Processing in Humans and Animals: Towards an Integrative Framework

6

Graham J. Hitch
University of Manchester

INTRODUCTION

It does not seem unreasonable to expect research on memory in animals to assist in our understanding of human memory and for work on humans to illuminate that on animals. Yet the two fields of inquiry appear to progress relatively independently of one another, even though many of the basic phenomena are the same. There is disappointingly little evidence for a fertile, two-way exchange of ideas and information, and indeed, conferences such as the one surrounding this volume are all too infrequent. It has been suggested that part of the problem arises from the use of quite different experimental paradigms and techniques with humans and animals. For example, there is a tendency for research on humans to be dominated by the use of verbal materials which, of course, cannot be used with animals. Perhaps more seriously, it has been noted that there is no agreed theoretical framework for generating hypotheses and relating data across species, despite an increasingly common tendency for researchers in both fields to adopt an information processing approach. The chapters by Lars-Göran Nilsson & Trevor Archer, Bob Crowder, and Endel Tulving cover these and other general issues in some depth.

The present chapter focuses on the topic of short-term memory, the retention of information over intervals of at most a few minutes or so. Human short-term memory has been quite extensively studied over the last two decades and consequently a good deal is known about some of the basic phenomena. Much less is known about short-term memory in animals, but the topic is currently attracting considerable interest and research effort. It is intended to show here that short-term memory provides a useful illustration of both some problems of linking

119

research on human and animal memory and the considerable mutual benefits that would undoubtedly spring from the establishment of such links.

The chapter is divided into three main parts according to the following plan. The first part considers the nature of short-term memory in humans. It is argued that the concept of a unitary short-term store is untenable and should be replaced by the more complex idea of a working memory comprising separate but interacting subsystems. Two aspects of working memory are discussed, passive registration processes responsible for recency effects, and active rehearsal processes involved in such phenomena as memory span. It is suggested that there are separate working memory subsystems for the rehearsal of verbal and visuospatial information and that there may also be more than one mechanism underlying recency. The second section is devoted to a brief consideration of recency effects and rehearsal processes in animals in the light of what is known about human working memory and attempts to show that this approach leads to some interesting and fruitful comparisons. The third and final section reflects on the nature of a general theoretical framework for analyzing memory in humans and animals. Some of the criteria for building a useful theory are discussed and it is suggested that choosing to analyze short-term memory in terms of relatively autonomous subsystems satisfies these criteria.

HUMAN SHORT-TERM MEMORY

Active vs. Passive Storage

In the late 1960s a number of arguments were put forward for distinguishing between separate memory systems for short- and long-term retention (see e.g., Atkinson & Shiffrin, 1968). The two systems were thought to differ in respect of operating characteristics such as storage capacity, coding format, and trace durability. Thus the short-term store was identified as a limited capacity system holding speech-coded information over relatively brief intervals. Two phenomena were of particular importance in suggesting a separate short-term store: the limited span of immediate memory and the 'recency effect' in free recall.

In free recall subjects are asked to recall a list of items, typically randomly selected words, without regard to the order in which they were presented. The recency effect is the tendency for the last few items in a list to be particularly well recalled when the memory test takes place immediately following list presentation. Recency involves processes that are separate from those mediating recall of items presented earlier in the list (see for example the excellent review provided by Glanzer, 1972). The critical evidence is that a range of task variables influence recall of recent but not early items, while other variables affect recall of early but not recent items. For example, a post-list delay filled with a distracting activity such as counting backwards by threes disrupts recency but leaves memory for early items unaffected, while manipulations of list length and presentation rate affect memory for early items but not recency. The small number of items contributing to the recency effect and its vulnerability to interference from subsequent stimulation suggest that it reflects output from a short-term store of limited capacity that is subject to overwriting.

The span of immediate memory is a limit on immediate recall of a random sequence of familiar items such as letters, digits or words. It is defined as the longest sequence that can be recalled accurately on some criterion proportion of occasions, and is typically somewhere between 5 and 9 items (Miller, 1956). Span contrasts sharply with our apparently unlimited capacity to remember well-learned materials over long intervals.

It was generally accepted within the two-store approach to human memory that both memory span and the recency effect in free recall reflect the limited capacity of a single unitary short-term store. However, a number of incongruities between these phenomena soon became evident, and dissatisfaction with such an interpretation began to appear. It was expressed most clearly, along with a number of other problems for the two-store approach, by Craik & Lockhart (1972) as part of the development of 'levels of processing' as an alternative theoretical framework. Subsequently, it has become quite firmly established that memory span and the recency effect reflect separate and distinct limitations within the memory system (Baddeley & Hitch, 1974; Hitch, 1980). Briefly, the evidence favoring such an interpretation is as follows:

1. In memory span, and in the closely related task of immediate serial recall of supraspan sequences, performance is sensitive to such variables as the spoken duration (word length) and phonemic similarity of the items, and is disrupted by irrelevant concurrent articulation (see e.g., Baddeley, 1983 for a review). These effects suggest that span tasks involve active subvocal rehearsal. There is no corresponding pattern of evidence for speech coding or the involvement of active rehearsal in the case of the recency effect in free recall (see e.g., Hitch, 1980 for a review). There is also evidence that recency can be observed in incidental learning (Baddeley & Hitch, 1977), as would be expected if it results from a passive registration process rather than an active strategy.

2. In dual-task experiments where a near-span immediate serial recall task is performed during presentation of a list of words for immediate free recall, there is no evidence of any selective interference with the recency component of the free recall task (Baddeley & Hitch, 1977). If recency and span both compete for a common limited capacity system, recency should of course be very markedly reduced.

3. Individual differences in memory span generally do not correlate with measures of the size of the recency effect (see e.g., Martin, 1978). A similar suggestion of dissociation comes from developmental data: memory span improves progressively during childhood but the size of the recency effect remains relatively invariant (see e.g., Hitch & Halliday, 1983 for a review).

In the light of this evidence the idea of a unitary short-term store responsible for both memory span and the recency effect in free recall is clearly untenable. These data are, however, consistent with the concept of working memory, a set of separate but interacting subsystems (Baddeley & Hitch, 1974; Hitch, 1980). This alternative approach emphasizes distinctions among the various subsystems and the functions they perform in everyday cognition. Memory span is thought to be mediated by a speech-based 'articulatory loop' involved in both subvocal rehearsal and normal speech production, while recency is quite independent of this subsystem. The following sections elaborate on the nature of the processes responsible for recency and active rehearsal, according to the working memory framework.

Varieties of Recency

It is now clear that recency is a fairly ubiquitous phenomenon. It can be readily observed over longer time intervals than the few seconds involved in immediate free recall in both everyday memory and laboratory tasks. For example, rugby players asked to remember details of games played during a season show better recall the more recent the game (Baddeley & Hitch, 1977). Similarly, university students asked to recall details of books borrowed from a library permitting only overnight loans also show a recency effect (see Fig. 6.1).

Recency extending over relatively long intervals has also been demonstrated under laboratory conditions in a variant of free recall known as the 'continuous distractor' paradigm. Here each word in a list including the final item is followed by a period of several seconds spent performing an irrelevant distractor task such

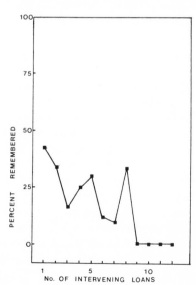

FIG. 6.1. Memory for library books borrowed on overnight loan as a function of number of intervening loans.

as backwards counting. Under these conditions there is a substantial and reliable recency effect in recall of the words even though the amount of distraction following presentation of the final item would be sufficient to abolish the recency effect in standard free recall (Bjork & Whitten, 1974; Tzeng, 1973).

How are such long-term recency effects to be explained? Although it seems clear that retrieval from a specifically short-term store can be ruled out, there remain a number of possible mechanisms. Two plausible and familiar candidates are trace decay and retroactive interference, each of which would lead to better memory for items or events later in a series. Another suggestion, made amongst others by Crowder (1976) and by Baddeley and Hitch (1977), is that items are encoded with tags representing their ordinal or temporal positions and that recency derives from the relative discriminability of such tags at retrieval. The general idea is that the more recently an item has occurred, the more discriminable will be its temporal or ordinal tag. A relationship of this sort would be expected if one assumed the discriminability of tags in memory to be analogous to perceptual discriminations which obey Weber's Law. An unpublished experiment by myself and two colleagues (Hitch, Rejman, & Turner, 1980), attempted to make a test of this idea.

Assuming Weber's Law, the ease of discriminating the tag of an item in a series will decrease with the size of the interval since its presentation and increase with the intervals separating it from adjacent items. On this view it is the ratio of the two sorts of interval that determines trace discriminability and hence the probability of successful recall. According to simple trace decay or retroactive interference it is of course only the interval following presentation that should influence the level of recall. Discriminating tags in memory can be thought to resemble the effect of spatial perspective obtained when looking along a row of telegraph poles (cf. Crowder, 1976). The visibility of an individual pole declines with distance from the viewer but increases with its spacing from adjacent poles.

We tested the importance of the ratio idea in an experiment using variants of the continuous distractor task in which the amounts of distractor activity between items and at the end of the list were independently varied. In one condition a between-item interval consisting of processing 2 distractors (numbers to be judged odd or even) was combined with a postlist interval filled with 3 distractors. In another, the same between-item interval was combined with a postlist interval of 15 distractors. Two further conditions comprised a between-item interval of 8 distractors combined with a postlist interval of either 15 or 60 distractors. We were interested in the effects of these combinations on the presence of long-term recency. A ratio rule would imply roughly similar recency in the low ratio '8:15' and '2:3' conditions and a corresponding absence of recency in the high ratio '8:60' and '2:15' conditions. A critical comparison is between the '2:15' and '8:15' conditions, since here the postlist delays are identical but the ratios of the between-item and postlist intervals differ. The results of the experiment are shown in Fig. 6.2. They confirm the prediction and hence provide support for the tag discriminability hypothesis. Processes that depend on only the postlist interval, such as simple trace decay or retroactive interference, cannot account for the results obtained.

A quantitative test of the tag discriminability hypothesis can be made by calculating the Weber fraction for items in the last few serial positions of each list in the various experimental conditions and seeing if this index is systematically related to levels of recall. Figure 6.3a illustrates the results and suggests there is indeed a systematic, functional relationship. Thus tag discriminability appears to provide a reasonably good account of the long-term recency effect in the continuous distractor task.

It is an important theoretical question whether long-term recency effects of the sort described here are fundamentally different from short-term recency in standard immediate free recall. In a further experiment (Hitch, Rejman, & Turner, 1980) we examined recall of the last few list items in immediate free recall, delayed free recall and the continuous distractor task, as a function of the Weber fraction. Figure 6.3b illustrates the results and shows that both short-term and long-term recency are consistent with a common tag discriminability process. On this evidence it would be parsimonious to propose a single mechanism for both

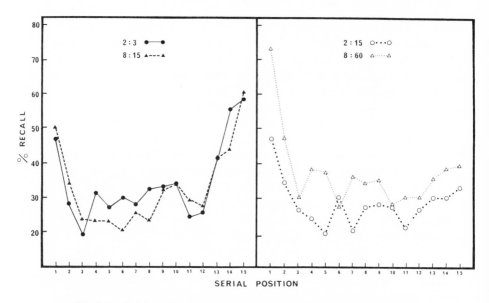

FIG. 6.2. Serial position curves in the 'continuous distractor' variant of free recall. Conditions specified in terms of no. of distractors separating adjacent list items and no. of post-list distractors (e.g. 2:3 corresponds to a within list separation of 2 distractors and 3 post-list distractors). Data from Hitch, Rejman and Turner (unpublished).

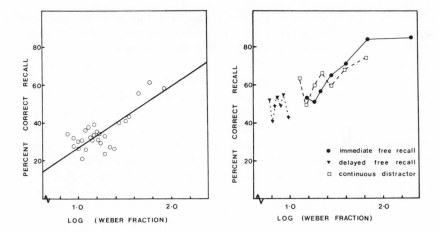

FIG. 6.3a.   Recall of items from the final 7 serial positions in variants of the continuous distractor task plotted as a function of an index of temporal discriminability. Data from Hitch, Rejman and Turner (unpublished).
FIG. 6.3b.   Recall of items from the final 7 serial positions in immediate free recall, delayed free recall and the continuous distractor task plotted as a function of temporal discriminability. Data from Hitch, Rejman and Turner (unpublished).

types of recency. However, other evidence suggests possible disparities between the two effects (see e.g., Hitch, 1980), so it must for the present remain an open question whether the mechanisms are the same or different.

Varieties of Rehearsal

It has been seen that memory span tasks appear to involve subvocal rehearsal since they are sensitive to phonemic similarity and word length of the materials and to concurrent articulatory suppression. All three effects appear to have a common basis since articulatory suppression removes the effects of phonemic similarity and word length (Baddeley, Thomson, & Buchanan, 1975; Murray, 1968). Within the working memory framework this common basis is identified with a specific subsystem known as the "articulatory loop". Detailed studies of the word length effect show that there is a simple linear relationship between amount of material recalled and the rate at which it can be articulated, suggesting that the articulatory loop has a well defined temporal capacity. The relationship is such that people can generally remember between 1 and 2s of "inner speech" using the loop.

Subvocal rehearsal of speech-based information is not however the only type of rehearsal process in which humans can engage. A further hypothetical subsystem of working memory specializing in the maintenance and manipulation of visual images has been proposed, known as the "visuo-spatial scratch pad" (see

Baddeley, 1983 for a recent overview). Early experiments by Brooks (1967) compared immediate memory for sequences of items that could readily be imaged as a spatial pattern with memory for more abstract, nonimageable sequences. Memory for spatial sequences was better when they were presented auditorily, whereas memory for nonsense sequences was better when they were presented visually. Brooks suggested that imagery involves a visuo-spatial coding system which is also involved in visual perception, while remembering abstract materials does not. Subsequent work by Baddeley and his colleagues has shown differential sensitivity of spatial and abstract short-term memory tasks to interference from a concurrent task, as would be expected if they involve separate processes. Spatial short-term memory is severely disrupted by tasks such as spatial tracking and making voluntary eye movements while non-spatial short-term memory is considerably less affected.

Other methods for studying nonverbal short-term memory have made use of abstract visual patterns that cannot readily be verbally encoded (see Phillips, 1983 for an overview). Phillips & Christie (1977a) found that in recognition memory for a list of such patterns there was a clear serial position effect such that the final pattern was remembered particularly well while the earlier patterns were remembered less well and roughly equally so. A number of task manipulations were found to have differential effects on memory for the final pattern and earlier patterns suggesting the presence of two distinct processes. Phillips & Christie attributed memory for the final pattern to ''visualization'', a limited capacity visuo-spatial rehearsal process capable of maintaining a single pattern for a few seconds or so depending upon its complexity. In a further experiment, Phillips & Christie (1977b) demonstrated the active nature of visualization by showing that instructions to rehearse a pattern other than the final one in a series led to enhanced memory for the selected pattern and poorer memory for the final pattern when compared with a control condition.

It is not yet clear how the process of visualization investigated by Phillips should be related to the visuo-spatial scratchpad of working memory and a good deal of further research is needed to explore this general area. However, the available evidence is highly suggestive of a human capability for rehearsing visuo-spatial information which, following Phillips' results, is limited to the maintenance of a single pattern at a time. Such a capability appears to be quite different from the capacity and use of the articulatory loop subsystem for the rehearsal of speech-based, verbal information.

Functions of Recency and Active Rehearsal

The functional significance of short-term memory processes in humans has been the subject of considerable speculation, and will probably continue so for some time yet. It is commonly assumed that such processes are important for general intelligence through providing temporary information storage during symbol manipulation. Indeed, assessment of memory span is a standard feature in routine methods of intelligence testing. Experimental studies have supported the idea of a common working memory system in such diverse activities as verbal reasoning, sentence comprehension, free recall learning, and mental arithmetic (Baddeley & Hitch, 1974; Hitch, 1978). Of further interest here is the possibility that the various subsystems of working memory have their own characteristic functional significance.

The clearest case is the articulatory loop, the subsystem thought to be involved in subvocal rehearsal. Part of its operational definition is that it is disrupted by irrelevant articulation, hence it seems unavoidable that the loop is closely concerned with processes of speech production. It is of course commonly argued that some form of output buffer is necessary for assembling the speech code. Identity of this buffer with the articulatory loop is strengthened by evidence of detailed correspondences between patterns of error in memory span tasks and in normal speech production (Ellis, 1980). By comparison, the functional significance of the human ability to maintain and manipulate visuo-spatial images is much less clear and consequently more open to speculation. Just two of the many suggested possibilities are the solution of spatial problems such as route finding and planning, and visual learning.

The role of processes responsible for recency effects has also attracted attention. One proposal is that the short-term recency effect in free recall of verbal materials reflects the operation of a buffer store necessary for language comprehension (Hitch, 1980). Such a store would hold surface constituents of a sentence prior to further processing for comprehension. Evidence consistent with this idea has been collected by Jarvella (1978) using a technique in which a meaningful message is interrupted and the listener asked for immediate recall. Jarvella observed a recency effect which was sensitive to the syntactic structure of the message rather than simply extending over a fixed number of words. It does not seem appropriate, however, to associate long-term recency for events spanning days, weeks, months, or even years with a psycholinguistic function. Recency spanning such intervals has been suggested as serving the primitive function of monitoring orientation in time and space by providing a basic mechanism for "keeping track" (Baddeley & Hitch, 1977).

These possible functions of working memory subsystems have yet to be fully elaborated and investigated and in any case are not an exhaustive list. The question of function is raised, however, because it may provide a useful basis for thinking about short-term memory in animals. For example, analogues of human speech input and output buffers would presumably be present in animals displaying appropriate communicative behavior, and would have capacities commensurate with the functional demands placed upon them. Animals operating with less sophisticated message systems involving only stereotypical sequences might, in the limit, not possess any analogue of such buffer storage. Analogues of nonverbal subsystems of working memory would, however, be expected to be much more wisespread and fully developed among animal species. The mechanism for monitoring orientation in time and space is a good example, as is the ability to perform spatial tasks.

These few suggestions obviously do little more than scratch the surface of a rich and potentially fruitful set of links and correspondences between working memory in humans and animals. The alternative of assuming a unitary short-term store and comparing parameters such as capacity and durability across species seems a considerably less interesting, even sterile approach in comparison.

To summarise the argument so far, it seems most unlikely that human short-term memory can be explained in terms of a single store. A more plausible hypothesis is that of a multicomponent working memory system. Within such a system processes of active rehearsal appear to be distinguishable from the passive processes which give rise to recency effects in unordered recall of serial lists. Furthermore, processes responsible for rehearsal and recency may themselves be subdivided. Speech-based and visuo-spatial rehearsal appear to be different from one another, and it may also be that a separate short-term recency process should be differentiated from a more general process giving rise to recency over longer intervals and a broader range of materials. A number of speculations have been made about the functions served by the various possible types of short-term memory processes. Some of these functions are closely tied to language and so have fairly direct implications for short-term memory in animals.

ANIMAL SHORT-TERM MEMORY

The treatment of short-term memory in animals will necessarily be highly selective and will focus on just two aspects: recency effects and rehearsal processes.

Recency Effects

There is fairly solid evidence for the existence of recency effects in animal short-term memory across a broad range of species. The experiments typically involve presenting an animal with a series of unrelated stimuli and then testing recognition memory by requiring a discrimination between test stimuli according to whether they are *old* (a member of the initial series) or *new* (not previously presented). Using such methods it has been demonstrated that rhesus monkeys show a recency effect in memory for series of photographs of familiar objects (Sands & Wright, 1980), colors and locations (Gaffan, 1977) and junk objects (Gaffan & Weiskranz, 1980). Similar effects have been reported in squirrel monkeys' memory for visual patterns (Roberts & Kraemer, 1981); dolphins' memory for sounds (Thompson & Herman, 1977; see Fig. 6.4) and pigeons' memory for colors (Macphail, 1980).

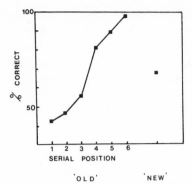

FIG. 6.4. Recognition memory judgments for 'old' and 'new' sounds in dolphins as a function of serial position of presentation. After Thompson and Herman, 1977.

Unfortunately, there has not been a great deal of analytic work on the processes underlying recency in animals. Such information as is available is rather fragmentary. For example, it appears (see Fig. 6.5) that the recency effect for visual stimuli in monkeys is reduced by an unfilled postlist delay, and that memory for earlier, nonrecency items is much less affected (see Gaffan & Weiskranz, 1980; Wright, Santiago, & Sands, 1983). Such results are compatible with recency in humans, except that it is usually necessary to fill the delay with distracting activity to abolish recency in the human case. It is also of interest that recency in animals is insensitive to variations in the length of the series being remembered. This has been found in both the dolphin (Thompson & Herman, 1977) and the pigeon (Macphail, 1980). There are of course conditions where the same is true in the human case. Despite these intriguing parallels, however, too little is known about the processes responsible for recency in animals to establish detailed correspondences with humans. It would be interesting, for example, to know if animals exhibit long-term recency, and to what extent recency effects in animals involve tag discriminability processes or buffer storage. For the present,

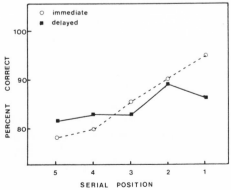

FIG. 6.5. Recognition memory for visual stimuli in rhesus monkeys as a function of serial position of presentation ("1" = most recent) for immediate and delayed testing. After Gaffan and Weiskranz, 1980.

it is worth noting that the existence of strong recency effects across a broad range of species is consistent with a fairly primitive function like keeping track. Certainly, many of the animal species mentioned here would not be expected to possess analogues of the human speech input buffer. In such terms, the mutual relevance of work on animals and humans is quite evident. As a postscript to this section, it is interesting to note that Ronald Cohen included recency in his chapter on general empirical laws believed to be true across species. (See chapter 12, this volume.)

Active Rehearsal

A great deal of interest has been shown in answering the general question "can animals actively rehearse material they are set to remember?" and in understanding the nature of any such rehearsal processes. Several lines of inquiry have been followed in pursuing these issues (see e.g., Hitch, 1983 for a review). Possibly the most direct and therefore most convincing are studies showing that forgetting is alleviated in the presence of observable mediating behavior during a retention interval.

In an experiment on pigeons using the delayed response paradigm (Jans & Catania, 1980) each trial began with presentation of one of two sample stimuli. Then after a variable retention interval a peck to either a left or right hand key was reinforced depending on which sample stimulus was presented initially. Performance in this type of task typically declines with increasing retention interval sugesting that forgetting is taking place. Jans & Catania found that if the response keys were illuminated during the retention interval but responding brought no consequences, pigeons tended to peck at the appropriate key and show less forgetting than control animals who performed irrelevant responses during the delay. Similar results have been obtained using the delayed matching to sample (DMTS) procedure. Here, each trial typically begins with presentation of one of two sample stimuli followed by a variable delay after which two comparison stimuli are simultaneously presented. The animal is reinforced for responding to the comparison stimulus which is physically identical to the sample. Zentall, Hogan, Howard, and Moore (1978) found that animals making clearly observable sample-specific responses during the retention interval forgot less rapidly than animals not doing so. It seems therefore that animals are capable of a type of rehearsal which involves using overt responses to bridge a retention interval and alleviate forgetting.

A potentially more powerful method for investigating rehearsal in animals uses the technique of directed forgetting (Grant, 1981). In a pigeon DMTS task Grant followed each sample with either a "remember" cue signaling that memory would subsequently be tested or a "forget" cue signifying no such test. Occasional probe trials following forget cues were used to assess their effectiveness. The results showed a clear tendency for less forgetting following remember cues, an effect which was greater the sooner the cue came after the sample stimulus. Both findings are consistent with the idea that the cues were successful in controlling active rehearsal processes capable of slowing forgetting.

These studies illustrate the type of evidence that supports the hypothesis that animals engage in active rehearsal processes in short-term memory tasks. What is rehearsed probably differs from task to task. In delayed response tasks, rehearsal appears to correspond to simple response repetition (Jans & Catania, 1980). On the other hand, in delayed symbolic matching tasks, where the comparison stimuli are symbolically rather than physically related to the sample, it has been suggested that animals remember an *instruction* to respond to a particular cue (Honig, 1978) or a representation of the correct comparison stimulus (Roitblatt, 1980).

Interestingly, none of the experiments on rehearsal in animals has demonstrated the ability to rehearse more than a single event, and none have shown that even with such a small load rehearsal can prevent forgetting from taking place for any appreciable time period. In both respects, animal rehearsal is grossly inferior to human verbal rehearsal using the articulatory loop. The contrast with human nonverbal rehearsal, on the other hand, is considerably less striking. Given different functions for these two types of rehearsal in humans, the animal data, such as they are, would seem to fit roughly with expectation. It also seems likely that animals' restricted rehearsal capabilities can be contrasted with the more extensive recency effects that can be observed. Such a disparity would be consistent with the hypothesis that rehearsal and recency are mediated by separate processes in animals as in humans.

It should therefore be evident that there is considerable scope for interesting, fairly direct comparisons between animal and human short-term memory, even if at present there is insufficient data to draw any strong conclusions.

COMMENTS ON AN INTEGRATIVE THEORETICAL FRAMEWORK

In attempting to illustrate how comparisons between aspects of short-term memory in humans and animals may be fruitful, data on animals have been considered in the light of certain ideas about human short-term memory. Some assumptions about the nature of memory systems in general are implicit in this exercise. These assumptions are discussed here in relation to the requirements of a general approach to the analysis of human and animal memory. First, it is necessary to make some remarks about the nature of an integrative theoretical framework for thinking about memory in different species. To do so involves some reflection on the nature of scientific methods.

The Nature of an Integrative Framework

One way in which scientific methods contribute to knowledge is through processes of analysis and synthesis. Complex problems are first analyzed in terms of simpler elements or constituents, then these constituents and their interactions are subjected to further investigation and scrutiny in their own right. Subsequently, the complex problem may be solved or understood by synthesis of the constituents. Evidently, for any particular problem, it is vital to select an appropriate set of constituents for analysis and to develop appropriate empirical and theoretical methods for investigating such constituents and their interactions. Furthermore, to construct a general theoretical framework for memory in humans and animals it is necessary to analyze memory systems in different species in terms of a common set of constituents (though empirical methods may differ). Endel Tulving refers to this as the "classification problem" in his chapter and draws attention to the large range of candidate categories (see chapter 4). It is also necessary to develop a superordinate "linking theory" for generating hypotheses about similarities and differences among the constituents of memory across species. Given such a characterisation of the problem, it follows that the constituents into which memory is analyzed should be elements that are suitable both for the description of memory in individual species and the linking theory. These requirements suggest criteria for evaluating different methods of analysis. For example, although it is not possible to go into the nature of potential linking theories here, it seems inescapable that such theories will be concerned with evolutionary perspectives on differences among species. If so, it follows that the functions of memory for the organism are likely to be important and therefore that analyses of memory systems must be such as to allow such functions to be clearly specified. A similar call for emphasis on the functional significance of memory is made in Bob Bolles' chapter; a different approach to linking theory and a fuller discussion of "connecting models" is presented in the chapter by Bill Estes.

Analysis of Short-term Memory

In this section, the suitability of the present analysis of short-term memory is considered in relation to a general integrative framework. Possible alternative approaches are also discussed briefly.

In adopting the concept of working memory and applying it to humans and animals it has been assumed that memory systems can be analyzed into relatively independent subsystems with characteristic properties. This amounts to the proposition that memory systems possess a high degree of modularity, and corresponds broadly with the position adopted by David Olton in his contribution (see chapter 5). A radical alternative is presented in Gus Craik's chapter in which he argues against separate subsystems and in favor of a unitary memory system capable of being used in different ways. A difficulty for Craik's view, however, is how to account for neuropsychological double dissociations (see below) without some appeal to structure.

A fundamental distinction within the modular approach, not defended here, is that between working memory and long-term memory. Working memory was analyzed in terms of separate subsystems for different types of rehearsal and recency and it was here that comparisons between human and animal research were particularly interesting. Subsystems can be regarded as specializing in the type of computation they perform and the form of information storage associated with them. The functions of subsystems derive from the uses given to their information storage or computational outputs. Having chosen to regard memory in humans and animals as comprising such subsystems and therefore having a modular structure, it can now be asked whether an analysis of this sort is (1) plausible, (2) tractable and (3) compatible with a linking theory for species differences.

In respect of plausibility, recall first that the evidence presented here has suggested that a multifaceted working memory goes some way towards capturing the many diverse aspects of human and animal short-term memory. Evidence for modularity also comes from the so-called natural fractionations observed in neuropsychological disorders of function. Thus the distinction between working and long-term memory systems in humans is supported by a neuropsychological double dissociation of function (see e.g., Shallice, 1979): amnesic patients show impaired long-term episodic memory but essentially normal short-term retention while other patients, typically conduction aphasics, show the converse pattern of deficit and sparing. Similarly, there is suggestive evidence from human neuropsychology that visual short-term memory can be selectively impaired while verbal short-term memory is unaffected (De Renzi & Nichelli, 1975), consistent with the idea of a modular working memory system. Other types of natural fractionation may be observed in developmental studies of normal individuals. For example, as mentioned earlier, it appears that recency effects in humans are fully developed at a relatively early age while memory span shows a considerable developmental increase. It must be noted, however, that there are no convincing a priori grounds for supposing that modularity is a necessary feature of complex information processing systems. For example, Fodor (1983) argues that while input and motor output systems are likely to be modular, central processing systems are not. Thus it seems likely to remain an empirical matter how useful the assumption of modularity will prove.

As regards tractability, it has been seen how neuropsychological and developmental fractionation can give valuable clues about the structure of cognitive and memory systems. In particular, neuropsychological double dissociations constitute powerful evidence for the identification of separate subsystems. Such dissociations may be supported and validated by means of converging operations applied to normal individuals. These are clusters of conceptually and empirically related manipulations which appear to converge on a particular subsystem, such as the set of operations for identifying the articulatory loop subsystem of human working memory discussed earlier. Converging operations may also help to clarify ideas about the nature of subsystems and their functional significance. However, while all these methods work well for separating pairs of subsystems, they are less well developed for identifying multiple subsystems. The tractability of the modular approach must therefore be accepted with some caution.

Turning finally to the question of compatibility with linking theory, there are just two points that can usefully be made. The first is simply that modularity enables functions to be specified for individual subsystems and thus fulfills a criterion for elements in a linking theory which makes reference to evolutionary processes. Second, it has been observed by Oakley (1983) that a possible advantage of modularity in the design of computational systems is that new or extended facilities can be added without necessitating a massive reorganization of the existing structure. Thus it may be fruitful to describe differences among species in terms of the presence or absence of specific subsystems.

Finally, one alternative approach to the analysis of human and animal memory is briefly considered in relation to the same criteria of plausibility, tractability, and compatibility with linking theory. This is the traditional analysis of memory in terms of separate processes of acquisition, storage, and retrieval. Adopting it here would entail attempting to compare human and animal memory in terms of the characteristics of these three fundamental processes. First, acquisition, storage, and retrieval are clearly plausible elements for an integrative theory of human and animal memory because it is difficult to conceptualize a memory system that could not be analyzed in this way. With regard to empirical tractability, however, it has proved surprisingly difficult to separate out the contributions of encoding, storage, and retrieval processes to several memory phenomena. A good example is the difficulty encountered by the levels of processing framework in demonstrating encoding effects which cannot be readily reinterpreted in terms of encoding specificity (see e.g., Tulving, 1979). Major sources of this difficulty are the causal dependencies which link acquisition, storage and retrieval in any memory task and therefore the difficulty of studying each process in isolation. Perhaps for these reasons it remains controversial whether neuropsychological disorders of human memory can be understood in terms of deficits specific to encoding, storage and retrieval. Finally, with regard to function, it is unfortunate that the traditional approach limits itself to the view that memory is a mental faculty which can be studied separately from cognition in general. It is not evident how issues about the functional significance of memory for the organism can be captured within the traditional approach and correspondingly difficult to see how to think about evolutionary changes in terms of the processes of encoding, storage, and retrieval.

Thus in conclusion it seems that an analysis of memory into subsystems may lead to interesting and fruitful links between research on humans and animals. It should however be very clear that a considerable amount of work is necessary, both empirical and theoretical, in order to take this suggestion further and demonstrate its usefulness to researchers in both fields of enquiry.

REFERENCES

Atkinson, R. C., & Shiffrin, R. M. (1968). Human memory: A proposed system and its control processes. In K. W. Spence & J. T. Spence (Eds.), *The psychology of learning and motivation: Advances in research and theory (Vol. 2)*. New York: Academic Press.

Baddeley, A. D. (1983). Working memory. *Philosophical Transactions of the Royal Society London, B 302*, 311–324.

Baddeley, A. D., & Hitch, G. J. (1974). Working memory. In G. H. Bower (Ed.), *The Psychology of Learning & Motivation: Advances in Research and Theory* (Vol. 8). New York: Academic Press.

Baddeley, A. D., & Hitch, G. J. (1977). Recency re-examined. In S. Dornic (Ed.), *Attention and Performance, IV*. New York: Academic Press.

Baddeley, A. D., Thomson, N., & Buchanan, M. (1975). Word length and the structure of short-term memory. *Journal of Verbal Learning and Verbal Behavior, 14*, 575–589.

Bjork, R. A., & Whitten, W. B. (1974). Recency-sensitive retrieval processes in long-term free recall. *Cognitive Psychology, 2*, 99–116.

Brooks, L. R. (1967). The suppression of visualization by reading. *Quarterly Journal of Experimental Psychology, 19*, 289–299.

Craik, F. I. M., & Lockhart, R. S. (1972). Levels of processing: A framework for memory research. *Journal of Verbal Learning and Verbal Behavior, 11*, 671–684.

Crowder, R. G. (1976). *Principles of learning and memory*. New York: Wiley.

De Renzi, E., & Nichelli, P. (1975). Verbal and non-verbal short-term memory impairment following hemisphere damage. *Cortex, 11*, 341–354.

Ellis, A. W. (1980). Errors of speech and short-term memory: The effects of phonemic similarity and syllable position. *Journal of Verbal Learning and Verbal Behavior, 19*, 624–634.

Fodor, J. A. (1983). *The modularity of mind*. Cambridge, MA: MIT Press.

Gaffan, D. (1977). Recognition memory after short intervals in fornix-transected monkeys. *Quarterly Journal of Experimental Psychology, 29*, 577–588.

Gaffan, D., & Weiskranz, L. (1980). Recency effects and lesion effects in delayed non-matching to randomly baited samples by monkeys. *Brain Research, 196*, 373–386.

Glanzer, M. (1972). Storage mechanisms in recall. In G. H. Bower (Ed.), *The psychology of learning and motivation: Advances in research and theory* (Vol. 5). New York: Academic Press.

Grant, D. S. (1981). Stimulus control of information processing in pigeon short-term memory. *Learning and Motivation, 12*, 19–39.

Hitch, G. J. (1978). The role of short-term working memory in mental arithmetic. *Cognitive Psychology, 10*, 302–323.

Hitch, G. J. (1980). Developing the concept of working memory. In G. Claxton (Ed.), *Cognitive psychology: New directions*. London: Routledge and Kegan Paul.

Hitch, G. J. (1983). Short-term memory processes in humans and animals. In A. Mayes (Ed.), *Memory in animals and humans*. Wokingham: Van Nostrand Reinhold.

Hitch, G. J., & Halliday, M. S. (1983). Working memory in children. *Philosophical Transcations of the Royal Society London, B 302*, 325–340.

Hitch, G. J., Rejman, M. H., & Turner, N. (1980). *A new perspective on the recency effect*. Paper presented to the Experimental Psychology Society, Cambridge, England.

Honig, W. K. (1978). Studies of working memory in the pigeon. In S. H. Hulse, H. Fowler, & W.

K. Honig (Eds.), *Cognitive processes in animal behavior*. Hillsdale, NJ: Lawrence Erlbaum Associates.

Jans, J. E., & Catania, A. C. (1980). Short-term remembering of discriminative stimuli in pigeons. *Journal of the Experimental Analysis of Behavior, 34,* 177–183.

Jarvella, R. J. (1978). Immediate memory in discourse processing. In G. H. Bower (Ed.), *The psychology of learning and motivation: Advances in research and theory* (Vol. 12). New York: Academic Press.

Macphail, E. M. (1980). Short-term visual recognition memory in pigeons. *Quarterly Journal of Experimental Psychology, 32,* 521–538.

Martin, M. (1978). Asssessment of individual variation in memory ability. In M. M. Gruneberg, P. E. Morris, & R. N. Sykes (Eds.), *Practical aspects of memory*. New York: Academic Press.

Miller, G. A. (1956). The magic number seven plus or minus two. *Psychological Review, 63,* 81–97.

Murray, D. J. (1968). Articulation and acoustic confusability in short-term memory. *Journal of Experimental Psychology, 78,* 679–684.

Oakley, D. A. (1983). The varieties of memory: A phylogenetic approach. In A. Mayes (Ed.), *Memory in animals and humans*. Wokingham: Van Nostrand Reinhold.

Phillips, W. A. (1983). Short-term visual memory. *Philosophical Transactions of the Royal Society B, 302,* 295–309.

Phillips, W. A., & Christie, D. F. M. (1977a). Components of visual memory. *Quarterly Journal of Experimental Psychology, 29,* 117–133.

Phillips, W. A., & Christie, D. F. M. (1977b). Interference with visualization. *Quarterly Journal of Experimental Psychology, 29,* 637–650.

Roberts, W. A., & Kraemer, P. J. (1981). Recognition memory for lists of visual stimuli in monkeys and humans. *Animal Learning and Behavior, 9,* 587–594.

Roitblatt, H. L. (1980). Codes and coding processes in pigeon short-term memory. *Animal Learning and Behavior, 8,* 341–351.

Sands, S. F., & Wright, A. A. (1980). Primate memory: Retention of serial list items by a rhesus monkey. *Science, 209,* 238–240.

Shallice, T. (1979). Neuropsychological research and the fractionation of memory systems. In L.-G. Nilsson (Ed.), *Perspectives in memory research*. Hillsdale, NJ: Lawrence Erlbaum Associates.

Thompson, R. K. R., & Herman, L. M. (1977). Memory for lists of sounds by the bottle-nosed dolphin: Convergence of memory processes with humans? *Science, 195,* 501–503.

Tulving, E. (1979). Relation between encoding specificity and levels of processing. In L. S. Cermak & F. I. M. Craik (Eds.), *Levels of processing in human memory*. Hillsdale, NJ: Lawrence Erlbaum Associates.

Tzeng, O. J. L. (1973). Positive recency effect in delayed free recall. *Journal of Verbal Learning and Verbal Behavior, 12,* 436–439.

Wright, A. A., Santiago, H. C., & Sands, S. F. (1983). On the nature of the primacy effect in memory processing: A reply to Gaffan. *Animal Learning and Behavior, 11,* 148–150.

Zentall, T. R., Hogan, D. E., Howard, M. M., & Moore, B. S. (1978). Delayed matching in the pigeon: Effect on performance of sample-specific observing responses and differential delay behavior. *Learning and Motivation, 9,* 202–218.

7 Short-Term Memory and Attention

Robert C. Bolles
University of Washington

INTRODUCTION

Once upon a time, and I cannot tell you just when it was, there was an angry god, and again I cannot tell you just which god it was, but he put a terrible curse on psychology. He cursed us with these words

> You will never ever discover anything about underlying causal processes, and you will never ever understand the overlying functional significance of anything. You will be forever doomed to be methodologists. You will content yourselves with teaching each other how to do experiments, and you will never know what they mean.

It seems clear that a lot of the people who work in the area of short-term memory in animals are indeed suffering under that curse. We certainly have learned how to do the experiments. One of our main techniques is the delayed matching to sample procedure, where we present, let us say, a red key to a pigeon for a few seconds. Then we take it away for a few seconds, and then we see if the bird can select red when it is presented again together with another color. We know how to do that. And we know how to vary all of the relevant parameters, so that we now have a pretty good idea of how long some representation of the initial key color, the sample, can stay in the pigeon's short-term memory. The problem is that we do not know how this is accomplished. We have no idea of what the bird is doing when it is remembering the color red. We don't know whether it has something like a concept of red, or whether it has some correlated body posture that tells it that red was the last color seen. We have no concept in the world of how red is represented to the pigeon. We do the experiments, we study the effect of this or that parameter, but we have no concept of the pigeon's concept of red. So much for the causal process.

Likewise, we have no idea of why the pigeon should be capable of such a performance. Why can a bird remember a color for a few seconds? Why can some mammals remember colors for much longer time periods? We do not know. We are inclined to say that mammals are smarter, or say that they are more highly evolved, or we say that they have bigger brains, but we do not know. The unhappy fact is that we have no theory of short-term memory. We do not understand how it works and we do not understand why it works. That curse lies heavily upon us. We know how to do the experiments but we do not seem to know what they mean.

We do have a little theoretical language, but most of it is the language of the methodologists. We anticipate a certain effect, so we vary this parameter. We anticipate other effects, so we look for an interaction between the two variables. That is theory of a sort, but it is not very satisfying because it does not tell us how and it does not tell us why. There is another small body of theoretical language, but it is largely the language of associationism. Consider, for example, that if we have two dimensions, perhaps a tilted line on a colored field, we typically find shorter memory for the relevant one of the two dimensions, than if we had used it all by itself. The introduction of the second dimension causes interference. The simple explanation of this effect is associative competition. No one knows just exactly what competition between associations consists of, but that is no matter because we always accept such an explanation. What happens next, of course, is that there comes along another methodologist who observes that whereas the stimulus dimensions were initially presented two at a time, in testing they were presented singly. Thus, some of the poor performance with the two dimension procedure can be attributed to stimulus generalization decrement. It appears that "stimulus generalization decrement" is a pseudo-theoretical concept that evolves from the pseudo-theoretical view of the associationists who, as often as not, turns out to be methodologists as well. Sure enough, other methodologists run further experiments with a new array of groups and find that there is, in fact, a stimulus generalization effect but there is also something else, which they call attention sharing (Roberts & Grant, 1978). Now, while we do not really know by what process two stimulus dimensions can share attention, that does not really matter either, because our associationistic language explains it almost automatically. The sharing of attention between two stimulus dimensions means lack of associative competition. We are right back where we started from. We have not gained any understanding of attention as a process. We have not learned anything about memory. But we have a number of new experiments.

EUPHEMISMS

I am supposed to say something here about short-term memory and attention. But I am stuck; I cannot help but point out that these terms are only euphemisms. Short-term memory is a euphemism for what the animal is thinking about. Calling it short-term memory is how the methodologists keep from having to think about what the animal is thinking about. In the same way, *attention* is a euphemism for what the animal is looking at and thinking about. Short-term memory and attention look like they might be processes, something that the animal is doing. But no, that is not the way the subject is handled in the animal experimental literature. We do not think about process, we think about how to do experiments. There is that curse. We worry about our experiments and not about how the processes work or what these processes mean in the overall scheme of things.

In his chapter, Tulving reminds us that there is an important distinction to be made between product and process. That is really what I am talking about, too. There is a set of memory processes and there is a set of attentional processes, but we do not study those processes. What we design our experiments to investigate is the product, the output, of those processes. We do that, I would contend, because our attention is mostly focused upon the methodology of the experiments and the product of psychological processes rather than upon the processes themselves. We ignore the processes; we pay no attention to them. It is as if we do not care what the processes are. We speak of attention, we speak of remembering, but we do not investigate those things. The methodologist has managed to focus our attention upon the product of these psychological processes.

Crowder, in his chapter, has suggested that, in contrast to the animal learning people, the human memory people have too many processes, they focus too much on process. He suggests there has been something like a boiling over of ideas about the kinds of things that are going on in the human mind in a short-term memory task. He is also concerned that a lot of the processes that have been postulated to operate in human memory are really no more than metaphors, rather than being identified processes per se. That may be true much of the time, but it has to be admitted that human mental processes are probably complicated enough that they have to be described in a metaphorical manner. The processes themselves may not be isomorphic with what is really happening, in much the same way as the basic processes in a transistor are not completely isomorphic to the functional properties of the thing. The electronics engineer's view of it does not correspond with the physicist's. There are holes and things in little bits of silicon that produce avalanche effects and other mysterious processes. That is what the physicist sees. But the output, the result of these physical processes, are amplification and gating and other kinds of outcomes the engineer understands, and that really look like metaphors. So the point is well taken that with processes there are different levels of analysis. What concerns me is that people in the animal learning business do not appear to be interested in theory at any of the possible levels of analysis. And that makes us distinct from the human memory folks, who have lots of processes, real or metaphorical, and who have maybe too many processes to think about. When Roger Shepard has his subjects rotating images in their mind, we can imagine that that is really what they are doing, or at least that that is what they are trying to do. I can imagine the use of body English, the twisting of the neck, to facilitate the twisting going on in the mind.

In the human memory literature there are processes like visualization and rehearsal and we have some idea of what these processes are because we do these things ourselves. Do rats visualize? Do pigeons rehearse? We do not know. We know how to do memory experiments, but little concept of what our subjects are doing in them. We have no concept of what the process is. Unfortunately, almost any foray into the animal experimental literature is likely to yield the same basic conclusion: There really are no psychological processes beyond the ability to associate one stimulus with another. One terrible implication of this doctrine is that attention is not something that the subject does, so it is not a process at all. It reduces to the relative salience of different environmental stimuli. So something like the *sharing of attention* is therefore not a process at all, it is just a quality of the impinging stimuli. In modern learning theory, different stimuli compete for participation in the associative process. But how the competition progresses depends on what is happening in the environment and not what is happening in the animal. And so on through the list of semitheoretical terms that associationism provides. An appropriate analysis would probably reveal that all the theoretical terms ultimately pertain to aspects of the environmental situation— something out there—rather than anything happening inside the subject. I am not sure that anyone really believes that animals (or humans) are quite that passive, quite that nonparticipating, but that is what our devotion to methodology and our continued use of the associationistic language have led us to.

It is partly a matter of language but it is also partly a matter of faith and ideology. I recently read an article by the contemporary Russian psychologist Zinchenko (1983) who said that there are those who would reduce everything psychological to associations but that, he said, is bourgeois psychology.

Before going on, I have to say something about an earlier work that bothered me. In his chapter, Rescorla, who is certainly one of our most distinguished and capable methodologists, tried to make the point that the only difference between conditioned taste aversion learning and other kinds of classical conditioning, is just a matter of degree; it is a quantitative matter. To be sure, the difference is substantial because conditioned taste aversions are formed over an interval of hours, whereas the limits of associability is in the order of seconds with most other kinds of conditioning paradigms. It is a matter of about a thousand to one, but Rescorla says that the thousand to one difference, while impressively large, is still only a quantitative matter. In commenting on this issue once before

(Bolles, 1985) I observed that ". . . one sees no leg bones on snake skeletons, but one does see on the skeletons of some snakes little bumps on certain vertebrae where the legs might be if the snake had legs. They are pelvic bumps, and it is my understanding that these bumps may be 1 or 2 mm in size. And I would observe that although a 1- or 2-mm leg [which does not move] is not much of a leg, it is actually about 1/1000th the length of the legs of a race horse. So the difference in legs between a snake and a race horse is really only a matter of degree" (p. 391). That is what a real methodologist would be likely to conclude. That is what associationists have to teach us about psychological processes.

It is clear that something is basically wrong. We appear to have been brought into a system, a way of thinking, and paradigms for conducting experiments and a language for describing them, that we do not believe in, but which nonetheless command all of our energies. It is obvious what is wrong. It is that curse which is hanging so heavily upon us. I think the time has come to defy that ancient god and break loose from his curse. I think that what we need to do is to encourage debate and discussion about what the processes are that operate in a memory task. We need more speculation about what the contents of memory are and how memories are coded and how they are represented. In what form does the pigeon hang on to a certain color? Or is it not a matter of hanging on at all? Is it perhaps that the animal recognizes the proper color when it reappears? Or perhaps what the animal keeps in mind is not some representation of the stimulus but some rule about how to respond when the next stimulus comes along. Perhaps everybody is wrong and all the animal remembers is some response rule. Perhaps what the bird is remembering is to peck again when the proper color is seen. Still another possibility is that the animal holds for a moment in short-term memory, that is, is thinking about, how a particular color means food. There are a lot of possibilities about the kinds of processes that are going on in short-term memory animal experiments. I am not going to advance my own ideas about this matter; what I want to do is invite people to begin worrying about and speculating about these processes, for a change.

CONTENTS AND PROCESSES

I want to come back to the discussion of processes, but first I have to say something about contents. Modern learning theory is deeply concerned with, obsessed, you might say, with predictiveness. Dickinson (1980) is quite open and frank about this. He begins his book with a quote from Hume, who was sort of a madman about predictiveness. And in the course of his book, Dickinson tells us that that is what learning is all about. Learning is really exhausted by discoveries of the sort where event one predicts event two. What the mind is full of, Dickinson assures us, is just that kind of predictive relationship. It is as if predictiveness is the only kind of associative process that exists, or at least the only kind that matters. However, even within associationism there are kinds of stimuli to be stuck together besides those that Hume was carried away with, where one thing leads to another. Thus there is John Locke's need to tie up all the primary and secondary qualities of perception into a unified percept, putting together a unified percept. One of the things I was relatively happy to see in Rescorla's presentation was his account of associative processes occurring *within* a stimulus compound, holding the compound together, as it were, in a Lockean way. (See chapter 3.)

We might suppose that the same sort of processes that lead to anticipation, or predictiveness (which we do not understand), are also involved in the Lockean kind of perceptual integration. We would like to believe in common principles; we would like to think that all of the paraphernalia of the modern experimentalists prevail in both realms, in both the Hume-type and the Locke-type of associationism. I think that is an important question, if we really are committed to being associationists, but an even more important question, I believe, is the question of whether or not other kinds of things can be learned. In human learning we have, for example, the famous story of the rock that rolled down the hill and crashed into the cabin. The exciting thing about that story, I think, is that if you ask subjects any kind of weird question about the incident, they can provide answers. You can ask them how big the rock was. You can ask them how much did the cabin cost. You can ask them how much noise did it make when the cabin collapsed, and they have answers, or they have a surprisingly good consensus about answers, to all of these weird questions—none of which was conveyed in the original stimulus material. And so you have the idea that humans learn propositions, they learn declarative stuff, they learn a logic. They learn to fit new stuff together with their general view of the universe. But animals, on the other hand, are alleged to simply hook one stimulus up with another, S_1 is associated with S_2. That's the only thing that animals can learn; it is the only thing they understand; it is the only thing that matters in the control of their behavior, we are told. And that is sheer nonsense.

We know, for example, that animals can learn about space. They can put pieces of space together, into a map. I was a little disappointed in David Olton's chapter because I was hoping he was going to talk about radial mazes, and he did not. So, let me tell you about Olton's discoveries with radial mazes (Olton, 1978). You put the rat in a maze that has a central hub and eight arms that radiate off in eight different directions. You put a little food out at the end of each arm, and you sit there quietly and leisurely with your stopwatch and your clipboard, and you record what the animal does. If you ask the simple minded question how many trips out from the central hub into the different arms does the animal have to make before it collects all eight pieces of food, the answer is about eight and a half. The rat makes very few errors, where an error is counted as repeating a run to an arm where it has already been. There is now enough data with this apparatus to tell us that what the animal is doing is putting together information about where the different arms are, and where it has recently been. But how does the associationist deal with the extraordinary ability of the rat to solve this problem? What would Hume have to say about the rat's proficiency? Or, for that matter, what would Locke have to say about how spatial information is integrated. Not very much; I suspect the methodologist really has nothing at all to say. He would simply vary the time interval, the number of arms, the richness of extra maze cues; he would grind out a number of experiments which in total would tell us what we already know, viz., that the rat is extraordinarily good at solving these kinds of spatial problems. The rat is a spatial integrator. It builds maps. It is extraordinarily good at remembering where it is, and where it has been. But how is that done? What is the process? It obviously is not simply an associative process. It is not a matter of one stimulus predicting another anymore than it is simple predictive relationship that underlies the learning of conditioned taste aversions. The methodologists would have you believe that, but we cannot believe it. The argument is absurd when it comes to rats learning either about bad foods or about a radial maze. Even when it comes to pigeons remembering what the last color was, the associationist really has nothing to say (Roitblat, 1982).

NONASSOCIATIONISTIC APPROACH

But there are nonassociationistic ways to approach radial maze behavior. One way to do it has been suggested by Staddon (1983). In Staddon's view, there are really three kinds of learning going on. One is that the animal has to learn a place code. Each of the eight arms is represented by a place code that the human spatialist would encode as north, north-east, and so on. The evidence indicates that this learning, the learning of places and where they are in space, occurs very rapidly and is really trivially simple for the rat. They are better at it than we are. The only thing we know in the learning literature that is comparable is the verbal labeling of humans; this is an ''a'' and that is a ''b''. We understand that, and we are extraordinarily good at learning that sort of thing. We will complicate problems enormously in order to stick verbal labels onto the material we learn. The rat will complicate problems enormously in order to be able to place spatial tags on different items. And that is because rats are extraordinarily good at learning about places.

The second thing that the animal has to learn, according to Staddon, is where it has been. That is where short-term memory is involved. The place code is in long-term memory because the maze does not change from day to day. What does change over time, and what causes confusion and occasional error is the animal having to remember where it has has been recently. Staddon's idea is that there is a memory trace for each place that it has visited recently. And what the animal must do in responding, is go toward places where the memory trace is weakest. If it has been, say, northeast in the last several minutes, then it does not go there again; it goes somewhere else. All the animal has to remember is that it has been there recently. What one gets, then, is a picture of a bunch of decaying traces, rememberance of places past, and the animal has the task of remembering which are the weakest traces. Staddon does not tell us how that weak trace is represented in memory, but no matter. From the formal analysis, that is what it looks like.

The animal also has a third thing to learn. It remembers where all the places are, it remembers perhaps where it has been last, maybe not in detail, but over the last several trials and then it also must have a response rule. It must remember *not* to go where it has been recently. That is to say, it must go places that have weak memory traces rather than those that have strong memory traces. Thus, Staddon has broken the radial maze problem up into a tripartite scheme, place code learning, the memory task of remembering where one has been, and then learning the appropriate rule. But the response rule is easy because the rat has a strong initial bias for a win-shift strategy. The place code learning is also very easy because the rat is such a great map builder. So, whatever errors it makes are attributable to confusion about the memory traces of where it has been recently. This is a nice neat analysis. One thing I find particularly nice about it is that it is not associative. In no way does Staddon's analysis look like a Locke type or a Hume type analysis of stimuli occurring together becoming linked associatively.

So much for the contents of short-term memory. I really cannot say much about what is in memory, that is, what representations look like, because we really do not understand about place codes, and where-the-animal-has-been codes, and response rules. We have never thought in those terms. And the reason we have never thought in those terms is that we have bought into an associatonistic and methodological paradigm where those kinds of analysis are not valid. All we really know how to talk about is how a CS calls up the memory of a US. We have no language and no concepts for dealing with what is actually happening in working memory.

Let us think for a moment in very general terms about the kinds of psychological theories that can be used to explain animal behavior. If one is an associationist then one is inclined to have a theory with very simple hypotheses. The internal working of the theory, more precisely, its syntactical rules, are most likely to be very simple. Rescorla has provided us with a nice illustration of this meta-principle: if one stimulus provides information about the occurrence of another stimulus, then the two will become associated. And we are asked to believe that that is the only essential psychological process, the only syntactical rule, that applies to learning. All the complexity of behavior is to be attributed to semantic difficulties such as defining the stimulus and extracting the response. That is where the difficulty and the unpredictability of behavior lies.

The issue is a very old and familiar one in behavior theory. We saw it in the great debate that occurred in the 1930s between Hull and Tolman. Hull was the associationist. He believed that the basic syntactical principle was that the response gets hooked up to the stimulus through reinforcement, which was a simple enough idea. All the difficulty in predicting behavior in a learning experiment resided in the fact that one could not be entirely sure what the stimulus was, and one could not be completely sure how to measure the response. The uncertainty was entirely semantic; the syntax was easy. On the other hand, Tolman's theory was semantically simple, almost trivial. If the animal pays attention to a stimulus that has meaning, it will respond to it. That is pretty simple; no trouble defining the stimulus. If the animal wants a particular outcome, it will approach that particular goal. Again, we see semantic simplicity, no problem defining the response. The complexity in Tolman's system was syntactical because Tolman's rats were reading maps, they were taking detours, they were learning where things were. So for Tolman, the internal psychological processes were very complex. For Hull, as for all associationists, the process was simple; this gets hooked up to that. And we know all about associationistic principles. It is easy to talk the associationist's language—even though it is not much fun because he rarely has anything very interesting to say. But it is not so easy to refer to complex syntactical terms. It is hard reading maps. We do not know how to talk about it.

It has been said that there really is no alternative to the associationistic position. But that is clearly nonsense. There are abundant alternatives. One of the fascinating things is that all of the alternatives invite us to look at and to speculate about psychological processes. John Staddon's analysis of what is happening in the radial maze is just one illustration. Animals, he says, are learning place codes and they are remembering where they have been, and they are learning response rules. There, right off the bat, you have three alternatives to the traditional associative analysis. How exciting that is! Suddenly we see syntactical complexity. Everyone is free to speculate about how rats read maps. And that is the kind of thing I am pleading for. Let us have some speculation about complex syntactical rules (e.g., Roitblat, 1982). We know that it is not just a matter of associative connections, and we know, or we should know, that is not just a matter of the animal remembering some biologically important stimulus that is impending. Let us defy that ancient curse. Let us stand up, shake our fist at that angry god, whoever he was, and let us start speculating about the psychological processes that operate in short-term memory and attention experiments. Let us start thinking about the syntax of the animal mind.

REFERENCES

Bolles, R. C. (1985). The slaying of Goliath: What happened to reinforcement theory. In T. D. Johnston & A. T. Peitrewictz (Eds.), *The ecological study of learning*. Hillsdale, NJ: Lawrence Erlbaum Associates.

Dickinson, A. (1980). *Contemporary animal learning theory*. Cambridge, Eng.: Cambridge University Press.

Olton, D. S. (1978). Characteristics of spatial memory. In S. H. Hulse, H. Fowler, & W. K. Honig (Eds.), *Cognative processes in animal behavior.* Hillsdale, NJ: Lawrence Erlbaum Associates.

Roberts, W. A., & Grant, D. S. (1978). Interaction of sample and comparison stimuli in delayed matching to sample in the pigeon. *Journal of Experimental Psychology: Animal Behavior Process, 4,* 468–482.

Roitblat, H. L. (1982). The meaning of representation in animal memory. *The Behavioral and Brain Sciences, 5,* 353–406.

Staddon, J. E. R. (1983). *Adaptive behavior and learning.* Cambridge, Eng.: Cambridge University Press.

Zinchenko, P. I. (1983). The problem of involuntary memory. *Soviet Psychology, 22,* 55–111.

V

CONNECTING MODELS

Lars-Göran Nilsson
Trevor Archer

A very basic question to be asked when attempting to integrate animal learning and human memory research is of course what we should look for when we seek commonalities. As discussed under the first topic about basic theoretical concepts one possibility is to look for commonalities in the concepts used within each of the two fields. However, as argued during the working conference after the presentations of each contribution this is a fairly passive form of integration in the sense that concepts have evolved separately within each field and those concepts which happen to be the same in the two areas may still have slightly different connotations for the animal learning and human memory researchers. The association is one such concept which may reveal similarities at one level, but which on the other hand also may conjure up quite different outlooks in the two areas. For example, it was argued in these discussions during the working part of the conference that it would be less meaningful to study whether associations as used in the animal learning area carry over to human memory. More meaningful, it was claimed, would be to see whether explicit models carry over. The model presented in the Dickinson and Shanks chapter may constitute a promising beginning in this direction and the Rescorla model on the Kamin blocking effect may be another example of this sort. The Estes conditioning model as dis-

147

cussed in our introductory chapter may be still another example of the same type and our own research of the role of context in taste-aversion learning provides another possible approach towards an integration which goes beyond the commonalities at solely a conceptual level. Another useful model consists of a reference memory and a working memory: Reference memory consisting of memory representations that are resistent to disruption whereas working memory incorporated the recently presented representations and is more easily disrupted (e.g., Honig, 1978; Olton, Becker, & Handelmann, 1980). Working memory seems to relate rather more directly to our notions of retrieval.

The theme of connecting models receives substantial elaboration in the chapter by Estes. The validity of assumptions, the usage of hypothetical constructs and intervening variables and the synthesis of a theoretical model applicable to human and subhuman species ought to be carefully attended. However, the pitfalls inherent to unrestricted parallel-seeking and concept-sharing between these two areas are implicitly and explicitly handled. The chapter by Dickinson and Shanks applies quite a different tactic. The authors used the conditioning phenomena from the field of animal learning to conceptualize a specific human learning and memory task. Previous applications of the human causality judgments procedure having proven their utility (Allan & Jenkins, 1983), Dickinson and Shanks show an ingenuous approach to realizing the generality between human and animal learning and memory. What is the relevance for the discussion on connecting models? Two points can be readily made: (a) Certain empirical questions seem to require development from an animal conditioning tradition. (b) The backward blocking effect observed in their result ought to prompt a search for similar effects in traditional animal conditioning experiments. Another, rather surprising, potential offered by the Dickinson and Shanks studies is that we are presented with a novel insight into the recurring and fundamental problem of how learning and memory processes are correlated to the measure of performance (cf. Rescorla & Holland, 1982).

Finally, some neuropsychological treatment of the topic of connecting models ought to be attempted. To date the vast collection of investigations pertaining to the neurophysiology, neuropharmacology, and neuropathology of learning and memory may allow some tentative speculations of the structural and chemical correlates of three hypothesized requirements for a successful act of remembering: attention, accumulation, and accessibility. Cortex-Hippocampal involvement in the attentional requirement seems clear whereas accumulation and accessibility may be localized to Hippocampal-Fornix-limbic areas. Neuropharmacological data seem to provide better scope for such speculation. Despite certain reservations, the putative neurotransmitter noradrenaline seems implicated in attentional processes regulating successful conditioning and performance (Archer, 1982a; Archer, Mohammed, & Järbe, 1983; Mason, 1981). A case for dopaminergic pathways in the accumulation of information could be argued. Since the accessibility requirement seems essential for successful retrieval much evidence seems to argue for the involvement of serotonergic (e.g., Archer, 1982b) and cholinergic (e.g., Walsh, Tilson, DeHaven, Mailman, Fisher, & Hanin, in press; Wirsching, Beninger, Thamandas, Boegman, & El-Defrawy, 1984) pathways. Recent evidence concerning cholinergic involvement in diseases leading to cognitive dysfunction in the aged (Winblad, Hardy, Bäckman, & Nilsson, 1985) are reinforced by the retrieval-accessibility deficits obtained. The quest for connecting models along these lines must eventually bring us to the issue of whether a symmetrical process underlies the outcomes of memory: remembering and forgetting.

REFERENCES

Allan, L.-G., & Jenkins, H. M. (1983). The effect of representations of binary variables on judgment of influence. *Learning and Motivation, 14*, 381–405.

Archer, T. (1982a). DSP4-(N-2-chloroethyl-N-ethyl-2-bromobenzylamine), a new noradrenaline neurotoxin, and the stimulus conditions effecting acquisition of two-way active avoidance. *Journal of Comparative and Physiological Psychology, 96*, 476–490.

Archer, T. (1982b). Serotonin and fear retention in the rat. *Journal of Comparative and Physiological Psychology, 96*, 491–516.

Archer, T., Mohammed, A. K., & Järbe, T. U. C. (1983). Latent inhibition following systemic DSP4: Effects due to presence and absence of contextual cues in taste-aversion learning. *Behavoral and Neural Biology, 38*, 287–306.

Honig, W. K. (1978). Studies on working memory in the pigeon. In S. H. Hulse, H. Fowler, & W. K. Honig (Eds.), *Cognitive processes in animal behavior* (pp. 221–248). Hillsdale, NJ: Lawrence Erlbaum Associates.

Mason, S. T. (1981). Noradrenaline in the brain: Progress in theories of behavioral function. *Progress in Neurobiology, 16*, 263–303.

Olton, D. S., Becker, J. T., & Handelmann, G. E. (1980). Hippocampal function: Working memory or cognitive mapping? *Physiological Psychology, 8*, 239–246.

Rescorla, R. A., & Holland, P. C. (1982). Behavioral studies of associative learning in animals. *Annual Review of Psychology, 33*, 265–308.

Walsh, T. J., Tilson, H. A., DeHaven, D. L., Mailman, R. B., Fisher, A., & Hanin, I. (in press). AF64A, a cholinergic neurotoxin, selectively depletes acetylcholine in hippocampus and cortex, and produces long-term passive avoidance and radial-arm maze deficits in the rat. *Brain Research*.

Winblad, B., Hardy, J., Bäckman, L., & Nilsson, L.-G. (1985). Memory function and brain chemistry in normal aging and in senile dementia. In D. Olton, S. Corkin, & E. Gamzu (Eds.), *Memory dysfunctions: An integration of animal and human research from preclinicial and clinical perspectives*. New York: New York Academy of Sciences.

Wirsching, B. A., Beninger, R. J., Thamandas, K., Boegman, R. J., & El-Defrawy, S. R. (1984). Differential effects of scopolamine on working and reference memory of rats in the radial maze. *Pharmacology, Biochemistry & Behavior, 20*, 659–662.

8

Some Common Aspects of Models for Learning and Memory in Lower Animals and Man

W. K. Estes
Harvard University

Why should we be interested in seeking connections between theories of animal and human learning? Perhaps the most commonly recognized source of motivation has to do with the common long-term goal of contributing to the understanding of brain, behavior, and cognition in human beings and thus to the solution of human problems. To the degree that we are guided by this purpose, we do research on animals that we would like to do but cannot do on human beings. The most conspicuous varieties have to do with attempts to unravel neural and biochemical bases of behavior and cognition. But at the strictly behavioral and cognitive levels we often turn to research on animals for similar reasons. We would like to understand how people adjust or fail to adjust to severe stress or trauma and how they learn when learning is instigated by truly important motives or when it extends over very long periods of time. In all such cases, we use animals as subjects, but such research is pointless unless we have some basis for making inferences from the results of animal research to processes of primary interest to human beings. Hence the need to develop a broad enough theoretical framework to permit the identification of significant correspondences between processes or mechanisms at the different phylogenetic levels.

It should be noted further that the payoffs are not all one way. Though we normally design investigations of animal learning in relation to the kinds of activities that engage animals in their ordinary environments, successive generations of animals often face drastically changing environments, just as do successive generations of human beings. We would like to understand the capabilities of animals for adjusting to circumstances that pose new problems, different from those that the same species have had to solve in the past. Thus, a recurring motif in animal research, and one that appears to yield increasingly interesting results, is that of confronting animals with tasks drawn from research on people and testing the limits to which the animal can approximate the problem solving or communicative accomplishments of human subjects. However, this kind of research, like the kind concerned with inferences from animal to human, is unlikely to yield important insights if guided only by superficial analogies between human and animal behaviors.

A framework for conducting and interpreting all of the varieties of research that entail inferences across phylogenetic levels is provided by information processing theory. Within the general theory of symbol-manipulating systems that is basic to much current research on artificial and natural intelligence, one can define the information processing requirements of tasks and the kinds of computations that must be carried out for problem solution regardless of the characteristics of the organism or machine engaged in the task (Marr, 1982; Newell & Simon, 1976). Ascertaining the degree to which different organisms or machines manifest the same capabilities for symbol manipulation and accomplish tasks by virtue of equivalent information processes does not in itself answer questions about underlying algorithms or mechanisms, but it can help the search for answers.

Rather than discuss this general strategy further at an abstract level, I propose in the remainder of this chapter to present a few illustrations from research that have in fact been carried out on animals and human beings within a common general information processing framework and point out some of the instances in which these specific theoretical models or mechanisms adduced to interpret information processing by either animals or people do appear to exhibit some approximation to isomorphism across animal, human, and even artificial information processors.

THE PROBLEM OF "CONNECTING MODELS"

Looking for correspondences between human beings and animals with regard to learning or memory is a special case of the general problem of establishing isomorphisms between systems. Roughly speaking, two systems are said to be isomorphic if they work in the same way so one can make predictions about one from knowledge of the other. A bit more formally, the two systems must have elements that can be set in correspondence in such a way that all relations among elements of one system are mirrored in the other and that, given the same starting points, they will run through the same sequence of states (see for example, Haugeland, 1981).

In science, as distinguished from mathematics and logic, isomorphisms are usually demonstrable only within limits and to some degree of approximation, as in the iron wire analogy of the nerve fiber or the use of model airplanes and wind tunnels to study the probable effects of turbulence on real airplanes in the atmosphere, but, as in these examples, even approximate isomorphisms often prove significant.

In the effort to relate human to animal learning, one surely does not expect to find extensive isomorphisms, but nonetheless being clear on the nature of the problem can help us avoid fruitless efforts. One can see, for example, that there is no point in asking whether a single concept (association, encoding, awareness, . . .) applies in both domains because the answer would make no difference as to what can be predicted in either. One can, however, meaningfully inquire as to whether models (that is, interrelated clusters of concepts) carry over from one domain to another.

How might theoretical connections between human and animal learning be achieved? Several possibilities suggest themselves.

1. Evolutionary theory might supply the framework for an orderly sequence of theoretical models of learning for animals at different phylogenetic levels, up to and including man. This goal is especially attractive to investigators who seek a biologically based theory of learning (e.g., Gould & Marler, 1984; Schneirla, 1959; Shettleworth, 1984). However, the hope of an orderly progression does not seem to be borne out. Rather, phenotypically similar forms of learning are accomplished by quite different mechanisms in different animal forms and sometimes quite sophisticated processes of learning appear in animals that are otherwise phylogenetically more primitive than some animals who lack them (Marler & Terrace, 1984).

2. Integration might be achieved by means of a deductive theory, axioms being established by research on animals and the deduction of theorems being adjusted to the animal and human cases in the light of environmental settings and species differences. Hull's programmatic behavior theory (1943) is a prime example. This goal was once taken up by many investigators with much enthusiasm, but the enthusiasm has waned as research results bearing on biological constraints on learning make Hull's vision seem increasingly unrealistic (Hinde, 1973; Shettleworth, 1972).

3. A more attainable goal than any form of comprehensive theory may be an organized collection of models for specific processes or mechanisms that may be common to theories for different empirical domains or phylogenetic levels. Though there must be varying degrees of similarity between animal and man in the anatomical, zoological, and biochemical bases, the hope is that, as in such disciplines as genetics and immunology, correspondences will prove close enough in some cases so that mechanisms of human learning can be illuminated by research on animals. This goal and strategy provide a justification for laboratory-based experimental approaches to learning, in contrast to the strong reliance on observations of learning in natural settings emphasized by some investigators. A principal objective of doing similar experiments on animals and human beings is to obtain detailed pictures of empirical functions, generally in quantitative form, which can provide evidence for common mechanisms where they exist and

lead to common physiological or biochemical explanations. Progress in this line has been achieved in some domains, for example, opponent-color systems and spatial-frequency analysis in vision. Thus there is some ground for hope that the strategy may pay off also in the study of learning and memory.

To offer more than hope, we need to adduce evidence of progress toward the development of models that can claim some credibility for the role of connecting links across varieties and levels of learning. I think that a case can be made for several candidate models, among them, associative networks with hierarchical organization and spreading activation, multidimensional memory representations, sampling variability and fluctuation in availability of units, probabilistic models to relate memory to choice, and discriminability/criterion models for detection and recognition (Green & Swets, 1966; Luce, 1963). In the remainder of this paper, I adopt a case-history approach, illustrating the potentialities of such models for connecting animal and human learning theory in terms of some current research efforts.

CATEGORY LEARNING

I would like to set the stage for further discussion of "Connecting Models" with a resumé of a current line of theory that is anchored in both animal and human research. The general paradigm is multidimensional classification learning, commonly studied with animals under the designation discrimination learning, and in human beings under the designation concept or category learning. A special virtue for our purposes is that the work of Medin (Medin, 1975; Medin & Schaffer, 1978) has generated closely related models for both the animal and human cases, thus providing convenient materials for examining some of the models or processes that play a role in connecting the two otherwise quite distinct domains.

In the class of animal studies considered by Medin (1975) a typical problem is to present the animal with two stimulus cards, perhaps one displaying a large black circle and the other a small white circle, and to reward a response to the large black circle (Fig. 8.1). Over a series of trials, the sizes of the cards are varied randomly and reward is consistently given for choice of the black card regardless of size. If, then, on a test trial the animal were presented with, say, a black and a white triangle, the most likely result would be choice of the black triangle, a result which would be taken to signify that what the animal had learned had at least some properties in common with what would be termed concept or category learning in human beings.

In a model proposed to interpret this form of learning, Medin assumed that, on any trial, information concerning the stimuli presented and their context is stored in memory with some probability and that the retrievability of the information on subsequent tests is reduced by changes in either stimulus or context from

	Sample Discrimination Problem	
	Reward Condition	
Trial	+	−
1	large black circle	small white circle
2	small black circle	large white circle
.		
.		
.		
test	small black triangle	small white triangle

FIG. 8.1. An illustrative sequence of trials for a discrimination learning problem. On each trial the indicated pair of stimuli is presented and the one under the plus sign is rewarded.

the original conditions. But even when test stimuli are not identical to those used during training, as in the example above, the animal would tend to choose correctly by selecting the stimulus that was more similar to one for which choice had been rewarded during previous training.

If the same training sequence were given to a normal human subject, we would expect rapid learning of a rule to the effect that "the rewarded category contains black objects," and thus might be led to a hypothesis-testing model quite different in form from the model for animal discrimination learning (see, for example, Levine, 1975; Trabasso & Bower, 1968). However, in the recent literature on human category learning, we have seen much emphasis on the fact that in ordinary life categories often resist definition by simple, verbalizable rules (Rosch, 1975; Smith & Medin, 1981). Thus we need models that can account for learning of "fuzzy categories," as, for example, games, furniture, weeds, as well as rule-defined categories.

The Exemplar Model

The way of meeting this need proposed by Medin and Schaffer (1978) was a model in which the learning process is assumed to be basically identical to that of the discrimination model. That is, on any trial, the subject is conceived to store in memory a representation of the exemplar of a category presented for observation, the representation taking the form of the values of the exemplar on a set of relevant dimensions or attributes. These representations are grouped in memory together with their category labels and on subsequent tests an individual is conceived to assess the similarity of the test exemplar to the clusters stored in memory and assign the exemplar to the category to whose stored representations it is on the average more similar. For example, in an experiment described by Medin and Schaffer (1978), subjects had the task of classifying stimuli by combinations of values on four binary valued dimensions—triangle versus circular form, red versus green color, large versus small size, and left versus right position in the display. If, say, a subject had been presented with a large, red triangle on the left and informed that it belonged to category A and a small green circle on the right with the designation category B, then if a small red triangle on the left were presented on a test, the subject would be likely to assign it to category A since it is more similar to the previously experienced A exemplar than the previously experienced B exemplar (Fig. 8.2). In a series of experiments with artificially contrived fuzzy categories, Medin and his associates have shown that the model accounts quite well for numerous properties of human category learning, including, for example, predicting particular exemplar patterns that should be especially easy or especially difficult for the learner. Recent work of Nosofsky (1984) shows that the model can account equally well for learning of rule-defined and fuzzy categories.

The exemplar model of Medin and Shaffer, and its extension by Nosofsky, is of special interest for this study in that, although the model as a whole was formulated to account primarily for category learning, it is in essentials a combination of two submodels both of which are of much greater generality. One of these is the conception of memory as a record of the attribute or feature values of a remembered item or event, first developed formally by Bower (1967) and applied widely in the human memory literature but also prominent in recent approaches to animal memory, for example, Spear (1976). The other component is the model for relating a state of memory to observable choice behavior. This component of the theory derives from the choice model of Luce (1963) and, as

Category of Exemplar	Dimension			
	Form	*Color*	*Size*	*Position*
A	Triangle	Red	Large	Left
B	Circle	Green	Small	Right
?	Triangle	Red	Small	Left

FIG. 8.2. An illustrative sequence of trials for a multidimensional classification problem. On the first trial the category of the exemplar, which is a large, red triangle on the left, is A, on the next trial the category of the exemplar is B, and the third trial is a test on which the subject must attempt to categorize the exemplar.

applied to the categorization problem, embodies the assumption that the probability that an individual will categorize a particular test exemplar i in category X is equal to the sum of the similarities, $s_{i,x}$ of the test exemplar to all of the remembered exemplars in category X divided by the sum of the similarities of the test exemplar to the members of category X and the members of alternative categories.

$$P(X/i) = \frac{s_{i,x}}{s_{i,x} + s_{i,\bar{x}}}$$

Formally, the choice model was originally presented by Luce as an abstract theory, but it has had applications to animal learning (Bush, Galanter, & Luce, 1959), psychophysics (Luce, 1963), and human memory (Estes, 1982a; Nosofsky, 1984).

The Problem of an Experimental Baseline for Assessing Models

The kinds of experiments that have been conducted hitherto to evaluate exemplar and related models have some rather severe limitations for purposes of analyzing the learning process. One of these limitations is that typically categories to be learned have not been generated in a systematic fashion that would enable the presentation of relatively large numbers of exemplars with objective and unambiguous criteria for category assignment even in the case of fuzzy categories. Another problem is that usually the categories and their exemplars have been so constructed that the features or attitudes differ both in perceptual salience and in validity as indicators of category membership. Consequently, the learning of categorization must typically involve processes of selective attention and the like in addition to processes more specific to category learning. This point is of special importance in that essentially the entire basis for category learning in the exemplar model is the development of selective attention to the most valid or diagnostic attributes of a class of exemplars. One might think that the sheer accumulation of exemplar information would be an important factor. Analysis of the exemplar model shows, however, that once a single exemplar of each category in a task has been stored in memory, the accumulation of additional exemplar representations modifies the variance of categorization performance but has almost no effect on mean accuracy.[1] Nonetheless, we would surely expect people to be able to learn categorization in situations where features or attributes of category exemplars are all of equal validity. If so, would we have to bring in

---

[1] It is assumed that exemplars are presented to a learner in a random sequence, as is virtually always done in experimental studies.

some new learning principle, which might be basically different for human and animal learners?

In order to be able to explore this problem further, I contrived an experimental situation in which exemplars of categories are defined by combinations of features that are equally valid indicators of the categories and at least very nearly equal in perceptual salience.

In my experiments, categories are defined, neither by rules that could be accessible to the subjects nor by arbitrary assignments, as in the Medin studies, but rather by probability distributions over sets of features. In the particular experiments I discuss, exemplars of categories are defined by values on eight binary-valued features. The task is presented to the subjects as a simulation of the problem of a diagnostician learning to diagnose diseases on the basis of symptom patterns, with exemplars representing the charts of hypothetical patients; the features, symptoms that might be used in diagnoses; and the categories, alternative diseases. In order to equate perceptual salience and validity across features, the displays presented to the subjects took the form of bar diagrams, with eight slots representing possible symptoms and bars extending above or below a horizontal base line denoting high or low values of particular symptoms. The bars were all of the same height and all features were equally valid indicators of category membership. A typical chart is shown in Fig. 8.3, and would be interpreted as indicating that the hypothetical patient had high values on symptoms 1, 2, 4, 5, and 8, and low values on the others. After viewing the chart and attempting to categorize it, the subject would be told that the hypothetical patient actually belonged to the disease category A. The experimenter's rule for generating the sequence of displays was that a subset of four randomly selected symp-

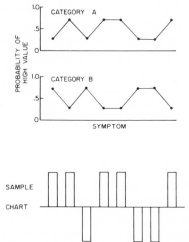

FIG. 8.3.   At the bottom is a sample chart as the subject would see it in the category learning experiment described in the text. The letters below the graph are the initials of a hypothetical patient who displays the indicated symptom pattern. The graphs above show the probabilities of high values (upward extending bars) and low values (downward extending bars) for each symptom associated with each of the two categories.

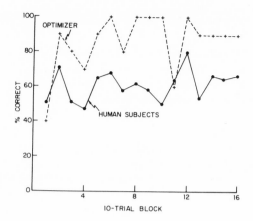

FIG. 8.4. Category learning function for human subjects in terms of percentage of correct categorizations per ten-trial block. The dashed line above shows the progress of learning the same sequence of charts by the Optimizer learning program.

toms had relatively high probabilities (.725) of having high values on trials when category A was the correct diagnosis and the other four symptoms the same probabilities on trials when B was the correct diagnosis. Thus, just as in actual diseases, individual symptoms were imperfect indicators of the disease categories. However, a learner who acquired full information about the probabilities of each of the features relative to each of the categories would in principle be able to generate diagnoses with high probability of being correct (approximately .90 in this study).

As may be seen in Fig. 8.4, a plot of proportion of correct diagnoses per ten-trial block for a group of subjects, progress was highly uneven over the sequence of trials but did lead to performance significantly greater than chance, even though below that achievable if all of the available information were acquired and used optimally. Some questions we would like to be able to answer are precisely what information was acquired by the learners, how it was encoded in memory, and how it was retrieved and used to generate decisions.

Progress toward a Model for the Learning Process

One of the strategies I tried in order to make a start toward answering these questions was to construct an optimal learner in the form of a computer program that could learn the categorizations and reach an optimal level of performance. I wanted to be able to compare the performance of the human subjects with that of the optimal learner and then try to determine just what aspects of the optimal learner would have to be modified and how in order to bring its performance closer to that of the human subjects. The program, which I will call Optimizer, was written in the LISP programming language and represents a version of what have been termed feature-validity models in the literature (Reed, 1973; Smith & Medin, 1981).

Optimizer's memory consists of a set of registers in which the outcomes of individual learning trials are tallied so as to yield, over a series of trials, cumulative counts of the frequencies with which each symptom occurred in conjunction with each category. In order to make decisions when presented with test exemplars, Optimizer converts its memory for symptom frequencies into probability estimates, computes the likelihood that a given exemplar would occur in either of the two categories A or B, and then assigns the exemplar to the category for which this likelihood is the higher. As may be seen in Fig. 8.4, Optimizer learns very rapidly and reaches a level of performance much higher than that of the human subjects.

However, the similarities between Optimizer's performance and that of the human subjects proved more interesting than the differences. In the experiment, all subjects received the same sequence of exemplars, and consequently the ups and downs of the learning function may be expected to reveal points of ease and difficulty in the trial sequence. Thus, it is interesting to note that the ups and downs of the learning functions for the human subjects and for Optimizer proved to be highly correlated even though the levels of performance reached are quite different.

If the similarity of patterns were due to some basic commonality in the learning process, then what might be the source of the large difference in performance level reached? One of the first possibilities that comes to mind is the strategy used by the individual to go from a state of knowledge concerning category probabilities to a decision on any individual test trial. Optimizer always makes the optimal decision, but it is easy to modify her strategy so that, instead, she computes the probability that a test pattern belongs to a category, then makes the choice of category with that probability (as in statistical learning models that predict probability matching [Estes, 1959, 1982a]). With this modification, the final level reached by the model, which we rename Categorizer-0, is brought down closer to the level of the human learner (Fig. 8.5), but she still learns too fast.

Here an obvious possibility is that Categorizer's memory is simply too good. On each trial Categorizer records all the information in the input and remembers all of it. The next step, then, was to weaken Categorizer's memory by allowing for the possibility that the learner may not attend to and encode in memory every feature displayed on a trial. Rather than modify the memory system in some arbitrary way chosen only to produce the desired effect, we take the course of generalizing the original, deterministic model by incorporating the sampling process of statistical learning theory.

The notion of element sampling was originally introduced into learning theory in relation to conditioning, to allow for the variability in learning and performance that must result from random changes in an animal's environment and internal state from moment to moment or trial to trial (Estes, 1950). The speed of learning in any situation is constrained by the extent to which the population of

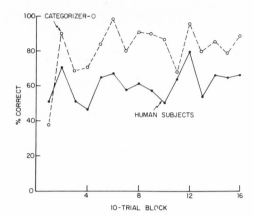

FIG. 8.5. The same learning function for human subjects shown in Fig. 8.4 is here compared with the performance of the computer model Categorizer-0.

stimulus aspects is sampled on any one occasion. Also, fluctuations over time in the availability of aspects for sampling influence both the rate of learning and the likelihood that learned responses will be evoked when the situation present on a learning trial recurs on a test for retention. Although initially the concepts of sampling and fluctuation were defined only in relation to stimulus properties or components, it later became clear that they should apply generally to units at all levels of the perceptual and memory systems (Bower, 1967, 1972; Estes, 1982b; Murdock, 1974). Currently, one finds formally identical models for sampling and fluctuations of availability of units entering into a variety of theories both for animal learning and for human memory.

With this modification and with an appropriate choice of the sampling probability, we arrive at a new, and more realistically endowed, entry in our sequence of models, displayed in Fig. 8.6 as Categorizer 1. Her memory system comprises two sets of registers, or bins, the rows corresponding to categories A and B and the columns to the symptoms on a patient's chart. Each bin contains a set of memory elements, each of which can be set to a high or a low value, corresponding to the value of the symptom. On each learning trial, each perceived symptom value on the chart presented has some probability of setting an element in the corresponding bin to its value. The computational mechanism takes the proportion of high- and low-valued elements in the bins as likelihood estimates and, when a particular chart i is presented for categorization, computes the probability of category A given the observed symptom pattern by the formula at the bottom of Fig. 8.6.

When Categorizer-1 is given the sequence of charts actually shown to the human subjects in our experiment as input, we obtain the simulated learning function shown in Fig. 8.7 along with the learning function for the human subjects. It may be seen that the correspondence between theoretical and observed functions is now surprisingly close.

CATEGORIZER 1

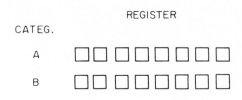

REGISTER

CATEG.

A   ☐☐ ☐☐ ☐ ☐☐ ☐

B   ☐☐ ☐☐ ☐ ☐☐ ☐

CHART i

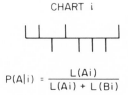

$$P(A|i) = \frac{L(Ai)}{L(Ai) + L(Bi)}$$

FIG. 8.6. Schematic summary of the memory system and response rule for Categorizer-1. For details see text.

But we have a new theoretical problem. Categorizer-1 is composed of processes, or submodels, that are quite general in that they have entered into many different theories of both animal and human learning, as is the case for the exemplar model of Medin and Shaffer. Also, Categorizer-1 and the exemplar model both show encouraging ability to describe human category learning. However, Categorizer-1 and the exemplar model are composed in part of different constituent processes. Both record input information in the form of a memory representation organized in terms of attributes, or feature values, but the retrieval processes are quite different. In the exemplar model the learner is presumed on a test trial to retrieve memories of individual previously experienced exemplars and compare these representations with the test stimulus, whereas Categorizer-1

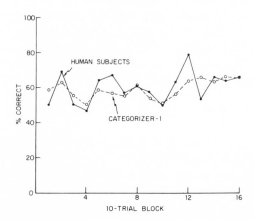

FIG. 8.7. Categorization learning function for human subjects compared with the learning of the computer model Categorizer-1.

retrieves only a computed probability that each feature of a test pattern would occur in an exemplar belonging to any given category. If human learners are built on the lines of Categorizer-1, then they do not have access to the memories of individual exemplars, only statistics of the whole collection of previously observed exemplars, whereas if they are built on the lines of the exemplar model they have access to memories of individual exemplars but not to relative frequency information about individual features. Finding ways of determining which approach comes closer to representing how human subjects actually learn fuzzy categories is a top priority activity in my current research, but pursuing it would take us outside the scope of this paper.

REFLECTIONS AND CONNECTIONS

In summary, we have seen that a number of aspects of classification behavior and learning relative to fuzzy categories can be shown to be accounted for quite well by models that go beyond sheer description and link category learning with other phenomena of learning and memory.

In the class of models we have illustrated, information perceived about individual category exemplars on learning trials is stored in memory in the form of a vector or list of attribute values. Then, decisions about categorization of new exemplars are based on mental computations of the relationships between these and the ensemble stored in memory. Within this class of models one subvariety, the exemplar model, is based on the idea that categorization is achieved by judgments of the global similarity of test exemplars to memory representations, whereas in the other main subvariety, cue validity models, categorization is based on computation of the likelihood of the category given remembered information about features of the test exemplar.

What is of special interest here is that the principal constituents, both general and specific, of these models have not been constructed ad hoc to account for particular kinds of data, but rather have been carried over as submodels or modules from other theories, some of which were originally developed in relation to animal learning, some in relation to human learning and memory.

I do not mean to imply that, given the same perceptual inputs, lower animals than man form memory representations that are the same or even similar in content. I do mean to suggest that the architecture of the system that enables these representations may be basically similar in important respects. Again, I do not mean to imply that the capacities for mental computations, regarding similarity, probability, or whatever, are the same at the lower and higher phylogenetic levels, but I do suggest that though the particular algorithms employed may differ, some general properties of mental computational procedures and some of the constraints to which they are subject may be similar for lower animals and man.

A severe limitation on the set of studies I have cited is that categorization performance has to be based wholly on information gained from experience with a particular sequence of category exemplars that the learner has an opportunity to observe within the experimental setting. Outside of the laboratory, an individual learning, say, to diagnose diseases does not depend entirely on his or her own past observations of relationships between symptoms and disease categories, but also brings to bear other kinds of knowledge, for example that drawn from studies of physiology or biochemistry. How should consideration of this fact affect our view of the significance of theoretical connections we have demonstrated between models for animal and human category learning? Several possible answers deserve consideration.

One important consideration is that even though human learners may often bring significant previously acquired knowledge to a particular task involving categorization, general knowledge always has to be tailored to specific situations. Prior knowledge provides us with expectations or hypotheses as to what categorizations are likely in a particular task, but these expectations still have to be checked out by observation. Again, prior knowledge may guide our choice of what attributes or features are likely to be relevant to a given type of classification problem, but we still have to make the observations and learn from the results. Thus it may well be that generally, in ordinary life, classificatory behavior depends on a combination of prior knowledge and specific learning. This prior knowledge probably varies greatly in form and content between lower animals and man, and at the human level between individuals with differing degrees of expertise in a particular subject matter, but the learning processes that implement and verify prior knowledge may have much greater generality.

Finally, it needs to be recognized that even the way lower animals achieve categorizations of objects and events in their environments may depend on mixtures of prior knowledge and specific learning. The degree to which prior knowledge is genetically programmed or gained from broader experience presumably varies greatly from lower to higher animal forms. Going up the phylogenetic scale, the importance of relatively unmodifiable preprogrammed knowledge or behavioral dispositions presumably declines with a commensurate increase in the importance of knowledge acquired by previous learning by the individual and modified by experience in each new situation.

How knowledge representations may differ between lower animals and man is a wide open question, and one that needs close examination. Though there are sure to be vast differences in the character of knowledge structures, owing to such things as the availability or nonavailability of language, there may also be basic commonalities. The differences are easy to demonstrate and the commonalities may be very difficult to tease out, but nonetheless, the greater effort needed on the latter tack may yield greater rewards. To the degree that we can use connecting models to help isolate common processes and mechanisms in the animal and human learning and memory systems, we open the way to studies bearing on the physiological and biochemical basis of human memory that could never be carried out on human beings alone.

ACKNOWLEDGMENT

Work reported in this paper was supported in part by Grant MH 37208 from the National Institute of Mental Health and Grant BNS 80-26656 from the National Science Foundation. Bradford Smith assisted with the experimental work and Hazel Rovno with the computations.

REFERENCES

Bower, G. H. (1967). A multicomponent theory of the memory trace. In K. W. Spence & J. T. Spence (Eds.), *The psychology of learning and motivation: Advances in research and theory*, vol. 1. (pp. 229–325). New York: Academic Press.

Bower, G. H. (1972). Stimulus-sampling theory of encoding variability. In A. W. Melton & E. Martin (Eds.), *Coding processes in human memory* (pp. 85–123). Washington, DC: V. H. Winston & Sons.

Bush, R. R., Galanter, E., & Luce, R. D. (1959). Tests of the "beta model". In R. R. Bush & W. K. Estes (Eds.), *Studies in mathematical learning theory* (pp. 382–399). Stanford, CA: Stanford University Press.

Estes, W. K. (1950). Toward a statistical theory of learning. *Psychological Review, 57,* 94–107.

Estes, W. K. (1959). The statistical approach to learning theory. In S. Koch (Ed.), *Psychology: A study of a science*, vol. 2. (pp. 380–491). New York: McGraw-Hill.

Estes, W. K. (1982a). Similarity-related channel interactions in visual processing. *Journal of Experimental Psychology: Human Perception and Performance, 8,* 353–382.

Estes, W. K. (1982b). *Models of learning, memory, and choice: Selected papers.* New York: Praeger.

Green, D. M., & Swets, J. A. (1966). *Signal detection theory and psychophysics.* New York: Wiley.

Gould, J. L., & Marler, P. (1984). Ethology and the natural history of learning. In P. Marler & H. S. Terrace (Eds.), *The biology of learning.* Berlin: Springer-Verlag.

Haugeland, J. (1981). Semantic engines: An introduction to mind design. In J. Haugeland (Ed.), *Mind design.* Montgomery, VT: Bradford.

Hinde, R. A. (1973). Constraints on learning—An introduction to the problem. In R. A. Hinde & J. Stevenson-Hinde (Eds.), *Constraints on learning: Limitations and predispositions* (pp. 1–19). New York: Academic Press.

Hull, C. L. (1943). *Principles of behavior: An introduction to behavior theory.* New York: Appleton-Century.

Levine, M. (1975). *A cognitive theory of learning: Research on hypothesis testing.* Hillsdale, NJ: Lawrence Erlbaum Associates.

Luce, R. D. (1963). Detection and recognition. In R. D. Luce, R. R. Bush, & E. Galanter (Eds.), *Handbook of mathematical psychology*, vol. 1. (pp. 103–189). New York: Wiley.

Marler, P., & Terrace, H. S. (Eds.). (1984). *The biology of learning.* Berlin: Springer-Verlag.

Marr, D. (1982). *Vision.* San Francisco, CA: Freeman.

Medin, D. L. (1975). The theory of context in discrimination learning. In G. H. Bower (Ed.), *The psychology of learning and motivation: Advances in research and theory*, vol. 9. (pp. 263–314). New York: Academic Press.

Medin, D. L., & Schaffer, M. M. (1978). Context theory of classification learning. *Psychological Review, 85*, 207–238.

Murdock, B. B., Jr. (1974). *Human memory: Theory and data.* Hillsdale, NJ: Lawrence Erlbaum Associates.

Newell, A., & Simon, H. A. (1976). Computer science as empirical inquiry. *Communications of the Association for Computing Machinery, 19*, 113–126.

Nosofsky, R. M. (1984). Choice, similarity and the context theory of classification. *Journal of Experimental Psychology: Learning, Memory and Cognition, 10*, 104–114.

Reed, S. K. (1973). *Psychological processes in pattern recognition.* New York: Academic Press.

Rosch, E. (1975). Cognitive representations of semantic categories. *Journal of Experimental Psychology: General, 104*, 192–223.

Schneirla, T. C. (1959). An evolutionary and developmental theory of biphasic processes underlying approach and withdrawal. In M. R. Jones (Ed.), *Nebraska symposium on motivation* (pp. 1–42). Lincoln: University of Nebraska Press.

Shettleworth, S. J. (1972). Constraints on learning. In D. S. Lehrman, R. A. Hinde, & E. Shaw (Eds.), *Advances in the study of behavior*, vol. 4. (pp. 1–68). New York: Academic Press.

Shettleworth, S. J. (1984). Animal learning in a functional context (foraging, food storage, and memory). In P. Marler & H. S. Terrace (Eds.), *The biology of learning.* Berlin: Springer-Verlag.

Smith, E. D., & Medin, D. L. (1981). *Categories and concepts.* Cambridge, MA: Harvard University Press.

Spear, N. E. (1976). Retrieval of memories: A psychobiological approach. In W. K. Estes (Ed.), *Handbook of learning and cognitive processes: Attention and memory*, vol. 4. Hillsdale, NJ: Lawrence Erlbaum Associates.

Trabasso, T., & Bower, G. H. (1968). *Attention in learning: Theory and research.* New York: Wiley.

9

Animal Conditioning and Human Causality Judgment

Anthony Dickinson
David Shanks
University of Cambridge

A major obstacle to interchange between students of animal and human learning remains the behavior-cognition divide. Thirty years ago the two fields were united by the behaviorist perspective, but over the intervening years the study of human learning has shifted its area of prime interest to cognitive and mental processes and, in doing so, has developed new procedures and terminology. This general shift can be easily illustrated by considering the minimal overlap that is found between the chapter headings of a contemporary general discussion of human learning and memory and a comparable text of the behaviorist period, for instance, McGeoch and Irion (1952).

The result of a similar comparison in the area of animal learning over an even longer time span is in striking contrast. Hilgard and Marquis (1940) and Mackintosh (1983), for example, structure the subject along similar lines, both having major chapters on classical conditioning, instrumental conditioning, and reinforcement processes. This similarity is not peculiar to Mackintosh's volume for the influence of Hilgard and Marquis can still be seen in almost every contemporary text. It is true that animal learning has thrown off the theoretical straight jacket of behaviorism; as Rescorla (see chapter 3) makes clear, no longer do we define learning in terms of behavioral change nor equate learning with reinforcement. Even so, behaviorism does seem to inform the paradigmatic and procedural distinctions we make in that the subject is still organized and presented almost exclusively in terms of behavioral rather than mental or cognitive criteria. The major distinction between classical and instrumental conditioning, for example, is maintained not because it is assumed that these two forms of conditioning involve different learning processes—in fact, Mackintosh (1983) argues explicitly that they do not—but rather because different principles of reinforcement are required. It is not that structuring the subject in terms of conditioning and reinforcement is in any sense wrong; in fact, it is entirely appropriate if we are primarily concerned with studying the control of behavior. Such an approach has two unfortunate consequences, however, if our focus is on the processes involved in the acquisition of knowledge.

First, the classification of our procedures by behavioral criteria tends to obscure some important commonalities from the point of view of learning. For instance, in terms of behavioral criteria alone classical inhibitory conditioning and instrumental avoidance conditioning would appear to have little in common, leading as they do to diametrically opposed behavioral effects. The inhibitory procedure endows a stimulus with the capacity to oppose the elicitation of a conditional response, whereas the avoidance procedure enhances the ability of a stimulus to control such behavior. For this reason it is not surprising that these two forms of conditioning are treated separately in texts of animal learning. And yet in terms of the type of relationship which the animal has to learn about, the two procedures are very similar. In both cases the animal is exposed to a negative temporal correlation between two events, the inhibitory stimulus and the Pavlovian reinforcer in one case and the performance of the avoidance behavior and the negative reinforcer in the other, and indeed the event correlation generated by one procedure is sufficient to bring about the other form of conditioning (Weisman & Litner, 1972). Thus, if we are primarily interested in mental processes and view the various forms of conditioning simply as alternative behavioral measures of the acquisition of knowledge, there is a lot of sense in treating inhibitory and avoidance conditioning simply as different measures of learning about negative event correlations. Dickinson (1980) has made an attempt to develop this approach to conditioning in general.

The second consequence of the behavioral perspective is of more direct relevance to our present concern, namely the relationship between human and animal learning. Because the two areas are organized in terms of different general paradigms, the behavioral and the cognitive, the relationship between their procedures and associated results and theory are not immediately obvious. Let us illustrate this problem by trying to identify the aspects of human learning that might be illuminated by current empirical and theoretical developments in animal conditioning. We suspect that one cannot start to answer this question properly without redescribing conditioning procedures in cognitive terms.

There are two steps involved in effecting this translation. The first is to abandon the conditioning and reinforcement terminology, which makes important behavioral distinctions but obscures knowledge-based ones, and to view conditioning as a technique for studying how animals detect and learn about certain event relationships, predictive ones in the case of classical conditioning and causal ones in the case of instrumental conditioning. The first event is either the presentation of the conditional stimulus in a classical procedure or the performance of a particular behavior during instrumental conditioning, and the second event the presentation of a reinforcer. Given this perspective, the analogous area of human cognition is obvious, namely the study of learning about predictive and causal associations on the basis of real-time observations of or interactions with such relationships.

The second step is to acknowledge explicitly that the conditional response may be treated as a behavioral measure of a mental process or state. Thus, if the strength of the response is taken as reflecting the animal's judgment of the event relationships involved in the conditioning procedure, a direct parallel can be drawn with the processes involved in human judgments of causal effectiveness. There is, of course, nothing particularly novel about this perspective on conditioning. For a number of years students of learned helplessness have recognized the possible relationship between animal conditioning and human judgments of control (e.g., Alloy & Abramson, 1979; Alloy & Tabachnik, 1984), but it is interesting to note that this parallel was also built upon a cognitive characterisation of animal conditioning (Maier & Seligman, 1976).

If one accepts this parallel, the study of the detection and judgment of event relationships would seem to be an area of human learning that might benefit from the procedures and theories that have been developed in animal conditioning. This is a possibility that we explore in the remainder of this chapter as an illustration of an interchange between the two areas.

EVENT CORRELATION

We already have some suggestive evidence that similar learning processes may underlie animal conditioning and human judgments of causal effectiveness from studies of the role of event correlation in these two forms of learning. Rescorla (1968; see chapter 3, this volume) was the first to demonstrate that animal conditioning is systematically sensitive to event correlation. He investigated the effect of varying the strength of a positive correlation between a tone and a shock reinforcer by holding the probability that a shock would occur in the presence of a tone, and hence the number of tone-shock pairings constant, while varying the likelihood of the shock in the absence of the tone, P(shock/no tone), across different groups of rats. Of course, an increase in the likelihood of shock in the absence of the tone decreases their correlation. After considerable exposure to these correlations, Rescorla assessed conditioning to the tone by measuring the extent to which nonreinforced, test presentations of the tone suppressed a positively-reinforced baseline behavior. Figure 9.1 illustrates the suppression ratios for the tone as a function of P(shock/no tone). Remembering that lower suppression ratios signify more conditioning, we can see that the conditional strength of the tone increased systematically as P(shock/no tone) was lowered, illustrating the sensitivity of simple conditioning to event correlation. These data represent but a subset of those presented by Rescorla showing the same effect at

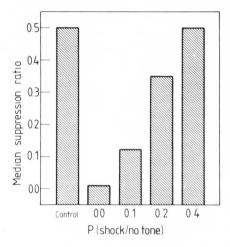

FIG. 9.1. The degree to which a tone suppressed baseline responding after various groups of rats had received different correlations between a tone and shock. The different correlations were brought about by holding P(shock/tone) constant at 0.4 per 2-min period for all groups and varying P(shock/no tone) across the different groups. A suppression ratio of zero indicates maximum suppression and hence strong conditioning, whereas a ratio of 0.5 indicates no suppression and no conditioning. (After Rescorla, 1968).

different probabilities of the shock in the presence of the tone. Moreover, this effect is not peculiar to the classical procedure employed by Rescorla since a comparable effect of event correlation has been observed in instrumental conditioning under positive reinforcement (Hammond, 1980).

What initially encouraged us to take the parallel between animal conditioning and human causality judgment seriously was their comparable sensitivity to event correlation. Although the early evidence suggested that we are surprisingly bad at judging causal effectiveness on the basis of event correlations (e.g., Jenkins & Ward, 1965), subsequent research modeled on Rescorla's procedure has reversed this conclusion (e.g., Allan & Jenkins, 1980, 1983; Alloy & Abramson, 1979; Wasserman, Chatlosh, & Neunaber, 1983). We shall illustrate the sensitivity of human judgments to event correlations using a video game task we have recently developed in which the subjects are asked to rate the effectiveness of a new type of shell in destroying a tank.

On each trial the subjects are presented with the representation of a tank moving across the video screen and are informed that in doing so the tank is moving through a minefield. At the outset of each trial the subject can choose whether or not to fire a shell at the tank by pressing a key on the console, and on some trials the tank *explodes* at a randomly determined point during its traverse of the screen, whereas on other trials it crosses the screen intact. The destruction of the tank is marked by a fragmentation of the image and the disappearance of its remains. If we regard the destruction of the tank as the outcome (O) and hitting the tank with a shell as the action (A), we are in a position to manipulate independently the probability of the outcome given the action, P(O/A), and the probability of the outcome in the absence of the action, P(O/-A). In this context variations in P(O/−A) reflect differences in the density of the minefield, whereas variations in P(O/A) can be due to differences in either the effectiveness of the shells or the minefield density. Because the point of the tank's destruction during the traverse of the screen is unaffected by whether or not the subject fires, the locus and time of a destruction provides no information about its cause. In addition, this procedure results in a variable delay between a firing and a destruction.

In one study using this task (Dickinson, Shanks, & Evenden, 1984), the subjects were presented with a number of sets of 40 trials during each of which P(O/A) and P(O/−A) were fixed. At the end of each set the subjects were asked to rate the effectiveness of the shell employed in that set in destroying the tank. The event correlations that we sampled are illustrated in terms of a contingency space in Fig. 9.2. We investigated whether causality judgments would show a sensitivity to event correlation that was similar to that exhibited by excitatory conditioning in Rescorla's study. To do so, we fixed P(O/A) at 0.75 and raised P(O/−A) from 0.25 (75–25) through 0.50 (75-50) to the case in which the two conditional probabilities were equal and the events uncorrelated (75-75). The parallel to excitatory conditioning predicts that ratings of the shell's effectiveness should have decreased systematically as P(O/−A) was raised.

In addition to the 75–75 set, we also measured judgments for another uncorrelated condition with a lower overall probability of destruction, the 25-25 set. In this set both P(O/A) and P(O/−A) were 0.25. The purpose of this comparison was to see whether judgments of causal effectiveness, like animal conditioning, are affected by the overall event frequency with an uncorrelated or random schedule. Animals tend to show more excitatory conditioning when the conditional stimulus and reinforcer occur randomly in time as the absolute frequency with which they occur is raised (e.g., Kremer, 1971; Rescorla, 1972). Consequently, we should expect our subjects to have rated the effectiveness of the

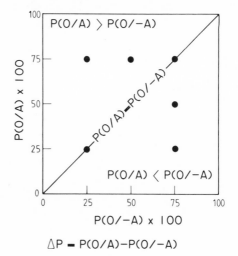

FIG. 9.2. A contingency space representation of the correlations between the action (A) and outcome (O) in terms of P(O/A) and P(O/−A). Along the diagonal the action and outcome are uncorrelated, above the diagonal positively correlated, and below the diagonal negatively correlated. The filled points represent the events correlations sampled in our first study.

shells more highly in the 75-75 set than in the 25-25 set, although in neither case did the shells actually have any effect.

Finally, animal conditioning is also sensitive to negative event correlations. We have already noted that such a relationship results in a form of classical conditioning that is opposed to that seen with a positive correlation, namely inhibitory as opposed to excitatory conditioning. The strength of inhibitory conditioning, like its excitatory counterpart, is determined by the degree of event correlation, in this case increasing in strength as the likelihood of the reinforcer in the absence of the inhibitor is raised (Rescorla, 1969) and the probability of their conjoint occurrence is lowered (Witcher & Ayres, 1980). Comparable sensitivity to event correlations is also seen in the instrumental analogue of inhibitory conditioning, namely avoidance learning (e.g., Kadden, Schoenfeld, & Snapper, 1974).

To investigate the parallels to inhibitory and avoidance conditioning, we measured the effects of varying both $P(O/A)$ and $P(O/-A)$ on judgments under a negative correlation or, in other words, when $P(O/A)$ was less than $P(O/-A)$. In the 25-75 set the negative correlaton was brought about by keeping $P(O/A)$ at 0.25 and setting $P(O/-A)$ at 0.75. This correlation was then reduced in the 50-75 set by raising $P(O/A)$ to 0.5. The possibility of a negative correlation was explained in the instructions by pointing out that, not only might the shell itself be unable to destroy the tank, but it might also alert the tank driver to the fact that he was in enemy territory and thereby cause him to drive with sufficient care so as to miss most of the mines.

The subjects were asked to express their judgments of the effectiveness of a shell in terms of a number between +100 and -100. They were informed that +100 indicated that the shell always destroyed the tank, zero that the shell was completely ineffective, and -100 that a correctly aimed shot actually prevented the tank from blowing up. Figure 9.3 illustrates these mean judgments for each set as well as the actual correlations experienced by the subjects as specified by one of the normative measures of contingency, ΔP, which is the difference between $P(O/A)$ and $P(O/-A)$ (Allan, 1980). As the nominal event probabilities acted as parameter values for a software random number generator in the program controlling the game, the actual correlations experienced by the subjects could differ from the nominal values for each set.

The three main features of animal conditioning were reproduced by our subjects' ratings. First, under a positive correlation with a fixed $P(O/A)$ the absolute magnitude of the judgments decreased as $P(O/-A)$ was raised. Second, the bias produced by varying event frequencies under uncorrelated schedules was observed in that the judgments were higher when the probability of the outcome was 0.75 rather than 0.25. And finally, negative contingencies yielded negative ratings which were sensitive to variations in the correlation brought about both by changes in $P(O/-A)$ and $P(O/A)$. It should be noted that in neither this experiment nor any of the subsequent studies did differences in the sampling of

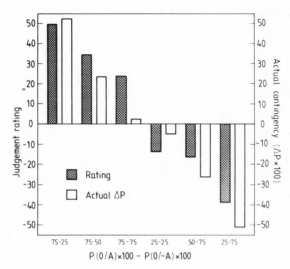

FIG. 9.3. Mean judgment rating and mean actual contingency (ΔPx100) as a function of P(O/A)x100 and P(O/−A)x100 during each set of trials.

P(O/A) and P(O/−A) contribute to the differences in judgment. There was never any significant difference in the number of trials on which the subjects fired in the various conditions and in all cases they sampled both probabilities.

To check that the judgments reflected the operation of cognitive processes that actually controlled decisions about whether or not to act, the subjects were asked to participate in a small behavioral test after they had given their ratings. This test consisted of 10 trials on which they had the opportunity to fire the shell. We were interested in how many times they would choose to fire when they were informed that each destruction of a tank had a certain value (3 points) and each shell a cost (1 point). The optimum strategy for scoring the greatest number of points with this payoff structure is to never fire when ΔP is less than 0.33, and then always to fire. Figure 9.4 shows, however, that our subjects, like those of Alloy and Abramson (1979), showed a graded strategy with the number of shots on target or hits being systematically related to the actual contingency in a manner comparable to the judgments, at least for the positive correlations.

The marked similarity between the effects of varying the event correlation on animal conditioning and human causality judgment encouraged us to consider seriously the idea that there might be common underlying processes and to pursue the apparent parallel further. In the first instance, we decided to concentrate on what we thought were the three most basic properties of conditioning and to investigate whether these same features characterise the judgment process. The first is the sensitivity of conditioning to event contiguity; it is well known that reducing temporal contiguity by delaying the reinforcer produces a systematic decrement in the strength of conditioning. Similarly, spatial separation of the

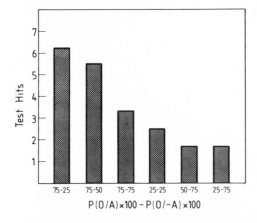

FIG. 9.4.   Mean number of test hits as a function of P(O/A)x100 and P(O/−A)x100 during each set of trials.

conditional stimulus and reinforcer also reduces conditioning (e.g., Rescorla & Cunningham, 1979; Testa, 1975). Second, conditioning typically shows a progressive growth function across a series of episodes or trials. And finally, conditioning is selective in the sense that the amount of conditioning accruing to a particular event, be it a stimulus or an operant, depends not only on its own correlation and contiguity with the reinforcer, but also upon the conditional status of other events that are present. As we shall see, human causality judgment does exhibit each of these features, although in one case, at least, the underlying process appears to differ from that mediating animal conditioning in an important and informative way.

EVENT CONTIGUITY

There is little doubt that in general the judged causal effectiveness of an event decreases with the temporal separation the putative cause and the effect (e.g., Gruber, Fink, & Damm, 1957). We felt, however, that it was important to establish a comparable effect in a procedure, such as our video game, in which we could also manipulate other important parameters of event relationships thereby, for instance, investigating the interaction between event contiguity and correlation. Our basic procedure restricted our ability to manipulate the contiguity between the action and outcome because the tank only took one second to cross the whole screen. Consequently, we decided to compare judgments at the extremes of the range that was available to us. In one set of trials, the Immediate (Im) condition, firings resulted in destructions that always occurred immediately the tank emerged from the gun sight. By contrast, following a firing in the other, Delayed (Del) condition the tank always blew up after it had traversed the whole screen and at the point just before it would have disappeared from sight anyway. The fragmentation of the image clearly distinguished a destruction in this location from a disappearance. The interval between a firing and a destruction was 250 msec in the Immediate condition and 700 msec in the Delayed condition. Finally, we also included a Random (Ran) set in which the point of destruction was determined randomly as in the previous study. In all these conditions the point of destruction was also random on trials on which an outcome was programmed and the subject chose not to fire. In all other respects the general procedure was similar to that employed in the previous study.

If causality judgment, like conditioning, is sensitive to contiguity, we should expect the ratings for the Immediate set to have been more positive than those for the Delayed condition. Our prediction for the Random set is less clear. As the action–outcome intervals in this condition are bounded by those in the Immediate and Delayed conditions, all we can predict for the Random set is that the ratings should be no more extreme than those in the other conditions. In order to check whether any such effects depends on the degree of event correlation, two groups of subjects received all three sets under either the 75-25 correlation for one group or the 75-75 relationship for the other. Figure 9.5 shows the mean ratings produced by each condition separately for Group 75-25 in the top panel and Group 75-75 in the bottom one. Also displayed in this and subsequent figures are the actual contingencies experienced by the subjects in each set to check that any rating differences are not a consequence of fortuitous differences in this variable.

The basic prediction of the conditioning model was fulfilled in that there was an overall significant effect of event contiguity with the Immediate condition producing higher ratings than the Random and Delayed sets which, in turn, did

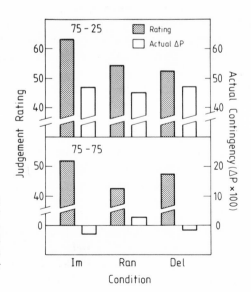

FIG. 9.5. Mean judgment rating and mean actual contingency (ΔPx100) for the groups experiencing the Immediate (Im), Delayed (Del) and Random (Ran) conditions under either the 75-25 (top panel) or 75-75 correlation (bottom panel).

not differ. We were worried that any effect of contiguity might be due to an effective change in the event correlation brought about by temporal and/or spatial marking of outcomes that follow actions, but this does not appear to be so. What we feared was that by making the tank blow up immediately after firing, the subject would be able to distinguish these outcomes from those on trials when he or she chose not to fire, thus increasing the rating by effectively reducing $P(O/-A)$ for the type of outcome that followed a firing. Two observations argue against the operation of this process. First, the outcomes following an action are also marked in the Delayed condition so that we should expect ratings for this set to have been higher than those in the Random set, which they were not. Second, the effect of such a process should be more pronounced when the $P(O/-A)$ is high because it operates by reducing the suppressive effects of such outcomes on the ratings. There was no significant interaction, however, between the effect of varying temporal contiguity and the overall event correlation. In conclusion, we argue on the basis of these data that event contiguity plays a functionally similar role in causality judgment and conditioning. Of course, we cannot determine on the basis of the present study whether it is the temporal or spatial factor that is critical, because our procedure confounds them.

THE ACQUISITION FUNCTION

The second claim, namely that causality judgments should show some form of acquisition function, is not as trivial as it might at first appear. Suppose that instead of asking for a rating of the shell's effectiveness after all 40 trials, we had requested a rating every five trials. Any procedure that bases the ratings on some normative measure of correlation, for example ΔP, would be expected on average to produce judgments that remained constant across trials. Although the variance of ΔP should decrease with the sample size on which it is based, and hence the number of trials, its expected value should remain constant. By contrast, the conditioning model anticipates that ratings should grow under a positive correlation and decline under a negative one from some starting point to their asymptotic value for that relationship, just as the strength of a conditional response shows a progressive change with training.

To test this prediction, we ran a second study under the same conditions as in the first experiment except that only four event relationships were investigated, the most extreme positive and negative correlations for which ΔP was 0.50 and -0.50 respectively, and the two uncorrelated cases with outcome probabilities of 0.75 and 0.25. In this study a linear scale was displayed horizontally on the screen below the gun sight and tank trajectory. This scale was calibrated from -100 on the left to +100 on the right, which points were defined by the same instructions as in the first study. At the start of each set of trials the subject was asked to specify a number on the scale reflecting their initial judgment of the shell's effectiveness, whereupon a pointer was displayed at this value. It was clearly explained to the subject that there was no rational basis for selecting any particular starting value. Thereafter the subject was given the opportunity to relocate the pointer to a new value after every five of the 40 trials comprising each set.

Figure 9.6 displays both the mean actual correlations experienced by the subjects and their associated judgments across the series of trials in each set. As we anticipated, the mean values of ΔP remained approximately constant across trials, and furthermore we replicated the pattern of terminal judgments seen in the first study. More interestingly, even if we exclude the contribution of the starting value, these terminal values appear to represent the cumulative effect of a series of increments in the case of the positive correlation and decrements in that of the negative relationship.

Clearly, the pattern of judgments is that anticipated by the conditioning analogy. This similarity might be regarded as artifactual, however, for two reasons. The first concerns the possible bias towards central values for initial ratings produced by requiring the subjects to give starting values. We do not think that this is an important factor for we have observed similar functions when no starting value was required and the initial rating was given after the first five trials.

The second possibility is that acquisition functions arose from the fact that our procedure might have forced the subjects to conflate their judgment of the strength of the event relationship with their confidence in this judgment by restricting them to a single rating. If we had allowed them to rate these two factors separately, we might have found that their judgment of the relationship

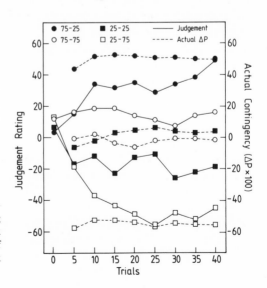

FIG. 9.6. Mean judgment rating and mean actual contingency (ΔP x 100) as a function of the number of trials for sets with different P(O/A) x 100 and P(O/$-$A) x 100.

would have remained constant on average across trials although their confidence in their judgment rose. Although this may be true, it does not invalidate the point of our demonstration. In instrumental conditioning, any knowledge about a contingency and the confidence in the reliability of this knowledge also would have to be expressed through a single variable, the propensity to act. As the point of the present studies is comparative, it seemed to us desirable that the judgment process should be studied under the same general constraints as those operating on a typical behavioral measure in a conditioning procedure. It is, of course, an interesting but separate question as to whether subjects would naturally distinguish between their judgments of the strength of a causal relationship and their confidence in their judgment when given the opportunity. None of our subjects have ever expressed any disquiet at not being allowed to do so.

SELECTIVE ATTRIBUTION AND BLOCKING

The third major feature of animal conditioning that we consider is its selectivity. This selectivity is most simply illustrated by Kamin's (1969) blocking effect. Pretraining to one stimulus by pairing it with the reinforcer, $X+$, in the first stage reduces or "blocks" the amount of subsequent conditioning that accrues to another stimulus, A, when a compound of A and X is reinforced, $AX+$, in the second stage. On a descriptive level, this finding suggests that, relatively speaking, conditioning favors more reliable predictors of the reinforcer at the expense of less reliable ones. Over the two stages of the blocking experiment a higher proportion of the reinforcers are signaled by X than by A. The analogous effect in causality judgments would be seen if it could shown that subjects selectively attribute an outcome to a more reliable potential cause at the expense of a less reliable one. We sought to investigate this possibility in a study employing Kamin's blocking design (Dickinson et al., 1984).

The subjects were given a set of trials consisting of two stages. In the first, observation stage, they could not fire the shell and simply observed tanks passing through a minefield that had a destruction probability of 0.75 for 30 trials. This stage is analogous to the pretraining of X in the first stage of the blocking experiment. In the second, firing stage, the subjects were able to fire the shell on 30 trials under an uncorrelated schedule in which the destruction probability remained 0.75. This second stage parallels the $AX+$ compound conditioning of the blocking procedure in that, at least on trials on which the shell hit the tank and it exploded, two potential causes, the shell and the minefield, were associated with the outcome. It will be recalled from the previous studies that exposure to such an uncorrelated schedule with a high outcome frequency tends to produce positive judgments of the effectiveness of the shell. If a blocking-like effect occurs, we expected pretraining to the minefield in the observation stage to reduce these positive judgments. Two control sets were examined, Con30 and

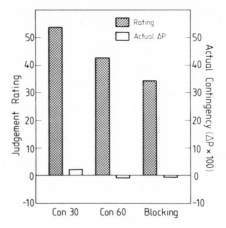

FIG. 9.7. Mean judgment rating and mean actual contingency ($\Delta P \times 100$) for the sets of trials in which the subjects were exposed to either 30 (Con30) or 60 trials (Con60) under the 75-75, random schedule or given 30 observation trials during which $P(O/-A)$ was 0.75 prior to 30 trials under the random schedule (Blocking).

Con60, in which subjects simply received either 30 or 60 standard firing trials, respectively, under conditions identical to those of the Blocking set. Thus, the number of firing trials was matched in the Blocking and Con30 sets and the total number of trials in the Blocking and Con60 sets. In this study we requested only a terminal rating of the effectiveness of the shells after each set.

Figure 9.7 shows that a clear blocking-like effect was observed in that the Blocking set yielded lower judgments than both control sets. Again, it is important to note that a normative procedure would not necessarily have anticipated this difference. As $P(O/-A)$ was the same in both stages, the addition of the observation stage should not have altered the value of ΔP, and Figure 9.7 also shows that, in fact, the actual ΔP calculated across all the trials was very close to zero and did not differ across the sets. These results point to the operation of a process of selective attribution in causality judgment which appears to be similar to the selective learning operating in animal conditioning.

RETROSPECTIVE REVALUATION

The type of selective learning seen in animal conditioning is usually assumed to be of a very restricted form in that it can only act prospectively. This restriction can again be illustrated by the blocking procedure. We have already noted that X+ training in stage one reduces conditioning to A during subsequent compound AX+ training in the second stage. But what would happen if we reversed these two stages so that the AX+ training precedes the X+ training to yield a backward, as opposed to forward blocking procedure? By any objective criteria the forward and backward procedures provide the same evidence about the relative predictive reliability of A and X, and so we might expect that the X+ training should reduce conditioning to A in both cases. However, this is not the result anticipated by current conditioning theories (e.g., Mackintosh, 1975; Pearce & Hall, 1980; Rescorla & Wagner, 1972) for, according to these accounts, once conditioning has been established to A, it should be impervious to any subsequent change in the status of X. To assess this prediction of the conditioning theories, in the next study we compared directly the magnitude of forward and backward blocking (Shanks, 1985).

The Forward Blocking (FB) and Forward Control (FC) conditions in the random, 75-75 group were identical to the Blocking and Con30 sets, respectively, of the previous study. The subjects received 30 firing trials under the uncorrelated schedule with a probability of destruction of 0.75, preceded in the case of the FB set by 30 observation trials with the same destruction probability. In the present study these forward sets were intermixed with two backward conditions, a blocking (BB) and control (BC) set. In the BB set the order of the two stages was simply reversed so that the observation stage now followed the firing stage. The BC set, like the FC condition, just consisted of the firing stage, although in the backward case an interval equivalent to that occupied by the observation stage in the BB set elapsed between the end of the firing stage and the request for a judgment.

In addition, we tested a second group of subjects to check that the blocking-like effects are not peculiar to judgments of the causal association between randomly related events. The design was identical to that of Group 75-75 except for the fact that there was a positive correlation during the firing stages. Whereas $P(O/-A)$ was 0.5 during both stages, $P(O/A)$ was 0.75 during the firing stage, giving a ΔP of 0.25 for Group 75-50.

Figure 9.8 shows that we were able to replicate the forward blocking effect in

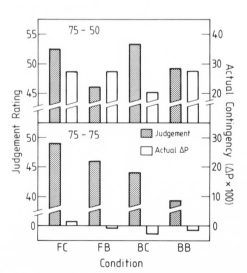

FIG. 9.8. Mean judgment rating and mean actual contingency ($\Delta P \times 100$) for the forward control (FC) and blocking (FB) sets and for the backward control (BC) and blocking (BB) sets. These data are shown separately for the groups experiencing the 75-50 (top panel) and 75-75 schedules (bottom panel).

both groups. There was also a backward blocking effect, however, that was at least as strong as that seen in the forward cases. In both cases the judgments for the blocking sets were lower than those for their respective control sets under each of the two correlations. These effects were not due to fortuitous differences in the actual correlations experienced by the subjects in the various sets; as Fig. 9.8 shows, what differences there were in the actual ΔP within each group were in the opposite direction to those of the judgments. It would appear that human causality judgment is subject to some form of retrospective revaluation process whereby subjects are capable of adjusting their judgments of the effectiveness of a shell in light of subsequently acquired information about the minefield.

Before accepting the clear challenge this conclusion presents to the parallel we have drawn between the conditioning and judgment processes, we must be certain that the backward blocking seen in this experiment is really due to retrospective revaluation. There are, at least, two examples in the animal conditioning literature of apparent backward blocking effects that on further analysis turn out not to be so. In his original studies, Kamin (1969) observed an apparent backward effect, but he claimed that this was simply due to the interval of time that elapsed between the end of AX compound training and the test for the conditional strength of A, rather than to the intervening training to X. The implication is that the apparent effect was caused by forgetting rather than some form of retrospective revaluation. An account in terms of forgetting could be advanced to explain our results. Although we left an equivalent time interval between the end of the firing stage and the request for a judgment in the BB and BC sets, this interval was filled with the attention-demanding stimuli of the observation stage in the BB, but not the BC set. If such stimuli enhance forgetting of information presented in the prior firing stage, an apparent backward blocking effect might result.

The second apparent backward blocking effect was reported by Rescorla (1983) in a study of pigeon autoshaping. What convinced him that this effect was not due to any form of retrospective revaluation was its insensitivity to the conditional status of X. This point can be illustrated by the design of one of Rescorla's experiments. As well as training to the AX compound, the birds were presented with reinforced presentations of a second, BY compound to yield AX+ BY+ training during the first stage. Then in the second stage he gave X+ Y− training in which X continued to be reinforced, whereas Y was nonreinforced. If retrospective revaluation occurs, this second-stage training should endow B with greater conditional strength than A; the reinforcement of X should reduce the strength of A, whereas the extinction of Y, if anything, should enhance the strength of B. In fact, Rescorla was unable to detect any difference in the strength of A and B on test, suggesting that his original observation of apparent backward blocking was due to a process other than retrospective revaluation. An analogous process may also be at work in the human causality judgment procedure.

We investigated this possibility in a judgment experiment employing a design similar to that used by Rescorla (1983). This required two distinct games to match the AX and BY compounds. The first was identical to that used in the previous studies, involving the destruction of tanks with shells in the causal context of a minefield. The second was formally similar except that in this scenario the subjects were asked to evaluate the effectiveness of missiles in destroying airplanes in the causal context of defending planes. When this game was operative, the target planes crossed the video display screen in the opposite direction to that of the tanks and in a higher trajectory. In each set of trials the firing stage consisted of two 30-trials blocks, one with each game. For both these games P(O/A) was 0.75 and P(O/−A) was 0.25. This stage was equivalent to the AX+ BY+ training in Rescorla's study, and was immediately followed by an observation stage again consisting of two blocks of 30 trials, one with each game. During these trials the subjects could not fire and simply observed either the tank or target plane traversing the screen with a fixed probability of destruction. The equivalent of X+ training was given by making the probability of destruction for one game 0.75 during the observation stage, while Y− training was matched by setting this probability at only 0.25 for the other game. The probability of destruction associated with each game was counterbalanced across two sets of trials. Furthermore, the order of the games during the firing and observation periods were counterbalanced across subjects.

We should be justified in attributing the backward blocking effect to retrospective revaluation only if the rating of the effectivess of the shell and the missile requested at the end of each set of trials was systematically affected by the destruction probability, P(O/−A), for that game during the immediately following observation period. Specifically, the lower the observation period P(O/−A) for a particular game, the higher should be the ratings for that game. The right-hand panel of Fig. 9.9 shows that this is just the pattern that we observed. In fact, the difference in ratings as a function of observation period P(O/−A) in this backward condition was statistically indistinguishable from that in an equivalent forward condition, even though a comparison of the panels in Fig. 9.9 shows that on average the difference was numerically smaller in the backward condition. The ratings in the forward condition were provided by a second group of subjects tested under an identical procedure to that of the backward condition except for the fact that the observation stages always preceded the firing stages.

Given these results, we have little option but to attribute the backward blocking effect in human causality judgment to retrospective revaluation. The effect cannot be due to differential forgetting or general interference for, on average, the destruction probability in the observation period was not confounded with the duration of the interval between the end of the relevant firing trials nor with the number of stimuli presented and actions required during this period. We seem to have identified a process of retrospective selective attribution that has no accept-

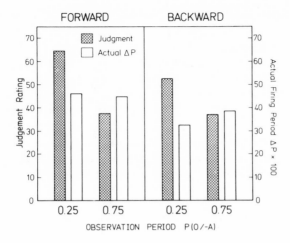

FIG. 9.9. Mean judgment ratings and mean actual contingency during the firing period (Δ P x 100) as a function of P(O/-A) during the observation period for subjects exposed to the backward (right-hand panel) and forward procedures (left-hand panel).

ed analogue in the field of animal conditioning. A caveat to this conclusion is necessary, however, for we must distinguish between theoretical and empirical claims.

There is no doubt that the attempt to explain human causality judgment in terms of contemporary animal conditioning theory, an enterprise we once endorsed (Dickinson et al., 1984), is untenable given these data. It is not that genuine backward blocking is a phenomenon that is tangential to these theories; rather it undermines one of their fundamental assumptions, namely that the associative strength of an event, and hence its conditional strength or rated causal effectiveness when applied to human judgments, can only change as a result of an episode involving that event (e.g., Mackintosh, 1975; Pearce & Hall, 1980; Rescorla & Wagner, 1972). This conclusion must be distinguished, however, from the empirical claim that animal conditioning does not exhibit backward blocking and therefore must be mediated by processes that differ from those underlying causality judgments. Based as it is upon a failure to disprove the null hypothesis, this claim is always vulnerable to a possible demonstration of the effect in animal conditioning under the right conditions, whatever they might be. It is true that, to the best of our knowledge, all attempts to demonstrate a genuine backward blocking effect with animals have been unsuccessful (e.g., Kalat & Rozin, 1972; Schweitzer & Green, 1982). But Kaufman and Bolles (1981) have reported what appears, at first sight anyway, to be a form of retrospective revaluation in a similar procedure. After AX+ compound training, the rats were given nonreinforced presentations of X. Relative to a group that did not receive this X-training, the experimental animals subsequently showed greater conditional responding to A when it was presented again. We must remain cautious, however, about attributing this difference to retrospective revaluation until it is replicated in a design which equates the animals' experiences following AX+ training except for the association that brings about the difference in the conditioned status of X in the two groups. When this has been done, albeit in a different conditioning preparation (e.g., Durlach & Rescorla, 1980; Rescorla & Cunningham, 1978), there has never been any evidence for a revaluation effect. Given this fact, we think we are justified in maintaining, at least provisionally, the conclusion that human causality judgment and animal conditioning differ in this fundamental respect.

HUMAN CONDITIONING AND JUDGMENT

But which aspect of animal conditioning is critical in differentiating it from causality judgment? Is it that the subjects are rats and pigeons or is it that the procedure is conditioning? At present, we can do no more than raise this issue for we do not have the evidence to resolve it. It is interesting to note, however, the strong correlation between human conditioning and the detection of the constituent event relationship. Baer and Fuhrer (1968), for instance, asked subjects to report their experiences during the intertrial interval of a differential conditioning experiment. Transcripts of these reports were then given to independent judges who were required to decide whether each subject was aware of the relationship between the conditional and unconditional stimuli. Following this classification, Baer and Fuhrer found that only aware subjects showed differential conditioning. The parallel between conditioning and awareness of the event relationship is not only correlational, but also occurs when the experimenter explicitly manipulates awareness. Using a masking procedure, Dawson (1970) gave subjects an auditory frequency perception task in which one of a number of tones was paired with a shock reinforcer. Only subjects that were informed of this tone-shock association prior to undertaking the task showed differential conditioning and were aware of the relationship at the end.

This type of evidence has led a number of authors (e.g., Brewer, 1974; Dawson & Furedy, 1976) to argue that awareness of the constituent event relationship is, at least, necessary for conditioning to occur. Thus, it may well be that conditioning in man is governed by the processes mediating causal judgments, which in turn differ from those controlling conditioning in other animals, or at least in rats and pigeons. The present analysis suggests that the critical question is whether or not backward blocking occurs in human conditioning. Unfortunately, we are not aware of any forward, let alone backward blocking studies in the human conditioning literature.

THEORETICAL IMPLICATIONS

Although the empirical parallel between animal conditioning and human contingency learning remains uncertain, we have already pointed out that the learning processes identified by current conditioning theories can not mediate the human judgments. There is no obvious way in which the conditioning models that we have considered can be modified to take account of backward blocking without offending one of their most fundamental assumptions. This conclusion should lead us to look elsewhere for an adequate account, but the problem is that, to the best of our knowledge, there are no well-formulated alternatives. It is true that in areas as diverse as social attribution theory (e.g., Kelley, 1967) and animal conditioning (e.g., Maier & Seligman, 1976), it has been argued that man and other animals are capable of acquiring some form of direct cognitive representation of the contingency, correlation, or covariation between events, and that this representation is a product of the interaction between prior expectations and currently available or *situational* information (Alloy & Tabachnik, 1984). The problem is that neither the nature of the representations nor the processes underlying their acquisition is sufficiently specified to allow an empirical test comparable to that undertaken for conditioning theories.

The main strategy employed in previous studies of human detection of event correlations attempts to identify the rule for combining the evidence upon which the judgment is based that yields the observed pattern of ratings. Typically, it has been found that the ΔP rule gives the best description of the judgments of the majority of subjects in tasks similar to our video game in which subjects are required to rate the effectiveness of an action, or action-related event, in controlling an outcome on the basis of real-time interaction with the causal process (Allan & Jenkins, 1980; Wasserman et al., 1983). As we have pointed out, however, in both the acquisition and blocking studies systematic variations in judgments were observed in the absence of any differences in ΔP or, for that matter, any function of $P(O/A)$ and $P(O/-A)$.

Performance in a number of related tasks such as probability learning (e.g., Estes, 1976) and causal inference based upon descriptive data (e.g., Schustack & Sternberg, 1981) suggest that judgments tend to be based on event frequencies rather than probabilities, and recently, Allan and Jenkins (1983) have argued for a rule based, for example, on some linear combination of the frequency of the different types of episodes in the case of judgment of control over an outcome by action. In such a rule, the frequency of episodes involving the joint occurrence and joint absence of the action and the outcome would receive a positive weighting, whereas the frequencies with which the action and outcome occur alone would be negatively weighted. We suspect that this general approach of trying to identify the contingency or correlation metric that best predicts the judgments is inappropriate if the implication is that subjects base their judgments upon such a metric, at least in cases in which judgments arise from direct interactions with or observations of a causal process in operation. This approach simply fails to encompass the dynamic factors that affect causality perception and judgment such as that revealed in our study of the role of event contiguity between an action and outcome. In cases where contiguity does not define the conjunction of the events, it is not clear why variations in their temporal relationship should affect the operation of processes involved in computing a correlation metric.

Thus, we seem to be left in something of a theoretical vacuum, and free to sketch the outline of a theory of real-time contingency learning primarily within the constraints provided by our studies. Such an outline must take two major factors into account. First, the theory must allow for both prospective and retrospective selective attribution as seen in forward and backward blocking. This problem could be handled by assuming that judgments of the effectiveness of some target event A, Ja, is determined by both a positive and negative factor, as in the ΔP rule. In the present case, however, the positive factor is the strength of the expectation of the outcome given the occurrence of any compound event involving A, say AX, or, in other words, the associative strength of AX, Vax. It should be noted that strictly speaking the putative cause A never occurs alone for there are always other potential background causes present, such as the minefield in our studies. We refer to these background causes as the causal context, X. The negative factor subtracted from this positive one is the associative strength of this causal context, Vx, so that:

$$Ja = Vax - Vx \qquad (1)$$

Forward and backward blocking follow directly from the fact that training to X alone in the observation periods increases Vx, thus reducing Ja.

The second relevant observation from the present studies is that Ja and so, by implication, Vax and Vx follow an acquisition function across a series of episodes involving these events. This suggests that we require incremental and decremental processes similar to those employed by standard conditioning theory to change the relevant associative strength on each trial as a function of the outcome on that trial. The joint occurrence of AX or X and the outcome on a trial increases the relevant associative strength, V, whereas the occurrence of AX or X alone decreases it. These changes in associative strength, ΔV, can be determined by the standard linear operator equation:

$$\Delta V = \alpha\beta\ (\lambda - V) \qquad (2)$$

where α is a learning rate parameter associated with putative causes AX and X, β an equivalent parameter for the outcome, and λ the asymptote of the associative strength. As it stands, this standard model does not specify the way in which increments in associative strength vary with the temporal and spatial contiguity between the events. Unlike the ΔP rule, however, the type of learning processes implied by Equation 2 is usually assumed to be sensitive, at least, to temporal

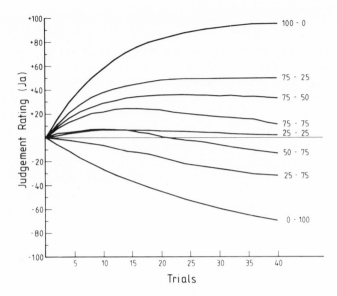

FIG. 9.10. Mean judgment ratings (Ja) provided by the Shanks theory as a function of P(O/A) x 100 and P(O/−A) x 100 during each set of trials. Each predicted value is the mean of 500 simulated subjects run under the same event correlations as the actual subjects in the first study and a probability of firing a correctly aimed shot of 0.5 on each trial. Ja equaled the difference between Vax and Vx where changes in Vax and Vx were controlled by the functions: $\Delta Vax = \alpha ax\beta\ (\lambda - Vax)$ and $\Delta Vx = \alpha x\beta\ (\lambda - Vx)$, where the learning rate parameter for the minefield and shell combined, αax, was 0.6 and that for the minefield alone, αx, was 0.2. The asymptote, λ, and learning rate parameter, β, for the outcome were 100 and 0.3, respectively, when the outcome was the destruction of the tank and 0 and 0.5, respectively, when the tank remained intact.

factors. Over the last few years, Wagner (1978, 1981) has developed a model that illustrates the way in which such a learning process might respond to variations in the temporal relationship between events.

Figure 9.10 shows that this simple model is capable of providing a set of judgments similar to those we have observed. The mean ratings are the mean values of Ja given by 500 simulated subjects run under the same conditions as the actual subjects in the first study with 40 trials under each correlation and a probability of firing a correctly aimed shell of 0.5 on each trial. The actual subjects in this study did fire on about half the trials. As Fig. 9.10 shows, a nonsystematic search of the parameter space of the model yielded a set of values that gave acquisition functions and terminal profiles that were broadly similar to those we observed.

Clearly, all we have done in constructing this model is to combine the advantages of conditioning theory and the Δ P rule. The parasitic relationship to conditioning theory is obvious, but there is also a close correspondence between the rule for determining Ja and that for ΔP; Vax corresponds to P(O/A) and Vx to P(O/$-$A). There are two important differences, however. The first is that the value of Ja, unlike that of ΔP, does not reflect directly the strength of an event correlation but confounds this factor with the amount of training. A given value of Ja can arise either after a limited exposure to a strong correlation or a more extended exposure to a weak correlation. The reason for preferring the Ja rule in this respect is empirical; the acquisition study showed that the ratings assigned to strong positive and negative correlations do in fact pass through intermediate values.

Second, the Ja rule, but not the ΔP rule, makes explicit the fact that information about the occurrence of the outcome in the absence of the putative cause, A, is important because it provides evidence about the effectiveness of the causal context, X, that is present whenever A operates. This information can then be used to determine the extent to which the effectiveness of A in the presence of the causal context is due to A rather than the context. In other words, the Ja rule implies the operation of a process of selective attribution, such as we saw in the blocking studies, which is modulated by the value of Vx. An objective measure of correlation or contingency, like the ΔP rule, of course has no such implications.

CONCLUSIONS

Whatever the merits of this particular theoretical approach, we hope that we have established a more general thesis, namely that the procedures and analysis developed in the field of animal conditioning can illuminate selected areas of human learning and cognition. We doubt whether a number of the empirical questions addressed in this paper would have been asked without the model of animal conditioning to work from. Moreover, the parallel human research may well feed back into animal conditioning. The strength of the backward blocking effect in the human studies, for instance, should encourage us to look more carefully for a comparable effect in animal conditioning.

Finally, it should be emphasized that, in the present case at least, the interchange between animal conditioning and human learning was dictated by parallels drawn on the cognitive rather than behavioral level. Traditionally, the relevance of animal conditioning to human psychology has been defended primarily on behavioral criteria; for example, animal aversive conditioning may illuminate human phobias, it has been argued, because similar behavioral reactions are involved. On behavioral criteria alone, however, there is little reason to draw any parallel between human causality judgments and say the autoshaped key peck of the pigeon, the conditional eyeblink of the rabbit, or even the conditional emotional response of the rat. It is only when a conditional response is seen simply as a behavioral measure of a mental state or process that the possible relationship between animal conditioning and human judgment becomes apparent.

ACKNOWLEDGMENTS

This work was supported by grants from the SERC and MRC. We should like to thank Cliff Preston and John Evenden for their advice and technical assistance, Alisande Martinez-Lainez for recruiting the subjects, and Peter Holland for his useful comments on an earlier draft of the chapter.

REFERENCES

Allan, L. G. (1980). A note on measurement of contingency between two binary variables in judgment tasks. *Bulletin of the Psychonomic Society, 15,* 147–149.

Allan, L. G., & Jenkins, H. M. (1980). The judgment of contingency and the nature of the response alternatives. *Canadian Journal of Psychology, 34,* 1–11.

Allan, L. G., & Jenkins, H. M. (1983). The effect of representations of binary variables on judgement of influence. *Learning and Motivation, 14,* 381–405.

Alloy, L. B., & Abramson, L. Y. (1979). Judgment of contingency in depressed and nondepressed students: Sadder but wiser? *Journal of Experimental Psychology: General, 108,* 441–485.

Alloy, L. B., & Tabachnik, N. (1984). Assessment of covariation by humans and animals: The joint influence of prior expectations and current situational information. *Psychological Review, 91,* 112–149.

Baer, P. E., & Fuhrer, M. J. (1968). Cognitive processes during differential trace and delayed conditioning of the GSR. *Journal of Experimental Psychology, 78,* 81–88.

Brewer, W. F. (1974). There is no convincing evidence for operant or classical conditioning in adult humans. In W. B. Weimer & D. S. Palermo (Eds.), *Cognition and the symbolic processes.* Hillsdale, NJ: Lawrence Erlbaum Associates.

Dawson, M. E. (1970). Cognition and conditioning: Effects of masking the CS-UCS contingency on human GSR classical conditioning. *Journal of Experimental Psychology, 85,* 389–396.

Dawson, M. E., & Furedy, J. J. (1976). The role of awareness in human differential autonomic classical conditioning: The necessary-gate hypothesis. *Psychophysiology, 13,* 50–53.

Dickinson, A. (1980). *Contemporary animal learning theory.* Cambridge: Cambridge University Press.

Dickinson, A., Shanks, D., & Evenden, J. (1984). Judgement of act-outcome contingency: The role of selective attribution. *Quarterly Journal of Experimental Psychology, 36A,* 29–50.

Durlach, P. J., & Rescorla, R. A. (1980). Potentiation rather than overshadowing in flavor-aversion learning: An analysis in terms of within-compound associations. *Journal of Experimental Psychology: Animal Behavior Processes, 6,* 175–187.

Estes, W. K. (1976). The cognitive side of probability learning. *Psychological Review, 83,* 37–64.

Gruber, H. E., Fink, C. D., & Damm, V. (1957). Effects of experience on perception of causality. *Journal of Experimental Psychology, 53,* 89–93.

Hammond, L. J. (1980). The effect of contingency upon the appetitive conditioning of free-operant behavior. *Journal of the Experimental Analysis of Behavior, 34,* 297–304.

Hilgard, E. R., & Marquis, D. G. (1940). *Conditioning and learning.* New York: Appleton-Century-Crofts.

Jenkins, H. M., & Ward, W. C. (1965). Judgement of contingency between responses and outcomes. *Psychological Monographs*, *79*, (1, Whole No. 594).

Kadden, R. M., Schoenfeld, W. N., & Snapper, A. G. (1974). Aversive schedules with independent probabilities of reinforcement for responding and not responding by rhesus monkeys: II. without signal. *Journal of Comparative and Physiological Psychology*, *87*, 1189–1197.

Kalat, J. W., & Rozin, P. (1972). You can lead a rat to poison but you can't make him think. In M.E.P. Seligman & J. L. Hager (Eds.), *Biological boundaries of learning*. New York: Appleton-Century-Crofts.

Kamin, L. J. (1969). Selective association and conditioning. In N. J. Mackintosh & W. K. Honig (Eds), *Fundamental issues in associative learning*. Halifax:Dalhousie University Press.

Kaufman, M. A., & Bolles, R. C. (1981). A nonassociative aspect of overshadowing. *Bulletin of the Psychonomic Society*, *18*, 318–320.

Kelley, H. H. (1967). Attribution theory in social psychology. In D. Levine (Ed.), *Nebraska symposium on motivation. Vol. 15*. Lincoln: University of Nebraska Press.

Kremer, E. F. (1971). Truly random and traditional control group procedures in CER conditioning in the rat. *Journal of Comparative and Physiological Psychology*, *76*, 441–448.

Mackintosh, N. J. (1975). A theory of attention: Variations in the associability of stimuli with reinforcement. *Psychological Review*, *82*, 276–298.

Mackintosh, N. J. (1983). *Conditioning and associative learning*. New York: Oxford University Press.

Maier, S. F., & Seligman, M. E. P. (1976). Learned helplessness: Theory and evidence. *Journal of Experimental Psychology: General*, *105*, 3–46.

McGeoch, J. A., & Irion, A. L. (1952). *The psychology of human learning*. New York: Longmans, Green.

Pearce, J. M., & Hall, G. (1980). A model for Pavlovian learning: Variations in the effectiveness of conditioned but not of unconditioned stimuli. *Psychological Review*, *87*, 532–552.

Rescorla, R. A. (1968). Probability of shock in the presence and absence of CS in fear conditioning. *Journal of Comparative and Physiological Psychology*, *66*, 1–5.

Rescorla, R. A. (1969). Conditioned inhibition of fear resulting from negative CS-US contingencies. *Journal of Comparative and Physiological Psychology*, *67*, 504–509.

Rescorla, R. A. (1972). Informational variables in Pavlovian conditioning. In G. H. Bower (Ed.), *The Psychology of Learning and Motivation* (Vol. 6). New York: Academic Press.

Rescorla, R. A. (1983). Effects of separate presentation of the elements on within-compound learning in autoshaping. *Animal Learning and Behavior*, *11*, 439–446.

Rescorla, R. A., & Cunningham, C. L. (1978). Within-compound flavor associations. *Journal of Experimental Psychology: Animal Behavior Processes*, *4*, 267–275.

Rescorla, R. A., & Cunningham, C. L. (1979). Spatial contiguity facilitates Pavlovian second-order conditioning. *Journal of Experimental Psychology: Animal Behavior Processes*, *5*, 152–161.

Rescorla, R. A., & Wagner, A. R. (1972). A theory of Pavlovian conditioning: Variations in the effectiveness of reinforcement and nonreinforcement. In A. H. Black & W. F. Prokasy (Eds.), *Classical conditioning II: Current research and theory*. New York: Appleton-Century-Crofts.

Schustack, M. W., & Sternberg, R. J. (1981). Evaluation of evidence in causal inference. *Journal of Experimental Psychology: General*, *110*, 101–120.

Schweitzer, L., & Green, L. (1982). Reevaluation of things past: A test of the "retrospection hypothesis" using a CER procedure with rats. *Pavlovian Journal of the Biological Sciences*, *17*, 62–68.

Shanks, D. R. (1985). Forward and backward blocking in human contingency judgement. *Quarterly Journal of Experimental Psychology*, *37B*, 1–21.

Testa, T. J. (1975). Effects of similarity of location and temporal intensity patterns of conditioned and unconditioned stimuli on the acquisition of conditioned suppression in rats. *Journal of Experimental Psychology: Animal Behavior Processes*, *1*, 114–121.

Wagner, A. R. (1978). Expectancies and the priming of STM. In S. H. Hulse, H. Fowler, & W. K. Honig (Eds.), *Cognitive processes in animal behavior*. Hillsdale, NJ: Lawrence Erlbaum Associates.

Wagner, A. R. (1981). SOP: A model of automatic memory processing in animal behavior. In N. E. Spear & R. R. Miller (Eds.), *Information processing in animals: Memory mechanisms*. Hillsdale, NJ: Lawrence Erlbaum Associates.

Wasserman, E. A., Chatlosh, D. L., & Neunaber, D. J. (1983). Perception of causal relations in humans: Factors affecting judgements of response-outcome contingencies under free-operant procedures. *Learning and Motivation, 14*, 406–432.

Weisman, R. G., & Litner, J. S. (1972). The role of Pavlovian events in avoidance training. In R. A. Boakes & M. S. Halliday (Eds.), *Inhibition and learning*. London: Academic Press.

Witcher, E. S., & Ayres, J. J. B. (1980). Systematic manipulation of CS-US pairings in negative CS-US correlation procedures in rats. *Animal Learning and Behavior, 8*, 67–74.

VI EXPERIMENTAL PARADIGMS AND ECOLOGY

Lars-Göran Nilsson
Trevor Archer

Systematic investigation of stimulus selection through the usage of associative learning procedures (Kehoe & Gormezano, 1980) has given rise to all manners of conditioned stimuli (CSs) and unconditioned stimuli (USs) combinations and vast numbers of compound stimulus conditioning experiments. It is possible that this trend has taken us in the direction of understanding more about stimulus selection principles necessary for a given organism's survival within its ecological niche. In spite of the constraint imposed by the arbitrary nature of conditioning procedures in general, the continual refinement of relatively simple methods has demonstrated that a high degree of complexity can be obtained from reexaminations of the basic Pavlovian concepts. The emerging importance of contextual or background stimuli, Pavlov's "synthetic environmental reflex" (1927), illustrates that this aspect of the organism's environment requires both a different (Bouton & Bolles, 1984) as well as the traditional conditioning approach (Balsam, 1982). We would like to suggest that an understanding and extrapolation of context effects is useful in a discussion of experimental paradigms and ecology.

The human memory approach to this topic appears to hinge open the symmetrical relationship between the encoding and retrieval events, and between task demands and cognitive capabilities of the individual. From the line of reasoning presented here it seems that we can consider a continuum whereby organisms lower down on the evolutionary scale rely more upon an environmental/contextual, procedural memory whereas humans and, perhaps, primates can also mobilize the self-generated, declarative memory. Certainly, we should be aware of some of the instances in which animals seem to display self-generated memory. One striking example is described by Premack (1973) and concerns the chimpanzee, Sarah's, generation of a stimulus/cue to represent the experimenter's cup of coffee. Consider Premack's (1973) description of this incident ''. . . We were sipping coffee, something we had not done previously in Sarah's presence, while staring balefully into the cage and paying less than the usual amount of attention to its occupant. Shortly, we noticed Sarah reaching out from the cage, more or less waving her arm at us. She proved to have a monkey pellet in her hand, an object about the size of her plastic words and the only object in her cage of those dimensions available to her. To guess what she had in mind required putting together the two novelties of the situation. We had not drunk coffee in her presence before, and she had not waved a monkey pellet at us before. We accepted the pellet from her and then offered her a sip of coffee. She accepted the sip and returned almost immediately with another pellet. . . . Ordinarily we would treat the above case as an impressive example of transfer, and would explain it in terms of stimulus generalization ''(p. 297). Later, Premack asks . . . ''is it possible that what we call discriminative stimuli are actually symbols, and would prove to be such if we made the proper tests?'' (p. 308). A more controlled example can be obtained from the phenomenon of sensory preconditioning. The demonstration of sensory preconditioning requires that two CSs (A and B) be paired prior to the pairing of one of these stimuli (A) with the US. Later the degree of conditioning strength accruing to the second stimulus (B) by itself is tested. Given the correct control procedures, sensory preconditioning has been reliably demonstrated (Rizley & Rescorla, 1972). In both these instances a case for contextual conditioning can be argued: (a) Sarah appears to have made her choice in the presence of the right contextual cue (experimenter), and (b) the contextual variable appears relevant to sensory preconditioning (Archer & Sjödeń, 1982).

The animal learning approach handled the very central issue of context function in encoding and retrieval. The tactic was equally critical since it involved proving that a particular demonstration of contextual control is that and nothing else. Thus, we found that caution must be exercised before accepting any of the numerous claims of contextual control of extinction whereas in the face of stringent experimental design contextual control of the latent inhibition, "Lubow," effect (Lubow, 1965; Lubow & Moore, 1959) was shown (but see also Baker & Mackintosh, 1979). Once again, the role of contextual cues in latent inhibition gives substance to the discussion of procedural and declarative memory. The human memory and animal learning discussions seem to suggest an important operational concept in the quest to unify the fields: emphasis upon a discussion of *remembering* rather than *memory*.

Although there is certainly some degree of continuity within both the animal learning and the human memory domains with respect to the empirical paradigms used there is also a considerable amount of inventiveness in creating new paradigms. In human memory research, for example, the distinction by Tulving (1972) between episodic and semantic memory has invoked a completely new set of semantic memory paradigms in parallel to all those episodic memory paradigms developed and used since the days of Ebbinghaus, and to the present. For one thing, studies on semantic memory have meant that we now know much more about the basic processes underlying remembering of general knowledge than we knew before solely on the basis of the traditional episodic memory paradigms. People may argue in turn that this is an important reorientation of at least some aspects of memory research, since thereby, it would be possible to understand how most people utilize their cognitive capabilities in more ecologically valid situations. For example, since most people go to school to acquire new knowledge and information for adequate use later in life, it could be argued that memory research should have something to tell us about such memory processes. Perhaps with some degree of exaggeration anyone could probably claim that the episodic memory tradition has given us very little in this respect. Nobody would probably have anything to say against such a reorientation per se; there is certainly no reason for not engaging in the study of memory in ecologically valid situations like, for example, in school. However, in the same sense, we concur with Tulving (1979) in stating "what is important is not whether observations about memory are made in the laboratory or in some natural setting, but rather the sense that one can make of the observations, and that there is no a priori reason to suspect that the sensibility of facts depends on the setting in which they are gathered" (p. 26). A reasoning of this sort would seem to hold true for human memory as well as animal learning. However, Craik (this volume) states in his thorough review of paradigms used in the human memory area that the principles studied must reflect central, general aspects of memory functioning in the person's day-to-day life.

A good example of the basic intention of Craik's words can be seen in a recent paper by Fagen & Rovee-Collier (1983) on time-dependent retrieval processes in 3-month-old infants. In an elegant way this paper describes how ecologically relevant aspects of memory or remembering can be studied in a meaningful way. This paper also brings to our attention a fact that we, maybe, should give some more thought when trying to integrate animal learning and human memory research. Rather than comparing theory and data in animal learning and human memory on the basis of experiments on the adult human being, who has a well-developed language, we should use data from human studies on infants or children. At least at face value, the basic compatibility between animal learning studies and human studies on infants should be much greater than that between animals and adult humans. This issue was touched upon implicitly several times during the discussions at the conference, but was not dealt with at any greater depth in any of the chapters. However, as stated in the final chapter Rönnberg & Ohlsson (this volume) this may be a major approach in future studies in comparative psychology.

REFERENCES

Archer, T., & Sjödeń, P. O. (1982). Higher-order conditioning and sensory preconditioning of a taste aversion with an exteroceptive CSI. *Quarterly Journal of Experimental Psychology, 34B,* 1–17.

Baker, A. G., & Mackintosh, N. J. (1979). Preexposure to the CS alone, US alone, or CS and US uncorrelated: Latent inhibition, blocking by context, or learned irrelevance? *Learning and Motivation, 10,* 278–294.

Balsam, P. (1982). Bringing the background to the foreground: The role of contextual cues in autoshaping. *The Harvard Symposium on the quantitative analysis of behavior: Acquisition processes.* New York: Ballinger.

Bouton, M. A., & Bolles, R. C. (1984). Context and cue predictability. In P. D. Balsam & A. Tomie (Eds.), *Context and learning.* Hillsdale, NJ: Lawrence Erlbaum Associates.

Fagen, J. W., & Rovee-Collier, C. (1983). Memory retrieval: A time-locked process in infancy. *Science, 204,* 1349–1351.

Kehoe, E. J., & Gormezano, I. (1980). Configuration and combination laws in conditioning with compound stimuli. *Psychological Bulletin, 87,* 351–378.

Lubow, R. E. (1965). Latent inhibition: Effects of frequency of nonreinforced preexposure of the CS. *Journal of Comparative and Physiological Psychology, 60,* 454–457.

Lubow, R. E., & Moore, A. V. (1959). Latent inhibition: The effect of non-reinforced pre-exposure to the conditioning stimulus. *Journal of Comparative and Physiological Psychology, 52,* 415–419.

Pavlov, I. P. (1927). *Conditional Reflexes.* Oxford: Oxford University Press.

Premack, D. (1973). Cognitive Principles. In F. J. McGuigan & D. B. Lumsden (Eds.), *Contemporary approaches to conditioning and learning.* Washington, DC: Winston.

Rizley, R. C., & Rescorla, R. A. (1972). Associations in second-order conditioning and sensory preconditioning. *Journal of Comparative and Physiological Psychology, 81,* 1–11.

Tulving, E. (1972). Episodic and semantic memory. In E. Tulving & W. Donaldson (Eds.), *Organization of memory.* New York: Academic Press.

Tulving, E. (1979). Memory research: What kind of progress? In L.-G. Nilsson (Ed.), *Perspectives on memory research.* Hillsdale, NJ: Lawrence Erlbaum Associates.

10 Paradigms in Human Memory Research

Fergus I. M. Craik
University of Toronto

The purpose of this chapter is to survey the experimental paradigms that have been used to study human memory. Because this is a large and somewhat unstructured brief, a considerable amount of selection is exercised to focus on paradigms with certain characteristics. I concentrate on those paradigms which (in my view) have been particularly useful in revealing details of memory processes and structures, those of current theoretical interest, and those that may help to bridge the gap between human and animal work. For the most part, I *comment* on the paradigms rather than simply describe them, and thereby hope to make contact with other chapters (e.g., by Cohen and by Crowder) that discuss theoretical issues in current work on human memory.

DESCRIPTION VS. ANALYSIS

In general, it may be suggested that paradigms in human memory research have been devised for two broad purposes: first, to provide a refined description of some phenomenon of memory, and second, to test some theoretically devised postulate about how memory operates. The two purposes thus serve, on the one hand, to enrich our descriptions of memory, and on the other to broaden our understanding of the processes that mediate memorial performance. Most current paradigms have been developed for the second purpose, and this review concentrates on them. Before turning to analytical methods and procedures, however, some brief consideration is given to descriptive paradigms.

Natural-history studies are more in the tradition of biology, and this tradition spills over into some areas of biological psychology. The interesting work on birds' ability to cache and later find seeds (Sherry, Krebs, & Cowie, 1981; Shettleworth & Krebs, 1982) is a case in point. Students of human memory have rather neglected descriptive paradigms, even though few would contest the notion that adequate theories can only be constructed on a base of careful, rich and valid observations and description. This neglect has been alleviated to some extent in recent years in response to theorists such as Bruce (1985) and Neisser (1982) who have argued for greater "ecological validity" in our work; my personal impression is that our field could profit by paying rather more attention to exploration and description.

It is still perfectly possible to describe striking phenomena of memory that come as a surprise to workers in the field. The "tip-of-the-tongue" (TOT) state explored by Brown and McNeill (1966) and the "flashbulb effect" investigated by Brown and Kulik (1977) are good examples. Such systematic observations of real-life remembering can often have important implications for theory, too. In the early 1970s it was widely believed that human subjects extracted the meaningful "gist" of written or spoken discourse, that the gist was remembered but the sensory or surface form was rapidly lost. Against this background, the demonstration of excellent memory for the exact words used in conversations 24 hours earlier (Keenan, MacWhinney, & Mayhew, 1977) or for the typescript in which passages were originally read, after weeks and months (Kolers, 1976; Kolers & Ostry, 1974) was both interesting and theoretically important.

The actual methods used in these descriptive studies have ranged from case histories (e.g., Luria, 1968) through questionnaire studies (Brown & Kulik, 1977; Harris, 1978) and the use of diaries (Linton, 1982) to measurements of number of items recalled and recognized under various experimental conditions—for example, Shepard's (1967) work on picture memory, studies of eyewitness testimony (Loftus, Miller, & Burns, 1978) and of story recall (Bower, 1976; Kintsch, 1974). By their nature, descriptive studies tend to use descriptive measures to assess performance, rather than to use standard paradigms; they also tend to focus on naturally occurring phenomena and on practical issues. My main point here is that descriptive studies have been relatively neglected by most students of memory—greater attention to the "natural history" of our area would help to keep our experiments focused on important issues and to enrich the basis of our theories.

In the more rigorously controlled studies that form the bulk of the human experimental literature, a number of basic paradigms recur in various forms. These studies typically involve linguistic materials, and are usually designed to test some hypothesis about the structures and processes that have been proposed to underlie memory performance. The common paradigms are free (unordered) recall of a list of items (e.g., words, pictures, objects), serial recall—in which the items must be recalled in the order of presentation, cued recall, recognition of the presented items among similar distractors, relearning of the materials to some criterion, and paired-associate recall and recognition. Whereas the first-named paradigms are tests of item information, the last two are tests of associative information. Specific forms of these basic paradigms have been designed to test various theoretical points arising from different models of human memory. These points address such questions as the type of representation (e.g., acoustic, semantic, procedural) relevant to a particular store or system, the nature of encoding processes, transfer from one part of the system to another, the capacity of various stores or structures, the time course and mechanisms of forgetting, and the nature and characteristics of retrieval processes.

Such analytical paradigms have clearly played the major role in extending our knowledge of human memory; however, all too often they depend for their usefulness on the validity of the underlying theory that they were designed to test. If the theory collapses, or becomes less relevant to prevailing views, the data may be of little value in their own right. One salient example is the colossal amount of work that was done on the Sternberg paradigm in the decade of the 1970s. Whereas the original demonstration and analyses of Sternberg (1966, 1969) represent the very highest level of thinking and empirical work in experimental psychology, I would say that the great bulk of subsequent work using the paradigm has made a relatively slight contribution to our understanding of human memory processes. This is not to argue that all paradigms must necessarily involve "ecologically valid" materials or situations; I believe with Tulving (1983) that important general principles can be elaborated and refined as well with artificial materials in the laboratory as they can be deduced from real-world phenomena. The important point, however, is that the principles themselves *must* reflect central, general aspects of memory functioning in the person's day-to-day life.

If some paradigms have told us rather little about how human memory works, there is even less reason to apply them routinely to animal research. "Because it is there" may be a perfectly sound reason for climbing Mount Everest, but it provides a less satisfactory rationale for measuring, say, short-term memory in the pigeon—unless of course it can first be demonstrated that pigeons use that type of short-term retention in their natural environment. The point is that satisfactory paradigms must be theoretically motivated, and the theoretical motivation in turn must be founded in valid general principles. Similarly, in order to bridge the gap between the areas of human memory and animal learning, the continuity should be at the level of principles, not paradigms. The paradigms themselves may well be modified in light of the particular organism's knowledge and capabilities, but the same general point can be attacked across species. The importance of the general points that merit this type of effort must be assessed in the context of what specific organisms use memory for.

So what are these centrally important general principles? How have they been studied in humans, and how might the paradigms be modified for animal work?

The chapters in this volume by Cohen and Crowder provide some answers. My personal reaction necessarily depends on my own idea of what memory is and how it works; the next section provides an outline of my present views.

WHAT IS MEMORY? A PERSONAL VIEW

Over the past 10 years my ideas have moved progressively away from a view of memory as a structural system — a "thing" in the head—and towards the viewpoint, advocated by Bartlett (1932) and others, of *remembering* as an activity. That is, the memory trace is perhaps not a specific structure located at some point (or even diffusely) within the central nervous system, but is rather an altered potential of the system to carry out certain mental activities provided that the context, task, goals, mental set etc. present at the time of initial learning are also reinstated, either "driven" by external stimulation or reconstructed internally by the rememberer. By this account, remembering is essentially a form of perceiving. Just as perceiving reflects an interaction between the stimulus array and aspects of previous learning (as well as genetically determined aspects of brain functioning), so remembering also reflects an interaction between some externally provided stimulus (either a general context or a specific retrieval cue) and relevant aspects of previous learning. Remembering is thus viewed as a recapitulation of the original experience, either in its relatively literal imaginal form (e.g., How were people in the group standing relative to others and to the furniture? What clothes were they wearing?) or in terms of higher-order information abstracted from the experience (How many people were in the group? What was the mood of person X? What was the gist of the conversation between X and Y?)

One crucial aspect of this position is that remembering is thought of *essentially* as an interaction between external events and mental activities. Just as it is not very sensible or meaningful to talk about the percept as a function of mental activity only (rather, it is by nature an interaction between stimulus information and specific "mental skills" of the perceiver), so it does not seem too useful to regard memory as a function of mind alone. Similarly, it is not very meaningful to ask about the characteristics of the percept when perception is not occurring; the percept is not a preformed "thing" waiting to be activated by appropriate input, rather it reflects a potential of the neural machinery to interact with sensory information in a lawful way, and so give rise to specific mental experiences. In just the same way, it is not sensible to inquire about the characteristics of the memory trace when remembering is not occurring (the memory trace "in repose" as Crowder, chapter 2, describes it); the experience of remembering may not reflect the activation of some preformed memory record so much as the interaction of specific inputs with the potential of the mental machinery. A further implication of this view is that it may be no more sensible for neurophysiologists to look for the engram within some neural memory bank than it would be to look for pictures in the circuitry of a TV set. Of course the circuitry does have the potential to *produce* pictures in interaction with highly specific incoming information, but the pictures are neither in the circuitry itself, nor in the electromagnetic radiation itself.

An important difference between remembering and the production of pictures on a TV screen, however, is that whereas the TV system passively reflects changes in the pattern of incoming stimulation, the human rememberer can reconstruct previous experiences on the basis of quite fragmentary incoming information. As discussed later in the chapter, different retrieval tasks vary in the extent to which such self-initiated reconstructive activities are required—free recall demands a great deal of reconstruction; recognition of pictures requires considerably less. One way of expressing these self-initiated remembering operations is that human subjects clearly *intend* to remember; that is, they are aware of some desired goal of the mental activity, and use various strategies to aid the reconstructive processes. An interesting point in the context of comparisons between human and animal memory is the degree to which animals also intend to remember. Can animals, like humans, improve their memory performance by attempting to recollect previously acquired information, or are their remembering activities driven more passively by changes in the incoming stimulus array interacting with current knowledge, drives, and goals? Do they function more like TV receivers with a learning capability?

I have called this synopsis a personal view, but it clearly owes a great deal to many other current researchers. In particular, the views just expressed are similar in many respects to those suggested previously by Bartlett (1932), Bransford, McCarrell, Franks, and Nitsch (1977), Jacoby (1983), Jenkins (1974, 1979), Kolers (1973), Nilsson (1984) and Tulving (1983). To return to the point of valid general principles—the present viewpoint suggests three sets of important questions that require answers at both the human and the animal level. First, how is the underlying system modified by the initial experience; what are the factors that constrain and modify encoding processes, what are the roles of attention and "working memory" in acquisition, how is new information related to the existing knowledge base, and what genetic constraints exist to bias the system to assimilate various types of information more or less easily? Second, what factors affect the reinstatement of the original mental operations; how do "reconstructive operations" work and what gives rise to the feelings of "pastness" that accompany remembering (and presumably enable the organism to distinguish remembering from perceiving)? Third, how do encoding and retrieval processes interact, and what are the necessary relations between them? What role, for example, does context play at acquisition and retrieval? The rest of the chapter will consider a selection of recent studies that address these problems, and evaluate the adequacy of the experimental paradigms that have been used to examine them.

PARADIGMS AND ISSUES IN SHORT-TERM
RETENTION

What is the role of short-term memory (STM) in perception and learning? Among the answers that have been given to this question is the notion that STM is essentially an input buffer that comes into play especially in situations of stimulus overload—STM holds "extra" information until the processing mechanisms are free to deal with the overload (e.g., Broadbent, 1958). With this point in mind, many early experiments used the dichotic listening paradigm in which two different strings of 3–4 digits, letters, or words were presented simultaneously, one string to each ear. In retrospect, the paradigm probably revealed more about attention than memory processes (e.g., Treisman, 1964) but work on dichotic listening was of great importance in formulating early views of auditory sensory storage, limited capacity processing mechanisms, and rehearsal processes (Broadbent, 1958, 1971).

But many (most?) information-processing situations do not appear to involve stimulus overload; does short-term storage play some further role? Two other suggested functions of STM are first, that it is a device to hold recently received information in a state of high accessibility so that the human or other organism can respond rapidly and effectively when some further event occurs (e.g., the warning provided by a bird's alarm call or by an orange traffic light). In the same vein, (Hollis, 1982) has suggested that a short-term storage mechanism is necessary for the successful association of stimulus and response in Pavlovian conditioning. Second, that STM serves to hold and integrate sequences of information that arrive over time—speech comprehension is a good example of an ability that requires such a device at the human level, and Harley's (1981) work on the learning of sequences of sites in foraging is an analogous case in the animal literature. Such views of STM lead to questions of capacity of the input buffer, the types of information that it can hold, the mechanism and time course of forgetting, and the characteristics of retrieval of information from the store. A great deal of research effort in the 1960s was expended on answering these questions, and appropriate paradigms were devised to tackle them. Capacity was assessed by span techniques, by Sperling's (1960) partial report method, and by measuring the size of the recency effect in free recall. The issue of coding was examined by means of the types of errors made (e.g., Conrad's, 1964, finding of "acoustic confusions" in recall of visually-presented letters), by considering the types of information that disrupt performance (Baddeley, 1966), and the types of retrieval information that are particularly effective at various retention intervals (e.g., Bartlett & Tulving, 1974). Retrieval characteristics were also studied by means of cued recall techniques, by the "release from PI" phenomenon (Wickens, 1970), and by Sternberg's (1966) recognition and sequential probe paradigms. The characteristics of forgetting from STM were explored using the Brown-Peterson paradigm (Brown, 1958; Peterson & Peterson, 1959), digit probe techniques (e.g., Waugh & Norman, 1965), the suffix effect (e.g.,

Crowder & Morton, 1969), and the displacement of items from recency positions by interference from further items (Glanzer & Cunitz, 1966).

Full reviews of this work are given by Craik and Levy (1976), Glanzer (1972), and Murdock (1974). The picture of STM that emerged from this decade of research was essentially one of a rather passive input buffer, dealing primarily with linguistic material and serving to prolong perceptual experience for a few seconds until the incoming material could be comprehended and integrated with existing knowledge. The term "primary memory" (James, 1890) was revived to describe this form of short-term storage (Waugh & Norman, 1965).

What role would the concept of STM play in a comparative psychology of learning and memory? Presumably, the study of primary memory in animals would explore interspecies differences in capacity, the types of codes used, forgetting functions, and so on. But would this be a useful exercise? Personally, I very much doubt it. One reason is that characteristics of primary memory that were originally considered structural and fixed, were later seen to depend heavily on the task and materials used (Craik & Lockhart, 1972). In this sense, "primary memory" might be better viewed as a set of related mental abilities rather than as a single structure to be measured and catalogued (Crowder, 1982).

A second reason for not applying the paradigms of 1960s STM research to animals, is that human memory researchers have adopted a progressively more active view of short-term retention since the late 1960s. Atkinson and Shiffrin's (1968, 1971) influential model of memory developed the notion that the short-term store was a structure within which various control processes were executed. By 1971 these control processes—rehearsal, coding, decisions, and retrieval strategies—were the essential stuff of the model, leaving the structural components with a rather vestigial role. This view of short-term retention involving a set of related active *processes* had been predated by Neisser's (1967) description of primary memory as "active verbal memory" and was developed more fully in Baddeley and Hitch's (1974) model of "working memory." (Interestingly, Atkinson and Shiffrin gave the short-term store the subtitle "temporary working memory" in their 1971 model.)

The idea of working memory emphasizes an active, functional role for short-term retention. Incoming information can be held, manipulated, and integrated with existing knowledge in a variety of ways, some quite novel. Thus working memory can be viewed as a forum in which a variety of higher-level cognitive functions—comprehending, learning, thinking, problem-solving, and remembering—can take place. It can also be viewed as a set of related processes, or (taking a somewhat more structural position) as "a heterogeneous array of independent storage capacities intrinsic to various subsystems specialized for processing in specific domains" (Monsell, 1984).

Whether working memory is regarded as a relatively fixed structure, albeit with a flexible "central executive" and several peripheral subsystems (Baddeley, 1983; Baddeley & Hitch, 1974; Hitch, this volume), or as an umbrella term for a set of storage capacities or processes, the concept has strong functional implications. Working memory is *for* something; it is a necessary component in a variety of complex cognitive functions such as reading (Daneman & Carpenter, 1980), comprehension of prose (Kieras, 1981; Kintsch, 1974; Miller, 1981) and problem-solving (Baddeley & Hitch, 1974). It also seems likely that working memory is crucially involved in learning—especially in cases in which the new information has to be held and comprehended prior to its integration with existing knowledge.

Because it is a relatively new concept, paradigms to assess working memory functioning are still few in number. My colleague Meredyth Daneman at the University of Toronto has suggested some methods for measuring working memory in the context of individual differences in language processes. In one paradigm, subjects read a series of sentences for comprehension and also attempt to remember the last words from each sentence. "Reading Span" is then the longest list of last words that the person can reproduce; this measure correlates well with results from tests of reading ability, especially with measures involving integration and inference (Daneman & Carpenter, 1980). In a related paradigm that Daneman calls "production span," subjects are first given a short list of unrelated words which they hold in mind; their task is then to produce a series of sentences, each successive sentence containing one word from the original list. Again "production span" is the longest sequence of sentences that the subject can produce. Daneman argues that whereas reading span taps complex receptive processes of reading and comprehension, production span assesses the ease with which subjects can access and produce words in discourse.

The fact that Daneman has developed two tasks (so far) to tap different aspects of working memory, reflects the assumption that "working memory" is not one structure or one process with fixed characteristics to be measured, but may be better thought of as a set of related cognitive skills (see also Crowder, 1982). Other tasks that involve holding, manipulating, and integrating information may also be considered working memory tasks, although they may again reflect somewhat different skills and abilities. For example, asking subjects to sort playing cards into suits, not with respect to the current card but with respect to the card one or two back in the series (Welford, 1958), might be considered a test of some aspects of working memory. Appropriate paradigms should reflect the particular function that the researcher is interested in.

If both "primary memory" and "working memory" are better regarded as descriptive categories rather than as separate stores or structures, what is the relation between them, if any? My suggestion is that primary memory tasks and working memory tasks may involve some of the same cognitive components, but whereas primary memory tasks stress the passive holding of information, working memory tasks involve more active manipulation and integration of information. But the two sets of tasks (or abilities) should probably be thought of as lying on a complex continuum as opposed to reflecting two separate systems, or discrete types of memory. By this account "appropriate" paradigms would be those tapping processes that are thought to be used in some real-world cognitive activity—reading, retrieval from long-term memory, problem-solving, or the like.

With respect to animal studies, my argument is that there seems very little point in simply adapting human memory paradigms to study the same aspects of short-term retention across very different species. The comparisons, rather, should be at the level of cognitive abilities with clear functional or adaptive significance for the animals studied, and the paradigms used should be designed specifically to assess these abilities or their hypothesized components. An excellent example is provided by Olton's studies of working memory in rats (Olton, Chapter 5; Olton & Samuelson, 1976). Olton's technique assesses the rat's ability to remember which arms of a radial maze it has already visited to retrieve food rewards. This type of temporary spatial memory appears to be trivially easy for the rat (although it might pose severe problems for human subjects!) presumably because it is highly compatible with the rat's specific cognitive abilities or "knowledge system" (Gallistel, 1980).

Two final comments on working memory: First, it may be more revealing to study the *knowledge systems* of various species directly, rather than various memory abilities; the latter may well be a function of the former (cf. Craik & Lockhart, 1972). Second, the "working memory" abilities revealed by Olton's tests appear to be somewhat different in kind from working memory abilities assessed in humans. In the human case, "working memory" almost always implies holding the information "in mind," and the ability is disrupted if the subject is severely distracted. This does not appear to be the case in Olton's paradigm; the animal can be confined to the central platform for several minutes halfway through its performance and then released to complete the task successfully (Olton & Samuelson, 1976). Perhaps a better parallel with human abilities would be the apparent skill of experts to remember some relevant set of information temporarily—for example, waiters remember complex sets of food orders over minutes or hours, real-estate agents remember detailed sets of facts about clients and houses on their current listings, chess masters can hold several games in mind at the same time. But these experts are clearly not rehearsing the current information continuously; it seems as if a subset of their knowledge can remain "primed" and thus easily accessed over minutes, hours, or days. Following Olton's work with rats, appropriate paradigms should be designed to evaluate this type of "working memory" in human subjects.

TRANSFER FROM SHORT-TERM TO LONG-TERM MEMORY

In multistore models of memory (e.g., Atkinson & Shiffrin, 1968; Murdock, 1967), an important issue concerns the transfer of information from one store to the next, especially transfer from the temporary short-term store (STS) to the permanent long-term store (LTS). Atkinson and Shiffrin's suggestion was that transfer depended on time in STS and the amount of attention paid to the information while in STS. They therefore developed paradigms in which these factors were varied and indeed they demonstrated lawful relations between time and attention on the one hand and LTS strength on the other (Atkinson & Shiffrin, 1968). However, this account turned out to be incomplete. Later work (Craik & Lockhart, 1972; Craik & Watkins, 1973; Woodward, Bjork, & Jongeward, 1973) suggested and showed that the *qualitative* type of rehearsal in the short-term store was crucially important as a determinant of later long-term retention. Maintenance rehearsal, involving for example the simple repetition of a word's phonemic characteristics, has little or no effect on later recall performance (although it does serve to increase *recognition,* as shown by Woodward et al., 1973) whereas elaborative rehearsal, involving "deeper" semantic and relational information, does enhance both recall and recognition.

This pattern of results was demonstrated in a recent, as yet unpublished, study by Zhu, Craik, and Olson. Subjects rehearsed groups of three unrelated words for intervals of 2, 4, 8, 16 and 20 sec and were later tested for both recall and recognition of the words. Four groups of subjects treated the words differently during the initial rehearsal intervals; one group held the words "incidentally" ostensibly to prevent them rehearsing lists of digits (after Glenberg, Smith, & Green 1977, and Rundus, 1977), a second group repeated the words for 2–20 sec, a third group formed a sentence involving the three words, and a fourth group constructed a visual image involving the words—all groups except the first were aware that a later memory test would be given. The results are shown in Fig. 10.1. In general, both recall and recognition benefitted from inten-

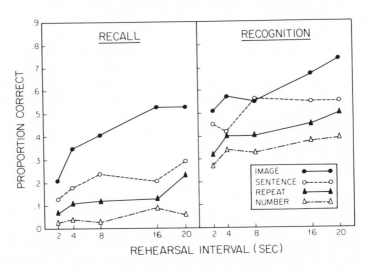

FIG. 10.1.   Recall (left panel) and recognition (right panel) as a function of type and duration of rehearsal (Zhu, Craik, & Olson, unpublished data).

tionality and deeper processing (in this case from "sentence" and "image" processing). For recall, type of processing interacted with initial rehearsal interval in that performance improved differentially for the deeper processing groups; but this interaction was absent in the case of recognition. One explanation of this result is that recall depends on interitem processing (Mandler, 1979), and that further rehearsal time allows the formation of particularly rich relational encodings in the deeper processing groups. Recognition, in Mandler's view, depends more on intraitem processing, and thus all processing groups benefit equally from extra rehearsal time.

One further important factor relating to "transfer" of information from STS to LTS, is that the effectiveness of different types of processing depends on the specific retrieval information present at the time of testing. This effect was demonstrated by Geiselman and Bjork (1980) in an experiment similar to the study just described. In their experiment Geiselman and Bjork had subjects rehearse the word triads in an imagined voice. Under maintenance rehearsal (but not elaborative rehearsal) conditions, later recognition performance was enhanced when the test words were presented in the same voice. Thus, performance depends on the compatibility between encoding and retrieval processes (e.g., Tulving & Thomson, 1973), but that general statement has to be qualified somewhat when various types of initial processing are considered.

What exactly is "transferred" in such studies? As I have argued previously (Craik, 1983), I do not find the notion of transfer particularly useful. Instead, it seems preferable to talk directly about the different types of encoding that can be carried out, and the effects of different encoding operations on memory performance after short or long retention intervals, and under different conditions of retrieval. Human subjects, with their rich and complex knowledge structures, may have a greater number of processing options open to them than other animals do—that is, humans may choose to process incoming information in a variety of ways depending on their goals and purposes. This degree of "optionality" appears to be especially true of linguistic material which can be processed in terms of its sounds (or visual characteristics) or in terms of its meanings and implications at various levels of elaboration and associative richness. Thus, if a person wishes to hold information temporarily, he or she may choose to merely repeat the sounds; if longer-term retention is required, however, deeper and more elaborate processing is carried out. But this distinction is not very usefully described as "transfer" of information.

For the same reasons, the notion of transfer may not be particularly useful in animal studies either. Even if animals do not possess the same range of "processing options" that humans do, the general principle may still hold that specific stimuli tend to be encoded in a given way, in light of the knowledge and experience of the animal in question. By this argument, instead of studying "transfer" in animals, paradigms should be devised to study how different encoding operations are carried out within and across species, and how these various types of encoding affect performance in a variety of retrieval situations.

ENCODING PROCESSES

It is generally agreed that encoding and retrieval processes cannot be studied in isolation—good encoding conditions depend largely on specific retrieval conditions and vice versa (Tulving, 1974, 1979; Tulving & Thomson, 1973). These interactive effects are dealt with in a later section. However, I also maintain that some encoding conditions *are* associated with superior levels of retention, given that compatible retrieval conditions are provided. That is, some ways of encoding information are potentially better than others, provided that the potential is realised by means of appropriate retrieval cues (Craik, 1979; Fisher & Craik, 1977; Moscovitch & Craik, 1976). In general these "superior" types of encoding are those that relate new information to an existing body of well-organized knowledge, and yet form an encoding that is *distinctive* from similar, previously encoded information (Eysenck, 1979; Jacoby & Craik, 1979).

The distinctiveness of a particular encoded episode facilitates its later retrieval by specific cues, and presumably increases the probability that the retrieved information will be identified and remembered as the original episode. Such distinctiveness is often conferred by the integration of event and contextual information; at the time of retrieval, the encoded "event plus context" can then be accessed either by providing some fragment of the original context and asking for retrieval of event information (recall) or by providing some part of the event and requiring retrieval of context (recognition). Some types of memory failure reflect the dissociation of item and context information. For example, a person may retain the general knowledge accrued from a specific event, yet be unable to say where or when the information was acquired—"source amnesia" (Claparede, 1911; Schacter, Harbluk, & McLachlan, 1984). In an analogous (though less dramatic) fashion, it is possible to remember a context yet forget the information that was acquired there or some specific event that occurred (Reed, 1979).

Encoding variables may thus be grouped under two headings—those variables that affect the (potential) memorability of items or events themselves, and those that affect the integration of focal events with other events or with the surrounding context. This distinction has been captured by Mandler (1979) in his contrast between "intra-item" and "inter-item" encoding. Some recent paradigms that explore the former set of variables are described briefly before considering variables that affect the integration of item and context.

When the emphasis in human memory research changed in the 1970s from quantitative variables (e.g., rehearsal duration, number of repetitions) to qualitative variables (e.g., expertise, types of encoding), new paradigms were devised to illustrate the new theoretical notions. For example, Craik and Tulving (1975) explored the consequences for later retention of various "levels of processing" of linguistic material. In an incidental learning paradigm, subjects were asked various questions about single words—e.g., is the word in capital letters?

Does the word rhyme with X? Is the word in Y semantic category? Answering these questions required different types (or "levels") of processing, and it was found that subsequent recall and recognition varied markedly as a function of the type of question asked. "Deep" semantic questions were associated with higher levels of retention than rhyme questions, which in turn were superior to questions concerning typescript. Later work (Rogers, Kuiper, & Kirker, 1977) showed that questions involving self-reference—e.g., "does this adjective describe you?" were associated with higher levels of retention than those following questions concerning semantic categories. The general principle appears to be that memory performance is a function of the degree to which the new information is related to pre-existing, organized, meaningful knowledge—to the subjects' general or specific areas of expertise.

Could this paradigm be usefully applied in animal studies? One drawback might be the restricted range of "processing options" in the animal's repertoire, but presumably higher mammals can deal with objects and events for different purposes and with different goals in mind. As a suggestion, monkeys can be trained to select the odd item in a group of three (Harlow, Meyer, & Settlage, 1951) and it may be possible to have the animal choose on the basis of different characteristics—e.g., color, shape, function, personal relevance. Performance on a later recognition test should then reflect the "depth" of the initial processing. If successful, this paradigm could be viewed as a means of exploring the animal's knowledge structures, as well as a way of assessing memory. The finding that rats have an excellent memory for the taste of "poisoned water" (Garcia & Koelling, 1966) is a good case in point.

Two encoding paradigms that have stimulated considerable interest in recent years are those giving rise to the "generation effect" (Jacoby, 1978; Slamecka & Graf, 1978) and the "transformation effect" (Kolers, 1973). In both cases, later retention is enhanced by an apparently trivial manipulation at the time of encoding. The generation effect is found in situations where subjects complete words with missing letters (e.g., R_BY) as opposed to simply reading them (e.g., PEARL); both recall and recognition levels are boosted by the act of generation. Kolers (1973) had subjects read passages of text that were transformed in various ways (e.g., inverted, mirror image) and again found superior retention of the transformed text relative to text that had been read in normal script. Kolers' original purpose was to demonstrate that recognition performance is a function of repeating the same pattern-analyzing operations (Kolers, 1973, 1979), but it seems likely that at least part of the effect is attributable to the more extensive *semantic* processes engaged by the reader attempting to decipher the transformed text (Graf, 1981; Masson & Sala, 1978). This account is supported by the finding that the transformation effect is not found with meaningless materials like anomalous sentences (Graf, 1981) or nonsense syllables (Glisky, 1983), but is not diminished when the recognition test is presented auditorily (Glisky, 1983). Given that the material was presented visually yet tested auditorily, there can be little if any overlap in the pattern-analyzing operations on the two occasions; the probable explanation is that more abstract, "semantic" operations are involved. Again, the generation and transformation effects appear to be cases in which greater involvement with the subject's knowledge systems are associated with higher levels of retention (Craik, 1981; Graf, 1981).

The generation effect, the transformation effect, and the "levels" effect of Craik and Tulving (1975) are examples in which the retention of single events is enhanced. What about paradigms to explore the integration of an event with its context? This important question has been relatively neglected, but there is evidence that interest in it is increasing (Mackintosh, Chapter 11). One relevant factor is the degree to which the context changes the interpretation of an event (Fisher & Cuervo, 1983; Godden & Baddeley, 1980). A second factor appears to be the amount of attention devoted to the situation. Preliminary evidence suggests that arousing or interesting events are better integrated with their contexts (Brown & Kulik, 1977; Rubin, 1984) and also that *reduced* attention is associated with poorer integration of event and context (Rabinowitz, Craik, & Ackerman, 1982). Other memory impaired groups also show poor memory for context (Huppert & Piercy, 1976; Schacter, Harbluk, & McLachlan, 1984; Stern, 1981) but whether these cases can also be attributed to attentional dysfunction or reduced processing resources remains problematical.

In any event, the role of context in both conscious recollection and in retention without awareness (Jacoby & Witherspoon, 1982) is not yet well understood, but seems likely to attract a lot of theoretical and empirical attention over the next few years. The topic appears to provide further common ground with studies of animal memory, and the distinction between intrinsic (interactive) and extrinsic (background) contexts is likely to provide further theoretical impetus (Geiselman & Bjork, 1980; Godden & Baddeley, 1980; Mackintosh, this volume).

RETRIEVAL PROCESSES

As outlined previously, I endorse the general view that the goal of retrieval processes is to reinstate the specific mental operations induced at the time of encoding the target event (Kolers, 1973; Tulving & Thomson, 1973). These encoding activities will typically include pattern analyzing operations reflecting perceptual aspects of the event and its context, but also operations that represent more abstract qualities concerned with the event's interpretation and significance in light of the organism's knowledge and previous experiences. It follows from this view that encoding processes and retrieval processes must be extremely similar, if not identical. Perhaps the major difference between the two sets of processes is their respective goals; that of encoding being principally to perceive and comprehend, that of retrieval being to reinstate aspects of some former percept, thought, or action (Craik, 1983; Craik & Jacoby, 1979; Jacoby & Craik, 1979). It is further suggested that the reinstatement of operations occurs partly through the system being "driven" by the current contextual and "cue" information, and partly by means of the subject's own reconstructive efforts, reflecting an *intention* on the subject's part to remember the previous event.

The helpful role of context in remembering is well documented (e.g., Godden & Baddeley, 1975, 1980); studies of state-dependent learning (Bower, 1981; Eich, 1980) make the same point. The ability to remember is clearly adaptive in that recurrence of a given set of circumstances will tend to evoke the operations (reflecting percepts, thoughts, conclusions, and actions) that occurred on similar occasions in the past, and thus provide some guidance with respect to present action. However, the present context may not provide sufficient guidance to "remind" the person (or animal) of the previous occasion, and further self-initiated reconstructive operations are then required to "jump the gap" between the current and desired states (Schank, 1982). To some extent the gap is closed by relatively automatic redintegrative processes; if retrieval cues plus background context drive the system close to some former state, there is a tendency for the system to move into that state. Although such redintegrative processes are not well understood they may be thought of as "pattern-completion" activities (Kintsch, 1974) in which a re-presentation of some fragment of a previously learned pattern serves to invoke the original pattern (Jones, 1976).

When contextual information is insufficient to drive the system back into the desired state, further constructive or reconstructive operations must be initiated by the subject (Bartlett, 1932; Neisser, 1967). I have previously suggested (Craik, 1983) that the degree to which such self-initiated activities are required, depends on the paradigm used. Free recall relies heavily on self-initiated reconstructive operations since very little guidance is provided by the request to recall. Cued recall provides more guidance, and recognition even more, and thus self-initiated processes are required less in these paradigms. In procedural memory tasks, self-initiated reconstruction of a previous episode is usually not required at all—the task calls merely for perception of a present event or execution of an action. Table 10.1 shows various memory paradigms ordered intuitively with respect to the degree of self-initiation required. The greatest degree of self-initiation may be needed when subjects must "remember to remember"; for example, when a person runs out of groceries he not only needs to remember the required items, but also (on the way home from work perhaps) to remember to stop at the store.

The scheme shown in Table 10.1 is in good agreement with the findings from studies of age-related deficits in memory. The large decrements shown by older people in free recall performance are typically reduced under cued recall or recognition conditions (Craik, 1977, 1983). Also, age differences are slight or nonexistent in procedural memory tasks such as priming (Howard, Lasaga, & McAndrews, 1980; Moscovitch, 1982). At the other end of the scale, everyday

TABLE 10.1
A Possible Classification of Retrieval Tasks

Task	Self-initiated activity	Environmental support
'Remembering to remember' Free recall Cued recall Recognition Relearning Procedural memory	↑ increases	increases ↓

forgetfulness provides many examples of the failure to "remember to remember" or of "prospective remembering" as Meacham and Leiman (1975, cited by Neisser, 1982) have termed it. My earlier suggestion (Craik, 1983) was that the different degrees of memory impairment shown by older people in various circumstances reflect the degree of self-initiated activity demanded by a particular task or paradigm, rather than the involvement of different memory systems (Tulving, 1983, this volume). Speculatively, the scheme may also be applicable to at least some other cases of memory dysfunction.

These notions provide some interesting questions for students of animal memory. Are there systematic differences in redintegration across species, for example? How do differences between the encoding and the retrieval context affect the animal's ability to produce a previously learned response? The ethologists have provided some information on this question—for example, in Tinbergen's classic studies of the digger wasp, in which the insect's ability to find its burrow was affected when salient visual cues were moved (see Gallistel, 1980). However, it could be argued that the behavior here is more a case of pre-formed actions being released provided that the contextual support is sufficient. Mackintosh's work (Chapter 11) can also be regarded as demonstrating the necessary role of contextual support at retrieval—especially in the "intrinsic" case, in which the encoding context serves to modify the initial encoding. This work clearly falls under the rubric of Tulving's (1983) encoding specificity principle, thereby providing a further link between studies of animal learning and human memory.

There is some evidence at the human level that whereas the notions of encoding specificity and contextual support are relevant across the lifespan, older children are somewhat less "context-bound" than are younger children. Ackerman (1981), for example, has demonstrated that when objects were presented for children to learn either as pictures of the objects or their names, younger children's later recognition performance depended strongly on the item being represented in the same form (i.e., picture-picture or word-word), whereas older children and young adults were less dependent on the exact form being reinstated. Thus the "encoding specificity" interaction between form at encoding and form at test, itself changes with age. Of course, the *mental operations* during retrieval are still likely to mirror those at encoding, even in adult subjects. The point is that with increasing age the child is less dependent on environmental cues driving the system back into the appropriate state; in addition, events are encoded in a less literal and more abstract form. In these ways the older cognitive system acts to modify the environmental input at both encoding and retrieval.

This interpretation provides a further interesting comparative question for students of animal memory—to what extent do different species actively modify the information provided at retrieval to reconstruct some previous representation? Is there a role for *intentionality* in animal memory? The likely answer is "yes" for higher mammals at least. For example, work on recognition memory in monkeys (Gaffan, 1976; Chapter 13) shows that the animals can solve a present problem by retrieving information from a previous occasion; in some sense the animal "knows" that the previous information is relevant and "intends" to retrieve it (see Dennett, 1983, for a fuller discussion of intentionality in animals). At a more general level, it would be interesting to demonstrate an increasing role for intentionality and active reconstruction in memory as the evolutionary scale is ascended; such a demonstration would show that higher animals are less bound to the contextual "here-and-now" and would parallel similar demonstrations in human ontogeny (Piaget, 1952).

PROCEDURAL MEMORY

In this final section I briefly mention some recent work on memory for skilled procedures. Because the procedures in question are often nonverbal, this area offers particularly good opportunities for developing paradigms common to man and other animals. Also, the retention of skilled procedures does not require conscious recollection of the original event and this fact too should facilitate comparative studies. The older work on learning perceptual-motor skills focused on the conditions that facilitate their acquisition and retention, but recent interest in the topic has been boosted by dramatic findings from studies of amnesic patients, and the focus of interest has changed accordingly. It has been known for some time that amnesics can learn and retain motor skills despite being grossly impaired in their ability to learn new verbal information (see Baddeley, 1982, for a review). However, the essential distinction is not between motor and verbal skills, since amnesic patients also fall within the normal range on eyelid conditioning (Weiskrantz & Warrington, 1979) and in their ability to recognize drawings when prompted by fragments of the original picture (Warrington & Weiskrantz, 1968). It is also clear that the patients are not simply learning a general skill, since they retain information about specific items (Baddeley, 1982).

Cohen and Squire (1980) suggested that the crucial distinction is between "knowing how" (procedural memory) and "knowing that" (propositional memory). In their study, amnesic subjects learned to decipher sets of words presented in inverted typography (following Kolers, 1973). Over several repetitions the patients improved their ability to read specific words, even in the absence of any conscious recollection that they had seen the words before. Such findings have led some theorists to postulate different memory systems underlying the conscious recollection of specific episodes and the often unconscious retention of procedural knowledge (Cohen & Squire, 1980; Tulving, 1983), although not all researchers take this view (e.g., Jacoby, 1983).

Regardless of the outcome of this theoretical debate, the revival of interest in procedural memory has already given rise to several new experimental paradigms. Following Warrington and Weiskrantz's work on picture fragments, Tulving, Schacter, and Stark (1982) had subjects learn a list of long, uncommon words and later tested retention of the information in one of two ways. The method tapping conscious episodic recollection was a standard recognition test; in the other test the subject was given word fragments (e.g., A_ _A_ _IN, _H_O_EM) and the task was to complete the word. Tulving et al. found that fragment completion performance was greatly enhanced by previous presentation of the whole word, but that this "priming" effect was independent from performance on the recognition memory test. In a somewhat similar demonstration, Jacoby (1983) found that recognition memory and perceptual identification were also independent; in the perceptual identification task, words were flashed briefly (for 35 msec) on a tachistoscope and the subject's task was to identify the word. Again, prior presentation of the word facilitated or primed performance on the identification task. A further ingenious paradigm to assess procedural memory was developed by Jacoby and Witherspoon (1982). In this task subjects were again presented with words to learn in an initial phase and were later given words to spell. In the first phase, words were presented visually, and the list contained some homophones (e.g., REED, READ; HARE, HAIR); in these cases the less common member of the pair was presented. The spelling task was given auditorily, and the interest lies in how frequently the subject responds with the primed word. It was found that amnesics showed as much priming (i.e., the spelling bias was as great) as did normals despite the fact that the amnesics showed little conscious recollection of the words.

In light of Tulving's (1983; this volume) suggestion that procedural memory is a relatively primitive system in terms of both evolution and ontogeny, comparative studies in this area would be particularly useful. Even at the human level, memory for procedures may actually be more pervasive and important for everyday functioning than the more salient forms of memory involving conscious recollection (Kolers & Roediger, 1984). It would be relatively easy to develop paradigms applicable to humans and animals, and interesting to explore the same abilities across species. Two theoretical points that seem particularly worthwhile are first the degree to which procedural memory is context specific (see Mackintosh, Chapter 11)—that is, are words or actions *primed* in some general absolute sense by recent experience, or does priming again reflect an interaction between a learned potential on the one hand and a specific set of contextual circumstances on the other? My own bias is towards the contextualist view, although the evidence is still quite fragmentary. The second theoretical point of interest concerns the degree to which procedural memory reflects the general principle that memory performance is tied to specific knowledge and expertise. Do experts in some perceptual-motor domain show particularly strong priming effects? Do they show *increased* contextual specificity? Do animals possess strong procedural memory abilities as part of their repertoire of biological adaptations? An exciting area of comparative research is just opening up.

CONCLUSIONS

In this chapter, I have surveyed some current ideas in research on human memory and commented briefly on the paradigms that have been developed to assess these ideas. My personal bias is to think of human memory as an activity to be understood in the person's biological and social context; by this account, we should talk in terms of underlying processes, as opposed to structures, and view the processes in terms of their evolutionary and functional significance (see also Bolles, chapter 7, and Hitch, chapter 6). A further bias is reflected in the suggestion that we should attempt to model the *interaction* between the organism and its environment, rather than think of memory as a property of the organism alone. In this regard, the role of context is crucial, both at encoding and retrieval, and this view is also shared by several other contributors to the present volume (e.g., Mackintosh, chapter 11; Rescorla, chapter 3).

With respect to the formation of closer ties between the areas of animal learning and human memory, recent developments in both fields make this goal appear realistic and worthwhile. In human memory research, there is increasing interest in nonverbal paradigms and in concepts such as procedural memory. Correspondingly, animal learning researchers are now more inclined to take a "cognitive" view of animal memory, and adapt concepts from human memory studies to their own ends (e.g., Mackintosh, chapter 11; Olton, chapter 5). One aspect of the establishment of a truly comparative science of memory is the development of common paradigms, and there are signs that this is now happening—stimulated by research in both areas (e.g., Dickinson, chapter 9; Gaffan, chapter 13). In the present chapter I have pointed out situations in which further common paradigms might usefully be established; in general, these are cases involving nonverbal "propositional" materials (e.g., pictures, spatial and temporal information) and cases of skilled procedures. A further area that could provide linking paradigms is the field of memory research in infants and young children (see Moscovitch, 1984, for a recent review).

Although the establishment of common paradigms appears to be a worthwhile goal, some warnings are in order. First, in contrast to the earlier ''learning set'' approach (Harlow, 1949) in which it was assumed that the evolution of some general learning ability could be measured across different species, the view advocated in the present chapter is that different species develop different kinds of knowledge about the world, and that memory performance reflects the specific knowledge of the animal in question. By this view it is not sensible to ask which has the best memory—bird, rat or man? Each species may show superior performance on its own ''natural'' task. Thus, it is more important to develop common principles than common paradigms. The primary objective is the establishment of a common *conceptual* framework for animal and human memory, and the experimental paradigms used should reflect the appropriate expression of the animal's memorial abilities within its own functional context. The Umeå conference has left me feeling optimistic that there is now sufficient common ground between the two fields of research to make the objective of a common conceptual framework both desirable and realistic.

ACKNOWLEDGMENTS

Preparation of this chapter was facilitated by a grant from the Natural Sciences and Engineering Research Council of Canada. I am extremely grateful to Mary Gick, David Sherry, and Endel Tulving for helpful comments on an earlier draft, and to Elizabeth Kelly for technical help in preparing the manuscript.

REFERENCES

Ackerman, B. P. (1981). Encoding specificity in the recall of pictures and words in children and adults. *Journal of Experimental Child Psychology, 31,* 193–211.

Atkinson, R. C., & Shiffrin, R. M. (1968). Human memory: A proposed system and its control processes. In K. W. Spence & J. T. Spence (Eds.), *The psychology of learning and motivation: Advances in research and theory, Vol. 2.* New York: Academic Press.

Atkinson, R. C., Shiffrin, R. M. (1971). The control of short-term memory. *Scientific American, 225,* 82–90.

Baddeley, A. D. (1966). Short-term memory for word sequences as a function of acoustic, semantic, and formal similarity. *Quarterly Journal of Experimental Psychology, 18,* 362–365.

Baddeley, A. D. (1982). Amnesia: A minimal model and an interpretation. In L. S. Cermak (Ed.), *Human memory and amnesia.* Hillsdale NJ: Lawrence Erlbaum Associates.

Baddeley, A. D. (1983). Working memory. *Philosophical Transactions of the Royal Society, London, B, 302,* 311–324.

Baddeley, A. D., & Hitch, G. (1974). Working memory. In G. H. Bower (Ed.), *The psychology of learning and motivation, Vol. 8.* New York: Academic Press.

Bartlett, F. C. (1932). *Remembering.* Cambridge: Cambridge University Press.

Bartlett, J. C., & Tulving, E. (1974). Effects of temporal and semantic encoding in immediate recall upon subsequent retrieval. *Journal of Verbal Learning and Verbal Behavior, 13,* 297–309.

Bower, G. H. (1976). Experiments on story understanding and recall. *Quarterly Journal of Experimental Psychology, 28,* 511–534.

Bower, G. H. (1981). Mood and memory. *American Psychologist, 36,* 129–148.

Bransford, J. D., McCarrell, N. S., Franks, J. J., & Nitsch, K. E. (1977). Toward unexplaining memory. In R. Shaw & J. Bransford (Eds.), *Perceiving, acting, and knowing.* Hillsdale, NJ: Lawrence Erlbaum Associates.

Broadbent, D. E. (1958). *Perception and communication.* London and New York: Pergamon.

Broadbent, D. E. (1971). *Decision and stress.* London: Academic Press.

Brown, J. (1958). Some tests of the decay theory of immediate memory. *Quarterly Journal of Experimental Psychology, 10,* 12–21.

Brown, R., & Kulik, J. (1977). Flashbulb memories. *Cognition, 5,* 73–99.

Brown, R., & McNeill, D. (1966). The "tip of the tongue" phenomenon. *Journal of Verbal Learning and Verbal Behavior, 5,* 325–337.

Bruce, D. (1985). The how and why of ecological memory. *Journal of Experimental Psychology, General, 114,* 78–90.

Claparede, E. (1911). Reconnaissance et moitie. *Archives de Psychologie, 11,* 79–90. In D. Rapaport (Ed.), *Organization and pathology of thought.* New York: Columbia University Press.

Cohen, N. J., & Squire, L. R. (1980). Preserved learning and retention of pattern-analyzing skill in amnesia: Dissociation of knowing how and knowing that. *Science, 210,* 207–210.

Conrad, R. (1964). Acoustic confusions in immediate memory. *British Journal of Psychology, 55,* 75–84.

Craik, F. I. M. (1977). Age differences in human memory. In J. E. Birren & K. W. Schaie (Eds.), *Handbook of the psychology of aging.* New York: van Nostrand Reinhold.

Craik, F. I. M. (1979). Levels of processing: Overview and closing comments. In L. S. Cermak & F. I. M. Craik (Eds.), *Levels of processing in human memory.* Hillsdale, NJ: Lawrence Erlbaum Associates.

Craik, F. I. M. (1981). Encoding and retrieval effects in human memory: A partial review. In J. Long & A. Baddeley (Eds.), *Attention and performance IX.* Hillsdale NJ: Lawrence Erlbaum Associates.

Craik, F. I. M. (1983). On the transfer of information from temporary to permanent memory. *Philosophical Transactions of the Royal Society, London, B, 302,* 341–359.

Craik, F. I. M., & Jacoby, L. L., (1979). Elaboration and distinctiveness in episodic memory. In L.-G. Nilsson (Ed.), *Perspectives on memory research.* Hillsdale NJ: Lawrence Erlbaum Associates.

Craik, F. I. M., & Levy, B. A. (1976). The concept of working memory. In W. K. Estes (Ed.), *Handbook of learning and cognitive processes, Vol 4.* Hillsdale, NJ: Lawrence Erlbaum Associates.

Craik, F. I. M., & Lockhart, R. S., (1972). Levels of processing: A framework for memory research. *Journal of Verbal Learning and Verbal Behavior, 11,* 671–684.

Craik, F. I. M., & Tulving, E., (1975). Depth of processing and the retention of words in episodic memory. *Journal of Experimental Psychology: General, 104,* 268–294.

Craik, F. I. M., & Watkins, M. J. (1973). The role of rehearsal in short-term memory. *Journal of Vebal Learning and Verbal Behavior, 12,* 599–607.

Crowder, R. G. (1982). The demise of short-term memory. *Acta Psychologia, 50,* 291–323.

Crowder, R. G., & Morton, J. (1969). Precategorical acoustic storage (PAS). *Perception and Psychophysics, 5,* 365–373.

Daneman, M., & Carpenter, P. A. (1980). Individual differences in working memory and reading. *Journal of Verbal Learning and Verbal Behavior, 19,* 450–466.

Dennett, D. C. (1983). Intentional systems in cognitive ethology; the "Panglossian paradigm" defended. *The Behavioral and Brain Sciences, 6,* 343–390.

Eich, J. E. (1980). The cue-dependent nature of state-dependent retrieval. *Memory and Cognition, 8*, 157–173.

Eysenck, M. W. (1979). Depth, elaboration, and distinctiveness. In L. S. Cermak & F. I. M. Craik (Eds.), *Levels of processing in human memory*. Hillsdale, NJ: Lawrence Erlbaum Associates.

Fisher, R. P., & Craik, F. I. M. (1977). Interaction between encoding and retrieval operations in cued recall. *Journal of Experimental Psychology: Human Learning and Memory, 3*, 701–711.

Fisher, R. P., & Cuervo, A. (1983). Memory for physical features of discourse as a function of their relevance. *Journal of Experimental Psychology: Learning, Memory, and Cognition, 9*, 130–138.

Gaffan, D. (1976). Recognition memory in animals. In J. Brown (Ed.), *Recall and recognition*. New York: Wiley.

Gallistel, C. R. (1980). *The organization of action: A new synthesis*. Hillsdale, NJ: Lawrence Erlbaum Associates.

Garcia, J., & Koelling, R. A. (1966). Relation of cue to consequences in avoidance learning. *Psychonomic Science, 4*, 123–124.

Geiselman, R. E., & Bjork, R. A. (1980). Primary vs. secondary rehearsal in imagined voices: Differential effects on recognition. *Cognitive Psychology, 12*, 188–205.

Glanzer, M. (1972). Storage mechanisms in recall. In G. H. Bower (Ed.), *The psychology of learning and motivation: Advances in research and theory, Vol. 5*. New York: Academic Press.

Glanzer, M., & Cunitz, A. R. (1966). Two storage mechanisms in free recall. *Journal of Verbal Learning and Verbal Behavior, 5*, 351–360.

Glenberg, A., Smith, S. M., & Green, C. (1977). Type I rehearsal: Maintenance and more. *Journal of Verbal Learning and Verbal Behavior, 16*, 339–352.

Glisky, E. L. (1983). *Encoding and retrieval effects in memory for inverted words*. Unpublished doctoral dissertation. University of Toronto, Toronto.

Godden, D. R., & Baddeley, A. D. (1975). Context-dependent memory in two natural environments: On land and underwater. *British Journal of Psychology, 66*, 325–332.

Godden, D. R., & Baddeley, A. D. (1980). When does context affect recognition memory? *British Journal of Psychology, 71*, 99–104.

Graf, P. (1981). Reading and generating normal and transformed sentences. *Canadian Journal of Psychology, 35*, 293–308.

Harley, C. B. (1981). Learning the evolutionarily stable strategy. *Journal of Theoretical Biology, 89*, 611–633.

Harlow, H. F. (1949). The formation of learning sets. *Psychological Review, 56*, 51–65.

Harlow, H. F., Meyer, D., & Settlage, P. H. (1951). The effects of large cortical lesions on the solution of oddity problems by monkeys. *Journal of Comparative and Physiological Psychology, 44*, 320–326.

Harris, J. E. (1978). External memory aids. In U. Neisser (Ed.), *Memory observed*. San Francisco: W. H. Freeman.

Hollis, K. (1982). Pavlovian conditioning of signal-centered action patterns and autonomic behavior: A biological analysis of function. In J. S. Rosenblatt, R. A. Hinde, C. Beer, & M. Busnel (Eds.), *Advances in the study of behavior*. New York: Academic Press.

Howard, D. V., Lasaga, M. I., & McAndrews, M. P. (1980). Semantic activiation during memory encoding across the adult life span. *Journal of Gerontology, 35*, 884–890.

Huppert, F., & Piercy, M. (1976). Recognition memory in amnesic patients: Effects of temporal context and familiarity of material. *Cortex, 12*, 3–20.

Jacoby, L. L. (1978). On interpreting the effects of repetition: Solving a problem vs. remembering a solution. *Journal of Verbal Learning and Verbal Behavior, 17*, 649–667.

Jacoby, L. L. (1983). Remembering the data: Analyzing interactive processes in reading. *Journal of Verbal Learning and Verbal Behavior, 22*, 485–508.

Jacoby, L. L., & Craik, F. I. M. (1979). Effects of elaboration of processing at encoding and retrieval. In L. S. Cermak & F. I. M. Craik (Eds.), *Levels of processing in human memory*. Hillsdale, NJ: Lawrence Erlbaum Associates.

Jacoby, L. L., & Witherspoon, D. (1982). Remembering without awareness. *Canadian Journal of Psychology, 36*, 300–324.

James, W. (1890). *Principles of psychology*. New York: Holt.

Jenkins, J. J. (1974). Remember that old theory of memory? Well forget it. *American Psychologist, 29*, 785–795.

Jenkins, J. J. (1979). Four points to remember: A tetrahedral model of memory experiments. In L. S. Cermak & F. I. M. Craik (Eds.), *Levels of processing in human memory*. Hillsdale, NJ: Lawrence Erlbaum Associates.

Jones, G. V. (1976). A fragmentation theory of memory: Cued recall of pictures and of sequential position. *Journal of Experimental Psychology: General, 105*, 277–293.

Keenan, J. M., MacWhinney, B., & Mayhew, D. (1977). Pragmatics in memory: A study of natural conversation. *Journal of Verbal Learning and Verbal Behavior, 16*, 549–560.

Kieras, D. E. (1981). Component processes in the comprehension of simple prose. *Journal of Verbal Learning and Verbal Behavior, 20*, 1–23.

Kintsch, W. (1974). *The representation of meaning in memory*. Hillsdale, NJ: Lawrence Erlbaum Associates.

Kolers, P. A. (1973). Remembering operations. *Memory and Cognition, 1*, 347–335.

Kolers, P. A. (1976). Reading a year later. *Journal of Experimental Psychology: Human Learning and Memory, 2*, 554–565.

Kolers, P. A. (1979). A pattern analyzing basis of recognition. In L. S. Cermak & F. I. M. Craik (Eds.), *Levels of processing in human memory*. Hillsdale, NJ: Lawrence Erlbaum Associates.

Kolers, P. A., & Ostry, D. J. (1974). Time course of loss of information regarding pattern analyzing operations. *Journal of Verbal Learning and Verbal Behavior, 13*, 599–612.

Kolers, P. A., & Roediger, H. I., III, (1984). Procedures of mind. *Journal of Verbal Learning and Verbal Behavior, 23*, 425–449.

Linton, M. (1982). Transformations of memory in everyday life. In U. Neisser (Ed.), *Memory observed*. San Francisco: W. H. Freeman.

Loftus, E. F., Miller, D. G., & Burns, H. J. (1978). Semantic integration of verbal information into visual memory. *Journal of Experimental Psychology: Human Learning and Memory, 4*, 19–31.

Luria, A. R. (1968). *The mind of a mnemonist*. New York: Basic Books.

Mandler, G. (1979). Organization and repetition: An extension of organizational principles with special reference to rote learning. In L.-G. Nilsson (Ed.), *Perspectives on memory research*. Hillsdale, NJ: Lawrence Erlbaum Associates.

Masson, M. E. J., & Sala, L. S. (1978). Interactive processes in sentence comprehension and recognition. *Cognitive Psychology, 10*, 244–270.

Meacham, J. A., & Leiman, B. (1975). Remembering to perform future actions. In U. Neisser (Ed.), *Memory observed*. San Francisco: W. H. Freeman.

Miller, J. R. (1981). Constructive processing of sentences: A simulation model of encoding and retrieval. *Journal of Verbal Learning and Verbal Behavior, 20*, 24–45.

Monsell, S. (1984). Components of working memory underlying verbal skills: A "distributed capacity" view. In H. Bouma & D. G. Bouwhuis (Eds.), *Attention and performance X*. Hillsdale, NJ: Lawrence Erlbaum Associates.

Moscovitch, M. (1982). A neuropsychological approach to perception and memory in normal and pathological aging. In F. I. M. Craik & S. Trehub (Eds.), *Aging and cognitive processes*. New York: Plenum Press.

Moscovitch, M. (1984). *Infant memory*. New York: Plenum Press.

Moscovitch, M., & Craik, F. I. M. (1976). Depth of processing, retrieval cues, and uniqueness of encoding as factors in recall. *Journal of Verbal Learning and Verbal Behavior, 15*, 447–458.

Murdock, B. B., Jr. (1967). Recent developments in short-term memory. *British Journal of Psychology, 58*, 421–433.

Murdock, B. B., Jr. (1974). *Human memory: Theory and data*. Hillsdale, NJ: Lawrence Erlbaum Associates.

Neisser, U. (1967). *Cognitive psychology.* New York: Appleton-Century-Crofts.

Neisser, U. (1982). *Memory observed.* San Francisco: W. H. Freeman.

Nilsson, L.-G. (1984). New functionalism in memory research. In K. Lagerspetz & P. Niemi (Eds.), *Psychology in the 1990's.* Amsterdam: Elsevier.

Olton, D. S., & Samuelson, R. J. (1976). Remembrance of places passed: Spatial memory in rats. *Journal of Experimental Psychology: Animal Behavior Processes, 2,* 97–116.

Peterson, L. R., & Peterson, M. J. (1959). Short-term retention of individual items. *Journal of Experimental Psychology, 58,* 193–198.

Piaget, J. (1952). *The origin of intelligence in children.* New York: International Universities Press.

Rabinowitz, J. C., Craik, F. I. M., & Ackerman, B. P. (1982). A processing resource account of age differences in recall. *Canadian Journal of Psychology, 36,* 325–344.

Reed, G. (1979). Everyday anomalies of recall and recognition. In J. F. Kihlstrom & F. J. Evans (Eds.), *Functional disorders of memory.* Hillsdale, NJ: Lawrence Erlbaum Associates.

Rogers, T. B., Kuiper, N. A., & Kirker, W. S. (1977). Self-reference and the encoding of personal information. *Journal of Personality and Social Psychology, 35,* 677–688.

Rubin, M. H. (1984). *Factors influencing memory for context.* Unpublished masters dissertation. University of Toronto, Toronto.

Rundus, D. (1977). Maintenance rehearsal and single-level processing. *Journal of Verbal Learning and Verbal Behavior, 16,* 665–681.

Schacter, D. L., Harbluk, J. L., & McLachlan, D. R. (1984). Retrieval without recognition: An experimental analysis of source amnesia. *Journal of Verbal Learning and Verbal Behavior, 23,* 593–611.

Schank, R. C. (1982). *Dynamic memory.* New York: Cambridge University Press.

Shepard, R. N. (1967). Recognition memory for words, sentences, and pictures. *Journal of Verbal Learning and Verbal Behavior, 6,* 156–163.

Sherry, D. F., Krebs, J. R., & Cowie, R. J. (1981). Memory for the location of stored food in marsh tits. *Animal Behavior, 29,* 1260–1266.

Shettleworth, S. J., & Krebs, J. R. (1982). How marsh tits find their hoards: The roles of site preference and spatial memory. *Journal of Experimental Psychology: Animal Behavior Processes, 8,* 354–375.

Slamecka, N. J., & Graf, P. (1978). The generation effect: Delineation of a phenomenon. *Journal of Experimental Psychology: Human Learning and Memory, 4,* 592–604.

Sperling, G. (1960). The information available in brief visual presentations. *Psychological Monographs, 74,* whole no. 498.

Stern, L. D. (1981). A review of theories of human amnesia. *Memory and Cognition, 9,* 247–262.

Sternberg, S. (1966). High speed scanning in human memory. *Science, 153,* 652–654.

Sternberg, S. (1969). Memory scanning: Mental processes revealed by reaction-time experiments. *American Scientist, 57,* 421–457.

Treisman, A. M. (1964). Monitoring and storage of irrelevant messages in selective attention. *Journal of Verbal Learning and Verbal Behavior, 3,* 449–459.

Tulving, E. (1974). Cue-dependent forgetting. *American Scientist, 62,* 74–82.

Tulving, E. (1979). Relation between encoding specificity and levels of processing. In L. S. Cermak & F. I. M. Craik (Eds.), *Levels of processing in human memory.* Hillsdale, NJ: Lawrence Erlbaum Associates.

Tulving, E. (1983). *Elements of episodic memory.* London: Oxford University Press.

Tulving, E., Schacter, D. L., & Stark, H. A. (1982). Priming effects in word-fragment completion are independent of recognition memory. *Journal of Experimental Psychology: Learning, Memory, and Cognition, 8,* 336–342.

Tulving, E., & Thomson, D. M. (1973). Encoding specificity and retrieval processes in episodic memory. *Psychological Review, 80,* 352–373.

Warrington, E. K., & Weiskrantz, L. (1968). New method of testing long-term retention with special reference to amnesic patients. *Nature, 217,* 972–974.

Waugh, N. C., & Norman, D. A. (1965). Primary memory. *Psychological Review, 72,* 89–104.
Weiskrantz, L., & Warrington, E. K. (1979). Conditioning in amnesic patients. *Neuropsychologia, 16,* 169–177.
Welford, A. T. (1958). *Ageing and human skill.* London: Oxford University Press.
Wickens, D. D. (1970). Encoding categories of words: An empirical approach to meaning. *Psychological Review, 77,* 1–15.
Woodward, A. E., Bjork, R. A., & Jongeward, R. H., Jr. (1973). Recall and recognition as a function of primary rehearsal. *Journal of Verbal Learning and Verbal Behavior, 12,* 608–617.

11 Contextual Specificity or State Dependency of Human and Animal Learning

N. J. Mackintosh
University of Cambridge

INTRODUCTION: THE ADEQUACY OF ASSOCIATIONISM?

Some of the contributors to, and perhaps even some of the readers of, this volume will have been originally introduced to the study of human learning and memory by McGeogh's classic textbook (McGeogh, 1942; McGeogh & Irion, 1952). But for someone who has entered the field within the last 20 years, McGeogh must give the impression of discussing issues not only from another time, but about a different place. Some of the topics he discusses will appear in a modern textbook, but the occasional similarities in topic are so few and their treatment so different, that they will seem more disconcerting than reassuring. The analysis of paired-associate and serial learning in terms of a theory designed to account for the results of animal conditioning experiments by the formation of stimulus-response associations, of interference between competing S-R associations, of unlearning and extinction, generalization and verbal discrimination, can find no counterpart in any book written in the last 10 years.

What has caused this change that it should now be necessary to call a special conference to bring together workers in animal learning and human memory to talk to one another, some of them probably for the first time? It is largely that animal learning theory has been identified with the theory used by McGeogh, and that there have seemed to be some obvious objections to S-R associationism as an account of human learning and memory: first, that it restricts attention to associations between particular elements, stimulus and response, i.e., that it is S-R; secondly, that it restricts attention to associations as the only form of learned relation, i.e., that it is associationist.

223

It is not necessary to rehearse the objections that students of human learning or memory might have on the former grounds (cf. Anderson & Bower, 1973). It is only necessary to note that S-R theory is no longer taken very seriously by many students of animal learning. Modern conditioning theory, as the Rescorla, Dickinson, and Gaffan contributions to this volume make clear, is relatively liberal in allowing associations between a quite wide variety of elements, between stimuli and stimuli and between responses and stimuli as well as between stimuli and responses. A plausible account of what happens in many typical conditioning experiments, indeed, would be to suggest that animals first detect that various relations hold between certain external stimulus events (between the CS and US in a Pavlovian conditioning experiment or between various stimuli and the occurrence of the reinforcer in an instrumental conditioning experiment), and thus form certain stimulus-stimulus associations; they later detect any salient relationship that may hold between their own actions and the occurrence of the US or reinforcer, and thus form certain response-stimulus associations with the consequent appropriate modification of their behavior; and only finally do they form certain stimulus-response associations when habitual and repeated responding in the presence of a particular set of stimuli results in a regular relationship which may be learned. Stimulus-response associations are allowed, but have no privileged status.

What of the second set of objections, those to associationism as such? These form a heterogeneous collection and some of them, at least, can perhaps be interpreted as saying only that the contents of associations are a great deal more complex than even this liberal stance of modern conditioning theory will allow. It is not events that are associated, but representations of those events, and the problem of how sensory input is encoded, processed, transformed, and recoded is largely ignored by conditioning theory. Rescorla's chapter ought to make it clear that this preconception is not wholly true: Conditioning theory can tolerate a significant degree of complexity here, and it is worth recalling that this insistence on the role of perceptual, attentional and encoding variables in animal learning dates back to the work of Lashley (1942) and Lawrence (1963).

But, as Crowder points out, it is obvious enough that animal subjects are not going to encode visually presented material verbally, or assign different meanings to homonyms depending on the sentence in which they are embedded. And although conditioning theorists pay some attention to the problem of encoding stimuli in different ways, they might have paid more attention if they were more inclined to use more complex stimuli and, possibly, more complicated animals. Rats and pigeons are probably not endowed with the most complex of perceptual processing systems (with the important exception of their ability to analyse spatial relations); that, at least, is our present conception of the matter. Pigeons, for example, have so far provided only meagre evidence of being able to respond to relationships between stimuli that transcend the actual stimuli to which they have been trained to respond (Mackintosh, Wilson, & Boakes, 1985). Primates, of course, can transfer matching and other rules across an indefinite set of stimulus changes (see Gaffan's contribution to this volume) and a chimpanzee such as Premack's Sarah can learn generalized matching discriminations where she is required to respond to a comparison stimulus not on the basis of its physical similarity to the sample, but because it instantiates some other relationship: an apple cut in half is matched to a half-filled jug of water in preference to a whole apple (Woodruff & Premack, 1981).

This is still to avoid the full force of the objection to associationism as an account of human learning and memory. Conditioning theory, as Rescorla has noted, remains firmly associationist in outlook and has chosen to add complexity not by allowing other relationships between events than their association to be learned about, but by suggesting that other relationships between events than their temporal contiguity are important in determining whether an association is established between them. An animal's knowledge about the relationship between two events, it is assumed, can always be summarised by a single number—the strength of the association between them. This must seem an implausible restriction to the student of human memory. Even when we are dealing with the relatively simple case where we wish our subjects to recall a target word learned as part of a list on an earlier occasion, there are numerous different ways of jogging their memory. We can present another word or nonsense syllable that had been paired with the target word during the earlier study trial; we can provide a category name, by saying that it's a bird; we can provide a more specific verbal description by saying that it's a red bird, or a yet more specific visual description by presenting a picture; we can provide various cues pointing to alternative meanings of the word by telling them to think of a red hat, a Roman Catholic prelate, a baseball team; we can provide skeletal letters: C–R–I–A–. Is it actually sensible or useful to say that all these cues are simply associated with the target word to a greater or lesser extent?

Once again, it is possible that the success of associationism as an account of animal learning reflects both the simplicity of the procedures and measures used in studying the behavior of laboratory animals, and, possibly, the simplicity of the animals studied. The student of conditioning allows his rat to press a lever in a Skinner box, to poke its nose into the food magazine, to freeze, to jump, to run, or to orientate towards a particular stimulus. This does not provide very much scope for the rat to display its knowledge of the world. The rather richer repertoire of the chimpanzee Sarah begins to raise new questions. Sarah has clearly associated, in some sense, various arbitrary symbols or tokens with various objects and can answer questions about an absent object when shown only the symbol (Premack, 1976). But conditioning theory hardly prepares us to expect animals to utilise stimuli associated with other events in quite the range of ways that Sarah uses her symbols.

CONTEXTUAL SPECIFICITY OF CONDITIONING AND
LEARNING AS A CASE STUDY

In spite of the obvious differences between the animal and human realms, and in spite of the doubts one may harbor as to the adequacy of associationism as a model for either, I, like David Olton, am encouraged by Tulving's belief that "words to the memory researcher are what fruit flies are to the geneticist: a convenient medium through which the phenomena and processes of interest can be explored and elucidated" (Tulving, 1983, p. 146). The conditioning theorist has his rats, pigeons and Skinner boxes: The question is whether the phenomena and processes in which he is interested overlap with those of interest to the student of human learning and memory. The only way to find out is to see if it is possible to apply similar analyses to the two sets of data. Does the probability of a human subject's correctly recalling a word studied on an earlier occasion respond in the same sort of way to the same variables and treatments as does the probability that a pigeon will peck an illuminated key in a Skinner box? And if it does, is the apparent parallel trivial or interesting? That too can be answered only by yet further analysis. In other words, it is necessary, I believe, to take a particular case and to treat it in some depth. The case I choose is that of contextual specificity or state dependency of learning and memory. The most obvious advantage it possesses is that there are at least superficial parallels between the human and animal data, for both humans and animals are more likely to retrieve previously learned information if tested for retention in the context or state in which they learned it. To that extent, we are not starting from a position that is self-evidently hopeless.

Contextual Specificity of Human Memory

The observation of contextual specificity or state dependency of human learning and memory is sufficiently ancient to have formed the basis of one of McGeogh's two main principles of forgetting (the other, of course, was interference). But it is still sufficiently important to form at least part of the basis for Tulving's principle of encoding specificity: "what is stored is determined by what is perceived and how it is perceived, and what is stored determines what retrieval cues are effective in providing access to what is stored" (Tulving & Thomson, 1973, p. 353).

There are, of course, differences both in the data on which McGeogh and Tulving primarily relied to formulate their principles and in the nature of those principles themselves. The sort of effect to which McGeogh was referring was that a list of paired associates learned in one room, at one time of day, with the items printed in a particular color of ink would be better recalled when subjects were tested in that room, at that time of day with the stimulus terms or cues for recall printed in the same color, than if any one of these conditions was changed. By contrast, the principle of encoding specificity is based on rather different observations: that a musical note may not be recognized as the same note if played as part of a different tune (Humphrey, 1933), or that the same word, cardinal, will be encoded quite differently when it is in a sentence about the habits of birds and in one about church offices, and will thus not be recalled if only the inappropriate retrieval cues are provided (Light & Carter-Sobell, 1970).

These rather obvious differences have encouraged some writers (e.g., Baddeley, 1982) to draw a distinction between intrinsic or interactive and extrinsic or independent effects of context. An intrinsic context determines the form or manner in which a target item is initially encoded and a change in context may therefore mean that subjects are required to recall or recognize something significantly different from that which they committed to memory. Perhaps the extreme case of this in verbal learning is where different verbal contexts impose different meanings on the same homonym, as in the cardinal example. But other, less extreme examples can be readily provided: The word "ground" may be encoded as rather different images when presented in conjunction with the word "cricket" and with the word "cold."

Extrinsic or independent contexts, such as the place where, or time when, an item was learned, the age, sex or attitude of the experimenter, the learner's emotional or pharmacological state at the time of learning, are assumed not to affect the subject's encoding of the target item and if they influence recall this must be established in some other way. The suggestion is that they themselves act as retrieval cues for the target item.

If the distinction between intrinsic or extrinsic contexts is a valid one, it must have behavioral implications, that is to say, there must be some behavioral criterion that will allow one to decide whether a particular context acted intrinsically or extrinsically. The suggested criterion is whether a change in context can affect both recognition and cued recall of a target item or only free, uncued recall. Tulving's principle of encoding specificity finds its most striking support from the demonstration that a target word learned as part of a sentence or paired with another word, may not be recognized when presented in isolation, but will be recalled if part of the original sentence or the word with which it was originally paired is presented as a retrieval cue. Such failure of recognition seems to imply that the original encoding of the target word was inextricably bound up with the context in which it was presented, or that this context interacted with, was an intrinsic part of, the subject's encoding of the target. Intrinsic contexts, in other words, are those which, if changed at the time of test, may prevent recognition of the target item. By contrast, a change in extrinsic context will affect only the recall of the target in the absence of other retrieval cues; since the role of the extrinsic context was only to provide a retrieval cue itself, in the presence of other retrieval cues, as in cued recall or, of course, recognition, a change in context will have no effect.

That there are contextual changes which affect only free, uncued recall is suggested by Eich's review of state dependent drug effects on human memory (Eich, 1980). Eich was able to show that the single variable that distinguished most clearly between successful and unsuccessful demonstrations of state dependency was whether the study had involved free recall on the one hand, or a cued recall or recognition test on the other. Of 26 studies employing uncued, free recall, 23 found an effect of a change in pharmacological state between study and test trials; of 24 studies that employed recognition or cued recall tests, only 3 found any evidence of state dependency. Baddeley's work with divers provides a second example: Free recall of a list of words learned either on the beach or under 15 feet of water was very much better when subjects were tested in the same place as that in which they had studied the list than if they were tested in the opposite condition. But the recognition of the target words was unaffected by a change in the place of testing (Godden & Baddeley, 1975, 1980).

In spite of this apparently neat division of outcome by type of contextual manipulation, there may be reason to question whether we are dealing with two quite distinct sorts of effects. In the first place, the notion that some contexts do, and others do not, affect the way in which a person encodes a target item seems suspect. Place of learning, for example, is said to be an extrinsic or independent context, which does not affect initial encoding. But it is not too difficult to believe that the word *ground* might be encoded rather differently by someone standing in the middle of a cricket pitch and someone in a diver's suit under 15 feet of water. And it seems equally probable that different emotional or pharmacological states might affect the image conjured up by a particular word and thus affect its encoding. Second, it is not clear that the distinction between contextual changes that affect recognition and those that affect only free recall always corresponds to one's intuitions about contexts which might affect initial encoding and those which would probably not. Consider, for example, Loftus' demonstration of the powerful effect of asking leading questions, which contain misleading information about the incidental details of a previously seen sequence of slides depicting successive scenes leading up to an accident (Loftus, 1979). What is measured is the subject's ability to recognize a target slide, and it is clear that such recognition can be seriously impaired. But there is evidence that reinstatement of more of the context of original learning, for example, by presenting the slides during the recognition test in the same order as they were presented during original learning, can mitigate the effects of the misleading information, that is, can increase the accuracy of recognition (Bekerian & Bowers, 1983). But it is not at all obvious that the order of presentation of the items should have interacted with the way in which such incidental features as the color of a car, the nature of a street sign or the name of a road were originally encoded.

The safest conclusion, I believe, is that contexts can affect encoding in a very wide variety of ways and that this can interact with the nature of the test for retrieval in a variety of ways. This conclusion may seem so safe as to be almost totally devoid of information—although it bears more than a passing resemblance to the encoding specificity principle. But it is surely not entirely vacuous to say that different contextual manipulations can interact to a greater or lesser extent with the encoding of different kinds of target item; that they should not be dichotomized into two classes, one interactive and the other solely acting as an independent retrieval cue; but that they form a continuum whose effects on retrieval also cannot be neatly divided into those observed only in free recall and those observed also in cued recall and recognition. At any rate, this is a conclusion that sits most comfortably with the data from studies of state dependency or contextual specificity in animal conditioning.

Contextual Specificity of Animal Conditioning

Changes in context may have marked effects on conditioning in animals. State dependency, evidenced by a failure of conditioning to transfer from drugged to undrugged state (or vice-versa) is well documented in animal studies (Overton, 1984). But numerous other factors, including time of day or the animal's motivational state have been shown to exert contextual control over conditioning (Spear, 1978), and in Capaldi's sequential theory a major role for the reinforcer is to provide part of the stimulus complex in the presence of which the animal learns to respond: thus the decline in responding seen in typical extinction conditions is largely attributed to the disappearance of this potent contextual stimulus (Capaldi, 1967).

What may seem to be quite minor changes in apparatus between original conditioning and subsequent test will also affect the level of responding seen on test. The absence of a background tone or a change in the angle of the floor will affect the rate of pecking by pigeons (Riccio, Urda, & Thomas, 1966; Welker, Tomie, Davitt, & Thomas, 1974). Thus, it is hardly surprising that a complete change of apparatus should have a marked effect on conditioning. Several studies have demonstrated that the effects of both conditioning and extinction trials may be largely confined to the apparatus or context in which they occurred. Animals conditioned in one context will be relatively unlikely to respond if tested in another. Similarly, if conditioning is extinguished in a different context from that in which it was established, there will be a significant recovery of responding if animals are tested back in the context of original conditioning. These effects have been reported in studies both of conditioned fear (Bouton & Bolles, 1979; Balaz, Capra, Hartl, & Miller, 1981) and of conditioned taste aversions (Archer, Sjödén, & Nilsson, 1984; see also Nilsson & Archer's introductory chapter to this volume).

A typical example of such contextual specificity is shown in Fig. 11.1 (Lovibond, Preston, & Mackintosh, 1984). This is a study of conditioned suppression in rats to a tone CS paired with a shock US. Two groups of rats received a series of conditioning trials to the tone in one apparatus and were then tested, in

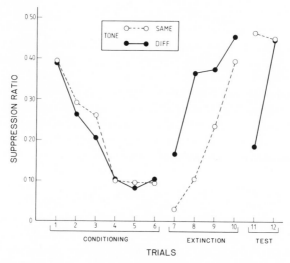

FIG. 11.1. Acquisition, extinction and final testing of conditioned suppression to a tone CS paired with a shock US. The two groups were treated identically throughout the experiment except that Group Diff received extinction trials, in the second phase of the experiment, in an apparatus different from that in which original conditioning had occurred. The measure of conditioning employed in this experiment is the suppression ratio, which divides the rate of food-rewarded lever pressing during the CS by the sum of rate of lever pressing during the CS and rate of lever pressing in an equivalent period of time immediately preceding the CS. A ratio of 0.50, therefore, indicates equivalent rates of lever pressing in the presence of the CS and in its absence, i.e., no conditioning to the CS; while a ratio of 0.00 indicates no lever pressing during the CS, i.e., complete suppression or strong conditioning.

extinction, for suppression to the tone either in the same apparatus as that in which they had been conditioned (Group Same) or in a different apparatus (Group Diff). It is apparent that Group Diff showed significantly less suppression to the tone during these extinction trials. But when both groups received a final pair of test trials back in the original context, this return to the scene of original conditioning reinstated suppression in Group Diff. The effects of both original conditioning and extinction are thus partly confined to the contexts in which they occur.

It is a simple matter to demonstrate contextual effects in animal conditioning. But if we are to understand these effects and are to relate them to those seen in human studies, we need to distinguish between a rather wide variety of possible causes, and we must specify how a conditioning episode and the experimenter's test for the effects of that episode are to be conceptualized. We need to map the terminology and procedures of the conditioning experiment onto the terminology and procedures of human experiments on contextual specificity.

My use of the term "conditioning episode" is, of course, deliberately intended to suggest that if we are forced to apply the distinction between episodic and semantic memory (Tulving, 1983), then animal conditioning experiments fall on the episodic side of the divide. The experimenter is usually more interested in what he has taught his animals on some specific occasion rather than in their general, previously acquired knowledge. The more important question to settle is the relationship between conditioning trials and tests for their effects on the one hand and the study and retrieval trials of a typical experiment on human episodic memory. I assume that a Pavlovian conditioning experiment, in which CS and US are initially paired and the ability of the CS alone to evoke a response is later tested, is analogous to a case of cued recall. What the experimenter is measuring is the ability of the CS, as a cue, to retrieve a representation of the US. But, when presented alone on the test trial, the CS will presumably not act as an effective retrieval cue unless it is recognized as the same stimulus that was paired with the US during original conditioning (study) trials. Thus, contextual specificity of Pavlovian conditioning might arise for either of two reasons: first, an extrinsic effect, because the conditioning context as well as the CS acts as a cue for retrieval of the representation of the US, and when the animal is tested in a new context, there is a reduction in the number of effective retrieval cues; second, an intrinsic effect, because the change in context affects recognition of the nominal retrieval cue (the CS) itself.[1] We have not come across this second possibility in our earlier discussion of contextual effects in human memory, for, as far as I know, it has not been taken very seriously by students of such effects. But if it is possible to fail to recognize the target item (the US) when it is presented out of context, it must also be possible to fail to recognize the list retrieval cue (the CS). And such a failure of recognition might carry with it a failure of that cue to retrieve the target item.

There is certainly evidence of such an effect in animal experiments. Certain changes in context act intrinsically or interactively to affect the CS itself. There are two ways in which they might do so, both no doubt somewhat simpler than the variety of encoding effects possible with verbal material and human subjects. First, a change in context can change the physical characteristics of the experimenter's nominally identical CS. A tone presented in one experimental chamber of a particular size and shape, constructed of particular materials, may simply not

---

[1]There are no data from any animal experiment to suggest that the encoding of the target item itself, the US, is intrinsically affected by the context in which it is presented in such a way as to cause a failure to retrieve the original US when animals are tested in a different context. The events used as USs in conditioning experiments do not, perhaps, lend themselves so readily to this sort of interactive effect, being salient, potent stimuli which elicit certain responses unconditionally (presumably, therefore, relatively independently of the context in which they are presented). It seems possible that certain pharmacological states might interact with a US to produce an intrinsic contextual effect when animals were tested in a different state, but I know of no evidence bearing on this possibility.

produce the same pattern of sounds when presented in a different sized chamber, constructed of different materials. This possibility forms the extreme case of an interactive contextual effect where the nature of the physical stimulus itself changes—even before the subject has encoded it. It may also seem too trivial a possibility to be of theoretical interest, yet has, there can be no doubt, simply not been properly controlled for or assessed in many animal experiments which have proposed much more elaborate explanations of contextual control of conditioning (e.g., Balaz et al., 1981; Bouton & Bolles, 1979). In our own experiments, we hoped that we could eliminate this possibility by using contextual changes that would not interact in this way with at least one of our CSs. Our two contexts were Skinner boxes of nominally identical construction, and the CS was a tone. The boxes differed by being located in different rooms, in being impregnated with different odors, and one being permanently illuminated, the other completely dark. Two further differences were that the rat's lever presses were reinforced by food pellets in one box and by sucrose pellets in the other; sessions in one box took place in the morning and in the other box in the afternoon. None of these changes should have altered the physical nature of the tone CS; one of them (the background illumination) might well interact with a second CS we used in some experiments, namely a flashing light. And certain slight differences we observed between the effects of contextual changes on tone and light CSs suggest that this may have happened.

A second possible intrinsic contextual effect in animal experiments would be to suppose that the context plus the experimenter's nominal CS are somehow combined to form a unique compound or configural stimulus. This idea conceals a number of different possibilities; for at least one there is quite good independent evidence. Rescorla (1973) has shown that where two separate CSs, A and B, each individually predicts the occurrence of a US, but when presented together signal the absence of the US, the animal solves this discrimination by attending to a unique configural stimulus produced by the *joint* presentation of A + B. Rescorla's data also suggested that this configural cue was not particularly salient and would not acquire control over the animal's responding unless explicitly correlated with the presence or absence of the US. But we do not know whether this would also be true of the putative configuration formed by presenting a CS in a particular context.

Although we hoped that the first intrinsic effect was not the cause of the contextual specificity of conditioning and extinction seen in our experiment, this second type of effect may certainly have been responsible. The alternative possibility is that the conditioning context acted as an extrinsic retrieval cue to assist retrieval of the target US and that a change in context reduced the number of appropriate retrieval cues. Further experimental analysis suggests rather clearly that this is in fact what was happening in our original experiment, and what may be responsible for contextual effects in a variety of other conditioning experiments. The argument is best understood by reference to Table 11.1. Part A of

TABLE 11.1
Two Designs for an Experiment
on Contextual Specificity of Conditioning
and Extinction

	A		
Groups	Conditioning	Extinction	Retest
Same	C_1 : T+	C_1 : T−	C_1 : T−
	C_2 : —	C_2 : —	
Diff	C_1 : T+	C_1 : —	C_1 : T−
	C_2 : —	C_2 : T−	

	B		
Groups	Conditioning	Extinction	Retest
Same	C_1 : T+	C_1 : T−	C_1 : T−
	C_2 : L+	C_2 : L−	C_2 : L−
Diff	C_1 : T+	C_1 : L−	C_1 : T−
	C_2 : L+	C_2 : T−	C_2 : L−

C_1, C_2 = Different Contexts; T, L = Tone and Light CSs; + = Reinforced trials; − = Nonreinforced trials.

this table illustrates the design of our first experiment: In the conditioning phase, the tone CS was paired with the US in Context 1, while animals were exposed to Context 2 without any conditioning trials occurring there. This allows Context 1, but not Context 2, to be associated with the US, and thus, when animals in Group Diff are extinguished in Context 2, that context does not act as a retrieval cue for the US and they show less overall fear than Group Same. By the same token, the fear of the US conditioned to Context 1 will itself extinguish during the course of this extinction test in Group Same, but not in Group Diff, so that when animals in the latter group are returned to Context 1 they now show the better retrieval of the US or greater fear.

The test of this analysis is to change the design of the experiment so that both contexts are equally associated with the US, as is shown in Part B of the table. Here, in the conditioning phase, animals are conditioned to the tone CS in Context 1 and to another CS, the flashing light, in Context 2. For Group Same, tone and light are then extinguished in their original contexts, while for Group Diff, the two CSs are switched to the opposite contexts for extinction, although back in their original contexts for a final test. The results of this new design are shown in Fig. 11.2. There is no longer any evidence of the contextual specificity of conditioning and extinction produced by the earlier design—with the possible exception of a small and statistically not significant effect in the case of the light CS on the final reinstatement test. Recall that the flashing light was the CS whose perceived characteristics might change with a change in context.

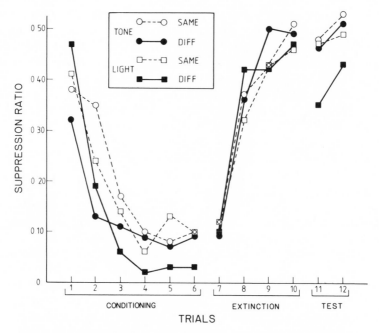

FIG. 11.2.   Acquisition, extinction and final testing of conditioned suppression to tone and light CSs paired with shock USs in an experiment of the design shown in Part B of Table 11.1. The effect of change in context in Group Diff, evident in Fig. 11.1, has disappeared.

The implication is that the contextual specificity of conditioning and extinction seen in Fig. 11.2 was an extrinsic effect, produced because one of the contexts, but not the other, had been established as an independent retrieval cue for the US. When the two contexts were equated in this respect, there was no context specificity of conditioning or extinction. A reader who has followed the argument to this point may recollect that this sort of extrinsic contextual effect in the human case, where the context was said to act as a retrieval cue for the target item, was supposedly distinguished from an intrinsic effect by the fact that it could be demonstrated only in the case of uncued recall, not in cued recall or recognition. If my analysis is correct, the animal data imply a clear effect on cued recall (i.e., Pavlovian conditioning). Rather than see this as a conflict between animal and human data, I believe it provides additional reason to question the analysis which said that the mark of an extrinsic effect is that it does not occur in a test of cued recall. If the context is a sufficiently important retrieval cue, and if the nominal retrieval cue is relatively ineffective, then a change in extrinsic context will certainly affect cued recall. There is no hard and fast distinction here, only a graded effect dependent on the relative importance of context and nominal retrieval cue.

There is, in fact, ample evidence from a variety of animal conditioning studies (see, for example, Rescorla's chapter), that contextual stimuli are rapidly associated with any US occurring in their presence. Contexts seem to be rather effective retrieval cues in animal conditioning. And there is little reason to doubt that the same is true of the pharmacological states used in animal studies of state dependency. The drug doses given to animals are usually orders of magnitude greater than those given to the subjects of human experiments on state dependency, and it is hardly surprising if they act as more powerful retrieval cues. The most plausible conclusion is that whether or not a change in context affects cued recall and recognition has rather little to do with whether that context is intrinsic or extrinsic. Extrinsic contextual changes may or not have an effect depending on the relative importance of the context and of other explicit retrieval cues as effective retrievers of the target information.

The results illustrated in Fig. 11.2 reveal no evidence of contextual specificity of conditioning or extinction - certainly not in the case of the tone CS. The disappearance of the effect when steps are taken to ensure that the two contexts are equally well associated with the US not only implies that contextual specificity of conditioning is a consequence of the ability of one context, but not another, to retrieve a representation of the US; it also argues against various alternative explanations of the phenomenon. A popular suggestion, surprisingly rather more widely canvassed in the animal than in the human literature, has been that contexts might act as conditional cues (e.g., Balaz et al., 1981; Bouton & Bolles, 1979). If a CS is paired with a US, it is supposed that the ability of that CS to retrieve a representation of the US is conditional on the presence of the contextual cues in which this conditioning episode occurred. If the CS is presented in another context, the animal will have no reason to believe that it predicts the US. Animals can, of course, learn conditional discriminations where one CS is paired with a US in one context but not in another, while a second CS is paired with the US in the second context but not in the first (Asratyan, 1965); but such learning normally requires explicit differential reinforcement and lengthy training. There is no particular reason to suppose that conditional control arises spontaneously simply from reinforcing a given CS in a given context, and our results suggest that it does not.

The absence of contextual specificity shown in Fig. 11.2 also makes it reasonable to infer that we were successful in our attempt to ensure that the two contexts did not interact with the tone CS in such a way as to alter its physical or perceived properties. Even when presented in a different context, the tone was apparently recognized as the same stimulus that had been paired with the US in the first context, and was fully capable of retrieving a representation of the US. Some further experiments, however, suggest that a different measure may yield clear evidence that the tone is not recognized as the same stimulus when presented in a different context. The measure in question is latent inhibition, the well-documented observation that conditioning proceeds more rapidly to a novel than to a familiar CS: if a stimulus is repeatedly presented to an animal with no further consequence, then conditioning to that CS will proceed relatively slowly when it is subsequently paired with a US (Lubow, 1973). Several experiments have suggested that such latent inhibition is context specific: A stimulus repeatedly presented in one context will be conditioned slowly when paired with a US in that context, but relatively rapidly if CS-US pairings occur in a different context (Channell & Hall, 1981; Hall & Minor, 1984; Lubow, Rifkin, & Alek, 1976). Few of these experiments have controlled for the possibility that a change in context may have altered the physical characteristics of the CS, and some have not even equated the familiarity of the two contexts. Our own results suggest that the context-specificity of latent inhibition survives such control. The design of our experiments is shown in Table 11.2, and the results of one, together with those of a second experiment demonstrating that with these contexts conditioning to a tone established in one context can transfer perfectly to the other, are shown in Fig. 11.3. The left-hand panel gives the results of the conditioning experiment: it is clear that suppression to the tone previously paired with shock was unaffected by whether the tone was presented in the context in which it had originally been conditioned or in the other context (where the light had been conditioned). The right-hand panel shows the results of the latent inhibition experiment carried out at the same time. There is equally clear evidence of a failure of transfer of latent inhibition: Suppression was conditioned to the tone significantly more rapidly when tone-US pairings occurred in a different context than when they occurred in the context in which the tone had previously been presented alone. If we take latent inhibition as a measure of the lack of novelty, i.e., of the familiarity, of a stimulus, then it appears that the tone was not recognized as a familiar stimulus when presented in a different context.

It is worth first pointing out that these results yet again call into question the generalization that contexts such as place of learning affect only uncued recall,

TABLE 11.2
Design for an Experiment
on Contextual Specificity of Latent Inhibition

Groups	Preexposure	Conditioning
Same	$C_1 : T-$	$C_1 : T+$
	$C_2 : L-$	$C_2 : L+$
Diff	$C_1 : L-$	$C_1 : T+$
	$C_2 : T-$	$C_2 : L+$
Control	$C_1 : -$	$C_1 : T+$
	$C_2 : -$	$C_2 : L+$

C_1, C_2 = Different Contexts; T, L = Tone and Light CSs; + = Reinforced trials; − = Nonreinforced trials.

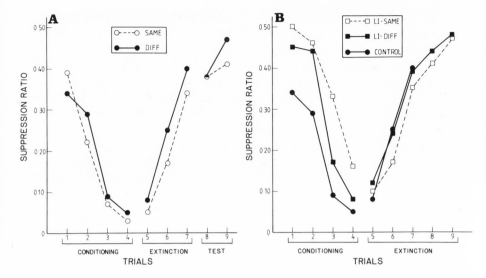

FIG. 11.3.   Panel A shows the acquisition, extinction and final testing of conditioned suppression to tone and light CSs in an experiment similar to that illustrated in Fig. 11.2. Panel B shows the acquisition of conditioned suppression to the tone and to the light after prior exposure to the stimuli either in the same (Group LI-Same) or in a different (Group LI-Diff), context. The Control Group had received no prior exposure to the stimuli in either context and conditioned more rapidly than either of the preexposed groups. But preexposure in the same context as that in which conditioning subsequently occurred had a more deleterious effect on conditioning than preexposure in a different context.

not recognition. But they also pose a further problem. In order to explain the perfect transfer of conditioning across changes of context illustrated in the left-hand panel of Fig. 11.3, we suppose that the CS is identified or recognized as the same stimulus as that paired with the US in another context. But the failure of latent inhibition to transfer across a change of context suggests a failure of recognition. What are we to make of this discrepancy? The least interesting possibility is that it reflects a difference in the sensitivity of our measures, that latent inhibition somehow provides a more sensitive measure of failure of transfer than does conditioning or extinction. It is not obvious how such a possibility is to be refuted, but then it is no more obvious why it should be true. A more interesting approach is to note some parallels with the human case. A variety of experiments have suggested that human subjects may report that they do not recognize an item as familiar, but nevertheless show by their behavior that they have in fact remembered some further information previously associated with that item.

The best known instances of this are those provided by amnesic patients, beginning with the woman studied by Claparède who, although unable to recognize him, was unwilling to shake hands with him again after Claparède had concealed a pin in his hand (Claparède, 1911). More formally, Weiskrantz and Warrington (1979) have demonstrated good eyelid conditioning in amnesic patients who confidently declare that they have never seen the experimental apparatus in which conditioning trials occurred. And several studies have shown that amnesics can correctly retrieve a target word given an appropriate cue for it, but have no confidence that they have seen it before (see Meudell & Mayes, 1982). However, as Jacoby (1982) and Meudell and Mayes (1982) themselves have persuasively argued, there is no reason to believe that this sort of behavior is the prerogative of amnesics. A number of experiments have demonstrated very similar findings in normal subjects. Recognition tests, judgments of familiarity, or ratings of confidence in the accuracy of their answer, may all reveal little or no evidence that subjects have ever been exposed to a specified item of information; but other measures of recall show unambiguously that the information is still, in some sense, available. The paradox has prompted some writers to draw a contrast between automatic and conscious memory (Baddeley, 1982; Weiskrantz, 1978), while others have talked of a difference between procedural and declarative memory (Cohen & Squire, 1980). The suggestion that such a contrast can apparently be demonstrated in experiments on conditioned suppression in rats may give one pause. Nevertheless, the parallel with our data seems too interesting to be dismissed out of hand. Information about the consequences of the tone must have been available to our rats, regardless of the context in which the tone was presented. But their readiness to associate the tone with a US seems to have required a context-dependent judgment of familiarity sensitive to any change in the place where it was presented.

CONCLUSIONS

The object of the exercise was to see whether there are experimental paradigms that reveal some commonalities between studies of human memory and animal conditioning. That there are parallels, of course, no one would surely deny. The question is whether they are more than superficial and whether they can be profitably analyzed in similar theoretical terms. In order to consider this question, I believe that it is necessary to take a particular case for study and to examine it in some detail. The case of contextual specificity or state dependency seems to have some advantages for such an exercise; there is little question but that similar experimental operations can be performed in human and animal experiments; and on the face of it the consequences of some of these operations are superficially similar. Has more detailed analysis yielded any further payoff?

The distinction between intrinsic contexts, which interact with the initial encoding of a target item, and extrinsic contexts, which affect recall by acting as independent retrieval cues for that item, first applied to human studies, is also readily applied to animal experiments. Indeed, animal experiments provide even clearer examples of the distinction than do human experiments. A contextual change which undoubtedly interacts with the subject's perception of a stimulus is one which alters the physical properties of that stimulus, as when the standing waves produced by a 1-KHz tone depend on the characteristics of the chamber in which it is presented. And relatively automatic and peripheral processes will ensure that a flashing light is initially perceived somewhat differently when it is turned on from a background of total darkness and when the background condition is one of strong illumination. But there are possibly less peripheral and automatic intrinsically acting contexts: the notion of configurational learning, where a CS presented against a particular background is analyzed in terms of a unique configural stimulus, captures something of this idea. In human studies, contexts which supposedly interact with the encoding of a target stimulus may do so in even more complex, and possibly even more optional ways. Whether or not the word *jam* is registered in different ways as a consequence of being paired with *strawberry* or *traffic,* for example, will depend on whether the subject knows English and is analyzing words for their meaning rather than for their number of letters or in terms of their rhymes.

This is one reason why it is dangerous to draw a hard and fast distinction between intrinsic and extrinsic contexts. But it is equally difficult to be confident in human studies that a context such as place of learning or the subject's pharmacological state at the time of learning are purely extrinsic and do not interact with his encoding of the target item. As noted earlier, pharmacological agents may well ensure that a word to be remembered is associated with different moods or feelings. (They also seem one of the few agents with the potential to alter an animal's encoding of the salient and biologically relevant events used as USs.) It is animal studies that provide the least ambiguous evidence that the place in which a learning episode occurs can act as an independent retrieval cue for the target item. Features of the apparatus in which conditioning trials are given become associated with the US and thus help to retrieve a representation of the US. There is no reason to suppose that the context of learning here is acting as anything other than an independent retrieval cue. The simplicity of animal experiments, the fact that the place in which a conditioning episode occurs is not rich in previous associations which might interact with the way in which events are encoded, and the simplicity, salience and relatively fixed properties of those events themselves, are all advantages for theoretical analysis. They leave little doubt that some effects of context on learning and retention are produced by the context acting as an independent retrieval cue, a conclusion rather harder to substantiate in the human case.

The difficulty of drawing the distinction in human studies is that there is no easy, independent way of verifying it. The suggestion that interactive contexts will affect recognition or cued recall, while independent contexts will affect only uncued recall, although attractively simple and supported by some theoretical and empirical considerations, is not in fact sufficient to handle the data even of human studies. And the results of animal experiments are quite inconsistent with any such simple division. If animals receive conditioning trials in one apparatus, but are tested for responding to the CS in another, where they have never been conditioned before, a marked effect of the change in context will be observed which can with some confidence be attributed to the failure of the new context to retrieve a representation of the US. Here then is an extrinsic effect, but one revealed in a test of cued recall. And similar changes of context will also affect latent inhibition or the speed with which a familiar, previously presented stimulus will be associated with a US. But latent inhibition is most readily conceptualized as a recognition test.

The further observation that contextual specificity of latent inhibition may occur under circumstances where conditioning and extinction transfer completely from one context to another provides a final example where animal studies may illuminate, and themselves be illuminated by, human studies. There is a suggestive parallel with the variety of dissociations, in human experiments, between the ability of subjects to use a stimulus to retrieve information previously associated with it, and their inability to recognize that stimulus as familiar. Whether this parallel is more than superficial can certainly not be answered with confidence from any existing data. But it is surely a spur to further research. And that is always a comforting note to end on.

ACKNOWLEDGMENT

Some of the work reported in this chapter was supported by a grant from the U.K. Science and Engineering Research Council.

REFERENCES

Anderson, J. R., & Bower, G. H. (1973). *Human associative memory*. Washington, D.C.: V. H. Winston.

Archer, T., Sjöden, P-O., & Nilsson, L-G. (1984). Contextual control of taste-aversion conditioning and extinction. In P. Balsam & A. Tomie (Eds.), *Context and learning* (pp. 225–271). Hillsdale, NJ: Lawrence Erlbaum Associates.

Asratyan, E. A. (1965). *Compensatory adaptations, reflex activity and the brain*. Oxford: Pergamon.

Baddeley, A. D. (1982). Domains of recollection. *Psychological Review, 89*, 708–729.

Balaz, M. A., Capra, S., Hartl, P., & Miller, R. R. (1981). Contextual potentiation of acquired behavior after devaluing direct context-US associations. *Learning and Motivation, 12*, 383–397.

Bekerian, D. A., & Bowers, J. M. (1983). Eyewitness testimony: Were we misled? *Journal of Experimental Psychology: Learning, Memory and Cognition, 9,* 139–145.

Bouton, M. E., & Bolles, R. C. (1979). Contextual control of the extinction of conditioned fear. *Learning and Motivation, 10,* 445–466.

Capaldi, E. J. (1967). A sequential hypothesis of instrumental learning. In K. W. Spence & J. T. Spence (Eds.), *The Psychology of learning and motivation* (pp. 67–156) (Vol. 1). New York: Academic Press.

Channell, S., & Hall, G. (1981). Facilitation and retardation of discrimination learning after exposure to the stimuli. *Journal of Experimental Psychology: Animal Behavior Processes, 7,* 437–446.

Claparède, E. (1911). Recognition et moïté. *Archives de Psychologie, 11,* 79–90.

Cohen, N. J., & Squire, L. (1980). Preserved learning and retention of pattern-analyzing skill in amnesia: Dissociation of knowing how and knowing that. *Science, 210,* 207–209.

Eich, J. E. (1980). The cue-dependent nature of state-dependent retrieval. *Memory and Cognition, 8,* 157–173.

Godden, D. R., & Baddeley, A. D. (1975). Context-dependent memory in two natural environments: On land and underwater. *British Journal of Psychology, 66,* 325–331.

Godden, D. R., & Baddeley, A. D. (1980). When does context influence recognition memory? *British Journal of Psychology, 71,* 99–104.

Hall, G., & Minor, H. (1984). A search for context-stimulus associations in latent inhibition. *Quarterly Journal of Experimental Psychology, 36B,* 145–169.

Humphrey, G. (1933). *The nature of learning.* New York: Harcourt Brace.

Jacoby, L. L. (1982). Knowing and remembering: Some parallels in the behavior of Korsakoff patients and normals. In L. S. Cermak (Ed.), *Human memory and amnesia* (pp. 97–122). Hillsdale, NJ: Lawrence Erlbaum Associates.

Lashley, K. S. (1942). An examination of the continuity theory as applied to discriminative learning. *Journal of General Psychology, 26,* 241–265.

Lawrence, D. H. (1963). The nature of a stimulus: Some relationships between learning and perception. In S. Koch (Ed.), *Psychology: A study of science,* (Vol. 5., pp. 179–212). New York: McGraw-Hill.

Light, L. L., & Carter-Sobell, L. (1970). Effects of changed semantic context on recognition memory. *Journal of Verbal Learning and Verbal Behavior, 9,* 1–11.

Loftus, E. F. (1979). *Eyewitness testimony.* Cambridge: Harvard University Press.

Lovibond, P. F., Preston, G. C., & Mackintosh, N. J. (1984). Contextual specificity of conditioning, extinction and latent inhibition. *Journal of Experimental Psychology: Animal Behavior Processes, 10,* 360–375.

Lubow, R. E. (1973). Latent inhibition. *Psychological Bulletin, 79,* 398–407.

Lubow, R. E., Rifkin, B., & Alek, M. (1976). The contextual effect: The relationship between stimulus pre-exposure and environmental pre-exposure determines subsequent learning. *Journal of Experimental Psychology: Animal Behavior Processes, 2,* 38–47.

McGeogh, J. A. (1942). *The psychology of human learning.* New York: Longmans, Green.

McGeogh, J. A., & Irion, A. L. (1952). *The psychology of human learning.* New York: Longmans, Green.

Mackintosh, N. J., Wilson, B., & Boakes, R. A. (1985). Differences in mechanisms of intelligence among vertebrates. *Philosophical Transactions of the Royal Society.* London, *B308,* 53–65.

Meudell, P., & Mayes, A. (1982). Normal and abnormal forgetting: Some comments on the human amnesic syndrome. In A. W. Ellis (Ed.), *Normality and pathology in cognitive functions* (pp. 203–237). London: Academic Press.

Overton, D. A. (1984). State dependent learning and drug discriminations. In L. L. Iversen, S. D. Iversen, & S. H. Snyder (Eds.), *Handbook of Psycho-pharmacology* (Vol. 18., pp. 59–127). New York: Plenum.

Premack, D. (1976). *Intelligence in ape and man.* Hillsdale: NJ: Lawrence Erlbaum Associates.

Rescorla, R. A. (1973). Evidence for "unique stimulus" account of configural conditioning. *Journal of Comparative and Physiological Psychology, 85,* 331–338.

Riccio, D. C., Urda, M., & Thomas, D. R. (1966). Stimulus control in pigeons based on proprioceptive stimuli from the floor inclination. *Science, 153,* 434–436.

Spear, N. E. (1978). *The processing of memories: Forgetting and retention,* Hillsdale, NJ: Lawrence Erlbaum Associates.

Tulving, E. (1983). *Elements of episodic memory.* Oxford: Oxford University Press.

Tulving, E., & Thompson, D. M. (1973). Encoding specificity and retrieval processes in episodic memory. *Psychological Review, 80,* 352–373.

Weiskrantz, L. (1978). A comparison of hippocampal pathology in man and other animals. in *Functions of the septo-hippocampal system* (pp. 373–387). CIBA Symposium 58. Amsterdam: Elsevier.

Weiskrantz, L., & Warrington, E. K. (1979). Conditioning in amnesic patients. *Neuropsychologia, 17,* 187–194.

Welker, R. L., Tomie, A., Davitt, G. A., & Thomas, D. R. (1974). Contextual stimulus control over operant responding in pigeons. *Journal of Comparative and Physiological Psychology, 86,* 549–562.

Woodruff, G., & Premack, D. (1981). Primitive mathematical concepts in the chimpanzee: Proportionality and numerosity. *Nature, 293,* 568–570.

VII GENERAL EMPIRICAL LAWS

Lars-Göran Nilsson
Trevor Archer

One fundamental prerequisite for claiming a close relationship between animal learning and human memory would seem to be the demonstration of similar empirical regularities within the two fields. Such similarities in data should in principle be more crucial than similarities in concepts and theoretical principles. Without any underlying empirical regularity, it would be difficult to argue for a theoretical similarity with any reasonable amount of sucess.

At present, however, there is hardly any consensus among researchers within the two fields as to the formulation of empirical laws, or their basic requirements. There is not even any consensus about what an empirical law is. With great care Cohen has reviewed the memory literature with respect to the occurrence of empirical laws in memory research. The total lack of such laws in the science of memory stands in sharp contrast to the existence of such laws in, for example, physics and chemistry. Cohen goes on to claim that if we pertain to the notion that memory research is a science claiming a similar status as that of those subjects mentioned, then, indeed, we need general empirical laws in memory research as well. Note that he does not actually suggest that memory research is a science or that it has a similar status; he simply entertains the notion of an independent entity.

After an enormous amount of research Cohen arrived at three plus one laws which are general enough to be referred to as laws rather than empirical effects or phenomena, which there are plenty of in memory research. Admittedly, these laws have generality but their existence is not a main point at issue; Cohen has treated this problem at the level of memory theory and data, a strategy that is justified by the results of this labour. In principle there should not be any difference between the practitioners of animal learning and human memory in this respect, but it seems reasonable to expect that those memory reseachers advocating a traditional entity view of memory (see Crowder, this volume; Roediger, 1980) will find them too general. The extent to which one can concur with Cohen is dependent upon personal conceptualizations of memory. An advocate of the entity view may find these laws far too general with too little reference given to properties of a hypothetical memory entity. As pointed out by Crowder the dominating contention of memory has, for many years, been that of a spatial entity—a receptacle in which information is encoded and stored and from which it is later retrieved when needed. Since the proponents of such a view claim that the identification and investigation of properties to this entity is essential for research in this field the empirical phenomena demonstrated are, for obvious reasons, also related to the memory entity and its hypothetical properties. The generality of Cohen's laws goes beyond such particulars and the entity view supporters may therefore find these laws too unspecific.

As noted elsewhere (Nilsson, 1980, 1984) recent years have witnessed a considerable reorientation in conceptualizations of memory. Whereas the emphasis previously was on structural properties, recent frameworks have focussed more on function in an attempt to understand memory and remembering in broader terms (e.g., Baddeley, 1982; Bransford, McCarrell, Franks & Nitsch, 1977; Craik, 1983; Craik & Lockhart, 1972; Jenkins, 1979; Nilsson, 1980, 1984; Tulving, 1983; Watkins, 1981). A common theme in most of these frameworks is that memory should be seen as an interaction between available cognitive capabilities of the rememberer and the demands of the particular task the rememberer is encountering. From this "functionalistic" or interactionistic point of view it may, in a sense, look quite paradoxical to search for empirical laws since the cognitive functioning in each particular case is assumed to depend on the specific task demands at hand in each situation. If they had been as specific as the advocates of an entity view claim they should be, it would indeed be a paradox to search for empirical laws from an interactionistic point of view. However, since interactions from this point of view are not only to be explained—they may be the explanation—it is not a paradox to search for general empirical laws and Cohen's laws are general enough to fit into this framework.

Gaffan, in his chapter, is less than sanguine about the possibility of finding general empirical laws in animal learning and human memory. Gaffan's argument is actually that we should not even look for such laws in psychological research in these two fields. This seemingly pessimistic standpoint should serve to caution us against falling into the trap of unrestricted or pretentious law-seeking, but we must, as scientists, seek to make some contribution to the formulation of general empirical laws. If one can accept the need to establish these laws, it is then necessary to decide at which level they ought to be sought. Cohen has outlined his laws at the level of data from memory experiments; this is perfectly valid. Gaffan's objection to the very idea of these laws has given us much food for thought. It would be quixotic to suggest that psychology can produce scientific laws of the same stature as those produced in physics and chemistry. We propose that these general empirical laws should be sought as biological rather than psychological entities.

REFERENCES

Baddeley, A. D. (1982). Domains of recollection. *Psychological Review, 89,* 708–729.

Bransford, J. D., McCarrell, N. S. Franks, J. J., & Nitsch, K. E. (1977). Towards explaining memory. In R. Shaw & J. D. Bransford (Eds.), *Perceiving, acting and knowing.* Hillsdale, NJ: Lawrence Erlbaum Associates.

Craik, F. I. M. (1983). On the transfer of information from temporary to permanent memory. *Philosophical Transactions of the Royal Society, London, B. 302,* 341–359.

Craik, F. I. M., & Lockhart, R. S. (1972). levels of processing: A framework for memory research. *Journal of Verbal Learning and Verbal Behavior, 11,* 671–684.

Jenkins, J. J. (1979). Four points to remember: A tetrahedral model of memory experiments. In L. S. Cermak & F. I. M. Craik (Eds.), *Levels of processing and human memory.* Hillsdale, NJ: Lawrence Erlbaum Associates.

Nilsson, L.-G. (1980). Methodological and theoretical considerations as a basis for an integration of research on memory functions in epileptic patients. *Acta Neurologica Scandinavica, 62* (Suppl. 80), 62–74.

Nilsson, L.-G. (1984). New functionalism in memory research. In K. M. J. Lagerspetz & P. Niemi (Eds.), *Psychology in the 1990's.* Amsterdam: North-Holland.

Roediger, H. L. (1980). Memory metaphors in cognitive psychology. *Memory & Cognition, 8,* 231–246.

Tulving, E. (1983). *Elements of episodic memory.* Oxford: Oxford University Press.

Watkins, M. J. Human memory and the information-processing metaphor. *Cognition, 10,* 331–336.

12 On the Generality of the Laws of Memory

Ronald L. Cohen
Glendon College, York University

This chapter essentially consists of three sections. The first section reviews the state of the human memory area vis-á-vis memory laws, according to some standard memory textbooks from the late seventies and early eighties. To anticipate somewhat, the outcome of this review is that memory laws are conspicuous by their absence.

The second section begins by questioning whether in fact we ought to have memory laws. The answer to this being yes, we probably ought; the remainder of the second section is devoted to a discussion of what such laws should look like.

The third section describes a set of three plus one possible memory laws. These laws evolved from a rather informal opinion survey taken in a class of seminaive undergraduate students. In order to optimize the generality of the proposed laws, each law encompasses several effects. This third section is really in the nature of a trial balloon. Is there any consensus as to whether there are in fact empirical laws of memory, and if so how these should be formulated? Should they be along the lines of the set of laws described in this third section?

SECTION 1: THE STATE OF THE MEMORY AREA WITH RESPECT TO LAWS

In order to gain some indication of the emphasis placed on laws in the memory area, I examined the indices of about a dozen textbooks, assuming that the books' contents would be accurately reflected in their indices. A review of the said indices netted virtually nothing, however. Adams (1976), Baddeley (1976) and Klatzky (1980) have neither laws nor principles listed in their indices.

Wingfield and Byrnes (1981), Kintsch (1977), Ellis, Bennett, Daniel, and Rickert (1979) and Hintzman (1978) make some mention of Thorndike's laws of learning, but these clearly belong to the learning area. The Gestaltist's Law of Prägnanz appears in Kintsch (1977) as a prelude to a discussion of chunking in short-term memory. This topic is also mentioned by Ellis et al. (1979) in their text under the aegis of the Perceptual Regrouping Hypothesis, promoted to the Perceptual Regrouping Principle in the index.

Regressing a few years, we find grouping treated as a law by Postman (1972) and by Bower (1972). In the same volume, Voss (1972) mentions the Law of Frequency and the Law of Contiguity. While these two laws, and especially the former, appeared more promising Voss fails to make a case for upgrading the Repetition Effect to a Law of Frequency.

Thorndike's Law of Disuse crops up occasionally in the texts, but is treated more as an historical curiosity than a viable law. The one exception to this is the use of Disuse in the special case of the decay principle in short-term forgetting (Wingfield & Byrnes, 1981).

A ray of hope, namely the entry "law" in the index to Loftus and Loftus' (1976) text was quickly extinguished when pages 157–163 proved to contain a discussion of eyewitness testimony. Strangely enough, none of the texts made so much as a mention of Jost's Laws, the only memory laws of which I had some prior knowledge.

Crowder's (1976) *Principles of Learning and Memory* lists no principles in the index, although it does list two laws, namely the Skaggs-Robinson Law which is a prediction without reliable empirical backing, and the Total Time Law, which is an upgarding of the Total Time Hypothesis. Crowder does, however, discuss the Encoding Specificity Principle in the body of his text (it appears in the index under its original guise of the Encoding Specificity Hypothesis).

In fact, the Encoding Specificity Principle is discussed in most of the textbooks, and would appear to be the only serious contender for a general laws title on the contemporary memory scene. The Encoding Specificity Principle's claim to the status of an empirical law of memory is discussed in the final section of this paper.

Although the recent standard memory texts appear to ignore the question of memory laws, references to such laws do crop up in the journals from time to time. For example, Roediger and Crowder (1976) consider the possibility that episodic and semantic memory "obey the same laws" with reference to the serial position effect (p. 275). In a similar vein, Anderson and Ross (1980) in discussing the episodic/semantic memory distinction also claim that "the two types of memory appear to obey the same laws" (p. 442). These laws are not, however, explicitly stated. I myself have written an article entitled *On the Generality of Some Memory Laws* (Cohen, 1981) in which I blithely described constraints on such things as the primacy effect and the levels-of-processing effect.

But is a law synonymous with an effect? If it is, then the memory texts are full of laws, the Primacy Law, the Recency Law, the Repetition Law, the Meaningfulness Law, the Similarity Law, the Spacing or Lag Law, the von Restorff Law, and so on. Although laws and effects are related, they are not synonymous. An effect is a general change observed when some variable is manipulated. A law, as I hope to show, is something more than this.

As earlier stated, the validity of my survey depended on the assumption that it is the practice of textbook authors to list existing laws in their indices. Although I had no way of testing this assumption in the specific context of memory, I could make a more general test by checking the indices of chemistry and physics books, I already knew that these disciplines have laws (the control condition, as it were). Laws are listed in the indices of chemistry and physics books. One rather slim chemistry text (Holum, 1969) lists 15 laws in its index (I was pleased to note that Avogadro's Hypothesis has been promoted to a law), not to mention a couple of principles and 3 or 4 rules. The index to a general physics text (Landau, Akheizer, & Lifshitz, 1967) yielded 24 laws, one principle and a rule.

Biology proved rather disappointing, however. Keeton's (1980) *Biological Science* mentions only 3 laws, 2 principles and 2 rules in its index to over 1,000 pages of text.

Judging from my brief forays into these other disciplines it certainly looks as if sciences that possess laws do advertise them in their textbook indices. My conclusion at this point was that psychology, like biology, being a young science had not had time to establish its laws. However, a scan of the index to *Perception: The World Transformed* (Kaufman, 1979) revealed no fewer than 13 laws and 3 principles.

Of course, memory is a more recent field of research than is perception, which could be one reason for the inequitable distribution of laws between the two. Or, of course, it may be that the study of human memory differs in some way from that of mechanics, solutions or visual perception—after all memory is still supposed to be preparadigmatic. This brings me to section 2 of the paper which considers the question of whether we should have memory laws, and if so what form these whould take.

SECTION 2: IS THERE A NEED FOR MEMORY LAWS?

In fact, there is no need for laws of memory, unless we aim to study memory phenomena in the traditional scientific manner. Bertrand Russell (1931) probably expressed it the most lucidly: "scientific method . . . consists of observing such facts as will enable the observer to discover general laws governing facts of the kind in question" (p. 15). Note, Russell does not say "observing facts" but "*observing such facts* as will enable the *observer to discover general laws*." There is an obvious interaction here: Our observations should be guided by their eventual importance in formulating a law. Toulmin (1953), in a similar vein, likens the ideal scientist (a physicist, naturally) to a traveller with a run-about rail ticket who has to travel from station to station in order to discover the limits of its validity. The ideal scientist should spend his time in discovering laws and then using empirical methods to test their limits.

Strictly speaking, the above only refers to the physical sciences. It has been suggested that biological scientists should shoot for different goals. Instead of seeking laws, biologists should spend their time seeking out and refining concepts (Mayr, 1982). This difference in goals depends on the argument that biological sciences can never have laws of the universal type possessed by the physical sciences, and that any empirical lawlike statement about biological phenomena should be designated an empirical generalization, and not a true law of nature (see e.g., Smart, 1963). Rather than simply expanding this argument to the more specific case of memory, however, I have opted to relax the strict definition of empirical law to include empirical generalizations. Using this expanded definition, it should now be possible to argue that the scientific study of memory should include the establishment of empirical laws.

The further question implied by Russell's statement is, of course, which phenomena should be observed in order to arrive at the laws? Again there is a consensus among the authorities. Einstein (see Mahoney, 1976) informs us that our *theories* tell us what we can observe. Toulmin (1953) agrees with this—for Toulmin, the lowest form of life is the natural historian who spends his time looking for regularities, that is in classification, but does not bother about the theoretical underpinning of his observations. Laws should be set against the background of the current theory in the area. So not only does memory need laws, it needs laws that fit the current theoretical state of the memory area.

Given then that memory should have laws, what should they look like? Before trying to answer this question for memory laws in particular, some mention should be made of criteria for scientific laws in general.

There are, of course, several kinds of laws. There are *de*scriptive laws (which tell how things are) and *pre*scriptive laws (which tell how things ought to be). Obviously, it is the former type of law which is appropriate.

There are low-level laws and high-level laws. For example, Leahey (1980) points out that operational definitions are low-level scientific laws since they make empirical statements whose generality must be tested by experiment. Obviously, we want something better for memory laws than operational definitions. High-level laws would be much preferable.

Then, there is the more specific question of what constitutes an empirical law. According to *The Century Dictionary* (1914), an empirical law is a formula that sufficiently satisfies certain observations, but which is not supported by any established theory or probable hypothesis, so that it cannot be relied upon far beyond the conditions of the observations upon which it rests. What this says, then, is that we can establish some kind of function, say $y = f(x)$, from a range of observations. Since we do not go beyond the empirical statement, however, we can be certain of our law only in and around the range of x and y values for which we have taken our measurements, but not far beyond this. An empirical law accordingly to this definition, allows for interpolation but not for extrapolation.

Further reading, showed this definition to be insufficient. *The Encyclopedia of Philosophy* (1967) extends this definition somewhat, emphasizing that the most fundamental distinction between a theory and an experimental law is that an experimental law contains only terms that are observables or which are operationally definable, whereas theories contain at least some terms which are not observables or operationally definable. *The Encyclopedia of Philosophy* further distinguishes empirical statements into accidental statements and lawlike statements. The statement "all ravens are black" is supported by confirming instances but has no connection with any statement of wider scope, and may be designated an accidental statement. On the other hand, "all species surviving in snowy regions are white," having both the support of instances and a connection with the Principle of Natural Selection, may be designated a lawlike statement. Although an accidental generalization satisfies one criterion for a scientific law—namely, it is a true statement of universal form—Hempel (1966) tells us that such a generalization does not qualify as a scientific law because it does not meet a second criterion. It does not meet the criterion that a law should bear some relationship to contemporary theoretical views, the same point as was made by Toulmin (1953). In fact Toulmin's dislike of natural historians is based partly on the fact that they are just as happy with accidental statements as with lawlike statements.

My old chemistry professor, James Kendall (1948) took a somewhat different approach, defining a law as the top rung of a three-stage ladder comprising hypothesis, theory, and law. An hypothesis is a statement that has received some empirical support; a theory is an hypothesis that has received a goodly body of support; and a law is a theory that has received so much empirical support that it looks like it is not going to be challenged in the foreseeable future. Toulmin (1953), by the way, disagrees with this approach, although it is the hypothesis end of the ladder with which he does not agree. For Toulmin, an hypothesis is not a junior law.

Leaving aside the question of a definition for an empirical law for the moment, let us consider the question of what is meant by *generality*. Schwarz (1978) in discussing laws of behavior, illustrates generality in terms of whether the effects of some situation on an organism's behavior can be generalized transspecies and transsituations. Luckily, in the human memory area we do not care whether our laws apply to racoons and quail (or at least we did not care up until this conference), but they should be transsituational.

One further point in connection with the notion of generality involves the classification of apparent exceptions to a law. An empirical relationship which is generally observed but which fails to appear in some studies may be classified either as a candidate for meta-analysis if the conditions for the observation and nonobservation of the relationship are similar, or as an exception to the law represented by the relationship if the conditions are dissimilar. It is only the second of these two alternatives which provides the basis for deeming the nonappearance of the relationship as a possible constraint on the law.

In view of the above, it appears that a memory law should be a statement about some empirical relationship in memory, which has transsituational generality and which looks like it will be around for some time to come. The statement should aim for something wider than an operational definition and should be lawlike rather than accidental; it should bear some relationship to current theory. Before going on to consider some possible candidates for memory laws, however, I should perhaps mention two further points.

The first point is that to exist as a scientific law, a law candidate must find consensus in the scientific community. The laws I propose in the next section do not have such consensus, although they do have the support of a class of seminaive undergraduates. Luckily, it is not necessary to have complete consensus—Newton's laws were still laws even although Laplace, Mach and Hertz did not accept them as such.

The second point is that an empirical law should be capable of being expressed as a mathematical function, which raises the question of quantification. If we have a law that states that some situation favors a good memory performance then we have to specify scales of measurement for our situation and for our memory performance. In perception the situation is often readily measureable in physical units, wavelengths, luminance, area and so on. In memory we sometimes have problems specifying a scale of measurement for the independent variable. Strictly speaking, I am of the impression that an empirical law should be a statement about a relationship between variables, each of which may be measured independently of the other variables involved in the relationship. Further, not only should the variables be independently measurable, but they should be measurable on something higher than a nominal scale. Lawlike relationships which do not conform to the independent measurement criterion I will designate definitional laws.

A prominent example of a definitional law is provided by Skinner's Law of Reinforcement. A reinforcer is defined by its effect in an operant learning situation. There is no independent measure of the effectiveness of the reinforcer other than performance. Even without Premack's Principle (Premack, 1965), however, Skinner's Law was extremely useful because of its transsituational generality. If food functioned as a reinforcer in one situation, it would function as a reinforcer in other situations too. By contrast, the Law of Generalization is an empirical law of conditioning, since the strength of the response and the degree of similarity between the conditioned and test stimuli on some dimension may be measured independently of each other.

It could also be noted in passing that Newton's Second Law was a definitional law; in fact much of its original importance lay in providing a method of defining force *(Van Nostrand's Scientific Encyclopedia,* 1976).

I come now to the third section of the paper, namely the proposal of a set of memory laws.

SECTION 3: POTENTIAL LAWS OF MEMORY

Each of the memory laws I shall describe is supported by several memory *effects.* Some of these effects conform to the empirical definition—both variables are separately measurable on ordinal scales or better, and others to the definitional definition—the variables are not independently measurable on ordinal scales. The result of this is that at least one of the laws is a hybrid in the sense that it encompasses both empirical and definitional aspects.

In interpreting the results of my student survey, my approach was to go for the general rather than the specific. The set of three laws deals with that well-known trinity, acquisition, retention, and retrieval.

> FIRST LAW: *The better something is learned, the greater the likelihood it will be remembered.*
> SECOND LAW: *The longer something has to be retained in memory, the less the likelihood that it will be remembered.*
> THIRD LAW: *The likelihood of remembering something depends upon the nature of the memory test.* (A more precise formulation of this law will be attempted later.)

In discussing these laws I take as my basis shopping-list memory, that is episodic memory for lists of words, and build on this where I am able. The reason for this is obvious. Most research in the memory area has used shopping-list procedures, either short term or long term. Consequently, although the use of this type of memory data strives against the rapidly growing craving for ecological validity in the area, it still makes a convenient place to start looking for lawful relationships.

Transsituationality will be tested in many cases by comparing word list memory with memory for series of minitasks enacted by the subject (subject-performed tasks, or SPTs). In the SPT procedure, the subject is given a series of simple verbal instructions such as *clap your hands* or *put the cap on the pen.* The subject enacts each instruction immediately following its presentation. At the end of the series the subject free recalls the events. It should be noted that, although they have a verbal component, SPTs are essentially nonverbal events (see Cohen, 1981).

Although the main focus of attention is on episodic memory, the possibility of generalization to semantic and procedural memory (see Tulving, this volume) is also considered in some instances.

First Law—acquisition

The better something is learned the greater the likelihood that it will be remembered. All that remains now is to define *better.*

Table 12.1 shows seven effects which feed into the First Law. This list is not, of course, exhaustive, but it includes some of the more prominent acquisition effects in the memory literature. The first three columns of Table 12.1 are self-explanatory; the fourth column, however, requires some comment. A question mark signifies that the effect has not yet been tested with SPTs; a *yes* or *no* signifies that SPT recall showed the presence or absence of the effect in question. Because of the rather recent introduction of SPT events into the memory area, the yes/no classification of the effects in the final column is sometimes based on the results of a single study, and should therefore be regarded as somewhat tentative.

The effects supporting the First Law involve two classes of variables, one class having to do with meaning or organization variables, and the other class with "strength" type variables (Jacoby, Bartz, & Evans, 1978). One effect feeding into the strength class is the repetition effect. The independent variables in this effect are, of course, readily quantifiable on an ordinal scale, since they use such units as number of item or list presentations. The meaning class, in which quantification is much more difficult, includes such effects as mnemonic effects and levels-of-processing effects. I consider the effects associated with the meaning class of variable first.

The basic purpose of a mnemonic device is to improve memory (usually free recall) for lists of items. At present, mnemonic effects tend to be definitional in nature, since the effectiveness of a mnemonic is defined by the level of recall it produces. (Mnemonics can be independently classified, of course, but only on a nominal scale.) Similarly, the basic levels of processing effect tends to be definitional since the depth or level of processing is defined by memory performance, in this case either recall or recognition. Thus, a graphemic processing of a word is more shallow than a phonemic processing. We know this because directing a subject's attention to phonemic aspects of a word during acquisition yields a

TABLE 12.1
Effects Feeding into the First Law

Effects	Effect Class	Words	SPTs
mnemonics	definitional	yes	?
levels of processing	definitional	yes	no
presentation rate	empirical	yes	no
frequency of item presentation	empirical	yes	yes
frequency of list presentation	empirical	yes	yes
primacy effect	empirical	yes	no
von Restorff effect	empirical	yes	?

higher level of recall or recognition than does directing his attention to the word's graphemic aspects (see Nelson, 1977).

In fact, both mnemonic and levels effects are on the way to becoming empirical. In the case of mnemonics, Bellezza (1981) has set out a series of rules which specify the properties to be desired in a good mnemonic and which are at least potentially testable empirically. For example, the three acquisition rules specify that the cognitive cues used in good mnemonics should be constructible (readily and reliably generated), readily discriminable, and have high associability. With regard to generality, some mnemonics appear to possess a certain degree of transsituational generality (the keyword procedure), while others appear to lack reliability, such as the first-letter mnemonic (a case for meta-analysis?). Limitations on mnemonic effects include short retention intervals (mnemonics are basically long-term memory aids), length of list (mnemonics show their advantage with long lists), and rate of presentation (time is required to fit items into a retrieval plan).

In the case of levels of processing, Seamon and Virostek (1978) have indicated at least the promise of an independent ordinal measure of depth or level of processing using subjective ratings. The ratings proved to be predictive of recall probability. What we can say, then, is that operations that involve semantic aspects of words produce better recall or recognition scores than do operations which involve "surface" features. Given this finding for words, what is the generalizability of this effect? Initially, this seemed to be quite a general phenomenon applying to words (Craik & Tulving, 1975), to prose (Marslen-Wilson & Tyler, 1976) and also apparently to facial recognition (Bower & Karlin, 1974). Later studies (Patterson & Baddeley, 1977; Winograd, 1976), however, suggest that all types of operations produce about the same facial recognition performance unless the subject's attention is directed to individual facial features at the cost of attention to the total gestalt. Further, one study which demonstrated a levels effect on the recall of action events performed by the experimenter, failed to yield a levels effect on the recall of these same events when they were presented as SPTs, that is when they were performed by the subjects themselves (Cohen, 1981). The levels manipulation would appear to be generally effective for verbal targets; the situation with regard to nonverbal targets is unclear.

One further constraint in connection with the levels manipulation is that if memory for target words is measured in terms of their priming effect on the probability of their identification in a tachistoscope (procedural memory), there is apparently no levels effect (Jacoby & Dallas, 1981).

The first empirical effect listed in Table 12.1 is the presentation rate effect. The original Total Time Hypothesis stated that the level of acquisition in some verbal learning task depends on the total amount of time spent in acquiring the material, regardless of how this time is divided up (Cooper & Pantle, 1967). Of interest in the First Law is the corollary of this hypothesis, namely that the more time spent in acquiring events, the better they will be remembered (Murdock,

1960). There are several ways of manipulating the acquisition time for events, for example, by varying the presentation rate, or the number of presentations. Variations in acquisition time may also be involved in the primacy effect and the von Restorff effect. These various effects are considered separately.

As demonstrations of the presentation rate effect may be cited Murdock (1962) and Glanzer and Cunitz (1966), who showed that the free recall of word lists varies inversely with presentation rate. To examine the transsituational generality of this effect we required subjects to free recall three 15-item lists of auditory words or of SPTs. Three groups of subjects were tested with word lists and three with the SPT lists (n = 12 subjects per group). The rate of presentation, and thus the total time for list presentation, was varied across the groups, by varying the interval between the items. For the SPTs these intervals were 1 sec, 5 sec or 10 sec giving total list presentation times of about 90 sec, 145 sec or 215 sec respectively; the use of 1 sec, 5 sec or 10 sec intervals gave total presentation times for the word lists of about 22 sec, 77 sec and 148 sec respectively. Two minutes were allowed for the written recall of each SPT list, and 90 sec for each word list.

The results of this study are shown in Figure 12.1. A 2 × 3 Anova showed the interaction between the types of items and the presentation times to be significant, $F(2,66) = 4.88$, $p < .05$. For the word lists, the fastest presentation condition yielded significantly lower recall than the two slower presentation conditions. The difference between the latter two conditions was not, however, significant. For the SPT lists, the slower rates yielded poorer recall performance than the fastest rate, although none of the differences was significant. The presentation rate effect apparently has its limitations; the effect occurs with word lists but not with SPT lists.

The obvious explanation for these data involves interpreting the presentation rate effect not in terms of the nominal time concerned, but rather in terms of the

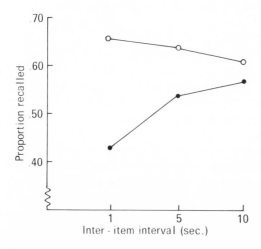

FIG. 12.1. Proportion of items recalled, as a function of length of inter-item interval. Words ●——●; SPTs ○——○.

time actually used in encoding the material into memory (see Cooper & Pantle, 1967). Thus, in the above study subjects in the word conditions reported that they had utilized the long intervals in trying to acquire the to-be-recalled items. Further, in the condition using the 10 sec intervals the subjects reported that they had tended to utilize only part of the interitem intervals for the purposes of memorizing the words. Consequently, if we consider utilized time, there may have been little difference between the two slow presentation conditions, which would account for the nonsignificant difference in recall levels between these two conditions. A similar finding is reported by Nelson (1977). In his study, subjects judged whether words contained an r or an n sound. The words were presented at either a 4 sec or an 8 sec rate. An unexpected recall test showed no difference in recall level as a function of presentation rate. Given that the subjects only utilized as much of the presentation time as was necessary to make their judgments, the extra time available in the 8 sec rate was worthless from the encoding viewpoint. Unfortunately, this notion does not quite explain the SPT results. In the two conditions having long interitem intervals, two-thirds of the subjects claimed that they used these intervals to try to memorize the SPTs. In spite of this, however, the longer intervals did not increase recall level.

A second constraint on the presentation rate effect is reported by Jacoby and Dallas (1981). Decreasing the presentation rate during acquisition, from one word/sec to one word/2 sec increased recognition performance but did not increase the priming effect in a tachistoscopic identification task.

The total time effect may also manifest itself in the primacy effect in free recall. Under conditions where the subject's strategy is to devote more time to the first few words in a list than to later items, this is reflected in superior recall of these primacy items (Rundus & Atkinson, 1970). Under conditions where the subject splits his time over the items evenly, the primacy effect does not occur. This latter result may be obtained with word lists where cumulative rehearsal is forbidden (Atkinson & Shiffrin, 1971) and with lists of SPTs where encoding is free (Cohen, 1981). Incidentally, I hesitated in including primacy effects in the First Law since these effects can also occur under conditions where the primacy events should not have had an advantage in acquisition time (see, for example, Glenberg, Bradley, Kraus, & Renzaglia, 1983, Experiment 5).

The von Restorff effect may also be an offshoot of the total time effect (Cooper & Pantle, 1967). If one item in a list differs from the others in some way, its probability of recall will be higher than that for the other items. Since the total amount of list learned is the same regardless of whether there is a stand-out item or not (Wallace, 1965), there is an obvious trade-off which may reflect increased encoding time being given to the stand-out at the expense of the time spent on the remainder of the list.

Similar effects may be obtained by directing the subject's attention to certain list items as being important-to-remember. The important items are better recalled than the unimportant items, again presumably through the subject investing more time in learning the important items at the expense of the unimportant ones. This has been demonstrated for word recall using paired associate lists (Cohen & Nilsson, 1974; Harley, 1965a, 1965b) and for free recall (Cohen 1983). Although this effect does not disappear completely when used with SPT events, the minimal size of the effect in this case suggests that we are close to the boundary condition (Cohen, 1983).

Probably the most consistent manifestation of the total time effect is the repetition effect. In its simplest terms, the repetition effect is shown when two presentations of an event yield better memory for that event than one presentation. This effect has an obvious relationship with Thorndike's Law of Exercise.

Event repetition would appear to be a robust method of improving memory for all sorts of events (see, for example, Hintzman, 1974). The effect is obtained for both recall and recognition, and also in priming for tachistoscopic identification, (Jacoby & Dallas, 1981). Further, the effect appears to be impervious to interference from other robust effects, such as the interactive context effect (see Third Law). For example, repetition of a homograph in an interactive context (a context which suggests one meaning of the word) boosts performance in a recognition test by about the same amount whether the homograph is tested in the same interactive context, or in a different interactive context, which suggests a second meaning of the target (Davis, Lockhart & Thomson, 1972). Similarly, Donaldson (1981) has reported comparable effects of repetition on recognition when homographs were presented twice in different biasing contexts and when they were presented twice in the same biasing context. Using cued recall, Slamecka and Barlow (1979) have also found that two presentations in different biasing contexts give the same size of repetition effect as two presentations in similar (although not identical) biasing contexts.

Some boundary conditions for the repetition effect are very clearly defined, however. If words are used as target events, the spacing of the repeated presentations is critical. The repetition effect is more reliable with long than with short lags. This is known as the spacing or lag effect (see Melton, 1970, and Hintzman, 1974, for reviews). When the two presentations occur with zero separation (zero lag), the repetition effect is minimal, if it occurs at all. Presentation lag then, defines one boundary of the repetition effect. We tested the generality of the lag constraint on the repetition effect using SPT events. Twelve subjects were each tested with two word lists and two SPT lists. Each list was composed of 7 buffer items (the 3 primacy and 4 recency items) and 12 critical items, 3 of which were presented once only and 9 of which were presented twice. Of the 9 twice presented items, 3 were repeated with a lag of zero, 3 with a lag of three, and 3 with a lag of six. Half of the subjects received the two word lists followed by the two SPT lists; the other half received the two SPT lists first. Word presentation was by audiotape, using a 2 sec rate. The SPTs were presented at a 5 sec rate. Ninety sec were allowed for written word recall, and two min for written SPT recall.

Free recall performance on the two types of list is shown in Figure 12.2. Collapsing over lag, a significant effect of repetition was found, $F(1,11) =$

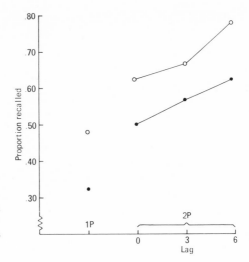

FIG. 12.2   Proportion of items recalled, as a function of number of item
repetitions (1P = 1 presentation; 2P =
2 presentations) and of lag. Words
●————●; SPTs ○————○.

19.27, $p < .05$; the interaction between the repetition variable and class of event
was not significant, $F < 1.0$. The effect of spacing is seen in the data for twice-
presented items. This effect was significant, $F(2,22) = 3.45$; again, the interaction between spacing and class of event was not significant, $F < 1.0$. Thus SPTs
behave like words in showing a repetition effect attenuated by the massing of the
repetitions.

A second procedure for demonstrating the repetition effect is to present the
total list of items more than once. Again a repetition effect occurs even if the
meanings of the words in the list are biased in two different ways on the two
presentations (Young & Bellezza, 1982). The effect did not occur, however,
when the subjects were instructed to use a completely different mnemonic on the
two list presentations, and to recall the list with the aid of the mnemonic device
used in acquiring the immediately preceding list.

The multitrial effect generalizes to SPT memory. Two groups of twelve
subjects were given either a 20-item word list or a 20-item SPT list in a multitrial
free recall test. Following each of four presentations the subjects were given a
recall test, being allowed 90 sec or two min for the words or SPTs, respectively.
Figure 12.3 shows similar multitrial effects for the words and SPTs; an anova
yielded a significant effect of trials, $F(3,66) = 33.21$, $p < .05$, but no significant
trials by class of item interaction, $F < 1.0$.

It should be noted that a basic prerequisite for a repetition effect is that the
subject should attend to the various occurrences of the target events. As Bekerian
and Baddeley (1980) have demonstrated, repetitions of a radio message spaced
over a period of weeks produced zero memory performance in most individuals
who had been exposed to, but had apparently not attended to, approximately
1000 occurrences of the message.

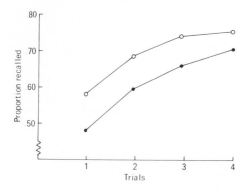

FIG. 12.3. Proportion of items recalled as a function of number of
study-test trials. Words ●———●;
SPTs ○———○.

In sum, the statement that better acquisition yields better memory performance would appear to have a fair degree of generality. This Law exhibits some
constraints, notably that the levels manipulation and presentation rate have not so
far shown effects in SPT recall, nor in procedural memory as measured by
priming effect. There are two ways of interpreting these constraints. One alternative is to suppose that the manipulations that affect word recall or recognition,
but not SPT recall, affect the acquisition of words but not of SPTs. If we take this
route, the First Law becomes definitional in nature, even in the case of independently measurable variables. (See discussion of the Third Law).

The other possibility is to simply accept the failure of the levels manipulation
and presentation rate in the case of SPT recall as a constraint on the Law, without
making any inferences as to whether or not these variables affect acquisition.
This second possibility is preferable on two counts. In the first place it leaves
much of the Law empirically intact. And, perhaps more importantly, the Jacoby
and Dallas (1981) data showing presentation rate to affect word recognition
memory, and thus presumably word acquisition, but not procedural memory
(priming), shows the danger of using memory performance data to make inferences about acquisition.

Second Law—forgetting

The Second Law, which is purely empirical, deals with the general phenomenon
that events are better remembered when they are recent as opposed to temporally
remote. Recency may be measured either in units if time as in retention intervals
of various lengths, or of lag as in the number of intervening items. If units of
time are adopted, then we are talking about forgetting in the tradition of Thorndike's Law of Disuse. If the units are lag units, then we are talking about the
recency effect that is more in the tradition of Watons's or Guthrie's recency.
Whether or not forgetting over time and recency are simply two facets of the
same phenomenon or two separate phenomena has little importance in the context of the second law. What is important is that *recent is best*.

In the short term, where the units are intervening items, the so-called recency effect appears to be a general recall phenomenon. In the free recall of word lists, the recency effect spans the last 2–8 items in the list (depending on the study). This result is obtained both under conditions where there is no effort made to separate the individual list items from each other (Murdock, 1962; 1974) and in the continuous distractor procedure, where the items (words, word pairs, word triplets) are separated from each other by some mental activity such as arithmetic (Aldridge & Farrell, 1977; Bjork & Whitten, 1974; Tzeng, 1973). In addition to unrelated words, a short term recency effect is obtained using proverbs (Glanzer, 1972) or other types of sentences (Cohen, 1981) as list events. Transsituational generality is also provided by the very reliable recency effect found in the recall of SPTs (Bäckman & Nilsson, 1984; Cohen, 1981). Other examples of short-term recency for nonverbal events are to be found in the literature, although such studies often favor a serial rather than a free recall procedure, which may limit the span of the effect. For example, blindfolded subjects were required to move a handle from a starting position to a stopping point. The handle was returned to the starting point and the subject again moved the handle to a new stopping point. This was repeated several times, after which the stopping point was removed completely and the subject attempted to replicate the series of movements. Using this serial recall procedure, a recency effect was found for the final list event, as measured by degree of correspondence between the original length of movement and the recalled length of movement (Magill & Dowell, 1977; Wrisberg, 1975).

A similar result was obtained in deaf subjects attempting to serially recall short lists of signed (ASL) words, namely a recall advantage of the last item (Shand, 1982).

Constraints on short-term recency effects fall into two categories. First, the method of testing appears to be critical. Apparently, the less the explicit cuing (comparing free recall, cued recall, and recognition) the greater the recency effect (Glenberg et al., 1983). In fact, there is some doubt as to whether recognition shows short-term recency at all (Glenberg & Kraus, 1981; Poltrock & MacLeod, 1977). One problem in trying to detect recency in short-term recognition memory is, of course, the very high level of performance attained for all list items, which often does not leave much room for an increase in performance for recency items. A convincing recency effect in short-term recognition memory has been reported, however, in Murdock and Anderson (1975). In this case, recency spanned the whole list of study-plus-test items.

The second constraint involves the limited span of the recency effect in short-term recall. In Murdock's (1962) studies, the probability of recall was highest for the final list item, next highest for the second last item, then for the third last, fourth last, etc. up to the eighth last word in the list. From that point on (or rather back) recency ceased to be an advantage. The eighth last word in the list was not recalled any better than the thirty-sixth, thirty-seventh or thirty-eighth last word. In other studies, recency has only spanned the final four items in lists of words, sentences (task instructions) and SPTs (Cohen, 1981). In Glanzer's (1972) study, only the last three proverbs in the list showed a recall advantage.

The span of the recency effect is also limited to the last few items in the continuous distractor procedure. Unfortunately, studies using this procedure have tended to use relatively short lists (10–12 items) which sometimes results in the recency effect running into a primacy effect. In such cases, primacy may have obscured some of the recency. This may have also occurred in the case of the nonverbal serial recall described earlier.

One clear failure to obtain short-term recency in recall was reported by Poltrock & MacLeod (1977) in an experiment in which four lists of words were presented using the continuous distractor procedure. The subjects were postcued to either recall or recognize the items in each list. The two lists which were recalled in this experiment showed a complete absence of recency. Whether this is simply a random anomaly or whether the nonrecall of the other two lists was responsible (as Poltrock & MacLeod believe), this failure to yield a recency effect is indeed a result outwith the range of common experience.

Recency in longer term free recall has also been convincingly demonstrated. Baddeley and Hitch's (1977) subjects who recalled rugby matches in which they had played, showed a recency effect spanning several matches (weeks). Glenberg et al.'s (1983) subjects who created a short story either once a day or once a week, for seven sessions, also showed a clear recency effect when tested for details of their stories one day after the final session.

Long-term episodic memory also shows strong recency effects, when recall is cued. Linton (1978), using herself as subject, recorded a couple of events every day of her life for several years. In testing her recollection for these events using written cues, Linton found clear evidence for long-term recency. Similar findings were obtained in Thompson's (1982) roommate study, which tested long-term retention for recorded real-life events not only in a group of event-recorders, but also in the recorders' roommates who had also experienced the events but were tested under conditions of incidental learning. In this case, the retention intervals were of the order of weeks, rather than years.

Although Glenberg et al. (1983) equate recency with forgetting over time, there does appear to be a difference between the two. For example, Baddeley and Hitch (1977) used a partial correlation technique to separate the effects of lag (number of intervening matches) and time (retention interval) in their rugby match study. Recall proved to be significantly correlated with lag, but not with time. Further, it is difficult to conceive of Linton's (1978) and Thompson's (1982) studies as involving lag rather than time. In particular, the roommates in Thompson's (1982) study, being unaware that the recorded events were to be tested until close to testing time, could hardly have separated these events into a shopping list.

Whereas it is at least possible to use lag as a measure in the Linton and Thompson studies, it would obviously have been impossible to use lag units to measure retention interval in a study that tested subjects' memory for details of their previous visit to the testing laboratories (Baddeley, Lewis, & Nimmo-Smith, 1978). While some types of information showed no loss over time, forgetting over time was reported for other types of information. Little or no forgetting was shown by subjects whose prior visit to the laboratories had occurred up to 120 days previously. The highest rate of forgetting (in fact, almost all of it) appeared to have occurred when the events aged from 120 to 180 days. Further aging, up to 240 days, had little effect on the events' memorabilities.

Although recency in short-term recognition memory is in some doubt, there is no doubt that episodic recognition memory shows forgetting over time. Shepard (1967), for example, convincingly demonstrated that the discrimination of *old* and *new* pictures decreases dramatically over retention intervals ranging up to 4 months.

The generality of forgetting over time also extends to semantic memory. For example, the more recent a news item, the better it can be identified. The same holds true for famous faces (Warrington & Sanders, 1971). Instead of news items, Squire and Slater (1975) tested knowledge of TV shows, each of which had run for only one season. Again, there was an advantage to the more recent shows, in the form of a recency effect which spanned a range of about 5–6 years, after which there appeared to be no further forgetting. A similar result was obtained by Bahrick (1984) in a study of foreign language proficiency. Forgetting was again limited to the first few years of the retention interval, although there was some further loss after a 30-year interval.

In the latter studies, it was tacitly assumed that the subjects being tested had actually experienced the events (news items, TV shows, etc.) first hand. There are also studies in the literature which have obtained recency effects in semantic memory from subjects who had first-hand experience of only the most (historically) recent of the recalled items. The recall of historical figures, for example, showed an initial sharp drop in the number of such figures recalled followed by a more gradual decline, as the historial remoteness of the figures increased (Riegel, 1973). A similar recency effect has been reported by Roediger and Crowder (1976) who required students to recall the names of U.S. presidents. Whether such recency effects should be included under our general recency/ forgetting law is questionable. While parsimony is an argument in its favor, the use of an historical time scale can hardly be equated with the personal time scales which constitute the independent variable in the traditional studies.

Finally, there remains the question of procedural memory as measured by priming procedures. Short-term recency effects have been reported in several priming studies. For example, Kirsner and Craik (1971) have demonstrated a priming effect in the time taken to repeat an auditorily presented word. Not only was response latency reduced by a prior presentation of the word, but this latency savings was found to be a function of the lag separating the test and priming presentations. The smaller the lag, the greater the latency saving. A similar effect has been demonstrated by Loftus (1973). In this case subjects were required to produce exemplars of categories beginning with specified letters. A savings in response latency was found on trials for which the specified category (but not the specified letter) had already occurred on a previous trial. Again the amount of savings was found to be an inverse function of the lag between the priming and test trials.

Although procedural memory appears to fit the short-term recency aspect of the Second Law, some published studies have failed to show forgetting over the long term. Jacoby and Dallas (1981) had subjects read aloud a long list of words. Subsequently, the subjects were given a tachistoscopic identification test which included words previously presented in the list and words not previously presented. A typical savings was reported—the previously presented words were identified more readily than the new words. What is of special interest here, however, is the finding that the priming effect did not appear to diminish significantly over a 24 hour retention interval. In Tulving, Schacter, and Stark's (1982) study subjects read a long list of words as priming for word fragment identification, tested either 1 hour or 1 week after priming. As in the Jacoby and Dallas (1981) study, there appeared to be no diminution of the priming effect during the 1 week (minus 1 hour) retention interval. However, a more systematic study has shown fast forgetting in priming over the first few minutes in the word fragment identification task, at which point the curve begins to flatten out somewhat; after 1 hour, rate of forgetting is very slow (Tulving, personal communication).

The Second Law, then, would appear to be fairly general.

Third Law—retrieval

For the Third Law we have available two possible candidates, namely the Encoding Specificity Hypothesis and the Encoding Specificity Principle. The encoding of target events and retrieval cues is guided partly by semantic memory (prior knowledge) but also by the episodic context. A completely empirical Third Law could be: *The closer the match between encoding and retrieval conditions (the greater the overlap in episodic contexts) the better the memory performance.* This statement, being empirically testable, is closer in spirit to the Encoding Specificity Hypothesis than to the Principle. Feeding into this law are context effects, state dependent effects, and cuing effects. In considering shopping-list memory, I found it useful to distinguish between context and cuing effects for several reasons, which will become apparent later. Context is here defined as the general state of the physical environment in which the list is learned or remembered; (retrieval) cues are considered as being specific to the items or events in the list, each item normally being related to a different cue. State dependency is defined along the lines of context, in that it reflects the general internal state of the subject during the acquisition and testing of the list.

Distinguishing between context and cuing effects in this way implies some measure of disagreement with Mackintosh (this volume). In fact, the difference in our approaches to context effects stems purely from a difference in emphasis. Since my area of specialization is human memory, the free recall of *lists* of items figures heavily in my thinking. Mackintosh, being an animal psychologist, concentrates more on the recall or recognition of individual events so that my distinction between context and cuing effects has little relevance for his discussion.

Context effects in memory refer to the phenomenon that performance is better when study and test occur in the same environments than when they occur in different environments. This is an old-established phenomenon in psychology which has earlier been stated in the form of a principle (Carr, 1925): "Recall depends on environmental conditions. . . . Practically, however, an experience can be recalled most readily in those environmental situations with which it has the most direct, the strongest, and the most numerous associations" (pp. 250–251).

Overviews of early studies show that context effects occurred in some studies but not in others (Smith, 1979; Smith, Glenberg, & Bjork, 1978). Nowadays, however, context effects appear to be quite reliable, at least in free recall. Baddeley and his colleagues have reported reliable context effects in the free recall of word lists by divers (see Baddeley, 1982). In particular, Godden and Baddeley (1975) found substantial effects across an underwater and an onshore context. Smith et al. (1978) also found reliable context effects in word-list recall, changing context through a change of rooms. In a follow-up study, Smith (1979) not only replicated the context effect but extended the earlier findings by demonstrating that mentally reinstating the learning context yielded just as marked an effect as did a physical reinstatement.

Context effects have also been demonstrated in the classroom. A rather weak effect was reported by Abernathy (1940); performance in this case concerned the recall of classroom material as measured by objective tests (cued recall). More convincing evidence for a context effect in the classroom has been reported recently by Metzger, Boschee, Haugen, and Schnobrich (1979), who tested recall of material from a physical geography course. Although the precise method of testing was not reported in this article, this would appear to be an example of a context effect in semantic rather than in episodic memory. A second example of a context effect in semantic memory is provided by Hunter (1957), who relates the true story of the non-Chinese man who lived in China for some years, thereby acquiring the language. At the end of a 2-year sojourn in his native land the man had almost completely forgotten all his learned Chinese. On returning to China, however, his fluency in Chinese spontaneously recovered—a clear case of a context effect in semantic memory.

Constraints on context effects appear to involve method of testing, at least in the case of word lists. Godden and Baddeley (1980) repeated their earlier diver study, this time testing recognition memory. Changing context had no effect in this study. In a similar vein, Smith et al. (1978) found little effect of changing context on word recognition, and no effect at all when the semantic sense of the words was disambiguated. Unfortunately, the literature is not consistent in its reported findings in this constraint on the Third Law. Malpass and Devine (1981) exposed students to an incident of vandalism. The students were tested 5 months later on their ability to select a head-and-shoulders photograph of the vandal in a photograph lineup. Those subjects who were simply given selection instructions showed a recognition hit rate of 40%; those subjects who were given a mental reinstatement of the original vandalism context (by verbal suggestion) showed a recognition hit rate of 60%. Since there was only one item (the vandal's face) involved in the Malpass and Devine (1981) study, it could be argued that the inclusion of their findings in the context effect section is inappropriate. If the effect of mentally reinstating the acquisition context is designated a cuing as opposed to a context effect, then the Malpass and Devine findings need no longer be considered anomolous. Indeed, in finding a cuing effect in facial recognition, Malpass and Devine (1981) may be considered as providing confirmation for the cuing effect on facial recognition reported by Watkins, Ho, and Tulving (1976) and by Thomson, Robertson, and Vogt (1982).

The generality of, and constraints on the Third Law as exemplified by state-dependent effects are more clear-cut. These effects are shown when a subject studies a list in either a drugged or nondrugged state and is subsequently tested, again either in a drugged or nondrugged state. Performance is better when the states of the subject are similar during acquisition and test. This effect appears to be reliable across several classes of target items, although it only occurs reliably if memory is tested using free recall; neither cued recall nor recognition can be relied upon to give state-dependent effects (see Eich's analysis of the state-dependent effect, 1980). Even in this case, however, the data are not entirely consistent. Among the 57 studies listed in Eich's article, two of 15 recognition studies obtained state-dependent effects, while three of 26 free recall studies failed to yield such effects.

In sum, then, environmental context effects and state-dependent effects appear to support the Third Law in the case of free recall but not of recognition. Because both these effects involve the interaction of encoding and test contexts or states, they fit well into the spirit of the Encoding Specificity Hypothesis, especially in the form it was conceptualized by Tulving (1974).

Unlike context and state-dependent effects, cuing effects are sometimes difficult to define. A context or state-dependent effect requires that free recall in context or in state is superior to that out of context or out of state. The problem with cuing effects is that free recall may not constitute the appropriate comparison condition. To illustrate this problem, consider two studies, one by Tulving and Watkins (1973) and the other by Bahrick (1974).

In Tulving and Watkins (1973) the recall of 5-letter words was cued with either the first two letters, the first three letters, the first four letters, all five letters, or else they were free recalled. Bahrick (1974) tested the recall of names presented together with pictures in a 6 × 6 array, either cued with the pictures, with the locations, with the pictures plus locations, or else free recall. In both studies the effectiveness of the cues as retrieval aids was demonstrated by the direct relationship between recall level and number of cues. The more cues provided, the higher the recall level. In neither study, however, did the minimal cuing condition yield better recall than free recall. Indeed in Bahrick's (1974) study two cues were required to match the performance attained in the free recall condition.

One difference between the context effect and the cuing effect procedures is that whereas reinstating the context does not hamper the subjects' own retrieval routes, cuing puts a constraint on free retrieval. Each item has to be recalled using the route indicated by the provided cue. Although this part of the discussion is theoretical, it is relevant to our empirical approach, since it suggests that even when cued recall does not top free recall, there may still be a cuing effect in the sense that some items which would not have been free recalled, may be recalled specifically through the use of provided cues. Bearing this problem of measurement in mind, let us examine the contribution of the cuing effect to the Third Law.

First, the clearly interpretable cuing effect, namely that the probability of recalling an item increases with the number of cues provided for it appears to have some degree of generality as illustrated by a study reported by Jones (1976). Jones presented a series of cards which varied according to the pictures of the objects they depicted, the color of the objects and the spatial positions of the objects on the cards. In addition, since the cards were presented sequentially, the cards also varied according to their sequential position in the series. The recall of each type of information, object, color, location, and sequential position, was tested using either one, two, or all three of the remaining types of information as cues. For all four types of information, recall level increased with the number of provided cues.

An alternative method of studying the cuing effect is to use a cross-over design in which two or more types of retrieval cue are crossed with two or more types of encoding directions. The purpose of such studies is to try to demonstrate an interaction between the cue type and encoding direction such that optimal performance would occur when the type of retrieval cue matched the encoding direction.

The data from several such studies clearly support the Third Law. In particular, two recent studies provide strong support. Reddy and Bellezza (1983) instructed subjects to encode a list of words by making a visual image of each word and elaborating on it. Subjects were required to think aloud during this phase.

Recall was subsequently tested under one of three conditions, namely free recall, recall cued by a written record of the subjects' own utterances made during encoding (cued recall condition), or recall cued by a written record of some other subject's encoding utterances (yoked condition). The efficacy of matching encoding and retrieval cues was shown by the close to ceiling performance of the cued recall condition as compared with the yoked condition which produced a performance level of less than 50%. Similar data have been reported by Mäntylä and Nilsson (1983). In this study, subjects were presented with a list of 30 visual words and asked to generate three qualities for each word. At recall, the subjects were given either their own verbalizations or else the verbalizations of other subjects. As in Reddy and Bellezza (1983), performance was close to ceiling for the subjects receiving their own verbalizations but only 58% when cued with the verbalizations of others.

Yet another procedure for demonstrating cuing effects uses a cross-over design and guided encoding. The subject's encoding is guided in one of two directions by experimental instructions. At test a cue is provided which matches the encoding encouraged during acquisition, or else the alternative encoding. For example, Ozier (1978) instructed subjects to memorize a word list for a later test in which cues would be provided. One group of subjects was told that recall would be cued by the initial letter of each word (and presumably paid attention to these letters during encoding); a second group was told that they would be cued by category names (and presumably paid attention to the semantic aspects of the words). The results of the study showed an interaction between encoding instruction and retrieval cue. A letter cue was more effective when the acquisition instructions had stressed letter encoding; a semantic cue was more effective when combined with a category encoding instruction than with a letter-encoding instruction. Again, then, performance was better when encoding and retrieval conditions were matched. One further aspect of Ozier's results might be mentioned at this point, namely that the semantic cues yielded just as good recall of letter-encoded words as did letter cues, which of course should not happen according to the Third Law.

If instead of the Encoding Specificity Hypothesis I were to base the Third Law on the Encoding Specificity Principle, the aforementioned aspect of Ozier's data would not contravene the law. The use of the Principle would result in a hybrid law. In its empirical aspect it would encompass context and cuing effects. In its definitional aspect it would state that a retrieval cue is effective only to the extent that its encoding is compatible with the stored representation of the episodic target. Consequently, the Principle would have no trouble with the equality of Ozier's semantic and letter cues following letter-directed encoding. The efficacy of the semantic cues would simply indicate that the subjects had encoded the targets semantically, in spite of the letter-directed instruction.

If valid and reliable, the hybrid law would obviously be of great importance in episodic memory research; for example, it would enable us to uncover what goes on in unguided encoding situations, by measuring the effectiveness of various kinds of retrieval cues. Tulving (1983) implies that the Principle is self-evident—obviously the retrieval cue should match the subject's original perception and stored representation of the target, if it is to be effective. The Principle is only self-evident, however, if episodic memory is indeed a separate system from semantic memory. If semantic memory plays a greater role in episodic recall than it is presently allowed by Tulving, the Principle is no longer self-evident. And indeed there are data in the literature to support the notion of access to episodic traces by means of a detour through semantic memory (see, for example, Santa & Lamwers [1974] and Postman [1975]).

At this point my inclination is to follow the same path I took in the case of the First Law, which is to opt for an empirical Third Law based on the Encoding Specificity Hypothesis.

In section 2 it was made clear that the main search for generality would take place across situations rather than across species. Given the goals of this conference (Nilsson & Archer, this volume), however, it is obviously desirable to make some comment on transspecies generality. The First Law is, of course, the basis of the animal learning area, which studies changes in behavior over (learning) trials. The Second Law has received only limited attention in the animal learning area. As Gleitman (1971) explains ''Most workers in the area have been so impressed by the fact that learned patterns persist, that few have asked whether they persist in full'' (p. 2). Short-term recency in free recall has, however, been shown by Lana the chimpanzee (Buchanan, Gill, & Braggio, 1981) and in recognition by Keakiko the bottle-nosed dolphin (Thompson & Herman, 1977). Forgetting over time has been shown by rats in some situations, if not in others (Gleitman, 1971), and by pigeons (Thomas, 1981).

In contrast, context effects have received, and are currently receiving, a fair amount of attention in the animal area. Such effects undoubtedly occur in animal subjects (Archer, Sjödén, Nilsson, & Carter, 1979; 1980. See also Mackintosh, this volume). As regards the acquisition, retention, and retrieval laws, then, there is some measure of agreement between the human memory and the animal learning literature.

Zeroth Law—Individual Differences

Thus far, I have described a set of three laws. I would like now to add one further law which I call the Zeroth Law of Memory. Laws normally deal with similarities. The Zeroth Law, deals with dissimilarities, but I feel that I must offer it anyway. This law, which is borrowed from Darwin, states that individuals differ reliably in their memory capacities.

In addition to aging effects in episodic and semantic recall (Burke & Light, 1981), developmental differences in episodic recall (Brown, 1975; Reese, 1976) and IQ effects in episodic recall (Campione & Brown, 1977; Detterman, 1979) there is clear evidence for reliable individual differences in episodic and semantic recall in samples of adult subjects drawn from the normal population (Cohen, in press; Underwood, Boruch, & Malmi, 1978) and also in recognition memory (Woodhead & Baddeley, 1981). Oddly enough, although reliable individual differences are also shown in SPT recall (Cohen, 1984), SPT memory does not appear to be affected by old age (Bäckman & Nilsson, 1984), nor by development from the age of 9 years (Cohen & Stewart, 1982). Further, the immediate free recall of SPTs shows minimal dependence on IQ (Cohen & Bean, 1983).

This law is not discussed further, here. I mention it mainly to draw attention to the existence of individual differences in memory, a fact of life ignored by most memory theorists. This state of affairs also appears to exist in the animal learning area. References to individual differences in the animal literature are rather sparse, and usually involve very small samples of subjects (see, for example, Dewsbury, 1978; Rilling, 1977).

EPI*LA*WGUE

Well, there you have my three plus one laws. In retrospect, they do not do a marvelous job of conforming to the criteria I described in my introduction. I have not mentioned a single mathematical equation. In addition, only some of the effects I have described have connections to current theoretical thought in the memory area—the Third Law obviously does; the strength effects of the First Law also have theoretical underpinnings, but perhaps of an earlier era, when trace strength theories were in vogue, although the study of the lag effect has been accompanied by a plethora of theoretical speculation in the contemporary literature. In the case of the Second Law the recency aspect is of current theoretical interest; the forgetting over time aspect is not. This failure to meet the current theory criterion may reflect a weakness in current memory research rather than in the Second Law, however. As Slamecka and McElree (1983) observe: "Our impression is that current theories are little suited and even little interested in focusing on the determinants of long-term forgetting rates . . . . this is to be noted and regretted" (pp. 395–396).

As I said in my introduction, the stated Laws were to be viewed as very rough approximations, which would hopefully act as bases for further more precise statements. What I envisaged was the kind of progression made in physics when Galileo's Law of Falling Bodies was improved upon and extended by Newton's Law of Gravitation, which in its turn was improved upon and encompassed by Einstein's General Theory of Relativity.

While it is true that Galileo's original law, being expressable as a mathematical function, was far more precise than any of the formulations I have described, we must remember that 20th century psychology has probably not yet caught up with 17th century physics. In fact my attempted formulations probably belong sometime between Aristotelean and Galilean science. Even so, it would appear that a progression towards greater precision is already underway even in the case of potential memory laws. For example, Glenberg and his associates are already working on a much more precise statement of the relationship between recall performance and recency than the one I have discussed here (Glenberg et al., 1983). Also, in spite of some interstudy differences in the shape of forgetting curves, Slamecka and McElree's (1983) research gives the promise of deriving a general forgetting function. And there already exists an exact formulation with regard to the recognition failure of recallable words, which has at least some theoretical linkage with the Third Law (Flexser & Tulving, 1978; Tulving & Wiseman, 1975). Indeed, the relationship expressed by this formulation has already been referred to as the Tulving–Wiseman law (Jones, 1984).

In conclusion I would like to make some comments on the relationship between laws and memory research, specifically in the context of two points raised by other speakers at this conference.

The twin goals of science would appear to be classification and the uncovering of laws. These two goals are not mutually exclusive of course, although the general approach to laws taken here stresses the search for similarities across classes or systems of memory rather than the differences emphasized by Tulving and by Olton (this volume). Thus, even although SPTs do not appear to exhibit all the properties shown by words (see, for example, Table 12.1) it is still possible to include SPT recall in the First Law since they do show some forms of acquisition effects.

The second point, which is to my mind much more difficult to deal with is that raised by Craik (this volume). As he has indicated, memory researchers often become fixated on some experimental procedure (often designated an experimental paradigm), such that research appears to concentrate on the procedure rather than on solving the mysteries of memory. As was discussed in the second section, establishing general laws also implicates testing the limits of these laws. The problem is to define where the testing of limits ends and fixation on an experimental procedure begins. While I have no ready solution to this problem, it is deserving of our attention. At the very least such a definition would be of inestimable value to journal editors.

ACKNOWLEDGMENTS

Preparation for this paper was supported by grant number A7023 from the Natural Sciences and Engineering Research Council of Canada.

Special thanks are due to Karen Griffiths for technical help with this project.

REFERENCES

Abernathy, E. M. (1940). The effect of changed environmental conditions upon the results of college examinations. *The Journal of Psychology, 10,* 293–301.

Adams, J. A. (1976). *Learning and memory: An introduction.* Illinois: The Dorsey Press.

Aldridge, J. W., & Farrell, M. T. (1977). Long-term recency effects in free recall. *American Journal of Psychology, 90,* 475–479.

Anderson, J. R., & Ross, B. H. (1980). Evidence against a semantic-episodic distinction. *Journal of Experimental Psychology: Human Learning and Memory, 6,* 441–465.

Archer, T., Sjödén, P.-O., Nilsson, L.-G., & Carter, N. (1979). Role of exteroceptive background context in taste-aversion conditioning and extinction. *Animal Learning and Behavior, 1,* 17–22.

Archer, T., Sjödén, P.-O., Nilsson, L.-G., & Carter, N. (1980). Exteroceptive context in taste-aversion conditioning and extinction: Odour, cage, and bottle stimuli. *Quarterly Journal of Experimental Psychology, 32,* 197–214.

Atkinson, R. C., & Shiffrin, R. M. (1971, August). The control of short-term memory. *Scientific American,* 82–90.

Bäckman, L., & Nilsson, L.-G., (1984). Aging effects in free recall: An exception to the rule. *Human Learning, 3,* 53–69.

Baddeley, A. D. (1976). *The psychology of memory.* New York: Basic Books.

Baddeley, A. D. (1982). Domains of recollection. *Psychological Review, 89,* 708–729.

Baddeley, A. D., & Hitch, G. J. (1977). Recency reexamined. In S. Dornic (Ed.), *Attention and performance* (Vol. 6., pp. 647–667). Hillsdale, NJ: Lawrence Erlbaum Associates.

Baddeley, A. D., Lewis, V., & Nimmo-Smith, I. (1978). When did you last . . . ? In M. M. Gruneberg, P. E. Morris & R. M. Sykes (Eds.), *Practical aspects of memory* (pp. 77–83). New York: Academic Press.

Bahrick, H. P. (1974) The anatomy of free recall. *Memory and Cognition, 2,* 484–490.

Bahrick, H. P. (1984). Semantic memory content in permastore: Fifty years of memory for Spanish learned in school. *Journal of Experimental Psychology: General, 113,* 1–29.

Bekerian, D. A., & Baddeley, A. D. (1980). Saturation advertising and the repetition effect. *Journal of Verbal Learning and Verbal Behavior, 19,* 17–25.

Bellezza, F. S. (1981). Mnemonic devices: Classification, characteristics, and criteria. *Review of Educational Research 51,* 247–275.

Bjork, R. A., & Whitten, W. B. (1974). Recency-sensitive retrieval processes in long-term free recall. *Cognitive Psychology, 6,* 173–189.

Bower, G. H. (1972). A selective review of organizational factors in memory. In E. Tulving & W. Donaldson (Eds.), *Organization of memory* (pp. 97–137). New York: Academic Press.

Bower, G. H., & Karlin, M. B. (1974). Depth of processing pictures of faces and recognition memory. *Journal of Experimental Psychology, 103,* 751–757.

Brown, A. L. (1975). The development of memory: Knowing, knowing about knowing, and knowing how to know. In H. W. Reese (Ed.), *Advances in child development and behavior.* Vol. 10. New York: Academic Press.

Buchanan, J. P., Gill, T. V., & Braggio, J. T. (1981). Serial position and clustering effects in a chimpanze's "free recall". *Memory and cognition, 9,* 651–660.

Burke, D. M., & Light, L. L. (1981). Memory and aging: The role of retrieval processes. *Psychological Bulletin, 90,* 513–546.

Campione, J.C., & Brown, A. L. (1977). Memory and meta-memory development in educable retarded children. In R. V. Kail, Jr. & J. W. Hagen (Eds.), *Perspectives on the development of memory and cognition*. Hillsdale, NJ: Lawrence Erlbaum Associates.

Carr, H. A. (1925). *Psychology, A study of mental activity* (pp. 250–251). New York: Longmans, Green.

Cohen, R. L. (1981). On the generality of some memory laws. *Scandinavian Journal of Psychology, 22,* 267–281.

Cohen, R. L. (1984). Individual differences in event memory: A case for nonstrategic factors. *Memory and Cognition, 12,* 633–641.

Cohen, R. L. (in press). Individual differences in event memory: A case for nonstrategic factors. *Memory and cognition.*

Cohen, R. L., & Bean, G. (1983). Memory in educable mentally retarded adults: Deficit in subject or experimenter? *Intelligence, 7,* 287–298.

Cohen, R. L., & Nilsson, L.-G. (1974). The effect of monetary reward and punishment on the repetition of responses under open and closed task conditions. *Quarterly Journal of Experimental Psychology, 26,* 177–188.

Cohen, R. L., & Stewart, M. (1982). How to avoid developmental effects in free recall. *Scandinavian Journal of Psychology, 23,* 9–16.

Cooper, E. H., & Pantle, A. J. (1967). The total-time hypothesis in verbal learning. *Psychological Bulletin, 68,* 221–234.

Craik, F. I. M., & Tulving, E. (1975). Depth of processing and the retention or words in episodic memory. *Journal of Experimental Psychology: General, 104,* 268–294.

Crowder, R. G. (1976). *Principles of learning and memory*. Hillsdale, NJ: Lawrence Erlbaum Associates.

Davis, J. C., Lockhart, R. S., & Thompson, D. M. (1972). Repetition and context effects in recognition memory. *Journal of Experimental Psychology, 92,* 96–102.

Detterman, D. K. (1979). Memory in the mentally retarded. In N. R. Ellis (Ed.), *Handbook of mental deficiency*, Second Edition, (pp. 727–760). Hillsdale, NJ: Lawrence Erlbaum Associates.

Dewsbury, D. A. (1978). *Comparative animal behaviour*. New York: McGraw-Hill Book Company.

Donaldson, W. (1981). Context and repetition effects in recognition memory. *Memory and Cognition, 9,* 308–316.

Eich, J. E. (1980). The cue-dependent nature of state-dependent retrieval. *Memory and Cognition, 8,* 157–173.

Ellis, H. C., Bennett, T. L., Daniel, T. C., & Rickert, E. J. (1979). *Psychology of learning and memory*. Monterey, CA: Brooks/Cole Publishing Company.

Flexser, A. J., & Tulving, E. (1978). Retrieval independence in recognition and recall. *Psychological Review, 85,* 153–171.

Glanzer, M. (1972). Storage mechanisms in recall. In G. H. Bower (Ed.), *The psychology of learning and motivation*. (Vol. 5, pp. 129–193). New York: Academic Press.

Glanzer, M., & Cunitz, A. R. (1966). Two storage mechanisms in free recall. *Journal of Verbal Learning and Verbal Behavior, 5,* 351–360.

Gleitman, H. (1971). Forgetting of long-term memories in animals. In W. K. Honig & D. H. R. James (Eds.), *Animal Memory* (pp. 2–44). New York: Academic Press.

Glenberg, A. M., Bradley, M. M., Kraus, T. A., & Renzaglia, G. J. (1983). Studies of the long-term recency effect: Support for a contextually guided retrieval hypothesis. *Journal of Experimental Psychology: Learning, Memory, and Cognition, 9,* 231–255.

Glenberg, A. M., & Kraus, T. A. (1981). Long-term recency is not found on a recognition test. *Journal of Experimental Psychology: Human Learning and Memory, 7,* 475–479.

Godden, D. R., & Baddeley, A. D. (1975). Context-dependent memory in two natural environments: On land and underwater. *British Journal of Psychology, 66,* 325–331.

Godden, D. R., & Baddeley, A. D. (1980). When does context influence recognition memory? *British Journal of Psychology, 71,* 99–104.

Harley, W. (1965a). The effect of monetary incentive in paired associate learning using a differential method. *Psychonomic Science, 2,* 377–378.

Harley, W. (1965b). The effect of monetary incentive in paired associate learning using an absolute method. *Psychonomic Science, 3,* 141–142.

Hempel, C. G. (1966). *Philosophy of natural science.* Englewood Cliffs, NJ: Prentice-Hall.

Hintzman, D. L. (1974). Theoretical implications of the spacing effect. In R. L. Solso (Ed.), *Theories in cognitive psychology: The Loyola Symposium* (pp. 77–99). Hillsdale, NJ: Lawrence Erlbaum Associates.

Hintzmen, D. L. (1978). *The psychology of learning and memory.* San Francisco: W. H. Freeman.

Holum, J. R. (1969). *Introduction to principles of chemistry.* New York: Wiley.

Hunter, I. M. L. (1957). *Memory: Facts and fallacies.* Harmondsworth Middlesex: Penguin Books Ltd.

Jacoby, L. L., Bartz, W. H., & Evans, J. D. (1978). A functional approach to levels of processing. *Journal of Experimental Psychology: Human Learning and Memory, 4,* 331–346.

Jacoby, L. L., & Dallas, M. (1981). On the relationship between autobiographical memory and perceptual learning. *Journal of Experimental Psychology: General, 110,* 306–340.

Jones, G. V. (1976). A fragmentation hypothesis of memory: Cued recall of pictures and of sequential position. *Journal of Experimental Psychology: General, 105,* 277–293.

Jones, G. V. (1984). Analyzing recognition and recall. *The Behavioural and Brain Sciences, 7:2,* 242–243.

Kaufman, L. (1979). *Perception: The world transformed.* New York: Oxford University Press.

Keeton, W. T. (1980). *Biological science* (3rd Ed.). New York: Norton.

Kendall, J. (1948). *At home among the atoms.* London: G. Bell and Sons Ltd.

Kintsch, W. (1977). *Memory and cognition.* New York: Wiley.

Kirsner, K., & Craik, F. I. M. (1971). Naming and decision processes in short-term recognition memory. *Journal of Experimental Psychology, 88,* 149–157.

Klatzky, R. L. (1980). *Human memory: Structures and processes,* Second Edition. San Francisco: W. H. Freeman and Company.

Landau, L. D., Akheizer, A. I., & Lifshitz, E. M. (1967). *General physics: Mechanics and molecular physics.* Oxford: Pergamon Press.

Leahey, T. H. (1980). The myth of operationism. *The Journal of Mind and Behavior, 1,* 127–143.

Linton, M. (1978). Real world memory after six years: An *in vivo* study of very long-term memory. In M. M. Gruneberg, P. E. Morris, & R. N. Sykes (Eds.), *Practical aspects of memory* (pp. 69–76). New York: Academic Press.

Loftus, E. F. (1973). Activation of semantic memory. *American Journal of Psychology, 86,* 331–337.

Loftus, G. R., & Loftus, E. F. (1976). *Human memory: The processing of information.* New York: Wiley.

Magill, R. A., & Dowell, M. N. (1977). Serial-position effects in motor short-term memory. *Journal of Motor Behavior, 9,* 319–323.

Mahoney, M. J. (1976). *Scientist as subject: The psychological imperative.* Cambridge, MA: Ballinger Publishing Company.

Malpass, R. S., & Devine, P. G. (1981). Guided memory in eyewitness identification. *Journal of Applied Psychology, 66,* 343–350.

Mäntylä, T., & Nilsson, L.-G. (1983). Are my cues better than your cues? Uniqueness and reconstruction as prerequisites for optimal recall of verbal materials. *Scandinavian Journal of Psychology, 24,* 1–10.

Marlsen-Wilson, W., & Tyler, L. K. (1976). Memory and levels of processing in a psycholinguistic context. *Journal of Experimental Psychology: Human learning and memory, 2,* 112–119.

Mayr, E. (1982). *The growth of biological thought*. Cambridge, MA: Belknap Press.

Melton, A. W. (1970). The situation with respect to the spacing of repetitions and memory. *Journal of Verbal Learning and Verbal Behavior, 9*, 596–606.

Metzger, R. L., Boschee, P. F., Haugen, T., & Schnobrich, B. L. (1979). The classroom as learning context: Changing rooms affects performance. *Journal of Educational Psychology, 71*, 440–442.

Murdock, B. B., Jr. (1960). The immediate retention of unrelated words. *Journal of Experimental Psychology, 60*, 222–234.

Murdock, B. B., Jr. (1962). The serial position effect of free recall. *Journal of Experimental Psychology, 64*, 482–488.

Murdock, B. B., Jr. (1974). *Human memory: Theory and data*. Hillsdale, NJ: Lawrence Erlbaum Associates.

Murdock, B. B., Jr., & Anderson, R. E. (1975). Encoding, storage, and retrieval of item information. In R. L. Solso (Ed.), *Information processing and cognition: The Loyola Symposium* (pp. 145–194). Hillsdale, NJ: Lawrence Erlbaum Associates.

Nelson, T. O. (1977). Repetition and depth of processing. *Journal of Verbal Learning and Verbal Behavior, 16*, 151–171.

Ozier, M. (1978). Access to the memory trace through orthographic and categoric information. *Journal of Experimental Psychology: Human Learning and Memory, 4*, 469–485.

Patterson, K. E., & Baddeley, A. D. (1977). When face recognition fails. *Journal of Experimental Psychology: Human Learning and Memory, 3*, 406–417.

Poltrock, S. E., & MacLeod, C. M. (1977). Primacy and recency in the continuous distractor paradigm. *Journal of Experimental Psychology: Human Learning and Memory, 3*, 560–571.

Postman, L. (1972). A pragmatic view of organization theory. In E. Tulving & W. Donaldson (Eds.), *Organization of memory*. (pp. 3–48). New York: Academic Press.

Postman, L. (1975). Tests of the generality of the principle of encoding specificity. *Memory and cognition, 3*, 663–672.

Premack, D. (1965). Reinforcement theory. In M. R. Jones (Ed.), *Nebraska symposium on motivation*. Lincoln: University of Nebraska Press.

Reddy, B. G., & Bellezza, F. S. (1983). Encoding specificity in free recall. *Journal of Experimental Psychology: Learning, Memory, and Cognition, 9*, 167–174.

Reese, H. W. (1976). The development of memory: Life-span perspectives. In H. W. Reese (Ed.), *Advances in child development and behaviour* (Vol. 11, pp. 189–212). New York: Academic Press.

Riegel, K. F. (1973). The recall of historical events. *Behavioral Science, 18*, 354–363.

Rilling, M. (1977). Stimulus control and inhibitory processes. in W. K. Honig & J. E. R. Staddon (Eds.), *Handbook of operant behavior* (pp. 432–480). Englewood Cliffs, NJ: Prentice-Hall Inc.

Roediger, H. L., III, & Crowder, R. G. (1976). A serial position effect in recall of United States presidents. *Bulletin of the Psychonomic Society, 8*, 275–278.

Rundus, D., & Atkinson, R. C. (1970). Rehearsal processes in free recall: A procedure for direct observation. *Journal of Verbal Learning and Verbal Behavior, 9*, 99–105.

Russell, B. (1931). *The scientific outlook*. London: Allen and Unwin.

Santa, J. L., & Lamwers, L. L. (1974). Encoding specificity: Fact or artifact. *Journal of Verbal Learning and Verbal Behavior, 13*, 412–423.

Schwartz, B. (1978). *Psychology of learning and behavior*. New York: W. W. Norton.

Seamon, J. G., & Virostek, S. (1978). Memory performance and subject-defined depth of processing. *Memory and cognition, 6*, 283–287.

Shand, M. A. (1982). Sign-based short-term coding of American Sign Language signs and printed English words by congenitally deaf signers. *Cognitive Psychology, 14*, 1–12.

Shepard, R. N. (1967). Recognition memory for words, sentences, and pictures. *Journal of Verbal Learning and Verbal Behavior, 6*, 156–163.

Slamecka, N. J., & Barlow, W. (1979). The role of semantic and surface features in word repetition effects. *Journal of Verbal Learning and Verbal Behavior, 18*, 617–627.

Slamecka, N. J., & McElree, B. (1983). Normal forgetting of verbal lists as a function of their degree of learning. *Journal of Experimental Psychology: Learning, Memory, and Cognition, 9*, 384–397.

Smart, J. J. C. (1963). *Philosophy and scientific realism.* London: Routledge & Kegan Paul.

Smith, S. M. (1979). Remembering in and out of context. *Journal of Experimental Psychology: Human Learning and Memory, 5*, 460–471.

Smith, S. M., Glenberg, A., & Bjork, R. A. (1978). Environmental context and human memory. *Memory and Cognition, 6*, 342–353.

Squire, L. R., & Slater, P. C. (1975). Forgetting in very long-term memory as assessed by an improved questionnaire technique. *Journal of Experimental Psychology: Human Learning and Memory, 104*, 50–54.

The century dictionary. (1914). New York: Century.

The encyclopedia of philosophy. (1967). P. Edwards (Ed. in chief). New York: Macmillan Publishing Co., & The Free Press.

Thomas, D. R. (1981). Studies in long-term memory in the pigeon. In N. E. Spear & R. R. Miller (Eds.), *Information processing in animals: Memory mechanisms* (pp. 257–290). Hillsdale, NJ: Lawrence Erlbaum Associates.

Thompson, C. P. (1982). Memory for unique personal events: The roommate study. *Memory and Cognition, 10*, 324–332.

Thompson, R. K. R., & Herman, L. M. (1977). Memory for lists of sounds by the bottle-nosed dolphin: Convergence of memory processes with humans? *Science, 195*, 501–503.

Thomson, D. M., Robertson, S. L., & Vogt, R. (1982). Person recognition: The effect of context. *Human Learning, 1*, 137–154.

Toulmin, R. E. (1953). *The philosophy of science.* London: Hutchinson University Library.

Tulving, E. (1974). Cue-dependent forgetting. *American Scientist, 62*, 74–82.

Tulving, E. (1983). *Elements of episodic memory.* New York: Oxford University Press.

Tulving, E., Schacter, D. L., & Stark, H. A. (1982). Priming effects in word-fragment completion are independent of recognition memory. *Journal of Experimental Psychology: Learning, Memory and Cognition, 8*, 336–342.

Tulving, E., & Watkins, M. J. (1973). Continuity between recall and recognition. *American Journal of Psychology, 86*, 739–748.

Tulving, E., & Wiseman, S. (1975). Relation between recognition and recognition failure of recallable words. *Bulletin of the Psychonomic Society, 6*, 79–82.

Tzeng, O. J. L. (1973). Positive recency effect in a delayed free recall. *Journal of Verbal Learning and Verbal Behavior. 12*, 436–439.

Underwood, B. J., Boruch, R. F., & Malmi, R. A. (1978). Composition of episodic memory. *Journal of Experimental Psychology: General, 107*, 393–419.

Van Nostrand's scientific encyclopedia. Fifth edition. (1976). D. M. Considine (Ed.) New York: Van Nostrand Reinhold Company.

Voss, J. F. (1972). On the relationship of associative and organizational processes. In E. Tulving & W. Donaldson (Eds.), *Organization of memory* (pp. 167–194). New York: Academic Press.

Wallace, W. P. (1965). Review of the historical, empirical, and theoretical status of the Von Restorff phenomenon. *Psychological Bulletin, 63*, 410–424.

Warrington, E. K., & Sanders, H. I. (1971). The fate of old memories. *Quarterly Journal of Experimental Psychology, 23*, 432–442.

Watkins, M. J., Ho, E., & Tulving, E. (1976). Context effects in recognition memory for faces. *Journal of Verbal Learning and Verbal Behavior, 15*, 505–517.

Wingfield, A., & Byrnes, D. L. (1981). *The psychology of human memory.* New York: Academic Press.

Winograd, E. (1976). Recognition memory for faces following nine different judgments. *Bulletin of the Psychonomic Society, 8,* 419–421.

Woodhead, M. M., & Baddeley, A. D. (1981). Individual differences and memory for faces, pictures, and words. *Memory and cognition, 9,* 368–370.

Wrisberg, C. A. (1975). The serial-position effect in short-term motor retention. *Journal of Motor Behavior, 7,* 289–295.

Young, D. R., & Bellezza, F. S. (1982). Encoding variability, memory organization, and the repetition effect. *Journal of Experimental Psychology: Learning, Memory, and Cognition, 8,* 545–559.

13 Human and Animal Amnesia

David Gaffan
University of Oxford

INTRODUCTION

The obvious place for the studies of human and animal memory to meet is in the brain, and particularly in the monkey brain. The monkey brain is anatomically similar to the human brain. In behavioral experiments monkeys are adept at learning a wide variety of tasks which enable their memories to be studied closely and comprehensively. The hippocampal system, which is thought to be important in human memory, is well suited to the investigation of behavioral effects of experimental lesions in monkeys because the monkey's fornix, the major output of the hippocampal system, can reliably be cleanly and completely transected in an operation which causes negligible damage to extra-hippocampal structures. On general grounds one should expect the organization of brain mechanisms of memory to be broadly similar in monkey and in man since the organization of some non-mnemonic processes such as vision or motor control, which are relatively well understood by comparison with memory, are themselves similar in the two species. On equally general grounds one should expect that as scientific understanding of memory progresses the theories of human and of animal memory should have more and more in common, since on the one hand our understanding of memory as a biological phenomenon must at some point in its progress be related to detailed brain mechanisms, and on the other hand purely physiological studies in experimental animals must at some point in their progress make contact with psychological facts because the principal initial reason for taking interest in the brain is that it controls behavior.

And yet, as is demonstrated by the rarity of scientific conferences, with the present mixed participation the developments that these general considerations should lead one to expect have on the whole failed to materialize. The hypotheses advanced by students of human memory are usually difficult to translate into any suggestion of underlying brain mechanisms, physiological studies make little reference to memory as a psychological phenomenon, and behavioral experimentation upon brain mechanisms of memory in monkeys is often seen as a rather narrow speciality.

The main reason for this state of affairs is well known. There are some tests of learning and memory in which performance is quite unimpaired by discrete damage to the hippocampal system in animals. Horel (1978) and Mishkin (1978) have argued that such damage therefore does not produce in animals an amnesia comparable to that of human amnesic patients, that even in patients there is some evidence against the supposedly preeminent importance of the hippocampal system in memory, and that some new hypothesis of the pathological basis of amnesia is required before amnesic effects can be directly compared between man and animals. My aim is to show the fallacy of this line of reasoning. The evidence that human memory can be normal after fornix transection is weak and inconclusive; the best available evidence is consistent with the doctrine that discrete hippocampal damage in people impairs memory. In monkeys, fornix transection leaves certain types of memory intact but does produce a severe impairment in one crucial aspect of memory. The behavioral study of monkeys' memory before and after fornix transection indicates how some fundamental memory processes may be identical in man and monkey even though those processes are revealed in superficially different memory tasks in the two species. The study of the hippocampus offers a link between the psychological understanding of human memory and the physiological understanding of memory mechanisms in experimental animals.

CLINICAL EVIDENCE

A number of well known and ancient lines of evidence, as reviewed by Delay and Brion (1969) and by Mair, Warrington, and Weiskrantz (1979), suggest that severe memory impairments are caused in man by damage to the hippocampal system. Recent evidence from surgical transection of the fornix in man is also consistent with this view (Hassler & Riechert, 1957; Heilman & Sypert, 1977; Sweet, Talland, & Ervin, 1959). However, there exist some reports of fornix transection or destruction in man which do not mention memory disorder as a consequence (Garcia-Bengochea, Delattore, Esquivel, Vieta, & Claudio, 1954; Woolsey & Nelson, 1975). It is therefore necessary to briefly consider the interpretation and assessment of the apparently contradictory clinical reports.

Two opinions at least are defensible. One is that the fornix is without any prominent function in man, that the reports of no psychological effects of fornix destruction in man are straightforwardly correct, and that the reports of amnesia following fornix transection (or damage to closely related structures) are to be attributed to inadvertent damage to some quite separate structures, which are themselves important in memory. The other opinion, which seems to me much more realistic, is that fornix transection does cause a severe memory impairment in man but that the impairment is not always noted because of the circumstances of the clinical observation. Woolsey and Nelson (1975) noted this possibility: Their patient had a rapidly growing tumor and during the last few weeks of his life, when he may have been amnesic, he was comatose. Garcia-Bengochea et al. (1954) reported very briefly that they had transected the fornix in some epileptic patients, and reported no mental changes in those patients that survived the operation. Here again, it is likely that these severely ill people, undergoing an experimental treatment for an intractable condition, were simply not in a position for their higher mental functions to be properly assessed. Certainly, Garcia-Bengochea et al. (1954) report no mental assessment.

This possibility, of unremarked memory impairment, may seem so obvious that it scarcely needs attention drawn to it. But there is one special reason why I think it has been neglected, that reason being the contrast between cases such as those of Garcia-Bengochea et al. (1954), on the one hand, and those of Scoville and Milner (1957), particularly the patient H.M.; or at least, the contrast between these cases as they are sometimes described in textbooks or reviews. The impression may be received that H.M.'s memory impairment, following bilateral medial temporal lobe resection, was so immediately and devastatingly obvious that it could not possibly have been overlooked, and therefore, that amnesia following fornix transection could not possibly have been overlooked by Garcia-Bengochea et al. if it had been qualitatively similar. This impression however does not accord with a careful reading of Scoville and Milner's report of their series of patients. Their amnesia, profound as it was, was revealed in the majority of cases only by careful testing in difficult medical circumstances; and even in the case of H.M., who because of the partial relief of his epilepsy was relatively healthy after surgery, the amnesic effects were not sufficiently obvious for the series of similar surgeries to be immediately terminated. In an influential textbook Shepherd (1983, p.565) has written of H.M.: "Needless to say, this operation was never performed again." But in fact the patient D.C. was given a similar operation some 8 months after H.M. (Scoville & Milner, 1957, pp. 16–17).

There is no reason to doubt that extrahippocampal damage contributed something to the psychological deficits in H.M. But the seeming paradox of normal learning and memory in some tasks by monkeys with experimental lesions arises not only with fornix transection (see below) and with mammillary body lesions (Saunders, 1983) but also with medial temporal lobe ablations designed to mimic those of H.M. (Orbach, Milner, & Rasmussen, 1960).

Though I have not reviewed these complex issues in detail, I hope that enough has been said to indicate that it is worthwhile to consider a quite different resolution than the anatomical hypotheses of Mishkin or Horel, namely a psychological hypothesis that the memory function of the hippocampus is the same in people and monkeys, and that the effects of hippocampal damage in the two species are apparently discrepant only because we do not adequately understand the memory processes of the entire organism in either of them.

EFFECTS OF FORNIX TRANSECTION ON MONKEYS' MEMORY

Fornix-transected monkeys are impaired when they need to learn to make one voluntary movement in one circumstance and a different voluntary movement in some different circumstance. The simplest example perhaps, and certainly the first discovered, was spatial reversal learning (Mahut, 1972) where the animals must first learn to go left (for example) to obtain food reward and then subsequently must learn to go right to obtain it. A similar impairment has been observed also in reversal learning with a manual, not a locomotor, movement, when the animals had to learn on one day to withdraw the hand from a stimulus and on the next day to make repeated manual contact with the same stimulus (Experiment 2 of Gaffan & Harrison, 1984). In reversal learning the different circumstances in which different movements are required are differentiated temporally and by their reinforcement contingencies, but the same impairment is observed in conditional response learning, where the circumstances are differentiated visually. Again, an impairment has been observed both with locomotor and with manual movements. In the locomotor case the animals must learn concurrently, for example, to go left on trials with one visual stimulus and to go right on trials with another visual stimulus (Experiment 5 of Gaffan, Saunders, Gaffan, Harrison, Shields, & Owen, 1984b). In the manual case the animals must learn to withdraw the hand from one visual stimulus to get food reward, and concurrently on trials with a different visual stimulus must learn to make repeated contact with it in order to get the reward (Gaffan & Harrison, unpublished observations).

In all these tasks learning is severely retarded by fornix transection, but is not completely abolished. In relation both to these experiments and to the further findings discussed below, the capacity for learning and memory that survives fornix transection gives rise to two separate and fundamental questions which need to be answered before the significance of the findings can be assessed.

The first question is: In what sense can one ascribe a psychological function to a brain structure if the function is not entirely abolished by ablation of the structure? A strong hypothesis of localization of function in the brain might require that a structure's function be absent, not just impaired, in the absence of the structure. But to my mind a more realistic approach to behavioral analysis of higher brain function is to assume that the function of a central structure is to improve the precision, accuracy, detail, and speed of some process that can be performed in a rudimentary fashion by other structures. This is, as I understand it, a doctrine of Hughlings Jackson (1884).

The second and apparently more practical question is: Are the impairments of fornix-transected monkeys as severe as the impairments of human amnesics? If we leave aside for the moment the question of the generality of the impairments, that is of the range of tasks in which they are observed, one can raise this question of severity within the area where deficits do appear. The apparent simplicity of the question is deceptive however, since it assumes a scale of measurement of severity that is valid across tasks and species. The only such scale would be a psychometric one. In principle, one could place the performance of a fornix-transected monkey in a task at some point on the distribution of normal monkeys' performance in that task. Given enough data, an impairment could thus be expressed numerically as a subnormal memory quotient. Needless to say, I have not enough data from normal monkeys to perform such a calculation. Nevertheless it is relevant to point out as a preliminary step to such an analysis that in the impairments referred to, the typical experimental result is no overlap between the performance levels of intact and of fornix-transected monkeys. In this sense the learning and memory of fornix-transected monkeys is in cetain tasks quite abnormally bad, just as in other tasks the memory of human amnesics is. At any rate, this type of answer to the second question is to be preferred to the evidently futile discussion of whether a trebling of trials to criterion, for example, represents in itself a mild or a severe impairment.

Given these or some other answers to the two question just considered, one can proceed to an analysis of the learning deficits described earlier. In those tasks the fornix-transected monkeys were impaired in learning what to do when faced with a stimulus that should elicit some particular movement. But they are also impaired in memory tasks which require them to remember, given a stimulus, the movement that that stimulus elicited on some previous occasion. For example, monkeys were trained to remember whether they had contacted and displaced an object, or had simply seen the object without displacing it. At the presentation trials in such a memory task the monkey sees and displaces a randomly selected object A, and sees another such object B without displacing it. At the subsequent retention test with those objects the monkey is given a choice between A and B and is rewarded for choosing, in one version of the task, the object that elicits the memory of having been displaced. In the other version of the task, learned by different monkeys, the presentation trials are the same but the rewarded object at the retention test is the one that elicits the memory of not having been displaced. These two versions of the task are examples of the memory-dependent performance rules which monkeys are generally adept in acquiring (Gaffan, 1985); more example are given below. Performance of both versions was impaired by fornix transection (Experiment 4 of Gaffan, Gaffan, & Harrison, 1984c; Experiment 2 of Gaffan, Shields, & Harrison, 1984c). In another example of this type of memory task, monkeys were trained to remember whether a visual stimulus had previously elicited a leftward-going on a rightward-going reaching response, and to reproduce that response at the rentention test. Our preliminary postoperative results suggest that fornix-transected monkeys were deficient in this memory performance.

These memory tasks show that the learning impairments of hippocampally damaged animals, in reversal learning and in conditional learning, can be related to memory impairments and thus potentially to human amnesic impairments. The reversal and conditional learning deficit in tasks requiring a choice between manual contact and manual withdrawal is related to the memory deficit for those responses in the tasks requiring memory for object displacement, and similarly, the deficit in learning whether to reach leftwards or rightwards, either in spatial reversals or in visual-spatial conditional responses, is related to the memory deficit for the direction of reaching to a stimulus.

From the point of view of animal learning theory, the relation between the learning impairments and the memory impairments suggests what might technically be called a hypothesis of the mechanism of reinforcement in habit formation (Gaffan, 1985). The hypothesis may be summarized as follows. An animal's memory of its own voluntary movements directs its exploration, such that an animal when exploring will produce in response to a stimulus a movement other than that which it remembers having produced to that stimulus on some previous occasion. But exploration is controlled also by other memories, such that, other things being equal, the memory of a recent unfavorable outcome associated with a stimulus will promote exploration and the memory of a recent favorable outcome will inhibit exploration. Thus, the memory of previous responses may not only direct exploration but may direct the converse of exploration, that is, repetition of the previous response, in circumstances where the memory of outcomes promotes that strategy instead of exploration. Therefore a memory deficit in memory for voluntary movements will impair (a) performance tasks formally designed to test that ability, as in the memory tasks described above; (b) exploration (Experiment 1 of Gaffan, Gaffan, & Harrison, 1984a); (c) habit formation, as in the learning impairments described at the beginning of this section.

But from the point of view of one interested in animal memory rather than in animal learning theory, the salient feature of the results from memory tasks given to fornix-transected monkeys is a contrast between memory for movements and memory for stimulus events. The control of monkeys' behavior by memory of environmental events is just as subtle, flexible, and indirect as its control by memory of movements. For example a monkey can learn to choose, given a pair of visual stimuli at a retention test, the stimulus that evokes the memory of having on a previous occasion flashed on and off (Experiment 4 of Gaffan et al., 1984b). In the Wisconsin box, a monkey may learn that a stimulus object has under it a white penny rather than a black penny (Gaffan & Bolton, 1983; Experiment 3 of Gaffan et al., 1984b). Additionally, as is well known, a monkey may choose between stimuli according to whether or not they have recently been presented, in delayed matching or nonmatching (Gaffan et al., 1984a; Gaffan et al., 1984c); and a monkey may learn for food reward to choose stimuli previously paired with food in preference to stimuli previously paired with no food, in the so-called "Congruent Recall" task of Experiment 2 of Gaffan et al., 1984b. In all these cases fornix transection in the experiments cited has been demonstrated to leave intact monkeys' ability to remember these aspects of the history of events in the environment rather than of the animal's behavior. Monkeys readily learn memory-dependent performance rules in terms of environmental history, as well as in terms of behavioral history; but the two types of performance differ in their susceptibility to the effects of fornix transection, as we have seen.

These varied abilities of the monkey, demonstrated in a wide variety of memory tasks, may be understood quite simply and straightforwardly if one adopts the point of view of Capaldi (1971). This is to treat memories in much the same way of percepts. Certain pairs of stimuli S1 and S2 have a different unconditioned effect from each other upon an animal's behavior; but if one takes a pair that does not have such an unconditioned differential effect, and gives it a differential effect by a training procedure, then one assumes not that the percepts of S1 and S2 have been introduced anew into the animal's awareness, but that the percepts which were present all along have now been given some significance. (Indeed the existence of one-trial learning provides a logical proof, if one were needed, that stimuli presented before the delivery of any reinforcer are perceived.) All that is proposed is to treat memories similarly: though some memories, to be sure, have an unconditioned effect, an animal may also be assumed to have some memories that have no visible behavioral effect unless their potential control of behavior is realized by some training that teaches the animal what to do about those memories. I stress this point, however obvious it may be once stated, because it seems to me that much of conventional learning theory by ascribing to associations an immediate power over behavior places a very heavy burden of explanation upon memories, giving them an exaggerated importance in their own right which is not compatible with the open-minded attitude towards them which I am advocating; and if that open-minded attitude is not taken then the concepts of memory-dependent performance rules and mediated habits may seem obscure, difficult and irrelevant. Perhaps the most extreme form of the exaggerated explanatory burden of associations in memory is in the Pavlovian principle of stimulus substitution. This essentially proposes that all memories have a single and inflexible effect, namely to endow the retrieval cue with the power to elicit behaviour that is normally elicited by the recall target. But in general, even in apparently atheoretical contexts, to describe an animal as having associated a tone with shock (for example) is taken to imply that the animal expects the shock given the tone, and the absence of such an expectancy is described as a failure to associate the tone with the shock; as if the association was the immediate cause of the expectation. To give just one more example, if a stimulus in the context of discrimination training is first paired with no reward and then subsequently paired with reward, the animal may conveniently be described as having acquired first an association between the stimulus and non-reward, and subsequently in its place an opposite association between the stimulus and reward, the second association canceling out the first in some sense. But in fact, however appropriate those descriptions may be to the observable behavior of a naive animal, the memory, strictly speaking, that the stimulus was paired with nonreward is affected hardly at all by the temporal ordering of the reward and nonreward acquisition trials (Experiment 2 of Gaffan, 1979).

If this Capaldian point of view is adopted, it is not surprising that the impairments in perceptually based habit formation are mirrored by impairments in memory-based habit formation. In both cases the impairments are prominent when the habit formation in question requires some degree of reversal or conditional learning. A clear example is "Incongruent Recall" (Experiment 1 of Gaffan et al., 1984b) where a monkey must learn to displace, at the retention trials of the task, whichever object is associated in memory with nonreward.

RESPONSE CODING

The evidence considered above establishes that hippocampal damage causes memory impairment in monkeys, and that their impairments in certain types of habit formation can be seen as an effect of their memory impairment. But that evidence is not by itself sufficient to establish that the monkeys' memory impairment is the same as the global amnesia which similar brain damage appears to cause in man, since the range of the memory impairments in people seems to be much broader than in monkeys. For example, Heilman and Sypert's (1977) fornix-transected patient was severely deficient in visual recognition memory, but it is now clear (see above) that fornix-transected monkeys can perform at normal levels in the visual recognition tasks of delayed matching or nonmatching. Data of this kind raise the question of the ubiquity of amnesia across tasks as opposed to its severity within a task, a distinction that has been drawn above. My purpose in this final section is to discuss a hypothesis that may explain the difference of ubiquity in psychological terms. The hypothesis is consistent with available results from monkeys and is also being elaborated in some monkey experiments that are currently in progress and are briefly described below. But the hypothesis also makes some assumptions and implications about human memory.

The tasks that test monkeys' memory for voluntary movements are tasks in which memory for movements aids and supplements purely sensory memory. Normally if stimulus A elicits movement 1 and stimulus B elicits movement 2 at acquisition trials, so that at a later retention test with A and B these can be said to act as retrieval cues for the memories of the movements which they formerly elicited, there exist also some stimulus properties alpha and beta which are present at acquisition and may be described as instructions in that their function in the experiment is to ensure that the arbitrarily chosen stimulus A really does elicit the movement 1 and B the movement 2. In addition, the movements will produce characteristic sensory feedbacks which are partly visual as well as kinaesthetic. Thus, the memory of movements is confounded both with memory of sensory feedbacks and with memory of the instructions alpha and beta. For example, in the case of spatially directed reaching, the most natural experimental arrangement is that a stimulus A at acquisition will elicit leftward reaching because it is placed on the left, that spatial position constituting in this case the instruction alpha. In the case of objects that are pushed or not pushed by the monkey in the Wisconsin box, the push produces a characteristic visual feedback namely the movement of the object; and in the arrangement of the experiments with this response that were summarized above, the instruction to the monkey that a push was not required was a visible foodwell just in front of the object, while the absence of such a foodwell was the instruction for a push that would then reveal it. The reason why these descriptions seem unnecessarily cumbersome is that in these cases the instructions and feedbacks are linked very naturally with the movements. But it is also possible to set up quite artificial and arbitrary confoundings of this kind. In a new task currently under development, the monkeys must remember at retention tests whether the stimulus then present was on its former appearance at acquisition presented in triplicate, three copies of it side by side, or in a single copy; and in addition the monkeys perform an overlearned conditional movement at acquisition trials, emitting a long steady "holding" response to any singleton stimulus but a series of short "hammering" responses to the center member of any stimulus presented in triplicate. Our expectation is that these characteristic conditional movements will increase the memorability of the singleton/triplicate dichotomy, and that the increased memorability will be impaired by fornix transection.

It is obviously not unreasonable to suppose that in the course of a relatively long, demanding and intelligent life, by comparison with that of the monkey, man develops a relatively greater number of arbitrary conditional movements (including those of speech), so that the question whether A was paired with alpha at an acquisition trial is often confounded, for very many possible alphas, with the question whether A elicited some alpha-characteristic movement. It may of course be objected that silent and motionless observation can result in the storage of the type of memories which are defective in human amnesia. But this objection is not fatal, given one more step in the argument.

Monkeys, like humans, can recall not only the motor response that a stimulus display elicited but also the motor response which the display indicated as being potentially necessary in the future. This was demonstrated in an experiment with a confusion matrix, formally similar to Conrad's experiment with visually presented letters of the alphabet in which it was demonstrated that "the majority of the subjects verbalise the stimuli, rather than attempting to store them in visual form" (Conrad, 1964). In the monkey experiment (Gaffan, 1977) the animals were first taught to emit characteristic spatially directed movements to a number of nonspatially differentiated colored lights. Subsequently in a recall experiment there was a delay between the presentation of a colored light (the acquisition trial) and the possibility of an opportunity to emit the movement appropriate to that light (the retention test). The errors induced at retention tests by this delay were systematically related to the mutual confusability of the recall responses rather than to that of the colors. Thus, the monkeys were not remembering the colors directly; instead they were remembering the response which the stimulus did not overtly elicit at acquisition, but indicated as being of potential appropriateness in the future. Perhaps this is how humans describe what they saw but did not describe in the past.

CONCLUSION

I have argued for the central role of neurology in linking animal with human memory mechanisms. This is of course not to deny that purely behavioral experimentation can make substantial advances in its own right; only to claim that one of the fruits of such progress is the application of behavioral methods and psychological insights to neurological problems. This kind of behavioral neurology needs to be distinguished from the mere search for double dissociations, and from the use of brain lesions only as a convenient source of independent variables in psychological experiments. For these latter purposes any process that affects the brain will suffice: for example, a naturally occurring disease. The use of precisely designed lesions in experimental neuropsychology can serve a more ambitious purpose, namely to link neuroanatomical and neurophysiological with neuropsychological findings. Although the brief review earlier of experiments with monkey hippocampus concentrated on behavioral findings, I have elsewhere (Gaffan, 1985) stressed the relation of these experiments and interpretations to the anatomical disposition of the fornix, connecting temporal lobe with thalamus, and to the electrophysiological correlation of hippocampal theta rhythm with voluntary movement. Thus, the effect of a brain lesion upon memory can be understood as depriving the animal of certain elementary memory processes which are constituted by the physiological activity of the brain regions disabled by the lesion, and which rely on the anatomical connectivity of those regions. Behavioral analysis of such lesion effects can not only identify specializations of function within the brain; it can also elucidate complex memory processes of the whole organism, by revealing the many varied ways in which an elementary memory process can contribute to behavior.

REFERENCES

Capaldi, E. J. (1971). Memory and learning: A sequential viewpoint. In W. K. Honig & P. H. R. James (Eds.), *Animal memory*. New York: Academic Press.

Conrad, R. (1964). Acoustic confusions in immediate memory. *British Journal of Psychology, 55*, 75–84.

Delay, J., & Brion, S. (1969). *Le Syndrome de Korsakoff.* Paris: Masson.

Gaffan, D. (1977). Response coding in recall of colours by monkeys. *Quarterly Journal of Experimental Psychology, 29,* 597–605.

Gaffan, D. (1979). Acquisition and forgetting in monkeys' memory of informational object-reward associations. *Learning & Motivation, 10,* 419–444.

Gaffan, D. (1985). Hippocampus: Memory, habit and voluntary movement. *Philosophical Transactions of The Royal Society, B308,* 87–99.

Gaffan D., & Bolton, J. (1983). Learning of object-object associations by monkeys. *Quarterly Journal of Experimental Psychology, 35B,* 149–155.

Gaffan, D., Gaffan, E. A., & Harrison, S. (1984a). Effects of fornix transection on spontaneous and trained non-matching by monkeys. *Quarterly Journal of Experimental Psychology, 36B,* 285–303.

Gaffan, D., & Harrison, S. (1984). Reversal learning by fornix-transected monkeys. *Quarterly Journal of Experimental Psychology, 36B,* 223–234.

Gaffan, D., Saunders, R. C., Gaffan, E. A., Harrison, S., Shields, C., & Owen, M. J. (1984b). Effects of fornix transection upon associative memory in monkeys: role of the hippocampus in learned action. *Quarterly Journal of Experimental Psychology, 36B,* 173–221.

Gaffan, D., Shields, C., & Harrison, S. (1984c). Delayed matching by fornix-transected monkeys: the sample, the push and the bait. *Quarterly Journal of Experimental Psychology, 36B,* 305–317.

Garcia-Bengochea, F., Delattore, D., Esquivel, O., Vieta, K., & Claudio, F. (1954). The section of the fornix in the treatment of certain epilepsies. *Transactions of the American Neurological Association, 79,* 176–178.

Hassler, R., & Riechert, T. (1957). Uber einen Fall von doppelseitiger Fornicotomie bei sogenannter temporaler Epilepsie. *Acta Neurochirurgica,* Wien, *5,* 330–340.

Heilman, K. M., & Sypert, G. W. (1977). Korsakoff's syndrome resulting from bilateral fornix lesions. *Neurology, 27,* 490–493.

Horel, J. A. (1978). The neuroanatomy of amnesia: A critique of the hippocampal memory hypothesis. *Brain, 101,* 403–445.

Jackson, J. H. (1884). Croonian Lectures on evolution and dissolution of the nervous system: Lecture 1. *British Medical Journal,* p. 591. (Reprinted in "Selected writings of John Hughlings Jackson", Vol. II, J. Taylor (Ed.), London: Hodder & Stoughton, 1932.)

Mahut, H. (1972). A selective spatial deficit in monkeys after transection of the fornix. *Neuropsychologia, 10,* 65–74.

Mair, W. G. P., Warrington, E. K., & Wieskrantz, L. (1979). Memory disorder in Korsakoff's psychosis: A neuropathological and neuropsychological investigation of two cases. *Brain, 102,* 749–783.

Mishkin, M. (1978). Memory in monkeys severely impaired by combined but not by separate removal of amygdala and hippocampus. *Nature, 273,* 297–298.

Orbach, J., Milner, B., & Rasmussen, T. (1960). Learning and retention in monkeys after amygdala-hippocampus resection. *Archives of Neurology, 3,* 230–251.

Saunders, R. C. (1983). *Some experiments on memory involving the fornix-mammillary system.* Doctoral thesis, Oxford University.

Scoville, W. B., & Milner, B. (1957). Loss of recent memory after bilateral hippocampal lesion. *Journal of Neurology Neurosurgery & Psychiatry, 20,* 11–21.

Shepherd, G. M. (1983). *Neurobiology.* Oxford University Press.

Sweet, W. H., Talland, G. A., & Ervin, F. R. (1959). Loss of recent memory following section of the fornix. *Transactions of the American Neurological Association, 84,* 76–82.

Woolsey, R. M., & Nelson, J. S. (1975). Asymptomatic destruction of the fornix in man. *Archives of Neurology,* Chicago, *32,* 556–568.

VIII SUMMARY AND INTEGRATION

14 The Challenge of Integrating Animal Learning and Human Memory Research

Jerker Rönnberg[1]
Kjell Ohlsson[2]
University of Umeå, Sweden

INTRODUCTION

The purpose of this final chapter is to select some of the most important and frequently debated issues and concepts at this Umeå conference, to summarize these issues and concepts, and finally, to supplement the summary with some ideas about task analysis and its application to animal learning and human memory. In the summary, we have focused on similarities rather than dissimilarities between animal learning and human memory. This means that we have given priority to conceptual analogues, and on the whole, to ideas that might link the two fields together. We have structured our summary and discussion into five sections: Animal perspectives, Human perspectives, Connecting perspectives, General perspectives and *Task analysis as an integrative perspective on learning and memory*. Each section comprises *theoretical concepts/issues* and *methodological issues*. The motif for this organization is that we would like to emphasize and identify some themes that *emerged* during the working sessions of the conference.

ANIMAL PERSPECTIVES

This section deals with two concepts basic to modern animal learning theory: the concepts of association and context. Parallels between the animal and human fields are emphasized. Inherent task constraints and its implication for theory are discussed, as well as the possibility of classifying contextual components.

---

[1]Now at the Department of Education and Psychology, University of Linköping, SWEDEN.
[2]Now at the Department of Technical Psychology, Luleå University of Technology, SWEDEN.

The Concept of Association

From its earliest beginnings the concept of association has had remarkable applicability (e.g., Rachlin, 1970). However, influences from cybernetics and the rapidly growing computer-industry caused a shift in emphasis for the human memory and learning theorists towards *communication,* whereas the animal learning theorists have remained biologically oriented and emphasized the *adaptive* aspects of behavior (Crowder, this volume). There is an inherent trade-off in the use or nonuse of the associationistic language. The obvious scientific merits of the use of such a concept lies in the fact that we deal with *observables,* stimuli and responses that are carefully defined, and that this approach optimizes procedural *parsimony.*

Rescorla (this volume) argues that for associationistic theory to cope with the fact that the animal is dealing with a rich world, it is necessary that (a) more attention is given to what conditions produce associations, (b) that we focus more on the range of events and complexity of contents that may become associated, and (c) how already formed associations influence, and give rise to, various types of behaviors. Rescorla dismisses contiguity as the sole basis for explanation but carefully elucidates the critical importance of the Kamin blocking experiment. The blocking theme is extended by Dickinson and Shanks (this volume). The concensus is that the complexity of the stimulus situation demands theoretical precision with respect to the associative mechanisms (see Rescorla & Wagner, 1972; Wagner, 1976). Rescorla illustrates range and complexity by reference to within-event (or within-compound) learning (cf. Rescorla & Durlach, 1981). If rats are exposed to multiple tastes for a period of time (e.g., sweet/sour or salt/bitter compounds), and then one element of each compound is paired with, for example LiCl, taste aversion will result when the animal is tested in the presence of the other taste-element as the CS. In other words, the animal has established a within-compound, as well as a compound-US association. Further, Rescorla elaborates the differential predisposition of any given CS in eliciting particular responses (CRs), that is, careful analysis of the nature of the responses in specific situations must be maintained.

Human memory theorists, in their turn, have hidden the explicit associative assumptions in their models. Closer scrutiny reveals that the association is alive and well established even in such models. A few examples may elucidate this general point. Following Collins and Quillian (1969), many semantic memory models are represented as networks or hierarchies (see Shoben, 1980 for a review). The association is a necessary constituent to build these kinds of structures. The HAM model of Anderson and Bower (1973) and the ACT model of Anderson (1976; 1983a) also build on previously established associative connections between concepts represented as nodes. Sophisticated distributed memory models incorporate notions such as convolution of associative information (Metcalfe-Eich, 1982; Murdock, 1982). The popular priming models on spreading activation, rely heavily on a hypothetical flow of "primed" information which spreads according to pre-established semantic networks (e.g., Anderson, 1983b). The association is a robust concept and perhaps necessary to the fields of learning and memory (Estes, 1976). Presently, there is a plethora of concepts *imported* from the information-processing and biological disciplines.

Task Constraints

Some general methodological constraints should be recognized. The Pavlovian theorist as well as the early verbal learning theorist, has often used pairs of simple stimuli (the CS-US or the stimulus and response words). This pairing procedure does not allow much more than the ocurrence of associations. That is, the task per se constrains the subjects' actions, which may not necessarily consist solely of *associating*. In general, there may be a correlation between operational capacity and task requirements (Brehmer, 1984). The nontrivial aspect of this correlation is that the theorist may easily overlook the possibility that his models and concepts indirectly are influenced by the correlation. The inference step that the theorist necessarily has to make, when a certain behavior in a certain paradigm is present, is by no means straightforward. Response quality and magnitude constitute dimensions which, irrespective of theoretical bias, pose a crucial problem for all psychological theorizing. This problem is not solved by performing a larger number of experiments, nor by introducing tighter controls (Bolles, this volume). One solution to this problem may be to focus more on the *processes* "behind" the association. Another approach may be to attempt to understand the nature of the broader context within which the behavior of the animal takes place.

The Concept of Context

From an animal learning theorist perspective, Mackintosh (this volume) has addressed the issue of context specificity in animals and humans. If the animals receive conditioning in one context (e.g., a dark compartment) and if they are subsequently subjected to extinction in either the same or a different context (e.g., a light compartment), then the group of animals for whom extinction took place in a different context show evidence of more suppression than the group tested in the same conditioning context. When the associative values are controlled for, that is, the relative ease with which the context retrieves the US, context specificity is eliminated (Lovibond, Preston, & Mackintosh, 1984). However, in the case of the latent inhibition procedure (Lubow, 1973), where prior exposure of a CS slows down subsequent conditioning of that particular CS, compared to a control group with no preexposure of the CS, context specificity between preexposure and conditioning still holds true (Lovibond et al., 1984). Mackintosh argues that context manipulations within the latent inhibition and conditioned suppression procedures resemble the manipulation of *extrinsic* context in the human case (Baddeley, 1982).

Extrinsic context effects refer to the global aspects of the environment (Godden & Baddeley, 1975), time and place of learning as well as the general state of the brain (Hewitt, 1977), for example, induced by pharmacological agents. Important to note is that the extrinsic effect *mainly* affects *free recall* but not cued recall or recognition (see also Eich, 1980). To this extent there seems to be a discrepancy between the animal and human data in that the latent inhibition procedure is sensitive to extrinsic context; latent inhibition rests critically on the animal's *recognition* of the CS. Moreover, the results obtained for conditioned suppression imply that the context has acted as independent retrieval cues; demonstrating an extrinsic effect for *cued recall* as well. An intrinsic context effect, on the other hand, actively modifies the subjects perception and encoding of the to-be-learned event, and affects both cued recall and recognition in the human case (Tulving & Thomson, 1973).

Mackintosh's argument runs as follows: Unknowingly, many animal learning experimentalists have ignored the possibility that the context actually acts intrinsically on the CS. An extreme example would be the case where the actual physical characteristics of the CS is *altered* by the context. In the case of tones, different compartments may absorb sound differentially and hence produce different CSs. Extreme drug states could probably also act interactively in the sense that they change the animals' entire perception and encoding of an event. Mackintosh seems to imply a continuum ranging from the extreme forms of extrinsic to extreme forms of intrinsic context effects. Essentially, most studies on animal learning have not controlled for the possibility that the context has acted intrinsically. If this were true, it would be easy to reconcile the animal data with the human data, since intrinsic effects on recognition are obtained in both cases. In the previously mentioned study on conditioned suppression (Lovibound et al., 1984), care was taken to eliminate intrinsic context-CS interactions, and when the associative value of the extrinsic context to the US was made equal, the context effect vanished. This extrinsic cued recall effect and the remaining extrinsic effect on recognition in latent inhibition erode the exact divide between extrinsic and intrinsic effects, and complicates context manipulations in retention tests with animals.

Whereas animal learning theorists speak of associations between the CS and the context, Tulving and Thomson (1973) dismiss associative accounts of the contextual effects inherent in the recognition-failure phenomenon. For example, in the associationistic account by Bilodeau (1967), it is tacitly assumed that the pre-experimental association that might exist between a target word and its cue is not modified at study. Recognition-failure of recallable words is exactly a case where the effectiveness of the low-frequency retrieval cues are enhanced due to the encoding operations performed. Tulving and Thomson (1973) thus conclude that the Encoding Specificity Principle (cf. Cohen, this volume) gives a more satisfactory explanation: "Specific encoding operations performed on what is perceived determine what is stored, and what is stored determines what retrieval cues are effective in providing access to what is stored."

Contextual Components

Although the notion of context has been invoked to explain a large variety of effects in both the human and animal case, its conceptual status is relatively uncertain. On the face of it, it should be possible to classify different contexts using schemes that enable the researcher to be more precise about what *type* of context is manipulated. Such a classification would indeed be of both theoretical and methodological value. There are, of course, different ways of approaching this problem. At present, most classificatory attempts are rather inchoate in the sense that they usually take the form of dichotomies (e.g., extrinsic versus intrinsic, Baddeley, 1982; global versus local, Lundberg, 1984). One systematic empirical attempt to tease out contextual components in taste aversion learning in rats is at hand (Archer, Sjöden, & Nilsson, 1984). The work was inspired by Estes (1973) model on conditioning. Even though taste aversion was considered to be a phenomenon independent of the external context (Garcia & Koelling, 1966), Archer et al. have surprisingly found very strong effects of the exteroceptive context. It was found that a contextual compound of bottles, compartments, and an odor element exerted strong control of context-dependent conditioning as well as context-dependent extinction. It was also found that these components could be ordered according to their relative increase in strength: odor, compartments, bottles. Systematic investigations of this kind ought to have high methodological and theoretical value. First, the experimental series gives an example as well as a procedural demonstration of how to empirically classify various components of context in relation to a specific phenomenon. Second, it may create a basis for comparisons across experiments. The relative saliency of the contextual components could namely be captured by a simple contiguity principle; the bottle was more spatially and temporally contiguous with the CS than was the compartment etc., (Rescorla, 1980). Third, it is important to note that the classification is based on the independent variables manipulated within the experiments. This method of classification may be contrasted with factor analytic attempts in the human literature (e.g., Underwood, Boruch, & Malmi, 1978). In their study a large number of subjects solved a large number of memory tasks, and on the basis of performance data, correlational matrices were constructed and subsequent factor analyses computed. Hence, the task dimensions were abstracted post hoc. This clearly represents a different strategy compared to the Archer-strategy, and this strategic question of what research enterprises converge on the most natural taxa is indeed a difficult one. Under General Perspectives, Tulving (this volume) addresses this issue of classification in a broad way and it is further addressed in a task analysis approach in the last section.

HUMAN PERSPECTIVES

In this section some important concepts within the human memory area are discussed and applied to the animal field. The concepts considered important are: working-memory, the procedural-declarative dichotomy, and "optionality." Related methodological issues are also discussed, and focus is placed on nonverbal tasks, prospective tasks, and ecological tasks, respectively.

The Concept of Working Memory

Working memory could be viewed from a definitional or classificatory standpoint. Do animal learning theorists mean the same thing when they discuss working memory as their colleagues on the human side do? That is to say: Which mechanism is working with what representation and for what purpose?

The term "working-memory" was first coined by Miller, Galanter and Pribram (1960). In Estes (1982) review on learning, memory and intelligence, he states that Posner and Rossman (1965) probably were first to use the term in its modern sense: Working memory referred to a collection of items that were activated from long-term memory and which were kept active during the solution of the task. The notion of working memory has been made popular by Baddeley and Hitch (1974). As Hitch (this volume) argues in his chapter: Recency performance in free recall (Murdock, 1962) is dissociable from span performance. On the basis of several kinds of data, it can be stated that (a) recency is not speech-based, whereas span performance involves active subvocal rehearsal, (b) concurrent distractor activities affect span but not recency and (c) individual differences in memory span do not correlate with recency. So, these two tasks seem to tap two quite different aspects of short-term memory performance.

Baddeley and Hitch (1974, 1977) argue that working memory is tapped by span performance. In particular, there seems to be an articulatory loop that can be manipulated in several ways (Baddeley, 1983). For example, if rehearsal is manipulated in a span task through the phonemic similarity of the items, by word-length or by irrelevant subvocalizations, output from this hypothetical articulatory loop is dramatically wiped out. Working memory can be decomposed even further. Phillips (1983) discusses evidence which indicate that there is a visuo-spatial scratch pad which can hold one representation (a visual pattern) at the time. This should be contrasted to the articulatory loop which is assumed to hold 3–4 items at the time. In the literature of modality effects on the presentation of verbal material, there are logically similar decompositions made of short-term memory into auditory and visual memory systems (e.g., Rönnberg & Ohlsson, 1980; Rönnberg, Nilsson, & Ohlsson, 1982), which also have been modeled on a bulk of data on qualitative and quantitative differences.

Recency, on the other hand, does not even seem to be confined to short-term performance. Recency can be demonstrated in long-term tasks such as rugby-players' memory for matches (Baddeley & Hitch, 1977), university students recall of their book-loans (Hitch, this volume), and in the continuous distractor paradigm (e.g., Bjork & Whitten, 1974). Currently, there is a hypothesis of temporal discriminability which is assumed to account for all recency phenomena (see Gardiner, 1983, for a review). More specifically, recall seems to be sensitive to the relative times of two events according to Weber's law (Hitch, this volume). Several demonstrations of recency effects with animals may be claimed, for example, monkeys (e.g., Gaffan, 1977), dolphins (Thompson & Herman, 1977), and pigeons (Thomas, Moye, & Kimone, 1984). However, if working memory really is dissociable from a more general short-term memory, then one must also expect to find some correlates in the animal literature on how animals actually process (rehearse) the to-be-remembered events (For relevant evidence, see Hitch, this volume; Jans & Catania, 1980; Maki, 1981).

In a series of experiments pertinent to the temporal discriminability hypothesis, Rönnberg (1980a, 1981, 1983) has investigated the effects of varying within-list interitem intervals. Recall of *recency* items was found to covary with both an increase and a decrease of recency interitem intervals as well as with the timing of the recall signal. These recency variations hold for precuing and postcuing procedures and have been hard to reconcile with traditional models of the serial position curve. In addition to this, there is a debate whether short-term memory can be separated from long-term memory on the basis of temporal discriminability. This is one of the pieces of evidence that Crowder (1982) cites as he argues against the concept of short-term memory.

Irrespective of the short-term/long-term controversy, it may be interesting to ask why the mechanisms of recency and working memory evolved? According to Hitch (this volume), the long-term recency mechanism should be regarded as a rather primitive function, mainly evolved to keep track of the ''when and where'' of the organism, whereas the short-term recency effects are to be associated with a short-term buffer necessary for language comprehension (Jarvella, 1978). Working memory, and in particular the articulatory loop, is on the other hand supposed to be engaged in the production of speech.

Craik (this volume) implies that working memory is part of the comprehension system. The functional importance of working memory is thus to keep something ''in mind'' to support the workings of higher level cognitive activities such as comprehension and thinking. To illustrate this point, Craik refers to two types of working memoy span test developed by Daneman and Carpenter (1980). The first is called ''reading span'' and the second ''production span.'' In the first task the subject typically has to read a number of sentences for comprehension and in addition to that they are to store the final word of each sentence. The number of words that the subject can reproduce in the correct order defines the ''reading span.'' In the second task the subject learns a list of words, and for each of those words, the subject is to produce a sentence ending with that particular word. ''Production span'' is defined as the longest sequence of sentences that the subject can produce in the correct order. As it turns out, reading ability is highly correlated to the "reading span" scores, while traditional straight span scores correlate to a much lesser extent. The "production span" test is highly correlated to the production of words in discourse. Craik's processing view of memory suggests a focus on the interaction between the task (i.e., the environmental support) and the demands on the subject's self-initiated activity, that is, the working memory approach (Craik, 1983). When the environmental information is insufficient for the solution of the task, the subject has to engage in "further self-initiated reconstructive operations" to "jump the gap" to a desired state of memory. Memory tasks may be classified along the continua of environmental support and self-initiated activity, where, for example, procedural learning tasks are assumed to be high on environmental support and low on self-initiated activity, recognition assumes an intermediate position, and free recall is low on environmental support and thus high on the demand of self-initiated activity. Working memory tasks may demand a high degree of self-initiated activity, but what types of information drives the subject to utilize working memory, and to which consequences?

Human memory theorists address the basic questions of which mechanisms or representations constitute working memory, and what functions are served. Bolles (this volume) suggests that the relatively strict adherence to the associationistic language has hindered conceptualizations of short-term memory or working memory in terms of function and representation; this is arguable but the point should be taken (cf. Olton, 1978; Roberts & Grant, 1978). To be sure, associationistic language can not handle such data. The phenomena (for example, stimulus generalization, and radial maze learning) must be explained by referring to the animal's ability to build certain representations or codes (Staddon, 1983). Spatial representation, temporal discriminability, and response strategy provide a much more complicated syntax for description and explanation. Thus, Bolles' animal learning theories would then attend more closely to the process behind the association. This way, Bolles comes very close to what Hitch and Craik advocate.

Nonverbal Tasks

According to Honig (1978), working memory associates an event with its temporal/"personal" context (cf. episodic memory). The lack of a verbal (articulatory) component of working memory in animals is understandable in lieu of verbal communication. The verbal limitation of animals appears to parallel that of humans with spatial patterns (Phillips, 1983). Verbal articulation enhancing rehearsal must then optimize working memory. We argue that the evolutionary aspect of learning/memory in terms of articulation, constitutes one of the fundamental differences between animals and humans. Working memory that lacks articulation should produce similar performance by humans and animals.

Examples of nonverbal tasks assumed to tap working memory in animals may be found in the extensive use of the delayed matching-to-sample procedure

(Roitblat, 1984). However, it is not always easy to make a clear distinction between working memory and reference memory (memory independent of temporal context; cf. semantic memory). For instance, when scrutinizing working memory pigeons can perform better in a delayed matching-to-sample task with long sample durations compared to shorter duration (Roitblat, 1980). How is that compatible with a short-term based working memory?

Another methodological problem of importance connected to nonverbal tasks, recognized here, is concerned with the dissociation of recency and working memory in animals. Normally, animals demonstrate an extended recency and simultaneously a low degree of rehearsal activity as compared to humans in a short-term memory task (see Hitch, this volume). However, an extra inference step seems to be required in the separation of working memory from recency in animals. That is, in animal studies inquiry of overt rehearsal seems to be an abortive enterprise. Accordingly, the diffuse nature of inherent sensory modality differences between different species does not facilitate the separation of recency from working memory.

Methodological analogues may open up for a rapprochement between the fields of animal learning and human memory. One tactic is to apply a nonverbal task from animal research to human research (e.g., Dickinson & Shanks, this volume). Another example of "connected tasks" comes from conventional "language training" in primates (e.g., Premack, 1983), which involves both verbal and nonverbal tasks. Analogous procedures have also been developed in the human memory research. One such procedure with nonverbal components, which recently has received noticeable interest is the subject performed task (SPT) (Cohen, 1981). SPTs consist of a series of simple instructions such as *clap your hands* and *put the cap on the pen*. These instructions are enacted immediately by the subject and at the end of the series, free recall of the events begins. Mainly due to the verbal instructions SPTs are not unequivocally defined as nonverbal tasks (Bäckman, 1984), but with respect to the type of responses required, and the type of rehearsal required, there seems to be important connections between the study of human memory be means of SPT's and conventional "language training" in primates.

Perhaps, the traditional dichotomy between verbal and nonverbal tasks is not such a great issue as we fear. It might well be that the dichotomy between procedural and declarative memory is the more critical and fruitful one (Cohen & Squire, 1980; Craik, this volume).

The Concepts of Procedural/Declarative Information Processing

In the neuropsychological literature on human amnesia, several theoretical dichotomies have arisen to account for the spared/unspared memory functions in the amnesic patient. One such dichotomy is that of procedural versus declarative memory. Procedural memory refers to the *how* of information processing and declarative memory to the *what* (Cohen & Squire, 1980). The former can only be recalled by one single retrieval mechanism, whereas the latter may be retrieved by many alternative mechanisms. Procedural memory precludes consciousness, whereas declarative memory requires conscious processing by the subject. Typical procedural memory tasks involve tests of sensory, cognitive, and motor skills. Declarative tasks refer to tests of specific facts, the meaning of words, spatial and temporal datedness of events. Amnesic patients demonstrate relatively unimpaired procedural memory, whereas the declarative memory system is impaired.

Animal studies appear to be based on procedural memory tasks, but it has also been postulated that instrumental behavior can be classified in a procedural and a declarative form (Adams & Dickinson, 1981; Winograd, 1975). The procedural form is of an S-R type, for example, "when in the operant chamber, press the lever," whereas the declarative form is an action-reinforcement type, for example, "a lever press causes sucrose delivery." The latter form of representation does not contain any behavioral commands; however, it describes a relationship between events in the animal's environment. Moreover, the procedural form is referred to as a habit, whereas the declarative form is referred to as action. Experimentally, it can be demonstrated (Adams & Dickinson, 1981) that habits are *functionally autonomous* and are not susceptible to the current value of the reinforcer, as evidenced by postconditioning devaluation of the reinforcer. By contrast, the actions are indeed susceptible to such contingencies.

This dichotomy of procedural versus declarative representations evidently does not rest on the involvement or noninvolvement of consciousness as it does in the human case. However, there seems to be similarities with respect to the procedural component: Both rest on the assumption that the procedures may be carried out irrespective of the learning context and they both represent automatic predispositions of the animal/human to carry out certain actions. This communality may warrant further comparative studies on animal learning and human memory.

Gaffan (this volume) suggests that the notion of habit must be revitalized and distinguished from conditioned S-R associations. The essential point is that some departure from a strict Pavlovian account is required. Thus, whereas Adams and Dickinson (1981) claim that procedurally based habits are independent of the value of the reinforcer, Gaffan emphasizes the flexible yet purposive aspect of habit, that is, this notion of habit appears declarative rather than procedural.

Tulving (1985a, 1985b) makes a three-fold classification between episodic-semantic (declarative) and procedural memory systems. Associated with each of these memory systems is a certain level of consciousness. The episodic memory system is assumed to be the most advanced form of memory and entails autonoetic consciousness. The subjects' ability to make self-reports of dreams, and reports of experienced memories in space and time constitute some defining characteristics of autonoetic consciousness. Knowledge about the world which is not bound to the self corresponds to noetic consciousness and characterizes the semantic memory system. The procedural memory system entails anoetic consciousness, and the organism's consciousness essentially reflects a state of unknowing about the external world. One example of anoetic consciousness would be classical conditioning.

An interesting point of contact between animal learning and human memory would be to ask how far an animal can climb the ladder of Tulving's memory systems with corresponding levels of consciousness? For instance, how are we to classify declarative competencies of an animal? Clearly, if declarative representations control behavior, the animal has to have some sort of inferential capability (Mackintosh & Dickinson, 1979), that is, the animal has to combine several propositions about the external world. For example, "a lever press causes sucrose delivery" and "eating sucrose causes an aversive event," may lead to the inference "a lever press causes the delivery of an aversive agent." Other declarative theorists such as Bolles (1972) talk about the animal's expectation that a certain action produces a particular outcome (see also Restle, 1975; Seligman, 1975). Thus, the critical question is to what extent declarative competences (defined in animal learning terms), map on to declarative memory systems (defined in human memory terms), and how this mapping relates to consciousness. Further, how are we to classify the stumbling attempt of a chimpanzee who can learn some rudiments of language? If the chimpanzee, as some claim (cf. Savage-Rumbaugh, Pate, Lawson, Smith, & Rosenbaum, 1983), can perform some feats and actually produce language-like behavior, how should the animal's behavior be classified? Moreover, do we mean to imply that the chimpanzee does not have any concept of self, or does not dream? If the chimpanzee possesses these abilities, is the animal still anoetic, or what level of consciousness does a chimpanzee actually reach? And the evidence of pigeons' ability to process (rehearse) events, how should that ability be classified (Maki, 1981; Grant, 1984)? And the fact that bottle-nosed dolphins can process both syntactic and semantic features of sentences (Herman, Richards, & Woltz, 1984)?

Prospective Tasks

Some methodological points of contact between the two fields, especially tasks that both animals and humans can solve, are of interest. Priming is a widely debated topic in human memory. Priming works very well in amnesics (e.g., Graf, Squire, & Mandler, 1984). Amnesics perform at a level on a par with normals, while they suffer considerably in recall/recognition tasks. It may therefore be hypothesized that priming taps a primitive system of human memory. If one were to think of the delayed matching-to-sample task in priming terms, it might be possible to manipulate the response alternatives in a fashion so to mimic a yes–no recognition response procedure in humans (cf. Olton, this volume).

Would it be possible to prime the animal to choose one or the other response through various similarity manipulations? If feasible one could study the time course of recognition performance and compare that with the time course for the priming effects (effect of similar versus nonsimilar lures). In humans, it has been found that priming effects last for a long time and that recognition performance declines much faster. Moreover, it has been found that recognition and priming effects are stochastically independent (Tulving, Schacter, & Stark, 1982). Or, would it be possible to prime the matching response (or the conditional response) through previously reinforced and in some interesting way similar stimulus?

Furthermore, incidental procedures, such as the manipulation of levels-of-processing, do not rest on a conscious effort of the subject to encode a certain stimulus in a particular way for subsequent retrieval (cf. the concept of ''optionality''). By simply training the animal (an orienting task) to discriminate objects on the basis of their physical characteristics (shallow level), compared to functional characteristics (deep level), subsequent recognition performance will be predicted to be better in the functional case (Craik, this volume).

As Olton states (this volume), it does not suffice to give the animal and the human the same task. In comparative studies we always have the problem of task equivalence (Craik, this volume). Although we employ different tasks, similar processes in the animal and the human may be under scrutiny, depending upon the interaction between the subject's knowledge-base and the task. The only remedy to this problem, it seems, would be to have some theoretical underpinning as to why we think that the task actually taps the same process in the animal as in the human (cf. Hitch, this volume). Both Estes (this volume) and Dickinson and Shanks (this volume), seem to have managed in both devising comparable tasks for animal and humans, and with concomitant theoretical underpinning.

The Concept of "Optionality"

Craik (this volume) argues that the options that the animal/human has or can use, for the encoding of an event, constitute an interesting feature which should be explored further. To what extent can you teach an animal to use various types of coding of information? And how does the encoding interact with different retrieval conditions? What are the boundaries for an animal compared to a human? In a ''free'' encoding situation a human can impose a large set of ''processing options,'' whereas it seems plausible that animals have a very restricted battery of ''options.'' Nevertheless, on the basis of developmental data on humans (e.g., Flavell, 1970), it may be possible to teach subhuman species a much wider range of coding strategies than was previously assumed. Analogous to these developmental data on human subjects, it may be the case that animals suffer from a production deficiency, whereas mediational capacities are spared. Appropriate teaching may reveal previously unknown abilities of the animal, as Gaffan (this volume) appears to imply. The basic argument that any memory can be put to practically any purpose is indeed an interesting claim. This also implies that the animal is not "restricted" to use a particular memory system with its special properties. Nor is the performance in, for example, the incongruent memory task easily captured by associationistic concepts. Thus, Gaffan's theoretical position seems to allow for greater flexibility in learning, and this would certainly agree with a great flexibility in the *use* of the memory record, and in the use of different codes.

Ecological Tasks

Craik (this volume) has stressed that paradigms which aim to study human memory and animal learning should pay increased attention to how the subject *uses* memory in a natural setting (descriptive paradigms). Questions of how and why a particular task is conducive to performance should be addressed (cf. Neisser, 1982). Gaffan's notion of memory-dependent performance rules seems to meet this need. Here, the emphasis is shifted away from studying memory per se to the study of how the animal, after having acquired a certain memory, can use this memory for a given purpose.

Recently, we (Rönnberg & Bäckman, 1984) have developed a task analysis system which critically rests on a division between two basic purposes of a memory task: a reproductive and a productive purpose (Rönnberg, 1980b, 1981, 1982, 1983). *Reproductive* cognitive tasks refer to the traditional memory experiment, wherein the subject is asked to reproduce previously presented material by means of different variations of the recall/recognition procedures. A *productive* task, on the other hand, refers to the activities taking place when the subject operates on a certain level of reproduced information with a task purpose not linked to remembering. When we speak of tasks of high productivity, we include tasks where the reproduced information (pre-experimentally and experimentally acquired) is *used* for productive purposes, and where the use of this information also *transforms* the reproduced information itself. For instance, in a problem-solving task such as the crypto-arithmetic problems introduced by Newell and Simon (1972), the initially reproduced information (knowledge-state) is typically transformed many times before the productive end result (the solution) is arrived at. The same process of transformation holds true for chess problems (de Groot, 1965).

The important point to make in this context is that a *productive memory* task differs from a productive task in the sense that the solution of the productive memory task is highly dependent on experimentally acquired information without which a solution of the task would be impossible. In a productive task (e.g., a problem-solving task), the successful solution is actually very much dependent on pre-experimentally acquired procedures/algorithms for solving problems. For example, studying a story until a high acquisition criterion is reached (tested by some reproductive measure), and thereafter answering questions based on the text, is regarded as a productive memory task. If the questions are of very inferential character, the subject typically has to go beyond the information given in the story to reach a satisfactory productive decision. The productive memory task resembles Gaffan's memory-dependent performance rules in at least two ways: The aim of the task is to study *memory-use,* and this necessitates that the human/animal bases the productive decision on the experimentally *acquired* information.

For conceptual and empirical details of this productive memory task, see Rönnberg and Bäckman (1984). Following, we note some features of the productive memory task which may have a bearing on the enterprise of the conference:

(a) A productive memory task may come close to what one would call a natural or ecological memory task. The first argument to sustain this proposal is that the "testing conditions" in a productive memory task, are hardly ever compatible to encoding conditions in the sense of encoding specificity (Tulving & Thomson, 1973). By the same token, what seems to be the rule in everyday life is that use (cf. Craik, this volume) of memory also involves transfer from *one* situation to *another,* a property which has been noted by others (e.g., Kinsbourne & Wood, 1982). A frequency argument may also be conjectured; several of our everyday usages of memory appear to be high both on acquisition of information and on productivity (e.g., orienting behavior, engaging in a conversation, operating a machine). Furthermore, it seems reasonable to assume that one of the media through which animal and human studies can converge is via the use of ecological tasks. This way, it may become easier to capture common adaptational, functional, and teleological aspects of learning and memory.

(b) A productive memory task does not necessarily have to entail conscious operations on behalf of the subject. Acquisition of information can be done without conscious awareness (cf. Wood, Ebert, & Kinsbourne, 1982; Weiskrantz & Warrington, 1979) as well as reproduction of previously primed target items (Graf, Squire, & Mandler, 1984; Tulving, Schachter, & Stark, 1982). Also, the productive behavior may be executed in a state of relative unawareness as long as these behaviors are familiar to and automatized by the subject. Several everyday life examples testify to this point. Thus, this feature of the productive memory task may open up for a possible development of a productive memory task for animals (cf. Gafffan, this volume).

(c) Evidently, a productive memory task does not have to entail the use of verbal material. Productive memory behavior can be based on the acquisition of a set of objects or pictures. If one were to develop a task for animal studies, it had to focus on the relation between a set of learned nonverbal materials, and how this set could be used given a range of different productive task purposes.

CONNECTING PERSPECTIVES

In this section we propose to summarize some aspects of the work presented by Estes (this volume) and Dickinson and Shanks (this volume). Both contributors have in common that they have chosen to tackle the problem of integration between the fields by transporting models and ideas which have arisen within the animal field and by subjecting these models to empirical test with humans. Methodological difficulties with respect to task compatibility are also noted.

Category Learning

Estes (this volume) investigates category learning by using the contextually based classification model of Medin and Schaffer (1978) to measure subjects' ability to utilize symptoms to diagnose a certain illness. The Medin and Schaffer (1978) model is based on discrimination learning in animals (Medin, 1975), and on hierarchical associations (Estes, 1975). It postulates that most natural categories are fuzzy (Rosch & Mervis, 1975) and resist categorization (Smith & Medin, 1981). The decision component in the Medin and Schaffer (1978) model is hence modeled on the fuzzy nature of category membership, and the choice rule is based on the similarity between a probe cue and the stored exemplars that it retrieves. Specifically, the probability of a category x response to the probe y is equal to the sum of the overall similarities of the probe y to the stored exemplars in category x, divided by the sum of the overall similarities of the probe y to all stored examplars (including category x exemplars). A given cue (probe) is represented in the memory system on a set of dimensions. The similarity of two cues is determined by a similarity parameter assuming values from 0 to 1 for each of the dimensions involved. The component dimensions are represented in a multiplicative fashion (as opposed to additive): The context and the cue interact in forming the event. Thus, the various cue dimensions comprising stimuli and some context (e.g., color equals context and form equals cue) are each multiplicatively combined to determine the overall similarity between the two events (stimuli). For example, a yellow circle and a blue triangle would be equal to the parameter multiplication color by form.

Estes' computer program used the similarity formula for categorization of diseases based on the symptoms as cue dimensions. To minimize the possible effect of selective attention to a particular dimension, each symptom was here equally valid as a category indicator. Moreover, the computer program (optimizer) also recorded the categorization trials using a perfect memory. Performance of the computer program was of course much higher (around 90% correct decisions) than that of the group of human subjects. The interesting features were that the humans could still learn, although all symptoms were equally relevant (salient) and that the ups and downs in performance data of optimizer was actually rather well mimiced by the human subjects. This suggests that the human subjects may entertain some mental categorization process according to the similarity formula. However, to bring the performance down to that of the human subjects, Estes endowed the computer program with an imperfect memory according to the principles of stimulus sampling theory (Estes, 1950). That is, variability in the representation were now introduced. If anything, the performance of the computer program (categorizer) was now even more similar in terms of the shape of the performance curve, and the performance level also converged on the level of the human subjects.

In sum, the similarity-based categorization process and sampling variability seem to be two principles that work well in this type of learning situation. Estes goes on to argue that in the present learning situation, that is, learning to categorize through observation may constitute a model situation on which both animal and human learning theorists can build. Even though different species bring different knowledge-bases to this task, there is always the element of learning and inferring from the sample stimuli observed. Estes' work represents a strong candidate for a ''linking'' theory (cf. Hitch, this volume) between animal and human cognition. Yet another interesting ''link'' or ''connecting'' perspective is provided by Dickinson and Shanks (this volume).

Contingency Judgments

In dismissing behavioral criteria as adequate indices for studying the *knowledge* that an organsim can acquire, Dickinson and Shanks (this volume) argue that the study of event correlations may prove to be a fruitful avenue for future convergence between conditioning and selected areas of human cognition and learning; in this case human causality judgment. Dickinson and Shanks argue that although classical inhibitory conditioning and instrumental avoidance conditioning appear to have little in common from a behavioral perspective, both involve the learning of a negative event correlation between the inhibitory stimulus and the Pavlovian reinforcer in the first case, and between the performance of the avoidance behavior and the negative reinforcer in the second. Given this communality in the acquisition of knowledge, that is, event relationships (predictive for classical and causal for instrumental conditioning), Dickinson and Shanks find that human causality judgment may prove to be an area wherein event correlations can be manipulated in the same manner as in animal conditioning.

In the experimental task (a video game), a tank is moving through a minefield. The subject is instructed to press a key on the console so to fire a shell at the tank (the action $= A$), and on some trials the tank explodes (the outcome $= 0$). This allows for a manipulation of the probability of an outcome give an action, $P(0/A)$, and the probability of the outcome in the absence of the action, $P(0/-A)$. This way Dickinson and Shanks were able to investigate whether the subjects' ratings of the shells effectiveness, +100 (maximum efficiency) to −100 (shell prevents the tank to blow up), would parallel conditioning data.

The human subjects showed that (a) under a positive correlation with a fixed P(0/A) the absolute magnitude of the judgments decreased as P(0/−A) was increased, (b) with uncorrelated events, an increase of the overall frequency tended to boost positive judgments, and (c) negative contingencies also evidenced negative ratings. In all these cases, the effects on animal conditioning increases and decreases in the same manner as the human causality judgments.

Dickinson and Shanks demonstrated further experimental parallels: Contiguity effects between action and outcome, acquisition functions, and an analogue to forward blocking (cf. Kamin, 1969). Backward blocking, apparently at odds with data on animal conditioning, prompted a general model for real-time contingency learning. Theory and data from the animal conditioning literature were essential for these manipulations. A rebound effect was obtained since backward blocking in humans suggests experimental reconceptualizations of the animal conditioning data; for this alone, Dickinson and Shanks' contribution is immeasurable.

Task Compatibility

Task compatibility is a multidimensional concept beset with potential methodological difficulties. Given a connecting perspective, *functionally compatible* tasks outweigh nominally compatible tasks (cf. Mackintosh, this volume). "Functional" refers either to the case where tasks serve the same behavioral functions for two individuals of different species or to the case where the same cognitive functions are activated in both species. *Test compatibility* is one important feature of task compatibility. One aspect of test compatibility is connected to the Encoding Specificity Principle, whereas the other aspect is connected to the dependent variables used in comparative research in general. The generality of the Encoding Specificity Principle (see Cohen, this volume) focuses upon the correspondence between encoding and test conditions. In contemporary research it seems desirable to reach compatibility not solely between tasks administered to animals and humans, but also between tasks employed both at encoding and retrieval. The second aspect embraces "causal attribution" (cf. Bolles, this volume) and possible links between dependent variables and certain behaviors. Is the response pattern determined by the task, or is the task determined by the response pattern? *Response strategies* seem pertinent since organisms are constrained by superordinate response stratiegies, which complicate task analysis. Finally, any *generalization* is accompanied by two major problems: (1) Assessment of task independent response systems. (2) Sampling procedures and assumptions about normally distributed attributes.

GENERAL PERSPECTIVES

This section deals with general scientific aspects of memory and learning research. The two topics are: general laws of memory (Cohen, this volume) and classification (Tulving, and Olton, this volume). These are fundamental scientific demands.

General Laws

As a starting point, Cohen (this volume) enumerated criteria for law status: (a) the law should be descriptive as opposed to prescriptive, (b) the law should be general (transspecies and transsituations) as opposed to low-level laws (operational definitions), (c) the empirical nature of a law should be distinguished from a theory in the sense that an empirical law only comprises terms which can be operationally defined, (d) the law should be "lawlike" rather than accidental, and (e) if the law is truly empirical, the variables involved in the law should each be possible to measure independently of the other variables involved in the relationship; if not, the law is denoted a definitional law (cf. Skinner's law of reinforcement), (f) the law preferably should match contemporary views on learning and memory and should, ideally, be quantifiable.

Cohen's First Law, states that "the better someting is learned, the greater the likelihood it will be remembered," using the repetition effect and the depth-of-processing effect. The difference between these two effects is that in the former the independent variables are readily quantifiable, whereas in the latter case the independent variables assume a definitional status. Some constraints exist, for example, the depth-of-processing manipulation does not hold for SPT-recall (subject-performed tasks, Cohen, 1981).

Cohen's Second Law, states that "the longer something has to be retained in memory, the less the likelihood that it will be remembered," using short-term and long-term recency effects. Short-term recency is typically found for the last few items of the serial position curve (Murdock, 1962), given that no delay or distractor is introduced before recall (Postman & Phillips, 1965). Long-term recency can be observed in a variety of situations, ranging from free recall of short stories occurring at the rate of one/day to rugby matches occurring at the rate of one/week (see also Hitch, this volume). Long-term recency for semantic memory tasks can also be demonstrated (e.g., Squire & Slater, 1975). Constraints include, recency insensitivity in short-term recognition (Poltrock & Mac-Loud, 1977), recency span limitation to a few positions in the continuous distractor paradigm, and recency in priming experiments (e.g., Jacoby & Dallas, 1981; Kirsner & Craik, 1971; Tulving, Schacter, & Stark, 1982).

Cohen's Third Law states that "the likelihood of remembering something depends upon the nature of the memory test." A large number of studies on context, state-dependency and cuing effects feed into this law. Context and state-dependency effects are constrained to hold true mostly for free recall tasks, but not for recognition tasks (Eich, 1980). Constraints on the Third Law may be exemplified by Ozier's (1978) study. The study employed a cross-over design, where the encoding conditions (the subject was told to *expect* a letter cue versus category name at test) were crossed with letter cue or category cue retrieval conditions. The results pointed to an interaction between encoding and retrieval conditions so that matching conditions produced the best performance in accordance with the encoding specificity hypothesis (Tulving, 1983; Tulving & Thomson, 1973). However, as it turned out, the category cues were as effective in retrieving letter encoded targets as the letter cues were. This result is at odds with the hypothesis. The principle, with its definitional aspect, could handle the data, though. Since the principle states that a retrieval cue is effective to the extent that its encoding is compatible with the representation of the episodic target, the efficacy of category-cues given a letter-cue encoding simply would indicate that the letter-cue instruction also provoked a semantic/categorical encoding. The example may favor a hybrid law, according to Cohen, based on both the encoding specificity hypothesis and the encoding specificity principle. However, in view of some other data at variance with the encoding specificity principle (Cohen & Griffiths, submitted; Santa & Lamwers, 1974), Cohen leans towards the encoding specificity hypothesis as the best candidate for an empirical Third Law.

Cohen's Fourth Law, concerns individual differences. It is generally found, within homogeneous samples of individuals, that individuals differ both with respect to episodic and semantic memory performance (Underwood, Boruch, & Malmi, 1978), not to mention reliable effects due to age and IQ.

Principles Versus Laws

The complexity of animal and human cognition defy present methodological standards, and one consequence is the overriding pragmatic bias. It is likely that there are no laws to detect (Gaffan, this volume). Empirically, there is a large bulk of "evidence" of the multifarious cognitive functioning that characterizes homo sapiens. From a neurophysiological perspective, it may be argued that more cognitions are geared by random neurophysiological processes than is previously thought of (cf. Hart, 1983). However, with an increasing knowledge-base and more refined instruments it may be possible to bring order into those random processes. Crowder (this volume) assumes that in psychology there are no general laws of interdisciplinary agreement. He avoids "First Principles," arguing that from a pragmatic point of view it seems sufficient to detect relevant explanatory principles for scientific problem solving. These basic principles concern issues such as representation, processing, and capacity limitations. Under these headings Crowder presents an historical review of concepts such as codes and schemata, spatial metaphors, spread of activation, strategies, procedural knowledge, and episodic memory, and he makes a vital point: Animal learning studies *require* the presentation of novel events.

Classification

Tulving (this volume) suggests that classification of the varieties of learning and memory may serve integration. Traditionally there has existed ambivalence towards classification stemming from an underlying assumption that all learning and memory are fundamentally the same. If this were true, there is consequently no need for classifying different kinds of learning (see also Tulving, 1984). Tulving advocates acceptance of differences in learning and memory, but focuses on the *relatedness* by construction of classificatory schemes reflecting *natural* categories. Natural denotes correlation between brain mechanisms and varieties of learning and memory.

Tulving notes the large number of techniques for observing brain function in vivo: for example, cerebral blood flow indices, evoked potentials, CAT/PET scans, etc. This strategy of classification of performance and functions is widespread (e.g., Mason, 1981). Preliminary to decisions about different memory systems, the question of what constitutes, for example, an "episodic" or a "semantic" task must be addressed as well as to what extent these (or other) memory components (attributes) mediate performance in a given task.

Olton (this volume) discusses a neuropsychological approach. Three basic techniques exist for investigation of the functional organization of the brain:

1. Lesion experiments: If one function is disrupted but not another, a dissociation between components of the brain is said to have occurred. A single dissociation indicates that the lesion of structure 1 (S1) might impair function 1 (F1), while a lesion of S2 might impair both F1 and F2. A double dissociation indicates that a lesion of S1 impairs F1 but not F2, while an S2 lesion provokes the opposite effect.

2. Stimulation experiments: A region or pathway is stimulated, activity in that region increased and function affected.

3. Recording techniques: Activity of a brain region is appropriately monitored (e.g., the work of Björklund and associates, see Archer, 1984). Observations of brain damaged patients performing learning and memory tasks suggest a dissociation for different types of memory systems and processes. Dissociations can be assimilated for classification: for example, procedural/declarative, working memory/reference memory, activation/elaboration, and episodic/semantic memory.

Another route for classification of learning and memory is an ethopsycological analysis of the natural habitat (Olton, this volume). What is, for example, the optimal *strategy* for food-seeking? Apart from the win-shift strategy, other strategies exist as a function of selection pressures that the environment has put on the animal. This "task" analysis may aid the classification of neuropsychological dissociations, since an ethological basis may give insights into the informational demands that the animal is attuned to. Olton also discusses laboratory tasks, and specifically with reference to Tulving's (1983) distinctions on recognition and recall. Recognition and recall may be distinguished on the basis of what information is present at retrieval (copy-cue or noncopy cue), and the second difference is about conversion requirements (familiarity judgment versus identification of the item). Recognition is characterized by familiarity judgments of copies of previously presented items, whereas recall may be characterized by the demand on identification of an item (i.e., production of a name) in the presence of noncopy cues. Most animal studies usually have employed copy cues, but in conjunction with an identification of the item by means of some pecking, picking up, or uncovering-of-the-item response. Olton proceeds to discuss some possible task developments based on Tulving's two-fold classification scheme, and this is done with reference to inferences about underlying cognitive processes in the animal.

Problems of Classification

Tulving's and Olton's classificatory schemes are timely, particularly in view of the preparadigmatic status of learning and memory. Consider the theoretical dichotomies invoked to explain the data on amnesia. Some theoretical interpretations take the form of process explanations (e.g., Graf, Squire, & Mandler, 1984) and others take the form of memory systems interpretations (Tulving, 1983). Given that the generalizations are based on similar sets of data and on similar types of patients, there may arise some problems as to the possibility of arriving at general taxa within the classificatory scheme. There might of course be other grounds for classification (task dimensions) which may unify the picture for the classifier (Moscovitch, 1985).

In the general field of memory dysfunction, it may be that some specialities lend themselves to certain types of explanations. For example, it may be that aging effects (Bäckman & Nilsson, 1984; Craik, 1983) are more easily interpreted in processing concepts than amnesia effects are. Could it also be the case that certain kinds of evidence (neuroanatomical versus neurotransmittor) inherently favor some kind of interpretations of a given dissocation with two tasks of memory? The problem of classification would certainly also depend on how many a priori kinds of systems we could conceive of. (cf. Hitch, this volume; Tulving, 1985a, 1985b). That is, when a certain dissociation is present between two tasks and two types of patients, can we dissociate the "relevant" systems? It is evidently so that the type of dissociation (single, double) also must be related to some theoretical structure. Tulving (this volume) seems to favor a single dissociation account based on a "monohierarchical" arrangement of procedural, semantic, and episodic memory. The modular approach advocated by

Hitch (this volume) seems to call for double dissociations (e.g., working memory versus long-term memory). The question is how Tulving and Hitch would view each others' "dissociation approaches"? Furthermore, and as Olton has indicated, we think that much is to be gained if information processing requirements of different tasks are contrasted. This may help distinguish relevant (with respect to different kinds of systems/processes) from irrelevant dissociations (interactions), and might also serve to resolve conflicting interpretations of obtained dissociations. This is also our bias, and in the last section we present some arguments in favor of tasks analysis, both with respect to animal learning and human memory.

TASK ANALYSIS AS AN INTEGRATIVE PERSPECTIVE ON LEARNING AND MEMORY

In this section we propose that task analysis (henceforth denoted TA) of the central paradigms used in animal learning and human memory may constitute a fruitful device or aid integration. Allowing for memory systems/processes/mechanisms associated with particular classes of tasks, a clear insight of the subject-task information base may optimize reduction of unnecessary assumptions regarding memories/processes which typically are task-specific or technique-specific. TA may be pertinent to the classification of different kinds of learning and memory as proposed by Tulving and Olton, as well as to a more detailed analysis of context (Mackintosh) and working-memory components (Hitch).

TA requires some assumptions: (1) A set of theoretically motivated task dimensions (see for example, Rönnberg & Bäckman, 1984) constituting a TA-system. Once motivated, it is assumed that any particular task, human or animal, may be assigned a value on each of the dimensions used. (2) The method for assigning values to dimensions could be either purely theoretically based, be accomplished through ratings by professionals familiar with the TA-system, or be complemented with a dimensional analysis of performance data (e.g., through factor analysis) in the tasks subjected to scrutiny. (3) Assigning values to a task dimension has as consequence that any given paradigm subjected to TA is in principle possible to characterize in terms of a profile of task attributes. It is important to note that the TA-dimensions employed should be chosen at a level of abstraction permitting a classification of tasks in terms of features defining a *class of tasks,* and not individual tasks (Tulving, this volume). Otherwise, a number of independent variables would enter into the definition and classification of a task.

The theoretical basis for choosing dimensions for a TA gains profitably by ecological and ethopsychological approaches to learning and memory (cf. Gibson 1979, and Olton this volume). Questions about everyday memory and learning tasks, as well as laboratory tasks, may be put into a functional perspective:

To what extent does the task represent an important task for the survival of the species? Is the information "out there" sufficient for a successful solution of the task? If not, to what extent does the animal or the human have to compensate for this "poor" information, and in what way can the animal or human compensate? Is the compensation done on the basis of previously stored information (phylogenetically or ontogenetically), or is it accomplished by means of the information learned during, or immediately prior, to the solution of the task? Is the purpose of the task relevant to, or compatible with, the knowledge-base of the subject? Can we consider the task to be representative of complex everyday life memory behavior?

One of the more important consequences of TA emerges when the task attributes of two tasks (according to the particular TA-scheme employed) are contrasted to the memory attributes, usually employed as explanatory tools for obtained performance data in the two tasks. Here, the term memory attribute refers to any memory/learning system, process or mechanism assumed to explain performance. Orthogonal combinations of the principal possibilities of *same* and *different* task attributes (T_s and T_d) with assumptions in the literature of *same* and *different* memory attributes (M_s and M_d), can be used for resolutions of conflicting interpretations of data and for development of theory. This is especially true when the outcome of the TA is in harmony with the behavioral data. That is, when a T_d or T_s outcome is obtained, it is important that the two tasks also reveal a behavioral difference or similarity in accordance with the TA. However, when the behavioral data conflict with the TA, but are in concert with previously assumed memory attributes, then the discrepancy may be hard to evaluate (see Rönnberg & Bäckman, 1984). In the principal cases where task and memory attributes agree ($T_s - M_s$, $T_d - M_d$), but where the behavioral data disagree, this behavioral discrepancy could be due to several factors such as the level of measurement, the relevance of the dependent variable etc. Table 14.1 presents the four principal outcomes, with respect to demands on theory.

In the $T_s - M_s$ cell then, the outcome of the TA confirms previously assumed similarities between the actual tasks with respect to activated memory attributes, and this conclusion is of course reinforced if the behavioral data agree with the TA.

TABLE 14.1
Demands on Theory
Assessed by Task Analysis

	M_s	M_d
T_s	None	Generality
T_d	Precision	None

In the $T_d - M_s$ cell, however, the two tasks now reveal different attributes, as compared to previous conceptualizations regarding the activation of similar (same) memory attributes. At this stage an ambiguity arises: It is of course logically possible that the same memory attributes are still engaged, although tapped by two different tasks. Equally possible, however, is that the two different tasks tap different memory attributes. The important point to be made is that both possibilities call for a reevaluation of the degree of *precision* of the particular theory for the two tasks. In the first case, the theory must state why the same memory attributes are still viable; and in the second case why they are not. In this context it is worth reemphasizing that the discrepancy between tasks previously assumed to be equivalent, and the presently obtained differences through TA, would be rather cumbersome and pointless to interpret, unless we adopted a theoretical rationale for TA. This means that the presently obtained difference should be conceived in terms of relevant ecological and ethopsychological informational demands; thereby stimulating development of theory for the interaction between task attributes and memory attributes. Below, we offer two examples with respect to the demand on precision, where the behavioral data also suggest a T_d outcome. To pinpoint the interaction between task attributes and memory attributes, we have chosen to optimize the subject variables by using one example from the aging literature, and one from the amnesia literature. Why is it, for instance, that old adults do not show a difference in performance compared to young adults in the Brown-Peterson paradigm (e.g., Keevil-Rogers & Schnore, 1969), while they do show a decrement in the Sternberg task (Anders, Fozard, & Lillyqvist, 1972)? Both tasks are assumed to tap the same memory attribute: short-term memory. Further, why is it that amnesics evidence repetition priming effects for short periods of time in a lexical-decision task, while for example, repetition priming of reading transformed script may last for long periods of time (Moscovitch, 1985)? Can these two examples be explained in terms of task differences, or do we have to complement the interpretation with some more precise division of spared memory attributes of the elderly or amnesics?

Analogous to the $T_d - M_s$ cell, the $T_s - M_d$ cell calls for a higher degree of *generality* of the theory in question. Tasks which previously were assumed to be different, and hence, considered to tap different memory attributes have now been found to cluster around the same task attributes. Again, we obtain an ambiguity: Two tasks which share the same task attributes may of course still engage different memory attributes; however, the other logical possibility is that they engage the same type of memory attributes. On a logical basis, it is impossible to decide between the two alternatives. We simply suggest that there exists an obvious basis for theoretical integration and generalization; it might be fruitful to "rethink" the data, since the tasks are similar in terms of the TA-system, and especially so when behavioral effects show similarities across tasks. For example, one important common attribute of tasks used to investigate the modality effect (i.e., short-term retention is better for auditorily as compared to visually presented information) may be captured by different predictability variations (e.g., the timing of item presentation and the timing of the recall signal, Rönnberg, 1980a, 1981, 1983). Many of the task-specific models in this area may be subsumed under this concept as an explanation of similarities in the size and the extent of the modality effect. Hypothetical memory attributes thus become more general when revised to be in consonance with the basic predictability variations, instead of being tailored to minutiae (Ohlsson, 1982; Rönnberg, 1980b).

The last cell, the $T_d - M_d$ combination, is similar to the first cell, $T_s - M_s$, in the sense that no discriminative information is added through TA. Thus, the $T_d - M_d$ cell only confirms previously hypothesized dissimilarities between the actual tasks regarding activation of different memory attributes. Again, the conclusion is further reinforced if the behavioral data are in line with the TA.

The principal analysis presented so far is assumed to hold true for both animal learning and human memory in general. However, the number of memory attributes commonly postulated as explanatory tools in the area of animal learning seems rather limited (e.g., Rescorla, this volume), compared to the tremendous number of memory attributes postulated for human memory (Underwood, 1972). There could be several reasons for this state of affairs. Although there are exceptions (Hinde, 1970), one likely candidate is the supposition that animals, as opposed to humans, have a generally lower capacity to encode, store, and retrieve various types of information.

The relatively lower capacity of animals has some important consequences for reanalysis of the demands of *precision* and *generality* on theory (see Fig. 14.1). On the abscissa the range in capacity of the animal/human varies from 2 to n (low–high) memory attributes. Two attributes are considered minimum; otherwise, no dissociation of attributes is possible through TA. On the ordinate we assign various degrees of demands on theory.

Need for Precision. When the subject pool typically has a low capacity to utilize different memory attributes (e.g., most animals) then we argue that it becomes increasingly important to use an obtained $T_d - M_s$ outcome as a means of detecting the few attributes there are to detect (see Fig. 14.1). Consequently, when there is a low potential for detecting differences between memory attributes

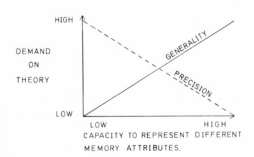

FIG. 14.1. Demands on theory (precision, generality) as a function of the organism's capacity to represent memory attributes.

(left-hand side of Fig. 14.1), each potentially dissociable attribute is considered to entail more scientific *"worth."* To understand the term *worth,* consider the following analogy: Imagine two accordions, (cognitive systems) one with, say, eight keys, and another with twenty-four keys, where keys correspond to eight and twenty-four memory attributes, respectively. Both are tuned according to the same musical scale. Furthermore, assume that a blind person (a scientist) is about to play (detect memory attributes) the first accordion (the animal), and another blind person is about to play the other accordion (the human); neither of the two blind persons have encountered this instrument before, and they share the same musical background (scientific background). As the first person haphazardly presses the keys of the first accordion, the seventh and the eighth keys will provide more discriminative information with respect to the possible tunes (models, theories) he can play, compared to the other person working on the twenty-third and twenty-fourth keys on the second accordion; he already has a reasonable idea of what he can do with accordion, and what he can not do.

Need for Generality.   Investigation of a subject pool which typically has been ascribed a large number of memory attributes (e.g., most humans), allows each potentially "new" discovery of an attribute considerably less scientific *worth* in tems of precision (see Fig. 14.1). That is, when TA has revealed a $T_s - M_d$ outcome, then by the principle of parsimony and the likely interpretation of $T_s - M_d$, the scientific *worth* of generalizing across memory attributes is high. As the number of attributes decreases, the possibility to generalize and to minimize the number of "superfluous" memory attributes also decreases.

The scope of TA is widened by presenting some additional advantages of this approach. Firstly, TA may:

(a) highlight previously "undiscovered" aspects of tasks; thus creating "new" links between tasks,

(b) sharpen the distinction between and the definitions of tasks,

(c) serve to put independent variables into perspective; viewing them as instances on more general TA dimensions,

(d) offer important information regarding constraints on response measures,

(e) shed light on, and give rise to, theorizing about ecological validity and representativity of tasks.

In view of an ecological/ethopsychological perspective, it might be fruitful to construct an overall mapping between task demands and types of responses with an ambition to sort out task-compatible versus task-irrelevant responses (cf. Rescorla, this volume) Moreover, since we do not always posess the knowledge about which function form that relates the independent variables to the dependent variables (Loftus, 1978), the crux of the matter may also be simplified through TA. In view of (a)–(e), TA may help the theorists to state more *precisely* under what conditions specific memory attributes are activated, and under what conditions they are not. General laws of learning and memory should display generality across species and situations (Cohen, this volume). In this vein, TA may guide the theorist to *generalize* the theory to a certain task domain, where the tasks share affinity with each other in terms of their respective task attribute profiles.

Second, our TA perspective does *not* imply that a task should be viewed as a *tool* for teasing out hypothetical properites of memory attributes. Rather, what is implied by our TA perspective is that focus should be put on what the task "affords" (Gibson, 1979) the animal/human in terms of "solvability." However, to accomplish this it seems inevitable that the theorist abandons the popular notion of memory viewed as a "receptacle" (Nilsson, 1980, 1984), or "thing" (Craik, this volume), which in its turn can be manipulated, stimulated or detected through means of task-specific independent variables (tools). If we instead accept the metaphor that any memory/learning task could be viewed as involving an act of *problem-solving,* perhaps rather different questions may be posed: (a) What are the minimal task requirements for a particular animal/human to solve a given task x? (b) Within what range (boundaries) of values on a task dimension (or a combination of several dimensions) can a particular animal/human solve x? (c) What memory attributes are necessary and what memory attributes are sufficient for the solution of x? Given the metaphor of problem-solving, then it also seems unavoidable that the solution of x may draw on other attributes of the cognitive system than memory attributes. For example, Olton's (this volume) ethopsycholological analysis of food selection strategy represents a case in point.

Third and finally, the issue of dissociation has already been touched upon. However, it is important to rephrase this issue in terms of TA. If a dissociation between a person variable (e.g. amnesic-normal) and two different tasks is present, and if the difference between the two tasks can be captured by the TA-system, then the inference need not exclusively be in terms of memory attributes (cf. the $T_d - M_s$ and $T_s - M_d$ cells). A striking example of this kind can be found in Moscovitch (1985), where he specifies a set of conditions which must be fullfilled for the amnesic to evidence learning. His TA accounts for much of the data and is more general than previous dichotomies based on spared and unspared memory attributes. It is also likely that such an analysis will generate broader research questions, which, at our preparadigmatic quest for knowledge, remain relatively neutral with respect to memory systems and processes.

To meet the challenge of integrating human memory and animal learning research, in the present preparadigmatic state of the art, *task analysis* offers *one* tool for integration.

ACKNOWLEDGMENTS

Writing of this chapter was supported by a grant (No 755/84) from the Swedish Council for the Research in the Humanities and Social Sciences to the first author and by another grant (No 724/84) to the second author. We would like to thank the editors, as well as

Lars Bäckman and Bo Molander, for encouragement and constructive suggestions during all phases of the work.

REFERENCES

Adams, C, & Dickinson, A. (1981). Action and habits: Variation in associative representations during instrumental learning. In N. E. Spear & R. R. Miller (Eds.), *Information processing in animals: Memory mechanisms*. Hillsdale, NJ: Lawrence Erlbaum Associates.

Anders, T. R., Fozard, J. L., & Lillyqvist, T. D. (1972). The effects of age upon retrieval from short-term memory. *Developmental Psychology, 6,* 214–217.

Anderson, J. R. (1976). *Language, memory, and thought*. Hillsdale, NJ: Lawrence Erlbaum Associates.

Anderson, J. R. (1983a). *The architecture of cognition*. Cambridge, MA: Harvard University Press.

Anderson, J. R. (1983b). A spreading activation theory of memory. *Journal of Verbal learning and Verbal Behavior, 22,* 261–295.

Anderson, J. R., & Bower, G. H. (1973). *Human associative memory*. Washington, D. C.: Winston.

Archer, T. (1984). Spontaneous recovery from damage to specific neurotransmittor systems. *Trends in Pharmacological Sciences, 5,* 263.

Archer, T., Sjödén, P.-0., & Nilsson, L.-G. (1984). Contextual control of taste-aversion conditioning and extinction. In P. D. Balsam & A. Tomie (Eds.), *Context and learning*. Hillsdale, NJ: Lawrence Erlbaum Associates.

Bäckman, L. (1984). *Age differences in memory performance: Rules and exceptions*. Doctoral dissertation, Umeå University.

Bäckman, L., & Nilsson, L.-G. (1984). Aging effects in free recall: An exception to the rule. *Human Learning, 3,* 53–69.

Baddeley, A. D. (1982). Domains of recollection. *Psychological Review, 89,* 708–729.

Baddeley, A. D. (1983). Working memory. *Philosophical Transactions of the Royal Society London, B302,* 311–324.

Baddeley, A. D., & Hitch, G. J. (1974). Working memory. In G. Bower (Ed.), *The psychology of learning and motivation, 8*. New York: Academic Press.

Baddeley, A. D., & Hitch, G. J. (1977). Recency reexamined. In S. Dornic (Ed.), *Attention and performance VI*, New York: Academic Press.

Bilodeau, E. A. (1967). Experimental interference with primary associates and their subsequent recovery with rest. *Journal of Experimental Psychology, 3,* 328–332.

Bjork, R. A., & Whitten, W. B. (1974). Recency-sensitive retrieval processes in long-term free recall. *Cognitive Psychology, 2,* 99–116.

Bolles, R. C. (1972). Reinforcement, expectancy and learning. *Psychological Review, 79,* 394–409.

Brehmer, B. (1984). Brunswikian psychology for the 1990's. In K. M. J. Lagerspetz & P. Niemi (Eds), *Psychology in the 1990's*. Amsterdam: North Holland.

Cohen, N. J., & Squire, L. (1980). Preserved learning and retention of pattern-analyzing skill in amnesia: Dissociation of knowing how and knowing that. *Science, 210,* 207–209.

Cohen, R. L. (1981). On the generality of some memory laws. *Scandinavian Journal of Psychology, 22,* 267–281.

Cohen, R. L., & Griffiths, K. (submitted). *Why are high associates better retrieval cues than low associates? A test of the Encoding Specificity Principle*.

Collins, A. M., & Quillian, M. R. (1969). Retrieval time from semantic memory. *Journal of Verbal Learning and Verbal Behavior, 8,* 240–247.

Craik, F. I. M. (1983). On the transfer of information from temporary to permanent memory. *Philosophical Transactions of the Royal Society London, B302,* 341–359.

Crowder, R. G. (1982). The demise of short-term memory. *Acta Psychologica, 50,* 291–323.

Daneman, M., & Carpenter, P. A. (1980). Individual differences in working memory and reading. *Journal of Verbal Learning and Verbal Behavior, 19,* 450–466.

Eich, J. E. (1980). The cue-dependent nature of state-dependent retrieval. *Memory and Cognition, 8,* 157–173.

Estes, W. K. (1950). Toward a statistical theory of learning. *Psychological Review, 57,* 94–107.

Estes, W. K. (1973). Memory and conditioning, In F. J. McGuigan & D. B. Lumsden (Eds.), *Contemporary approaches to conditioning and learning.* Washington DC: Winston.

Estes, W. K. (1975). Structural aspects of associative models for memory. In C. Cofer (Ed.), *The structure of human memory,* San Francisco: W. H. Freeman.

Estes, W. K. (1976). Introduction to Volume 4. In W. K. Estes (Ed.), *Handbook of learning and cognitive processes, 4,* Hillsdale, NJ: Lawrence Erlbaum Associates.

Estes, W. K. (1982). Learning, memory and intelligence. In R. J. Sternberg (Ed.), *Handbook of human intelligence.* Cambridge: Cambridge University Press.

Flavell, J. H. (1970). Developmental studies of mediated memory. In H. W. Reese & L. P. Lipsitt (Eds.), *Advances in Child Development and Behavior, 5.* New York: Academic Press.

Gaffan, D. (1977). Recognition memory after short retention intervals in fornix-transected monkey. *Quarterly Journal of Experimental Psychology, 29,* 577–588.

Garcia, J., & Koelling, R. A. (1966). Relation of cue to consequence in avoidance learning. *Psychonomic Science, 4,* 123–124.

Gardiner, J. M. (1983). On recency and echoic memory. *Philosophical Transactions of the Royal Society London, B 302.* 267–282.

Gibson, J. J. (1979). *The ecological approach to visual perception.* Boston: Houghton Mifflin.

Godden, D. R., & Baddeley, A. D. (1975). Context-dependent memory in two natural environments: On land and under water. *British Journal of Psychology, 66,* 325–331.

Graf, P., Squire, L. R., & Mandler, G. (1984). The information that amnesic patients do not forget. *Journal of Experimental Psychology: Learning, Memory, and Cognition, 10,* 164–178.

Grant, D. S. (1984). Rehearsal in pigeon short-term memory. In M. L. Roitblat, T. G. Bever, & H. T. Terrace (Eds.), *Animal cognition.* Hillsdale, NJ: Lawrence Erlbaum Associates.

de Groot, A. D. (1965). *Thought and choice in chess.* The Hague: Mouton.

Hart, E. (1983). *Windows on the mind. Reflections on the physical basis of consciousness.* New York: Quill.

Herman, L. M., Richards, D. G., & Woltz, J. P. (1984). Comprehension of sentences by bottlenosed dolphins. *Cognition, 16,* 129–219.

Hewitt, K. (1977). *Context effects in memory: A review.* Unpublished manuscript. Cambridge University Psychological Laboratory.

Hinde, R. A. (1970). *Animal behaviour: A synthesis of ethology and comparative psychology.* Tokyo: McGraw-Hill, Kogakosha Ltd.

Honig, W. K. (1978). Studies of working memory in the pigeon. In S. H. Hulse, H. Fowler, & W. K. Honig (Eds.), *Cognitive processes in animal behavior.* Hillsdale, NJ: Lawrence Erlbaum Associates.

Honig, W. K. (1981). Working memory and the temporal map. In N. E. Spear & R. R. Miller (Eds.), *Information processing in animals: Memory Mechanisms.* Hillsdale, NJ: Lawrence Erlbaum Associates.

Jans, J. E., & Catania, A. C. (1980). Short-term remembering of discriminative stimuli in pigeons. *Journal of Experimental Analysis of Behavior, 34,* 177–183.

Jarvella, R. J. (1978). Immediate memory in discourse processing. In. G. H. Bower (Ed.), *The psychology of learning, and motivation: Advances in research and theory, 112.* New York: Academic Press.

Jacoby, L. L., & Dallas, M. (1981). On the relationship between autobiographical memory and perceptual learning. *Journal of Experimental Psychology: General, 110,* 306–340.

Kamin, L. J. (1969). Selective association and issues in associative learning. Halifax: Dalhousie University Press.

Keevil-Rogers, P., & Schnore, M. (1969). Short-term memory as a function of age in persons of above average intelligence. *Journal of Gerontology, 24,* 184–188.

Kinsbourne, M., & Wood, F. (1982). Theoretical considerations regarding the episodic-semantic memory distinction. In L. S. Cermak (Ed.), *Human memory and amnesia,* Hillsdale, NJ: Lawrence Erlbaum Associates.

Kirsner, K., & Craik, F. I. M. (1971). Naming and decision processes in short-term recognition memory. *Journal of Experimental Psychology, 88,* 149–157.

Loftus, G. R. (1978). On interpretation of interactions. *Memory & Cognition, 6,* 312–319.

Lovibound, P. F., Preston, G. C., & Mackintosh, N. J. (1984). Contextual specificity of conditioning, extinction and latent inhibition. *Journal of Experimental Psychology: Animal Behavior Processes, 10,* 360–375.

Lubow, R. E. (1973). Latent inhibition. *Psychological Bulletin, 79,* 398–407.

Lundberg, I. (1984). *Språk och läsning.* Malmö: Liber förlag.

Mackintosh, N. J., & Dickinson, A. (1979). Instrumental (Type 2) conditioning. In A. Dickinson & R. A. Boakes (Eds.), *Mechanisms of learning and motivation.* Hillsdale, NJ: Lawrence Erlbaum Associates.

Maki, W. S. (1981). Directed forgetting in pigeons. In N. E. Spear & R. R. Miller (Eds.), *Information processing in animals: Memory mechanisms.* Hillsdale, NJ: Lawrence Erlbaum Associates.

Mason, S. T. (1981). Noradrenaline in the brain: Progress in theories of behavioral function. *Progress in Neurobiology, 16,* 263–303.

Medin. (1975). The theory of context in discrimination learning. In G. H. Bower (Ed.), *The psychology of learning and motivation: Advances in research and theory, 9,* New York: Academic Press.

Medin, D. L., & Schaffer, M. M. (1978). Context theory of classification learning. *Psycholgical Review, 85,* 207–238.

Metcalfe-Eich, J. (1982). A composite holographic associative recall model. *Psychological Review, 89,* 627–661.

Miller, G. A., Galanter, E., & Pribram, K. H. (1960). *Plans and the structure of behavior.* New York: Holt, Rinehart and Winston.

Moscovitch, M. (1985). The sufficient conditions for demonstrating preserved memory in amnesia: A task analysis. In N. Butters & L. R. Squire (Eds.), *The neuropsychology of memory.* New York: Guilford Press.

Murdock, B. B. Jr. (1962). The serial position effect of free recall. *Journal of Experimental Psychology, 64,* 482–488.

Murdock, B. B. Jr. (1982) A theory for the storage and retrieval of item and associative information. *Psychological Review, 89,* 609–626.

Neisser, U. (1982). Memory: What are the important questions? In U. Neisser (Ed.), *Memory observed: Remembering in natural contexts.* San Fransisco: Freeman.

Newell, A., & Simon, A. S. (1972). *Human problem solving.* Englewood Cliffs, NJ: Prentice-Hall.

Nilsson, L.-G. (1980). Methodological and theoretical considerations as a basis for an integration of research on memory functions in epileptic patients. *Acta Neurologica Scandinavica, 62,* 62–74.

Nilsson, L.-G. (1984). New functionalism in memory research. In K. Lagerspetz, M. J. (P. Niemi (Eds.), *Psychology in the 1990's.* Amsterdam: North Holland Publishing Company.

Ohlsson, K. (1982). *A functionalistic view of remembering: Interpretation of modality effects.* Doctoral dissertation, Umeå University.

Olton, D. S. (1978). Characteristics of spatial memory. In S. H. Hulse, H. Fowler, & W. K. Honig (Eds.), *Cognitive processes in animal behavior.* Hillsdale, NJ: Lawrence Erlbaum Associates.

Ozier, M. (1978). Access to the memory trace through orthographic and categoric information. *Journal of Experimental Psychology: Human Learning and Memory, 4,* 469–485.

Phillips, W. A. (1983). Short-term visual memory. *Philosophical Transactions of the Royal Society B 302,* 295–309.

Poltrock, S. E., & Macleod, C. M. (1977). Primacy and recency in the continuous distractor paradigm. *Journal of Experimental Psychology, 3,* 560–571.

Posner, M. E., Rossman, E. (1965). Effect of size and location of informational transforms on short-term memory. *Journal of Experimental Psychology, 76,* 496–505.

Postman, L. & Phillips, L. (1965). Short-term temporal changes in free recall. *Quarterly Journal of Experimental Psychology, 17,* 132–138.

Premack, D. (1983). The codes of man and beasts. *The Behavioral and Brain Sciences, 6,* 125–167.

Rachlin, H. (1970). *Introduction to behaviorism.* San Fransisco: Freeman.

Rescorla, R. A. (1980). *Pavlovian second-order conditioning: Studies in associative learning,* Hillsdale, NJ: Lawrence Erlbaum Associates.

Rescorla, R. A., & Durlach, D. J. (1981). Within-event learning in Pavlovian conditioning. In N. E. Spear & R. R. Miller (Eds.), *Information processing in animals: Memory mechanisms.* Hillsdale, NJ: Lawrence Erlbaum Associates.

Rescorla, R. A. & Wagner, A. R. (1972). A theory of Pavlovian conditioning: Variations in the effectiveness of reinforcement and nonreinforcement. In A. H. Black & W. F. Prokasy (Eds.), *Classical Conditioning II.* New York: Appleton-Century-Crofts.

Restle, F. (1975). *Learning: Animal behavior and human cognition.* New York: McGraw-Hill.

Roberts, W. A., & Grant, D. S. (1978). Interaction of sample and comparison stimuli in delayed matching-to-sample in the pigeon. *Journal of Experimental Psychology: Animal Behavior Processes, 4,* 68–82.

Roitblat, H. L. (1980). Codes and coding processes in pigeon short-term memory. *Animal learning and behavior, 8,* 341–351.

Roitblat, H. L. (1984). Representation in pigeon working memory. In H. L. Roitblat, T. G. Bever, & H. S. Terrace, (Eds.), *Animal cognition.* Hillsdale, NJ: Lawrence Erlbaum Associates.

Rönnberg, J. (1980a). Predictability as a task demand in single-trial free recall. *Scandinavian Journal of Psychology, 21,* 83–95.

Rönnberg, J. (1980b). *Conceptions of remembering as task-skill interactions.* Doctoral dissertation, Uppsala University.

Rönnberg, J. (1981). Predictability and recall strategy for nominal serial position curves. *Scandinavian Journal of Psychology, 22,* 189–195.

Rönnberg, J. (1982). On the tracing of auditory and visual support systems for remembering. *Scandinavian Journal of Psychology, 23,* 113–117.

Rönnberg, J. (1983). A framework for reproductive memory tasks. *Scandinavian Journal of Psychology, 24,* 45–56.

Rönnberg, J., & Bäckman, L. (1984). Attributes of memory tasks. Umeå Psychological reports, No 179. Umeå, Sweden: University of Umeå, Department of Psychology.

Rönnberg, J., Nilsson, L.-G., Ohlsson, K. (1982). Organization by modality, language, and category compared. *Psychological Research, 44,* 369–379, Springer-Verlag.

Rönnberg, J., & Ohlsson, K. (1980). Channel capacity and processing of modality specific information. *Acta Psychologica, 44,* 253–267.

Rosch, E., & Mervis, C. B. (1975). Family resemblances: Studies in the internal structure of categories. *Cognitive Psychology, 7,* 573–605.

Santa, J. L., & Lamwers, L. L. (1974). Encoding specificity; Fact or artifact. *Journal of Verbal Learning and Verbal Behavior, 13,* 412–423.

Savage-Rumbaugh, E. S., Pate, J. L., Lawson, J., Smith, S. T., & Rosenbaum, S. (1983). Can a chimpanzee make a statement? *Journal of Experimental Psychology: General, 4,* 457–487.

Seligman, M. E. P. (1975). *Helplessness: On depression development and death.* San Francisco: W. H. Freeman.

Shoben, E. J. (1980). Theories of semantic memory: Approaches to knowledge and sentence comprehension. In R. J. Spiro, B. C. Bruce, & W. F. Brewer (Eds.), *Theoretical issues in reading comprehension.* Hillsdale, NJ: Lawrence Erlbaum Associates.

Smith, E. D., & Medin, D. L. (1981). *Categories and concepts.* Cambridge. MA: Harvard University Press.

Squire, L. R., & Slater, P. C. (1975). Forgetting in very long-term memory as assessed by an improved questionaire technique. *Journal of Experimental Psychology: Human Learning and Memory, 104,* 50–54.

Staddon, J. E. R. (1983). *Adaptive behavior and learning.* Cambridge: Cambridge Universtiy Press.

Thomas, D. R., Moye, T. B. & Kimone, E. (1984). The recency effect in pigeon long-term memory. *Animal Learning and Behavior, 12,* 21–29.

Thompson, R. K. R., & Herman, L. M. (1977). Memory for lists of sounds by the bottle nosed dolphin: Covergence of memory processes with humans? *Science, 195,* 501–503.

Tulving, E. (1983). *Elements of episodic memory.* Oxford: Oxford University Press.

Tulving, E. (1984). Multiple learning and memory systems. In K. M. J. Lagerspetz & P. Niemi (Eds.), *Psychology in the 1990's.* Amsterdam: North-Holland.

Tulving, E. (1985a). How many memory systems are there? *American Psychologist,* in press.

Tulving, E. (1985b). Memory and consciousness. *Canadian Journal of Psychology, 26,* 1–12.

Tulving, E. & Thomson, D. M. (1973). Encoding specificity and retrieval processes in episodic memory. *Psychological Review, 80,* 352–373.

Tulving, E. Schacter, D. L., & Stark, H. A. (1982). Priming effects in word-fragment completion are independent of recognition memory. *Journal of Experimental Psychology: Learning, Memory, and Cognition, 8,* 336–342.

Underwood, B. J. (1972). Are we overloading memory? In A. W. Melton & E. Martin (Eds.), *Coding processes in human memory.* Washington, DC.: Winston.

Underwood, B. J., Boruch, R. F., & Malmi, R. A. (1978). Composition of episodic memory. *Journal of Experimental Psychology: General, 107,* 393–419.

Wagner, A. R. (1976). Priming in STM: An information processing mechanism for self-generated or retrieval-generated depression in performance. In T. J. Tighe & R. N. Leaton (Eds.), *Habituation: Perspectives from child development, animal behavior, and neurophysiology.* Hillsdale, NJ: Lawrence Erlbaum Associates.

Weiskrantz, L., & Warrington, E. K. (1979). Conditioning in amnesic patients. *Neuropsychologia, 17,* 187–194.

Winograd, T. (1975). Frames, representations and the declarative-procedural controversy. In D. G. Bobrow & A. Collins (Eds.), *Representation and understanding.* New York: Academic Press.

Wood, F., Ebert, V., & Kinsbourne, M. (1982). The episodic-semantic memory distinction in memory and amnesia: Clinical and experimental observations. In L. S. Cermak (Eds.), *Human memory and amnesia.* Hillsdale, NJ: Lawrence Erlbaum Associates.

Author Index

Subject Index

DATE DUE

MAY 3 1 '88			
	261-2500		Printed in USA